D1601795

IMAGES OF ANCIENT AMERICA

Visualizing Book of Mormon Life

IMAGES OF ANCIENT AMERICA

VISUALIZING BOOK OF MORMON LIFE

John L. Sorenson

RESEARCH PRESS
FOUNDATION FOR ANCIENT RESEARCH
AND MORMON STUDIES
PROVO, UTAH

Frontispiece: This magnificent portrait, one of the few preserved wooden sculptures from southern Mesoamerica, is about fourteen hundred years old. It tells us something of what we are missing because the climate has not been kind to perishable objects. The bearing and costume of this man indicate his social prominence. Interestingly, the published description of this figure notes that his elaborate handlebar mustache "raises the often argued question as to whether the Mongoloid American Indian could have had sufficient facial hair to grow a heavy beard—or a mustache such as this—and as to who might have been the model for this figure" (Gordon F. Ekholm, *A Maya Sculpture in Wood* [New York: Museum of Primitive Art, 1964], 152).

Research Press
a publishing arm of the
Foundation for Ancient Research and Mormon Studies
P. O. Box 7113
University Station
Provo, UT 84602

Printed in the United States of America
06 05 04 03 02 01 00 99 98 10 9 8 7 6 5 4 3 2 1

Library of Congress Cataloging-in-Publication Data

Sorenson, John L.
Images of ancient Mesoamerica : visualizing book of Mormon life / John L. Sorenson
p. cm.
Includes bibliographical references and index.
ISBN 0-934893-28-4
1. Book of Mormon—Geography. 2. Book of Mormon—Evidences, authority, etc. I. Title
BX8627.S644 1998
289.3'22—dc21
97-39237

Dedicated to all those ancient artists, builders, and recordkeepers, as well as modern researchers, who have helped bring to light "those who have slumbered in the dust."

Contents

Introduction

The Book of Mormon in a Mesoamerican Setting 1

The Land and the Peoples

Mesoamerica 6

The Variety within Mesoamerica: *Environments* 8

The Variety within Mesoamerica: *Cultures* 14

The Variety within Mesoamerica: *Ethnic Groups* 16

A Gallery of Ancient Faces 18

A Gallery of Modern Faces 22

The Variety within Mesoamerica: *Languages* 24

Mesoamerican Civilization

Cultures and Civilization 26

Level of Civilization 28

Life's Routine

The Seasonal and Daily Round 32

Foods 36

Luxury Consumption 42

Animal Use 46

Crafts and Tools 50

Markets and Commerce 54

Transport 56

Houses and Furnishings 60

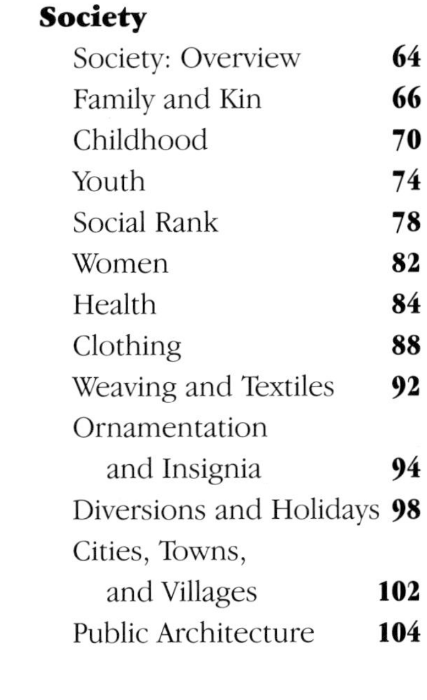

Society

Society: Overview 64

Family and Kin 66

Childhood 70

Youth 74

Social Rank 78

Women 82

Health 84

Clothing 88

Weaving and Textiles 92

Ornamentation and Insignia 94

Diversions and Holidays 98

Cities, Towns, and Villages 102

Public Architecture 104

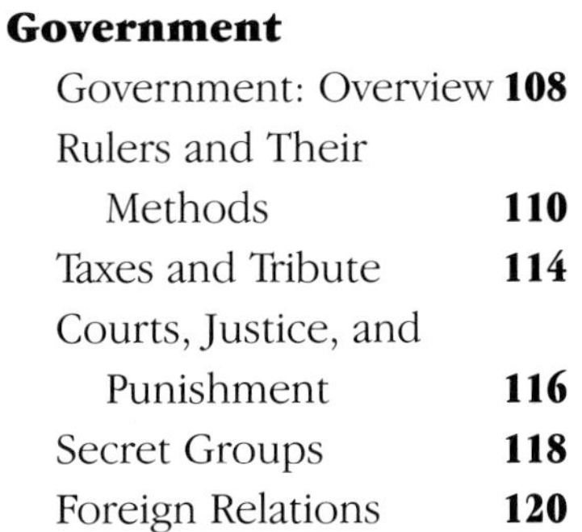

Government

Government: Overview 108

Rulers and Their Methods 110

Taxes and Tribute 114

Courts, Justice, and Punishment 116

Secret Groups 118

Foreign Relations 120

War and the Military

War: Overview 124

Military Organization 126

Battle and Conquest 128

Weapons and Armor 130

Fortifications 132

Belief and Worship

Belief and Worship: Overview **134**
Deities and Other Supernaturals **138**
Sacrifices **142**
Sacred Places **144**
Priests, Prophets, and Shamans **148**
Personal Worship **152**
Burial and Afterlife **154**

Knowledge Systems

Knowledge Systems: Overview **158**
Writing and Records **160**
Calendar, Astronomy, and Astrology **164**

Arts and Symbols

Art and Beauty: Overview **168**
Feather Work: A Special Case of Art **172**
Oratory and Poetics **174**
Music and Dance **178**
Symbolism: *Trees* **182**
Symbolism: *Felines* **184**
Symbolism: *Reptilian Figures* **186**

Book of Mormon Peoples and History

Mormon's Map in Relation to Mesoamerica **188**
Nephite History **190**
Book of Mormon Peoples in Terms of Mesoamerica **192**
The Early Nephites in the Land of Nephi **194**
The Land of Zarahemla **196**
The Lamanite Land of Nephi **198**
The Land Southward at the Time of the Great War **200**
Into the Land Northward **202**
The Crucifixion Catastrophe **204**
The Golden Age **206**
Apostasy **208**
The Nephites' Fall **210**
Nephites, Lamanites, and Successor Peoples **212**
The Jaredites **214**

Appendix I: Crossing the Oceans

Old World Connections with the New **224**

Appendix II: How We Learn About the Past

Archaeology **218**
Complementary Studies **222**

Endnotes **228**
Illustration Credits **233**
Scripture Index **238**
Subject Index **240**

Acknowledgments

This book could not have been produced without the support and assistance of a number of people. I am grateful for the professional contributions, goodwill, and kindness furnished by all the following and by others who cannot be named here. Melvin J. Thorne, Executive Editor of the Foundation for Ancient Research and Mormon Studies (FARMS) and of Research Press, gave encouragement at many points in the development of the work and spearheaded publication arrangements. He also personally improved the style, form, and content of the volume by his helpful editing. Mary Mahan ably assisted him. Scott Knudsen added greatly to the realization of my concept by his design skill. M. Gerald Bradford, Research Director at FARMS, has believed in the project all along and has made his belief concrete by providing funds for assistants and other necessary expenses. The Board of Trustees of FARMS, as well as Brent Hall, FARMS Director of Operations, and his staff, particularly Tracy Lytle, also have been supportive.

Without the long-term help of my friend and colleague Martin H. Raish, of the Bartle Library at the State University of New York at Binghamton, most images would never have been located and approved for use in this volume. His pursuit of elusive artists and photographers has gone far beyond that expected of a consultant. Bryan De Witt and Stewart Brewer, my student assistants, have carried out several related assignments. Andrea Darais and Michael Lyon provided valuable art services. Bruce W. Warren read the manuscript and made helpful comments. My wife, Helen Lance Christianson, has constantly spurred me with her enthusiastic yet critical reading of drafts. But only the author is responsible for the contents.

Finally, all those who have allowed images under their control to be used are thanked for their professionalism, courtesy, and patience. (See the credits list at the end of the book.)

Introduction

Alfred Percival Maudslay, an English gentleman archaeologist, is shown at work in a room in the Monjas structure at Chichen Itza in 1891. This classic scene epitomizes both the drudgery and the glamour of traditional archaeology in Mesoamerica.

This volume is primarily about ancient civilization in Mesoamerica (Mexico and Central America). It also shows ways in which that civilization relates to the life of peoples described in the Book of Mormon. The connection will be unclear to two types of readers, who come to the book with contrasting assumptions. The first consists of those (generally not members of the Church of Jesus Christ of Latter-day Saints) who do not consider the Book of Mormon to be factual. The second are religious believers ("Mormons") who reverence that book as scripture but are not well acquainted with what is known about the ancient world. How, both groups may ask, can what has been learned by scholars about ancient America help in visualizing Book of Mormon life, as the title of this volume implies? An explanation of what the author sees as the connection will help readers get off on the right foot.

The author has studied, taught, and published on ancient Mesoamerica at a professional level for nearly five decades. This book's discussions and choice of images reflect that experience. Yet most of his career has been as a sociocultural anthropologist, not as an archaeologist. From his perspective even the best books describing the civilization of Mesoamerica are disappointingly narrow, being far more concerned with material remains than with the people who left them behind. This volume tries to redress that failure by constructing a picture using striking visual materials and words that communicate a fuller scope of Mesoamerican culture and society.

Latter-day Saints in the past have often grasped at archaeological straws in supposing that all the ruins are somehow "Nephite" or "Lamanite." Moreover, few readers of that record compiled by Mormon have gained from it an accurate picture of how the Nephites or Lamanites may have lived.

Latter-day Saints accept the Book of Mormon as scripture, comparable in importance to the Bible. Most secular scholars of course have a different view. Historically most of the scant attention they have paid to the Book of Mormon has focused on the dispute about its origin. Few of the critics of the LDS position consider the volume ancient; most have claimed that it is merely a literary product of young Joseph Smith, or of some other nineteenth-century New Englander.

In recent decades, a growing cadre of Mormon (and a few non-Mormon[1]) scholars have approached the book as an ancient text that deserves analysis in its own right, without particular concern for its status in Latter-day Saint religion. This development has shifted some attention from the apology/criticism conflict toward research that follows the canons of conventional scholarship as applied to the study of other ancient documents. Although non-Latter-day Saint researchers remain largely unaware of this work, these studies have demonstrated that there is indeed new light to be shed on and by the volume. It is not implausible now to view the book as a source from and a neglected window on ancient life and history.[2]

Dr. Hugh Nibley began this type of analysis forty-five years ago in his work *Lehi in the Desert.* He carefully examined the initial portion of the Book of Mormon and documented that what it says about the departure of Lehi and his family from the land of Judah soon after 600 B.C. and their subsequent history includes details about the ancient Near East that even scholars could not have known until after publication of the Book of Mormon in 1830.[3] Subsequent studies have done the same thing in reference to the American scene; the text presents facts about the geography, history, and cultures of the peoples of America that could not have been known to Smith or any other nineteenth-century writer.[4] These studies have also demonstrated an internal consistency in the Book of Mormon text that would not be expected in a work of historical fiction.[5]

What portion of America was the scene for the Nephites and other peoples treated in the Book of Mormon? Nearly all qualified scholars who have dealt with that question have come to agree on Mesoamerica, that is, the area of high civilization in central and southern Mexico and northern Central America. Despite some disagreement over specifics, a significant consensus among LDS researchers now correlates the central lands spoken of in the Nephite record with the territory between Guatemala City and the city of Veracruz, Mexico.[6]

Some of the features of culture and history mentioned in the record are still puzzling when compared with modern scholarly knowledge about Mesoamerica. Still, a large majority of the record's statements are reconcilable, and in fact are congruent, with secular findings on Mesoamerican civilization. Striking and subtle agreements are found between certain details in the book and those uncovered by the work of scholars.[7]

A more extensive treatment of how the Book of Mormon relates geographically to Mesoamerica is given in the last quarter of this book.

The research just sketched has shown that we can be certain that only Mesoamerica could have been the scene on which the events recorded in the Nephite account were played out. A premise of this book, *Images of Ancient America*, is that the Book of Mormon account (aside from its short treatment of founding events in the Near East) is an ancient record mainly of certain events in part of Mesoamerica between approximately 600 B.C. and A.D. 400.

This does not mean that the scripture constitutes "a history of Mesoamerica." Mormon edited the account in the late fourth century A.D. from earlier documents, and apparently the form and content of the record from which the Book of Mormon was translated by Joseph Smith were similar in important ways to a Mesoamerican codex or native book.[8] Mormon was the last leader of the Nephites, the central people he described and with whom he was destroyed in battle. His abridged account treats events spanning a thousand-year period that was of key concern to his royal lineage, the Nephites.[9] Yet the text of the Book of Mormon makes clear that other peoples were on the scene besides his line and descendants of the other parties who arrived from the Old World by boat as reported in the record.[10] In short, while Book of Mormon groups were involved in Mesoamerica, there had to remain much that was Mesoamerican not alluded to in the Nephites' lineage history.

Agreement between information in Mormon's text and facts known from scholarship can shed light in three ways. First, ideas, motives, behavior, social roles, sites, and artifacts mentioned in or implied by the Book of Mormon text may be clarified by reference to facts known about Mesoamerica. Second, relating Book of Mormon statements to the world known from external research can bring to readers as they consult the Book of Mormon a sense of realism that they could not have experienced by relying on the text alone. Just as books that connect Bible scenes, events, and characters to ancient Near Eastern life benefit readers of the Bible who study them, the present work can enlighten anyone seeking contextual information about the world in which Book of Mormon events took place. And third, when they read with sufficient care what we might call Mormon's codex, Mesoamericanist scholars can discover unexpected information about the area of their concern at an early time period.

The most ambitious work showing how the peoples and cultures in the Book of Mormon articulate with groups and scenes in Mesoamerica is the author's 1985 book, *An Ancient American Setting for the Book of Mormon*.[11] Many readers have found it a useful resource in linking the two bodies of data. But its nature and scope did not allow doing justice to the visual dimension. The present volume aims to make up that lack.

The word *visualizing* in this book's subtitle is intended to suggest that when readers carefully study the verbal sketches and visual images, they will equip themselves better to picture the conditions under which the Nephites and Lamanites lived. Those who do so can understand Mormon's record more completely. I particularly hope that artists, filmmakers, pageant producers, and writers who deal with the Book of Mormon will enrich and discipline their creative work by use of the information in this book. The subtitle does not mean, however, that I think the illustrations show specifically Nephite artifacts or scenes.

Unfortunately, high-quality visual images are not available on every relevant subject. The more subjective areas of any people's culture, such as beliefs and feelings, are hard to document from objects. It would have been ideal had the pictures that are available come exclusively from the portions of Mesoamerica where the Nephites most likely lived and had they dated specifically from their era. Instead, it has often been necessary to use illustrations from pre-Nephite and post-Nephite times and from localities where that people probably did not live. Yet it is as reasonable to use those complementary resources as for books on Bible lands to use pictures of, say, modern desert-dwelling Bedouins to illustrate certain lifeways that may not have changed basically since the days of the Old Testament patriarchs thousands of years ago. Similarly this book takes advantage of illustrations of Aztec or Maya (i.e., clearly non-Nephite) and even modern-day scenes and objects to show what some elements of Nephite culture could have been like generally. Until a more specific identification can be made of who the Nephites were in Mesoamerican terms, we must often be satisfied with generic pictures of their culture that accessible sources provide us.

In any case the burden of picturing Book of Mormon scenes, or of Mesoamerican scenes as such, remains on the user of this book. May your visualizing be both accurate and exciting.

The Land

Mesoamerica

The highest civilization in the Western Hemisphere before the arrival of the European conquerors was in the area we know today as central and southern Mexico and Guatemala. Until the middle of the twentieth century vague or awkward terms—like *Middle America*—were used to distinguish this civilized area between the North and South American continents. In 1943 anthropologist Paul Kirchoff identified more than a dozen features—for example, writing systems, sacred temple towers, tribute-collecting governments, and bloody sacrifice—that were shared by cultures throughout this area. He proposed that the area where those features occurred be called Mesoamerica ("in between America").[12] Most scholars liked the clarity of his definition and soon adopted the name.

The term *civilized* clearly applies to this area. Only in the Andean zone of South America was there a possible New World rival, but the lack of clear evidence for writing (one of the usual diagnostic traits of civilization) in that zone has left its civilized status questionable. All other areas in the Americas were inhabited by less complex societies. During several time periods Mesoamerican culture strongly influenced both North and South America. To some degree, too, actual population movements spread Mesoamerican genes over those continental territories.

VISUALIZING BOOK OF MORMON LIFE

Research on the text of the Book of Mormon over the past half century has made a convincing case that the New World events involving the Nephites, Lamanites, and Jaredites of that record took place in Mesoamerica. The geographic, climatic, and cultural characteristics of the Nephite and Lamanite "land of promise" (1 Nephi 2:20) laid out in the Nephite record demonstrate that only a limited territory a few hundred miles in extent was involved in their history and that what the text says about that setting fits very well in central and southern Mexico and Guatemala.[13]

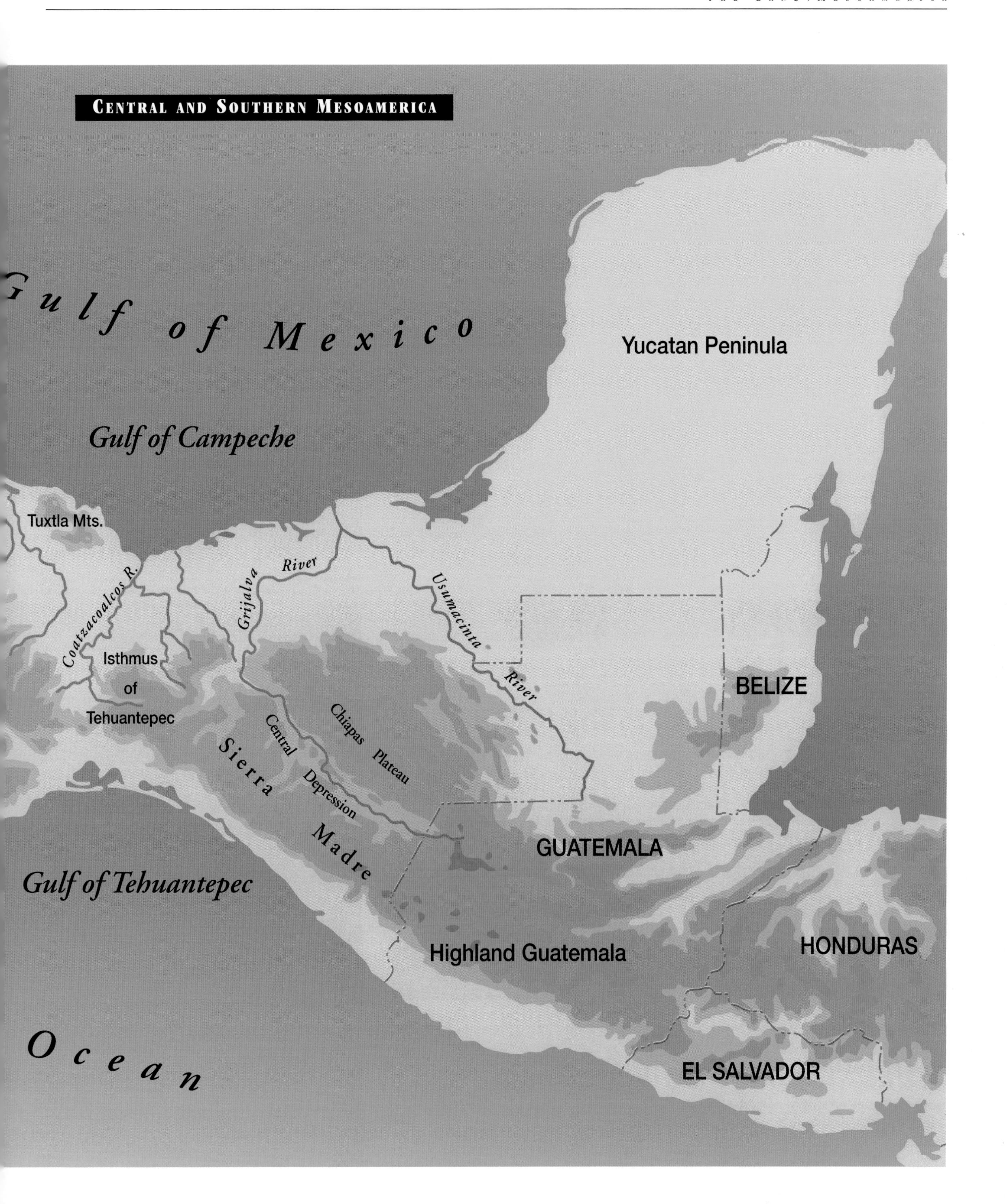
CENTRAL AND SOUTHERN MESOAMERICA
Gulf of Mexico
Yucatan Peninula
Gulf of Campeche
Tuxtla Mts.
Coatzacoalcos R.
Grijalva River
Usumacinta River
Isthmus of Tehuantepec
Central Depression
Chiapas Plateau
Sierra Madre
BELIZE
GUATEMALA
Gulf of Tehuantepec
Highland Guatemala
HONDURAS
Ocean
EL SALVADOR

The Variety within Mesoamerica

Environments

While certain features were found throughout Mesoamerica, each region showed peculiarities based on the fact that the people of each locality faced differing environmental conditions and had their own local histories as guides. The history and cultural development of pre-Columbian Mesoamerica overall was complex and had varied local effects. For example, a people located near the center of the civilization typically borrowed ideas and behavior from their neighbors much sooner than people located out on the margin. Also, populous territories were more likely to generate specialists who could develop, exploit, and pass on advanced skills and knowledge.

Undisturbed tropical forest is no longer extensive, as it was in the lowlands long ago, but less lofty, second growth jungle like this in the Tuxtlas Mountains zone of Veracruz is common. It illustrates the bountiful vegetation found in much of the hot lowlands, or *tierra caliente*.

A large segment of the state of Oaxaca, seen here, displays wildly broken terrain. Only a few favorable settlement spots appear amidst predominant wilderness. One observer has described the topography of Mesoamerica as being "like a piece of crumpled paper."

Uplands like these near Chimaltenango, Guatemala, were also agriculturally rich and the high elevation made for a pleasant climate. A sizable ancient population lived here, although the irregular topography discouraged the growth of large cities.

A few valleys and plateau areas with a temperate climate *(tierra templada)* offer sizable settlement areas where agriculture could support considerable numbers of inhabitants. The wide, flat Cintalapa River valley of western Chiapas was one such area. Its strategic position made it a major route for travelers headed northward to the isthmus, and so it remains today.

In some lowland areas extensive boggy wetlands are common. However, small elevations in the midst of the swamps provide excellent soil for cultivation and settlement, such as at the site of La Venta, Tabasco, an islet from which this photo was taken.

Mesoamerica constituted a more complex mosaic of environments and cultures than many other culture areas. China, for example, was characterized anciently by comparative cultural unity, as conquerors or rulers in that huge territory imposed similar ways of doing things in whatever parts they controlled. But probably no such politically dominant empire ever existed in Mesoamerica; conquests by or contacts between localities tended to be relatively temporary and to produce only modest changes in the territories affected. In fact most Mesoamericans lived out their lives acquainted only with the miniculture of their locality—ways of life whose details were shared in a single valley or limited tribal area. The mass of people who lived as little as fifty miles, let alone three hundred, from another group rarely encountered any of them.

The fragmented physical environment discouraged uniformity among the peoples and their cultures. Far more of the territory consisted of hard-to-traverse mountains or jungle than of lands readily usable for settlement and cultivation. Rivers were short or segmented by nature so they were of little use as aids to travel. Nowhere in Mesoamerica do we find an equivalent of, for example, Egypt's Nile River, whose agriculturally rich floodplain stretched continuously for hundreds of miles and whose smooth course favored communication by boat. Mesoamerica could more appropriately be compared to a scattered archipelago, its smallish "islands" of culture and settlement separated by a difficult "sea" of wilderness.

The physical environment in Mesoamerica that most impresses visitors from temperate lands is tropical forest, or jungle. There are large areas of this heavy vegetation in the eastern portions of the area. Winds coming inland from the Gulf of Mexico or Caribbean Sea produce abundant rains there as the moist air is raised and cooled when it encounters inland mountains. The result is giant trees and thick undergrowth that make cultivating the soil difficult. The heavy rain also washes many nutrients from the soil; thus only a thin layer of productive soil remains after the heavy plant growth has been cleared off. Building up large, stable populations and settlements in this setting was a real challenge. The discomfort of high

humidity and temperature still imposes obstacles to the development of stable civilized life there, as it did anciently.

Spots within the mountainous areas provided more favorable environments for settlement. Certain areas in elevated valleys and on plateaus permitted intensive settlement, but the extent of those favored territories was limited. In many mountain zones the climate was drier and more temperate than in the wet lowlands, with more marked seasonal variation in the rains. People in the Mesoamerican area typically speak of three types of environment, basing their classification on temperature, which usually relates to elevation: hot lands (essentially the flat lowland), temperate lands (mostly intermediate in elevation), and cold lands (high elevations). Of course, crops and cultivation techniques as well as building materials and house forms tended to differ from zone to zone. Because of the mountainous nature of the terrain, two or even all three of the temperature/land types could exist within a few miles of each other.

Throughout Mesoamerica, distinct wet and dry seasons are experienced. In the summer months (May through September) the tropical sun heats the land, causing the air to rise. The rise pulls in moist air from neighboring oceans and that causes the rains already mentioned. While the moisture is essential for the growing crops, the damp, cloudy conditions result in cooler temperatures; thus "summer" feels like winter could be expected to feel. Furthermore, the rain impedes travel by making trails muddy and by flooding low areas. In the drier part of the year (November to April) first harvesting and later new planting take place, and obviously travel becomes easier then. Anciently wars were fought in the dry period.

The variety in local environments fostered variations in culture. In the most diverse areas, several ecological niches existed in close proximity to each other, which allowed different peoples to exist near each other without necessarily clashing over use of the same resources. For example, farmers who lived only a few

Because few large bodies of water or easily navigable rivers are found in Mesoamerica, boat transportation was little developed and fishing was not a major occupation. Beautiful Lake Atitlan in highland southern Guatemala is an exception; a network of villages at the few viable settlement spots along its steep shore still take advantage of this rich resource.

miles from the sea might have cared nothing about fishing but would have happily exchanged goods with coastal dwellers who exploited the maritime resources. The groups might even have spoken very different languages. Given how Mesoamerican territory is broken into many ecological zones, it is no surprise that at the time of the Spanish Conquest in the 1520s as many as two hundred languages were spoken in Mesoamerica, and many cultural details distinguished the peoples thus set off from each other. Yet local differences were bridged by a veneer of shared concepts and customs we call Mesoamerican civilization.

Visualizing Book of Mormon Life

The Book of Mormon pictures its peoples settled in a tropical area where travelers were regularly reported as moving up or down over broken terrain. Wilderness surrounded or abutted on settled areas. For instance, a Lamanite army only a few days from its homeland could not find the way back without guidance from its enemies (see Mosiah 23:30, 35–6); another party was lost for "many days" (Mosiah 8:8), wandering hundreds of miles without ever fully realizing where they had traveled (see Mosiah 8:7–11; 21:25–7); wilderness lairs afforded guerrilla outlaws safe haven, while authorities from nearby settled lands who sought to control them were unable to do so (see Helaman 11:25, 27–33).

The Grijalva River Depression

One major river system that played a significant role in the lives of ancient Mesoamericans was the Grijalva in the Mexican state of Chiapas. Its upper basin, called the Central Depression, begins where the river's headwaters descend precipitously from the band of mountains in western Guatemala. Along the stream's northwestward course through the enclosed, semiarid depression, the narrow strip of good soil laid down by the river's flooding and the sure water supply furnished by the stream encouraged the building of towns and cities at such sites as those today called La Libertad, Santa Rosa, Chiapa de Corzo, and so on (nobody knows their ancient names).

A generation ago a hydroelectric dam was built that flooded the upper part of the Central Depression, including hundreds of archaeological sites.

At the northwest end of the Central Depression, the river has cut a spectacular canyon with nearly vertical walls. Through it the stream descends toward the coast in the state of Tabasco. There the river branches to form an immense, swampy delta before it reaches the Gulf of Mexico.

Visualizing Book of Mormon Life

The only river mentioned in the Book of Mormon is the Sidon. Analysis of the extensive textual references to it and its relation to the land of Zarahemla shows that the land essentially constituted a major portion of the drainage basin of the river. For the Nephites the river took on its identity as the Sidon near its head, upstream from the land of Manti where it emerged from a narrow strip of wilderness (see Alma 22:29; 43:22, 24, 27, 31–5, 40–2). Tributaries obviously swelled the stream somewhat as it passed adjacent to the city and immediate land of Zarahemla (see Alma 2:1). No mention is made about the course of the river in the lowlands as it approaches the sea, which could have been because the river lost its identity as it forked into channels that formed a delta near the coast.

Upon reaching the flat Central Depression after emerging from the strip of mountains that separates Guatemala from Chiapas, the river is still only a small stream.

As tributaries swell the flow, the Grijalva becomes a full-fledged, impressive river. In some years heavy seasonal rains upstream caused damaging floods along its course through the basin. Major dams control the floods today.

At El Sumidero (The Drain) the stream runs three thousand feet below the crest of this canyon rim where the river exits the Central Depression. A modern dam downstream has now backed up lake waters through most of the canyon, stilling what used to be entirely impassable rapids.

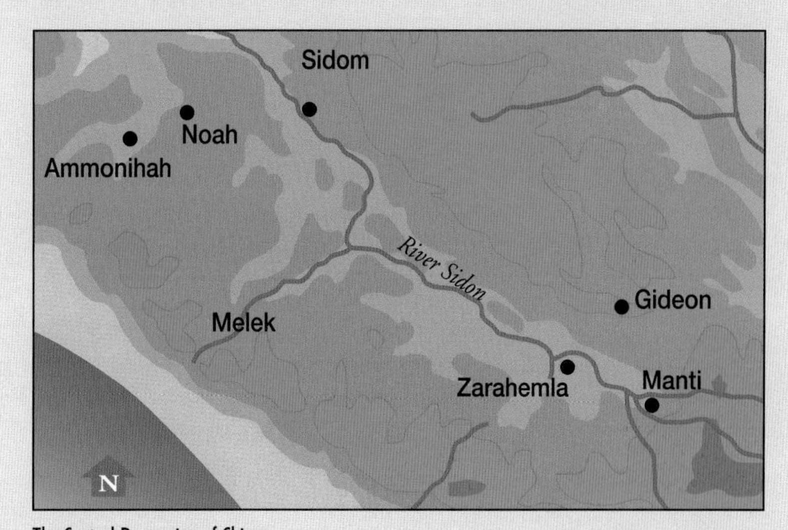

The Central Depression of Chiapas

The Variety within Mesoamerica

Cultures

Most people have heard of the Aztecs, the Zapotecs, the Maya, and so on. Less is known about how much variety sometimes hid beneath such cultural labels. For example, the Aztec heartland, the Valley of Mexico and its environs, included dozens of languages and groups who were ruled by a multitribal combine (the Triple Alliance) settled in a metropolis, Tenochtitlan, that had once been three rival cities. Many of the inhabitants of this cosmopolitan area in central Mexico knew two, three, or four tongues. East of the metropolis lived the Tlaxcalans, whose boundary lay only thirty miles from the Aztec capital. The Tlaxcalans had maintained independence from their hated neighbors for centuries. Then on the west of the great capital lay the Tarascans; they too had never been conquered. Each of these peoples (and others not mentioned here) were as different from the others as the English from the French or the Germans from the Italians.

Cultural variety also prevailed in more distant Mesoamerican territories. For example, the Zapotecs in what is today the state of Oaxaca dwelt cheek by jowl with Mixtecs, Amuzgos, Triques, Cuicatecs, etc. Meanwhile, "the Maya" so often spoken of in relation to Mesoamerica's history were speakers of at least thirty languages that were spread over eastern and southern Mesoamerica. Many differences in environmental settings, styles of art and architecture, religious systems, social arrangements, and governmental forms were manifest among these groups. So we need to be reminded frequently that what we for convenience term ancient Mesoamerican civilization was no more a uniform entity than was ancient Near Eastern civilization.

A good deal of the variation consisted of details on widely shared themes. It is because there were basic commonalities that we can speak of Mesoamerica as an overarching culture area. People of one group knew, for example, that a certain god or custom among their neighbors was more or less equivalent to one of their own. Knowledgeable individuals, such as merchants who had traveled about, were capable of making translations between their own cultural ideas and those of other groups on a "when in Rome, do as the Romans do" basis. Thus the pattern of life was somewhat similar for all groups, especially within a given region, and not startlingly different throughout the rest of Mesoamerica, despite the fact that locals had their own ways of acting and thinking.

This fragmentation means that exceptions can always be pointed out whenever we try to generalize about

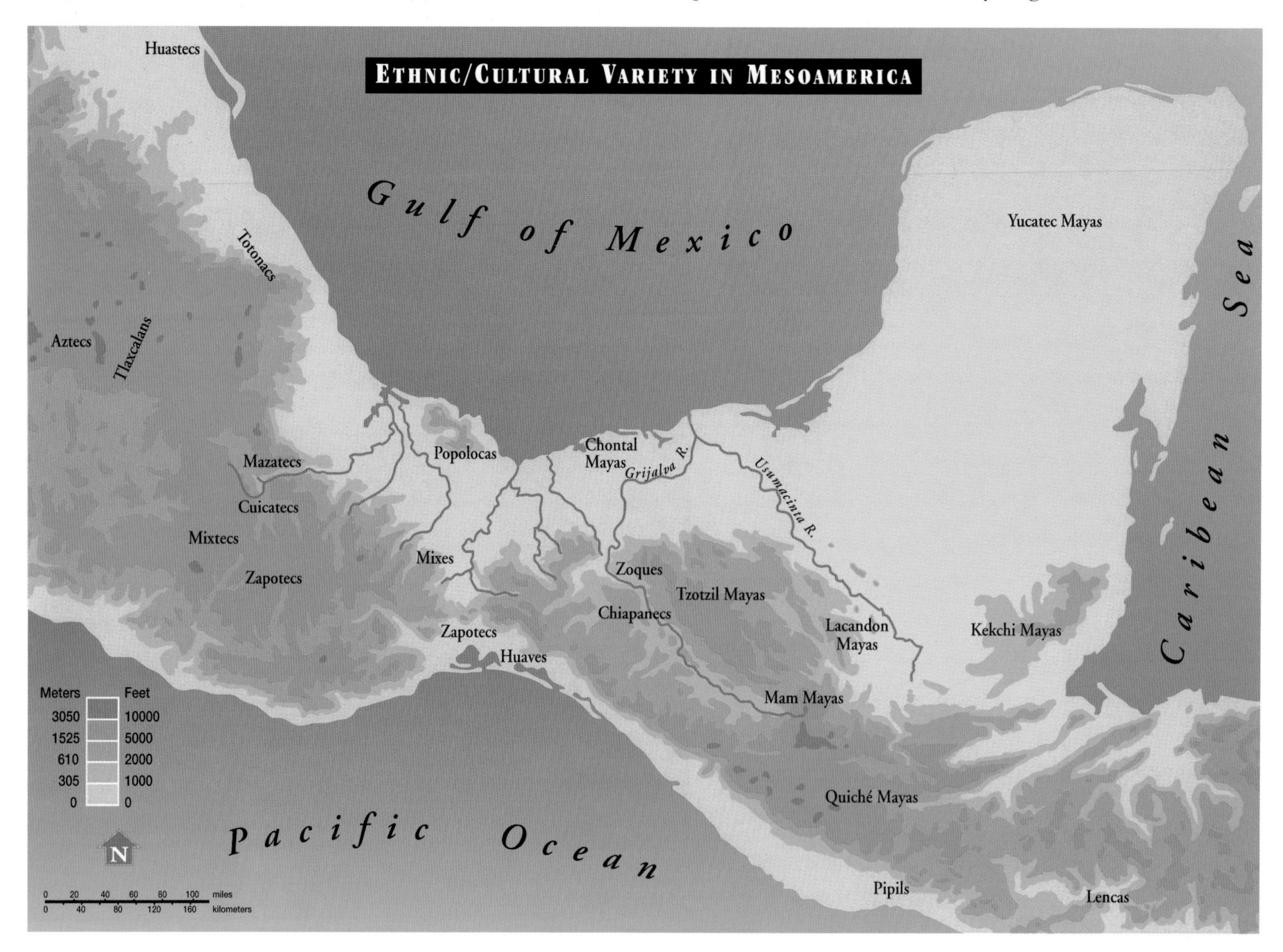

things Mesoamerican. All that can be done in the brief compass of this book is to make statements about what is more or less typical. Readers can understand the essential information without mastering all the intricacies of the diverse ancient scene.

It is also important to realize that some major patterns of Mesoamerican life did not change in their fundamentals over a period of two thousand or even three thousand years before the Spaniards arrived. Such comparative continuity means that when we look at clothing, houses, cultivation techniques, or customs of community cooperation in one period, we can gain valuable clues about how life went on in both earlier and later times as well.

The map on page 14 suggests some of the cultural groupings in Mesoamerica that are often referred to, although the details are impossible to show on a map.

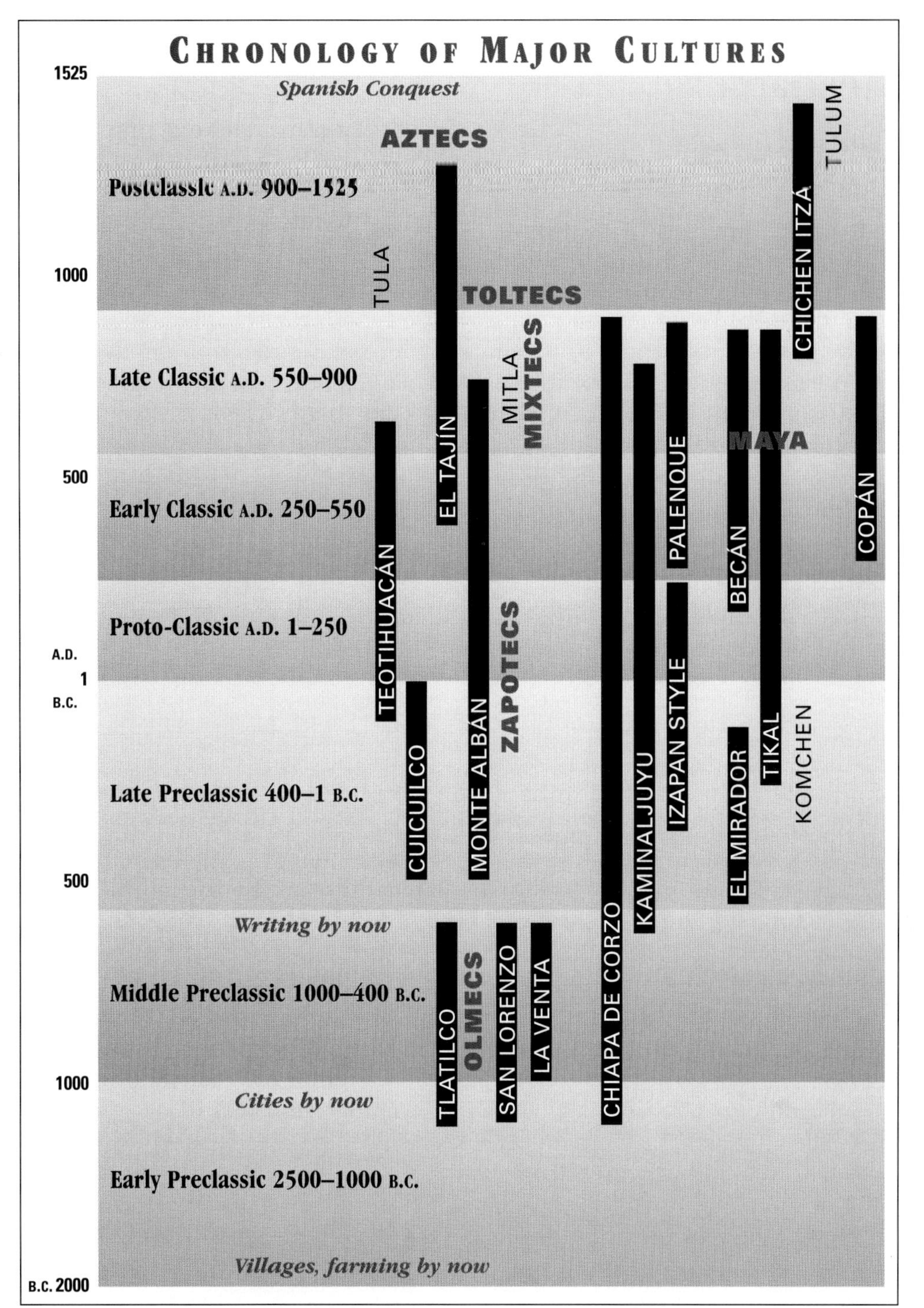

VISUALIZING BOOK OF MORMON LIFE

The groups who participated in Book of Mormon history were represented in that record as varying culturally in details even while a core of widely shared ideas and lifeways allowed them to interact with each other on a predictable basis. The social and physical isolation and separatism of groups we have seen in Mesoamerica was matched among Nephites and Lamanites. Within the land of Zarahemla, for instance, although a common government held control, in name at least, over all local lands, the people in the land of Ammonihah virtually thumbed their nose at the ruling powers in the nominal capital city (see Alma 8:11–3, 17). The Zoramites provide another case: we are first told of their pursuing strange religious customs and holding weird beliefs (weird, that is, to someone from Zarahemla), and soon they went even further and seceded politically in order to join the Lamanites (see Alma 31:59; 31:1–4). Rebel groups sprang up repeatedly at no great distance from the Nephite capital city (see Alma 2:2, 13; 51:16–20; 61:3–5). Each saw themselves as significantly different from those who ruled them. One of the causes of this fragmentation was that geographical separation and travel difficulties resulted in poor communication; even the chief military commander of the Nephites, Moroni$_1$, did not learn for several years what had been going on with some of his forces at the borders of the nation just a few hundred miles away (see Alma 56:1–2; 58:8–9; 59:2; 60:1–3).

The Variety within Mesoamerica

Ethnic Groups

When the first Europeans arrived in the New World five centuries ago, they didn't write in much detail about the biological traits of the inhabitants, although some did refer to particular groups as having "white" or nearly white skins. Other groups were noticeably darker.[14] Columbus himself claimed that there were "black" people in Central or South America.[15]

Physical anthropologists, who are concerned with humanity's biological variations, have argued the issue of American Indian unity or variation for over a century. At the beginning of the twentieth century, the notion was widespread that a number of different races had migrated to America from the Old World, but soon the weak logic, data, and methods that had been used to support this theory were decisively attacked. Anthropologists generally came to argue for the basic similarity of all American Indians, although some European and Latin American experts found the evidence for a single ancestry less persuasive than the North Americans did.

Full consensus has continued to evade the scholars. The more numerous and more powerful wing still claim that all American Indians are essentially similar in biological makeup, with only minor exceptions, and that a single, very ancient origin (except for a few latecomers to northern North America via Alaska) is the explanation for the uniformity. A minority of competent specialists protest that the uniformitarian view is based on insufficient evidence and that it is too early to rule out the possibility that different groups arrived in the Americas to enter into the makeup of the American Indian.

For example, a conference held in 1990 still encountered the conflict. The argument for a straightforward origin of Amerindians via the Bering Strait was said to have been "undone" by certain archaeologists, linguists, and geneticists. One study reported at the meeting used the recently developed DNA technique to show "that there were at least 11 major lineages [or biological lines in the Americas], possibly more."[16]

The experts use three sources of data about ancient racial or ethnic features. First they study preserved skeletal material or tissue, but good specimens are scarce and interpretations can differ,[17] even though a majority see relative uniformity.[18] A second source is pre-Columbian art. Ancient artists sometimes showed striking differences in the appearance of human figures, including skin color. Were the differences they showed due just to the artist's whim? Was the use of body paint the reason for the different skin shades, or were the differences due to variable ethnic and racial origins? The third source of data on the question, the appearance of the living descendants of the ancient peoples, seems to some observers to confirm that the variations were biologically real, for they also show wide differences in skin color and overall appearance, beyond what can be accounted for by any late mixing with the Spanish conquerors.

Differences of degree of skin darkness may be manifest in this mural from Bonampak in the ninth century A.D., although some believe that body paint may explain the different hues represented. Yet it is reasonable that differences in skin pigmentation were present long ago when we consider the diverse ancient faces displayed in the next section.

About A.D. 1100 a mural painter at Chichen Itza in Yucatan plainly distinguished degrees of darkness of skin color on the men in this boat. The scene that includes this detail has been interpreted by some (non-Mormon) observers as showing a military defeat and ravaging of the light-skinned folks by the darker-skinned group.[19]

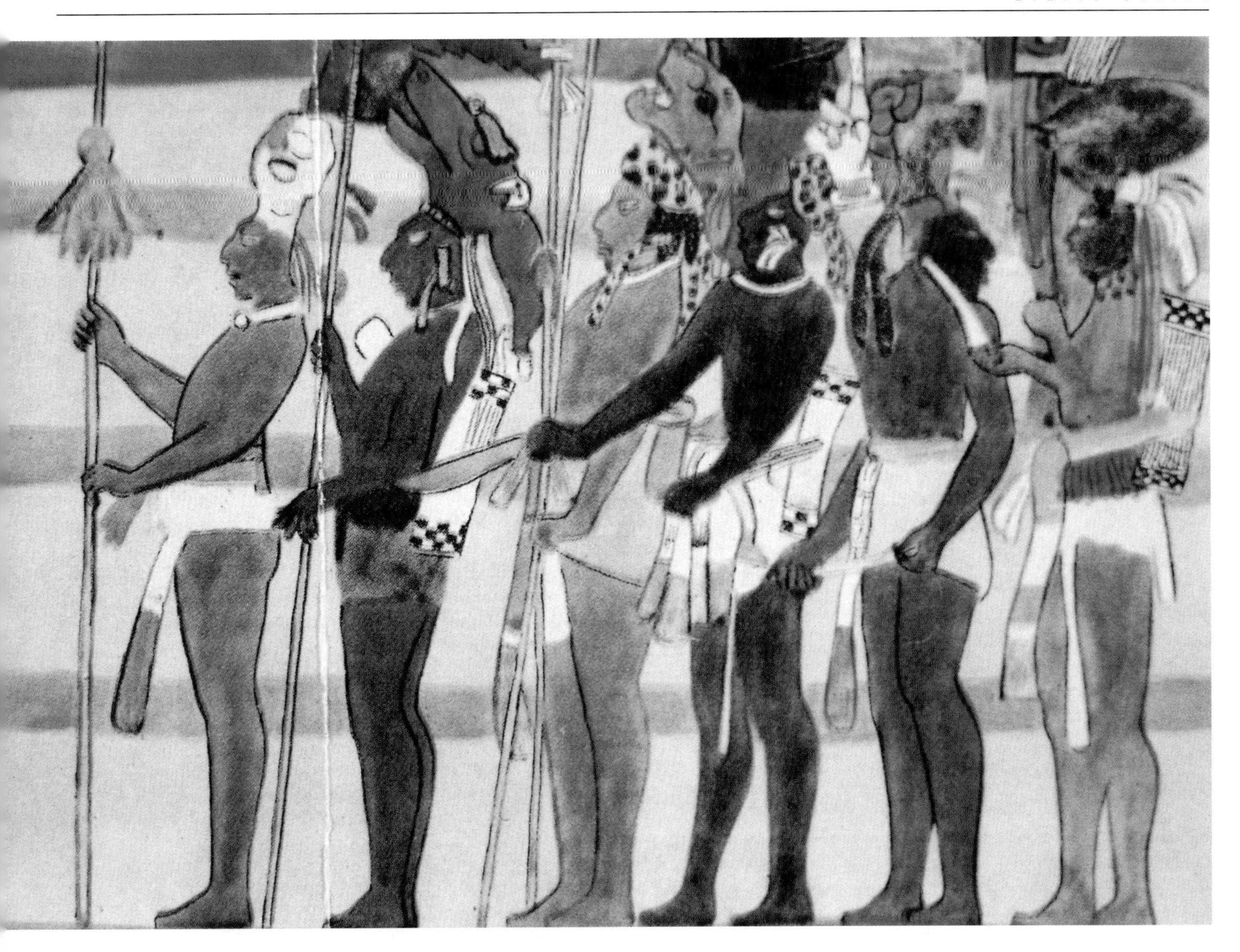

VISUALIZING BOOK OF MORMON LIFE

Mormon's record gives only minimal information about what Nephites or Lamanites looked like. Statements about skin color are made at a couple of points. The earliest Nephites were said to have been "white" or "fair" (2 Nephi 5:21),[20] while Lamanites were stereotyped as "dark" (1 Nephi 12:23). Later, however, certain Lamanite descendants were considered white like the Nephites (see 3 Nephi 2:15–6), while no hint is given that the skins of the numerous Nephite dissenters who became Lamanites darkened. We cannot develop an objective picture from the subjective statements that are all the text gives us. That leaves the question of biological variety open and complicated.

Other peoples were evidently present in the area when Nephi's and Mulek's parties arrived.[21] For all the text indicates, they could have included Mongoloid types. Very probably they involved unacknowledged descendants of the Jaredites, for personal names, plants, and cultural elements known among that earlier group show up among the Nephites without any historical explanation.[22] We have no way to know the biology of those Jaredite descendants. The numerous people of Zarahemla (commonly called "Mulekites" in LDS discourse, although not in the Book of Mormon text itself) shared the land of Zarahemla with the Nephites and became part of Nephite society. No facts about their biology are given in the text.

Throughout most if not all of Book of Mormon history, the terms *Lamanite* and *Nephite* signaled political and cultural affiliations, not biology. Skin color and other biological features within either faction could have varied considerably. Then, too, puzzling groups show up in Nephite history without adequate explanation. Who the Amalekites were and where they came from are questions never clarified; and the Amulonites in only a single generation are said to have become almost as numerous as the Nephites![23] Obviously, much more was going on and more peoples and cultures were involved in Book of Mormon history than modern readers usually detect when reading Mormon's terse, one-sided account. Given such uncertainties, it is well to remember Hugh Nibley's caution, "There is not a word in the Book of Mormon to prevent the coming to this hemisphere of any number of people from any part of the world at any time."[24]

A Gallery of Ancient Faces

The faces shown here are not claimed to be representative of the population of Mesoamerica at any particular time. Collected art objects can never provide a satisfactory basis for establishing what was representative. Rather, these countenances have been selected to demonstrate that anciently a surprising variety of human types coexisted in the area. A different selection of figures would have to be made to support the claim, common among experts, that Mesoamericans had only northeast Asian ancestors. Certainly many early figures display Mongoloid characteristics (see especially many faces to be seen in other sections of this book). But the present point is that types of people from many other parts of the world were also present in Mesoamerica. The faces shown here are portraits of such individuals, although their very presence is Mexico and Central America is ignored or denied by conventional physical anthropologists. Apparently the genes of those unexpected ancestors from other areas of the earth failed to survive on as wide a scale as those sprung from northeast Asian ancestry.

These ceramic heads are mainly specimens in private artifact collections in Mexico. The late Alexander von Wuthenau and other investigators have been struck with the variety of human types revealed by these objects and have drawn attention to this variety by photographic documentation.[25] They maintain that this is all the evidence needed to demonstrate that a wide variety of ethnic or racial types were present in Mexico and Central America.[26]

From the Classic era comes this lowland Maya bearded face with a notable nose.

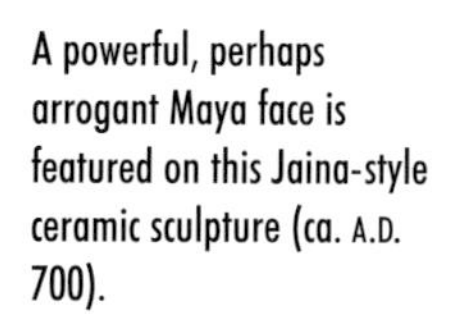

A powerful, perhaps arrogant Maya face is featured on this Jaina-style ceramic sculpture (ca. A.D. 700).

A rare arrangement of facial hair is seen on this racially unclassifiable portrait.

One of Palenque's greatest Classic rulers is shown in this magnificent plaster mask.

A Late Classic Maya (A.D. 600–900), from Guatemala.

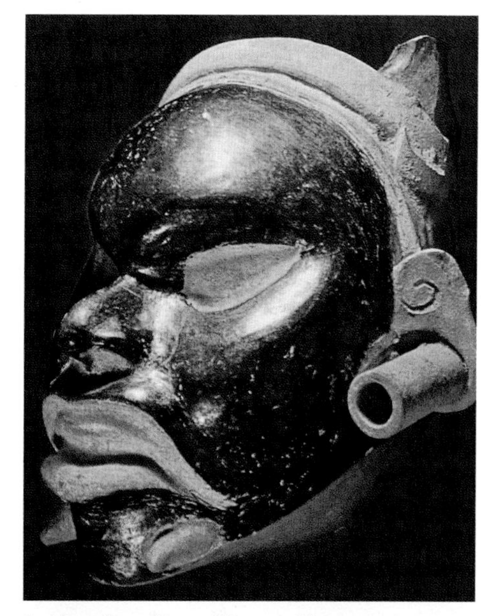

An African face, after A.D. 800, state of Oaxaca.

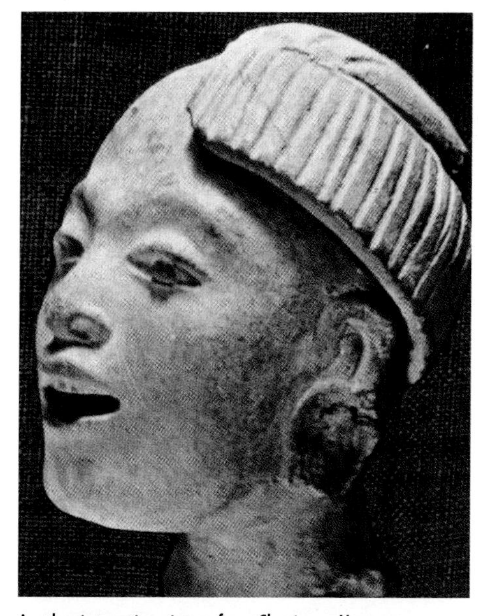

Another interesting visage, from Classic-era Veracruz.

A man in Olmec style from Puebla, central Mexico.

A Teotihuacan-style face from Veracruz, ca. A.D. 400.

A Semitic face, highland Guatemala, before A.D. 300.

A clearly Mediterranean type of face from Veracruz, of Classic age.

An Olmec jade mask that might be matched in, say, Korea.

Another Classic-age head from Veracruz that is very Mediterranean.

Another pensive woman from central Veracruz, A.D. 300–900.

An intensely Mongoloid face from the Veracruz Classic.

This head of Classic date from central Veracruz looks virtually Southeast Asian.

This "pretty lady" type was common in central Mexico in the first millennium B.C.

Young Mixtec woman, northern Oaxaca

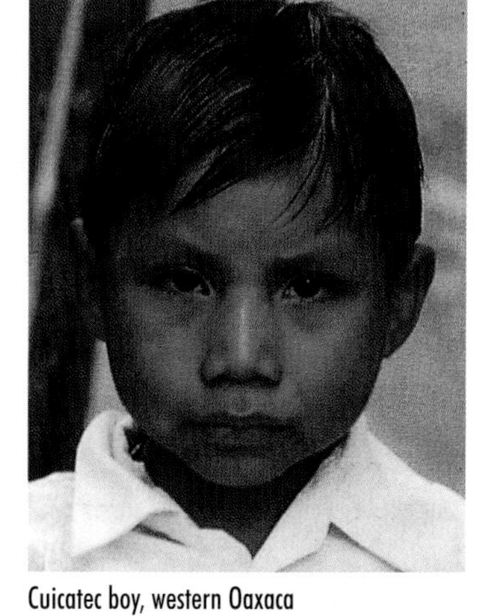

Cuicatec boy, western Oaxaca

Ixcatec girl, northern Oaxaca

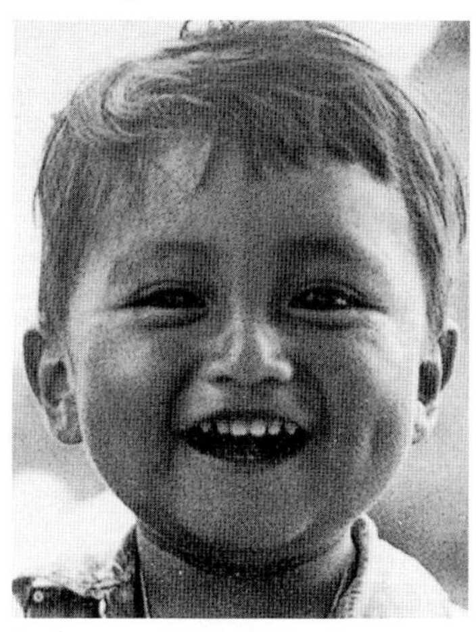

Another young Cuicatec, western Oaxaca

Zoque matriarch, central Chiapas

Old Zoque man, central Chiapas

Ixcatec man, northern Oaxaca

Mazatec woman, northern Oaxaca

A Gallery of Modern Faces

With so much biological variety present anciently, we should expect that some of those varied genes were passed down to Mesoamerica's modern native peoples. They indeed show substantial diversity in appearance. Of course, many problems complicate any attempt to penetrate the matter. For example, because the Spaniards and their diseases destroyed many Indian groups, the remnants of native peoples now to be found in Mexico and Guatemala represent only a sample of the range of groups that once inhabited the area. And the wars conducted by the Aztecs and earlier conquerors no doubt long before greatly modified whatever genetic composition was present, say, two thousand years ago. Mixing with the European newcomers may have further obscured the picture. Nevertheless, we still find evidence in living Mesoamerican groups of some of the ethnic complexity that prevailed anciently.

The pictures in this section are of individuals who still identify with their Indian tribal groups. They live in relatively remote areas of Mexico where native peoples continue to have a strong social presence. It is possible, though not likely, that the appearance of some has been influenced by their having had an incidental Spanish progenitor.

Zapotec woman, Tehuantepec

Mixtec madonna, southern Oaxaca

The Variety within Mesoamerica

Languages

It is logical to expect that the array of environmental settings and the multiple peoples occupying them would be reflected in the number and distribution of languages spoken anciently in Mesoamerica. Around the world, the more broken the terrain, the more fragmented is the distribution of languages. It is impossible to know precisely how many tongues were used in Mesoamerica, but two hundred would not overstate the number. (These were distinct languages, each one unintelligible to speakers of other languages, not merely dialects.)

Linguists are far from united on how these tongues related to each other. Some reckon that five or six major, independent families were involved. Those families differ from each other as much as, say, the Semitic family (including Hebrew) differs from the Indo-European family (including English and Latin). But other language experts are less willing to lump diverse languages into such gross families. The number of groupings they recognize is closer to two dozen, each seemingly independent from the others. Certain single languages have no apparent relatives at all in the area. No evidence hints that there was ever one dominant language or language family throughout Mesoamerica.

The accompanying map shows something of both the variety in and similarities among the languages of this area. On a map of Mesoamerica are plotted some of the words that mean "corn." Languages of the Mayan family, on the right side of the map, demonstrate how a particular early word (probably pronounced something like "eesh") ultimately varied from region to region as, over thousands of years, daughter languages split off and spread. The map also makes clear that in addition to the ancestral Mayan term, many other terms for corn were used, probably from early times.

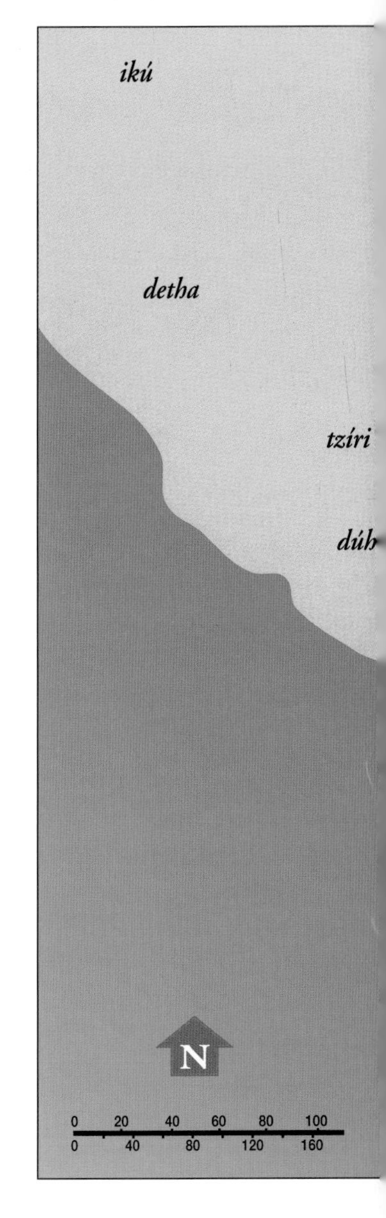

Corn in the Codex Borbonicus

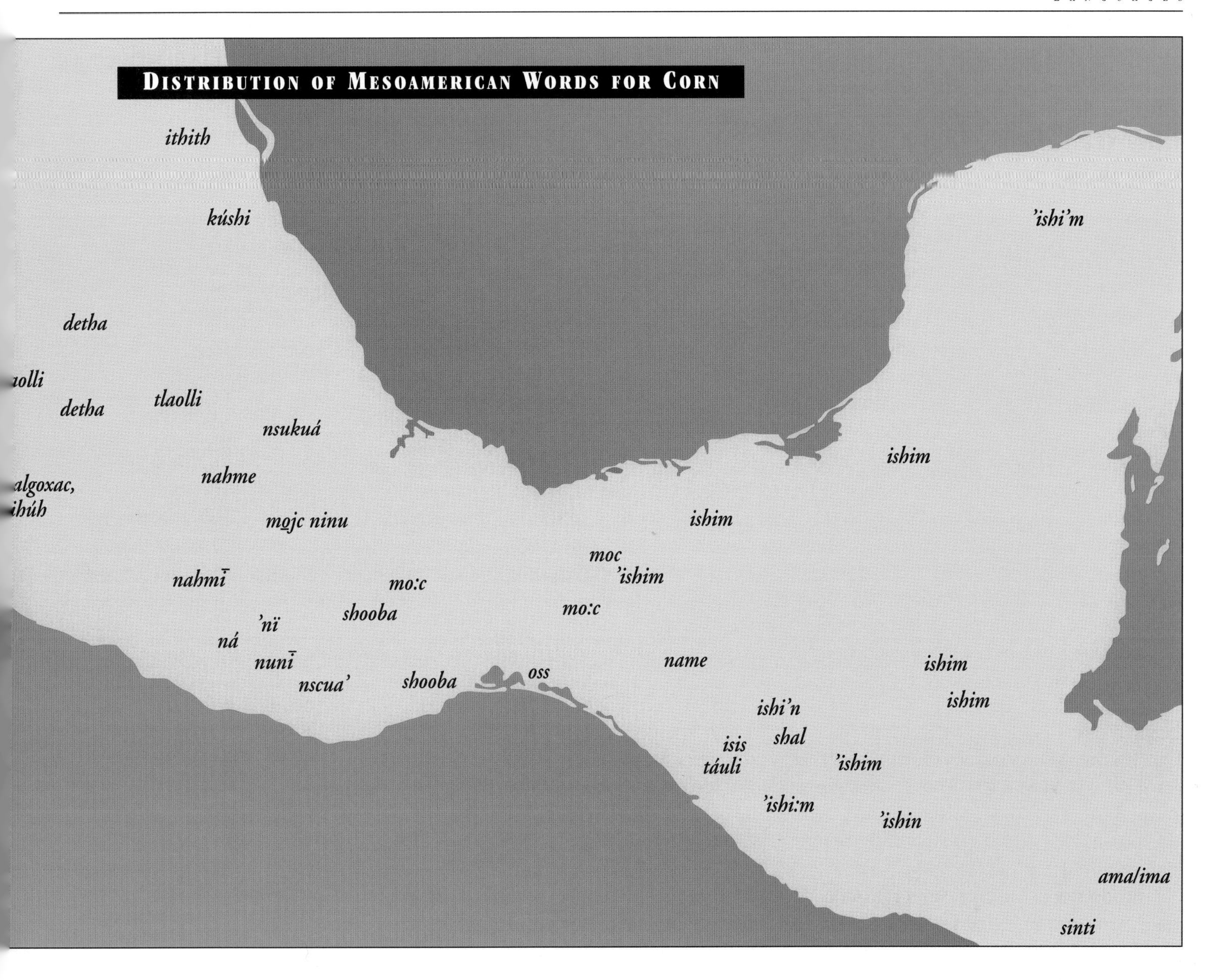

VISUALIZING BOOK OF MORMON LIFE

The Book of Mormon says extremely little about its peoples' languages. Lehi and his group initially spoke Hebrew, of course, but the brevity of the record does not allow us to determine if their descendants made an unreported change. (Keep in mind a potential parallel. The daily speech of Jesus' day in Judea was Aramaic, a language related to, yet different from, the Hebrew tongue that had been in use in Lehi's time. Yet if we did not have nonbiblical sources with which to reconstruct the history of the Semitic languages, we would not know the historical process by which Aramaic replaced Hebrew in Judea.)

We know that the spoken language of the people of Zarahemla in Mosiah$_1$'s day was not the Hebrew that had been spoken by Mulek's father, King Zedekiah, in Jerusalem. Omni 1:17–8 emphasizes that Mosiah$_1$'s Nephites and the people of Zarahemla spoke distinct languages when they first met. The Nephites assumed that Zarahemla's group had "corrupted" (Omni 1:17) their original Hebrew, yet research by linguists assures us that two branches from a common parent language would not change as rapidly as the Nephites supposed. The people of Zarahemla would still have been able to make recognizable sense of Nephite speech after only four hundred years of separation, if both had simply kept on using their own naturally evolving version of Hebrew. Instead, the Mulekites or the Nephites, or both, seem to have switched to a different tongue in those few centuries. Possibly they picked up a language spoken by survivors from the Jaredite era. And since the Mulekites greatly outnumbered their Nephite rulers, it is probable that the latter came to speak the majority tongue as the generations moved on.

The Book of Mormon gives no hint whether additional languages were used or not, though they might have been. Perhaps such a subtle matter was ignored in the very brief historical sketch we have for the early centuries of their history.

There is much to be learned yet. A few linguists have shown that a significant portion of Hebrew vocabulary and grammar is mixed into certain Mesoamerican languages.[27] Studies on that interesting matter continue.

Mesoamerican Civilization

Cultures and Civilization

Over a century ago people began speaking of the set of customs or ways of behaving that characterize each people as a *culture.* At first the term was only applied to the lifeways of tribal groups—"uncivilized" peoples with relatively simpler technologies and societies. In the nineteenth century, European and American explorers had busily penetrated every portion of the earth not previously directly examined by their countrymen. In the process they encountered hundreds of cultures; many of them were puzzling to European minds. The challenge of making intellectual sense out of this mishmash fell to an emerging group of scholars called anthropologists. Their core question became, "What is the range of possibilities—biological, cultural, and linguistic—for being a human being, and how can we explain the differences and similarities that have been discovered?" The development of methods for doing archaeology added the possibility of asking, "How did peoples differ in the past?"

Studies of living and extinct groups have demonstrated that tens of thousands of cultures have existed on the earth throughout history, each of them distinguished from all other groups in particular ways. Each culture can be thought of as constituting a set of rules for getting along in life; each is based on a different elaborated theory about the nature of humans and the world. Children, for instance, require years of experience and instruction to master the ins and outs of the culture in which they are reared, so that they can respond to situations unthinkingly, "naturally." Rules become second nature to them to guide them through such problems as when, if, how, and whom to fight or to embrace, how and whom to marry or divorce, and what to believe or to doubt.

Each ancient people in Mesoamerica followed its distinct cultural pattern. But as the descriptions of those patterns have multiplied at the hands of modern scholars, the notion of many separate cultures has increasingly clashed with an older concept—*civilization*. Historians, to whom the concept of civilization is old hat, are not very comfortable dealing with the idea of hundreds of cultures in an area. After all, the integrative concept of "Roman civilization" seems more useful than mere "Roman culture," used to refer to the unique ways of the early settlers of the city of Rome. Both terms, *civilization* and *culture,* have value but both can be confusing.

In this book, Mesoamerican civilization is considered the veneer or overlay of cultural patterns that were shared by the local cultures in the area. For example, an ancient Maya traveler who visited peoples beyond the boundaries of his own region would have noted that certain of their rituals, gods, social customs, foods, and taboos were enough like those of his home territory that he sensed an essential similarity. When the Spaniards arrived, even they could detect some cultural equivalents; they could see that a certain political role, a tradition, a ceremony, or a piece of art in one place was basically like what they had discovered elsewhere. Modern anthropologists and archaeologists are trying to reconstruct, clarify, and interpret what it was that the different Mesoamerican tribes or peoples had in common as well as how they differed, from each other and the rest of the world.

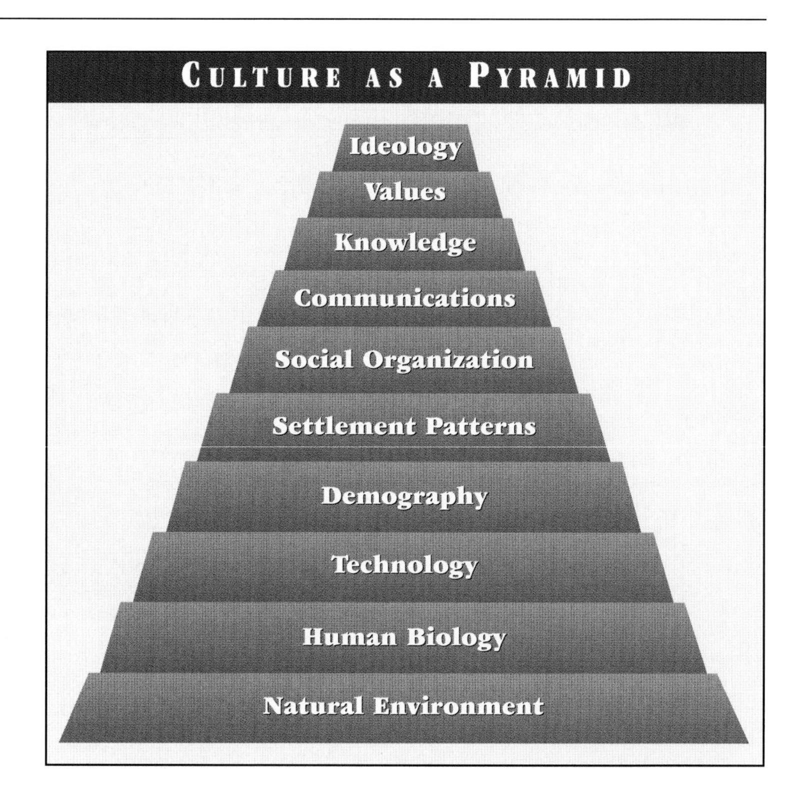

One convenient way to represent a culture is as a set of factors and conceptual rules that can be sorted into levels somewhat like a Mesoamerican pyramid structure. Aspects of a people's life situation at a lower level are more fundamental and harder to change than those higher up. Yet each "cultural pyramid" has solidified over its history to become an integrated whole. In the actual lives of people the categories are not like layers of a cake that can still be separated.[28]

Culture as Distilled History

Clifford Geertz, a noted anthropologist, has used a different image to represent culture.[29] A culture is something like an old city, he suggests. In part it contains old concepts and behavior patterns, symbolized by the quaint streets and courtyards in the plan of the city that still mark what once were cow paths and scattered hamlets. But cutting through those markers of the historical past may now be modern boulevards or even freeways. The cultural equivalent of those would be features like blue jeans, cola drinks, and computers which are superimposed atop hundreds of traditional cultures from Mozambique to Mongolia. Finding one's way around effectively in either an aged city or a mature culture can best be done on the basis of experience, not merely by consulting a guide book, Geertz thinks.

The lower sketch map shows Jerusalem at the time of Jesus. Its unique combination of Israelite, Greek, and Roman features symbolizes the historically unique mix of cultural patterns that ordered the lives of its inhabitants.

The Aztec capital, Tenochtitlan, shown in the upper map, displays another one-of-a-kind settlement and culture. This map was prepared in 1524 by one of Cortez's party to send to the Spanish king.

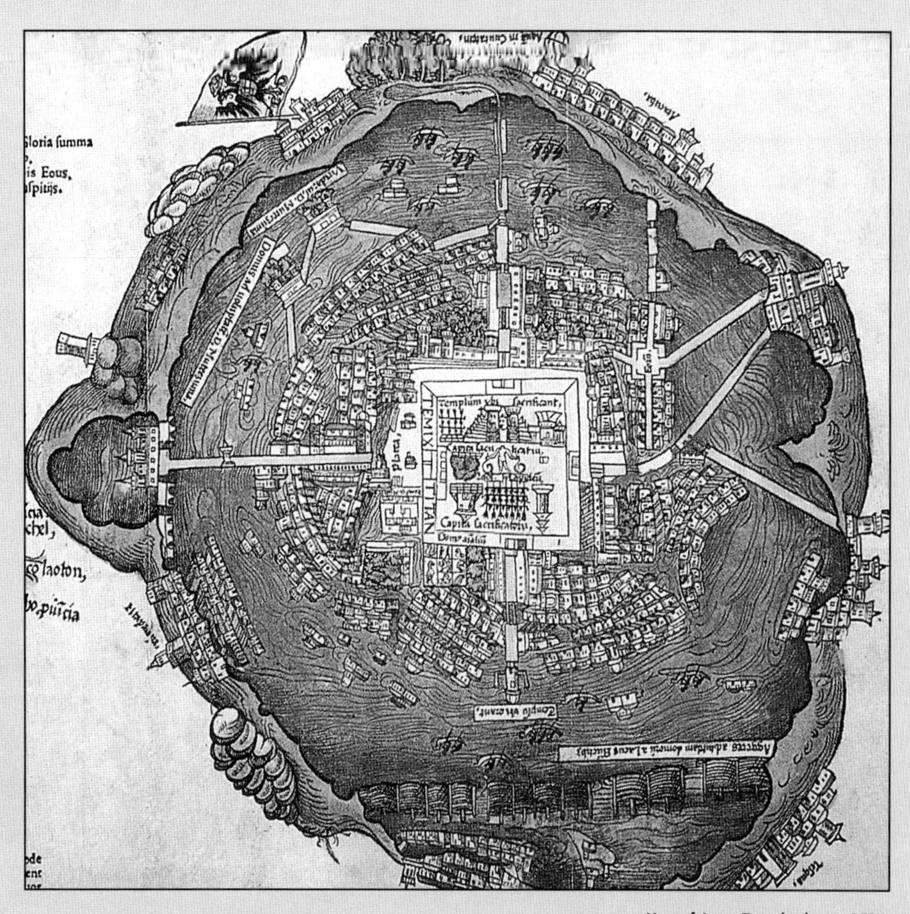

Map of Aztec Tenochtitlan in 1524

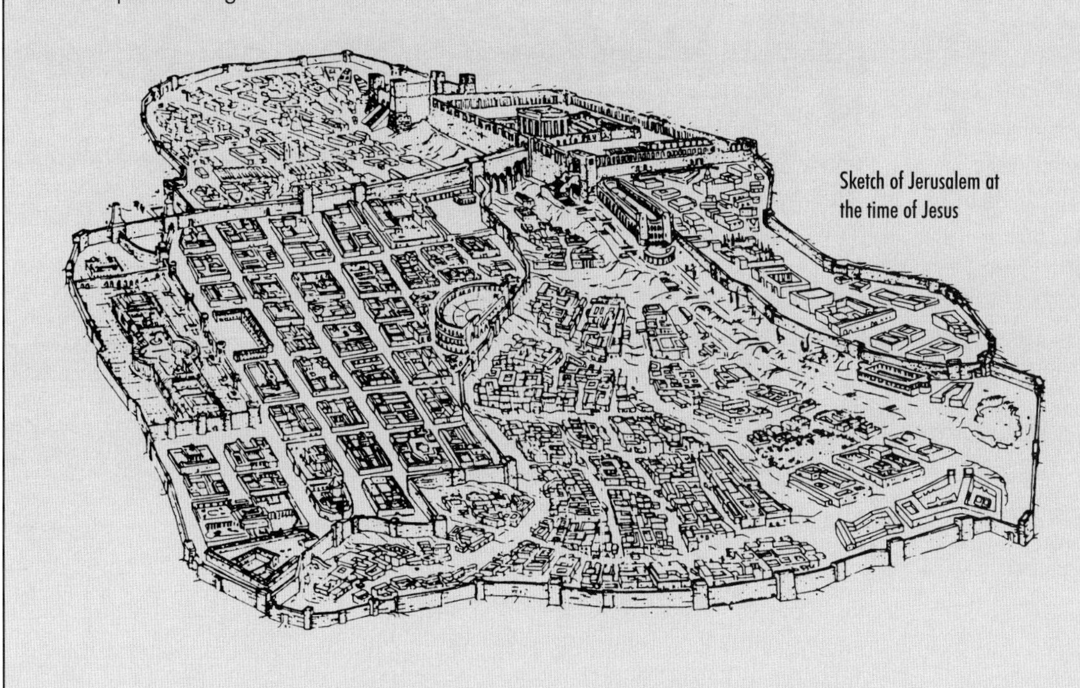

Sketch of Jerusalem at the time of Jesus

Level of Civilization

When the Spaniards arrived in Mexico they were surprised to find such a complex way of life. Their first encounters in America, with much simpler societies in the Caribbean islands, did not prepare their minds for what they would find on the mainland. They were taken aback by the Aztecs, who were the dominant political and cultural force in the area at the time of the Conquest. Shockingly barbaric in their massive human sacrifices, they nevertheless lived in large cities and employed highly effective technology and an intricate social system. Yet there is good evidence that thousands of years earlier there were cultures that were at a similar level of sophistication. Mesoamerican society in those times was at the same general level of development as the archaic civilizations of the Old World—Babylonia, Egypt, Greece, China, and India.

Cortez, the original Spanish conquistador in Mexico, wrote to his king about Mexico's capital city, Tenochtitlan, the seat of the Aztec empire, in this way:

> In the service and manners of its people their fashion of living was almost the same as in Spain, with just as much harmony and order; and considering that these people were barbarous, so cut off from the knowledge of God, and other civilised peoples, it is admirable to see to what they attained in every respect.[30]

About Cholula, a city in what is now the state of Puebla, Cortez noted that it consisted of perhaps twenty thousand houses in the body of the city and as many more around the outskirts. He commented:

> The city seen from the outside is more beautiful than the cities of Spain, because it is very level, and contains many towers . . . I counted from a mosque [sacred pyramid tower] four hundred and odd towers in the city, and all belonged to mosques.[31]

The Spaniard lamely summed up his awestruck impression in this report to his king:

> I know . . . (I) will hardly be believed, because even we, who see [these sights] here with our own eyes, are unable to comprehend their reality.[32]

This is the sacred precinct at the urban core of the Aztec capital, Tenochtitlan. The artist's reconstruction was made on the basis of Spanish eyewitness accounts and archaeological findings.

Not only was the scale of the civilization impressive, so were the qualitative aspects of it. Spanish craftsmen who arrived later were amazed by the sophisticated skills, ingenuity, and taste that Mesoamerican workers displayed. The Spanish military force, with the use of guns and horses that the Amerindians lacked, was barely able to eke out victory over its brave and resourceful opponents. (Had it not been for the new diseases the invaders brought with them, which quickly devastated the native peoples, the Europeans might have been driven off, which would have resulted in a very different scenario for subsequent history.)

The invaders were struck, as modern archaeologists are, by the simplicity of the tools and techniques employed by the ancient Mesoamericans. For example, the superb sculptures in green jadeite stone that so fascinate art aficionados today were made by a slow process of grinding, using nothing more than simple wooden drill bits. (The tool was rotated by wrapping the string of a bow around the bit and moving the bow back and forth; quartz sand beneath the bit was the actual cutting medium.) With plenty of manpower and thousands of years of craftsmanship to draw upon, Mesoamerican artisans were making giant stone statues and erecting vast cities using what seems to our modern age to have been primitive methods.

Beyond technology, the Mesoamericans also possessed immense bodies of systematized lore in astronomy, mathematics, engineering, medicine, botany, literature, art, philosophy, cosmology, and other fields of knowledge and creativity. For years language barriers, combined with the subtlety of much of the source material, hid its depth and quality from scholars and scientists brought up in the very different western European tradition. But in the last few decades a corps of investigators, mainly from Mexico, has been able to probe these sources. The result has been a stream of studies on esoteric matters that is, if anything, more impressive than the better-known work by archaeologists who have been showing through material evidence that a complex civilization existed in ancient Mesoamerica.

VISUALIZING BOOK OF MORMON LIFE

Book of Mormon writers describe for both the Nephites and the earlier Jaredites (and to some extent for the Lamanites) what they consider to have been elements of elaborate cultures. They report on successful agriculture, many arts and crafts (such as weaving), great cities, political states, class distinctions, populations in the millions, extensive records, widespread commerce, massive armies, and organized systems of religion, as well as "precious things of every kind and art" (Helaman 12:2) and "curious workmanship" (Ether 10:27; see Helaman 6:11; and, more broadly, Helaman 6:7–13 and Ether 10:5–6, 12, 22–7). The original leaders of the LDS Church as well as subsequent generations of members have held that study of this civilization would be valuable. In the 1842 words of Joseph Smith Jr. or a close associate, upon reading the account of explorations in Central America by John Lloyd Stephens, "It will not be a bad plan to compare Mr. Stephens' ruined cities with those in the Book of Mormon."[33]

Eerily beautiful artifacts called eccentric flints were chipped, ever so carefully, from common obsidian by the hands, brains, and eyes of master craftsmen. Such oddities exemplify how Mesoamericans imposed their unique ideas on materials that would have been handled only in utilitarian ways in other places in the world. No one knows for sure what eccentric flints signified, but surely they carried a heavy freight of sacred meaning.

Life's Routine

The Seasonal and Daily Round

A large majority of the inhabitants of Mesoamerica did not live in cities but in villages and hamlets. They had to be near their fields, for agricultural work was central to the activities of most households. The crucial crop was maize (corn). If enough maize could be provided, the remainder of life's necessities could be eked out by drawing upon a variety of other resources for additional food and for clothing and other essentials.

Land was prepared for planting strictly by men's hands. No animal power was employed in agriculture or in any other work. Clearing a field involved hand-cutting trees and bushes and then burning the debris when it had dried out. The intensity of the heat generated by burning the dry trash killed off the smaller plants and grass. About when the rains were predicted to begin, the unplowed, unleveled plot was planted (the thick ash served as fertilizer). Several kernels of seed corn were dropped into each hole poked in the earth with a sharp stick. The seeds were covered by a push of the sower's foot. Sometimes beans and squash would be planted in the same plot with corn; the different crops matured at different rates, so they did not interfere with each other. Fruit and seed trees as well as special garden crops were also carefully tended, usually close to the family's residence.

Timing was vital in this type of cultivation. The vegetation had to be cleared during the dry season to ensure a proper burn, yet the seeds needed rain soon after being planted if they were to germinate properly and keep growing. (The timing problem is thought to help explain the intense concern with the calendar in Mesoamerica; astrological predictions were made to try to anticipate when or whether the sacred powers would send moisture in timely fashion.) Where special soil and climatic settings prevailed, two or occasionally even three corn crops per year might be obtained. Where that was possible, a heavier population could be supported. However, there was never

An artist's sketch reconstructs aspects of daily activity in a community on the northern Yucatan peninsula. The scene is based on archaeological findings at the Komchen site that date to the middle of the first millennium B.C. The basic pattern of life shown was broadly similar elsewhere in Mesoamerica and would stay much the same for the next two thousand years. Even when cities arose, people preferred to live as near as possible to the style of life of villagers.

Families dwelt around, rather than in, their houses, preferring to spend time out in the light and fresh air. This west Mexican ceramic model (probably dating A.D. 100–600) illustrates the pattern. To be cramped up in a small dwelling, which was usually filled with smoke (there were no stoves or chimneys), was acceptable mainly at night or during unpleasant weather.

enough good farmland for long. The growing population exerted pressure on the system of cultivation, aggravating social disputes and reducing the adequacy of the diet.

From the settlements men and women spread over the countryside to catch or collect a wide variety of useful wild products—from fish, game animals, and edible insects to honey, dyes, minerals, and wood. Prized products were exchanged in markets and some were carried to other localities by traders. Only rarely was the transport of bulk foods or goods outside a local area feasible, since virtually all was carried on human backs.

Men's work revolved around the crops. That activity made heavy demands on their time only at certain seasons, yet those needs were so vital that they set the schedule for everything else in the year. During slack periods wars were fought, trading journeys were undertaken, and houses were built or repaired, for instance.

For women, turning corn and other staples into food was the most determining labor. In most cases, every single day of her adult life a woman could expect to rise before light and hand-grind fresh cornmeal using a stone roller atop a hard, flat stone. From this grist she made the day's food in some form of bread—chiefly in the form of tortillas (toasted on a griddle), or tamales (wrapped in a leaf and boiled), or as a wet ball of cooked dough that could be diluted with water and drunk during the day like modern instant breakfast. Basic food preparation had to be done early in the day because custom decreed that the first meal be the most substantial one. Men set off to work very early (they might have to travel several miles to their fields) to avoid the midday heat, so women's toil began even earlier. For women, too, there were routine tasks like weaving cloth and making garments, gathering firewood, toting water, caring for children, manufacturing or repairing household equipment, and so on.

When darkness came, so did sleep for all. Leisure was not a daily but an occasional thing, usually in connection with the frequent religious events.

Fish and other aquatic products were valued as sources of protein, which was scarce in the usual diet. A majority of settled areas did not have bodies of water nearby that yielded many of those products, but in a coastal area like this part of Tabasco state, fishing was routine.

Wherever fishing was possible, it received regular attention, as in the Valley of Mexico with its major lake. This scene from the Codex Mendoza says that an Aztec youth was expected to know how to fish effectively by age fifteen.

The most common spot for the hearth was on the floor. The tortilla-making housewife squatted or knelt next to it. No conveniences were thought necessary in these rudimentary kitchens.

Kitchen gardens were planted near dwellings where women could do the occasional tending they required and also have convenient access to the produce.

VISUALIZING BOOK OF MORMON LIFE

In a record like the Book of Mormon that was devoted mainly to sacred matters, it is no surprise that little is said about the people's daily activities. The comments are general: "they did raise grain in abundance" and kept "many flocks and herds" (Helaman 6:12). Ammon helped tend his master's flocks and drive them to water (see Alma 17:25–6); "their women did toil and spin, and did make all manner of cloth" (Helaman 6:13). About such mundane tasks as cooking, getting wood and water, making pots, or repairing roofs, no statements are made. We are left to infer such routine, obvious matters.

Cultivation of Corn

Typically the best land to plant was what had been in forest for a number of years. Shade would have killed out grass and weeds. Once the tall plant cover had been cut and burned off, grass would start to return. After two or three years in corn, a plot would have to be abandoned because of competition from the thickening grass. That plot would be abandoned to let trees and brush come back and again shade out the problem plants. After a dozen years or so of forest regrowth, the cycle could be repeated. However, in some areas with comparatively rich soil, a corn field could be cultivated almost continuously with the help of vigorous weeding.

Mature corn cobs were bent downward so that rain would not get in them and cause mildew. Sometimes the dry cobs were picked and taken straight to the kitchen as needed; in other situations storage bins were built. Loss of grain to birds and vermin was often high.

When the dried vegetation on the corn plots that are being prepared is set ablaze, typically in March or April, the atmosphere over wide regions is obscured by smoke. If this manner of burning was widely carried out in Jaredite times, it may have been a cause of the lack of timber noted by their successors (see Helaman 3:5–6). This scene is in southern Chiapas.

Hand-planting of the seed required no laborious plowing or other soil preparation, just time and patience.

Grass and other weeds had to be curtailed by hand labor during the early stages of the crop's growth, but the competition invariably won out in the long run.

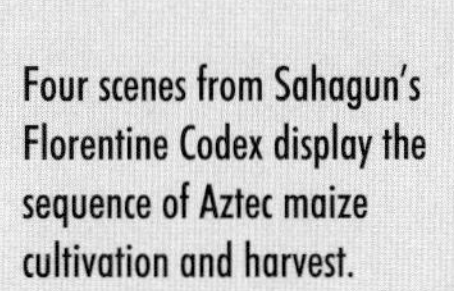

Four scenes from Sahagun's Florentine Codex display the sequence of Aztec maize cultivation and harvest.

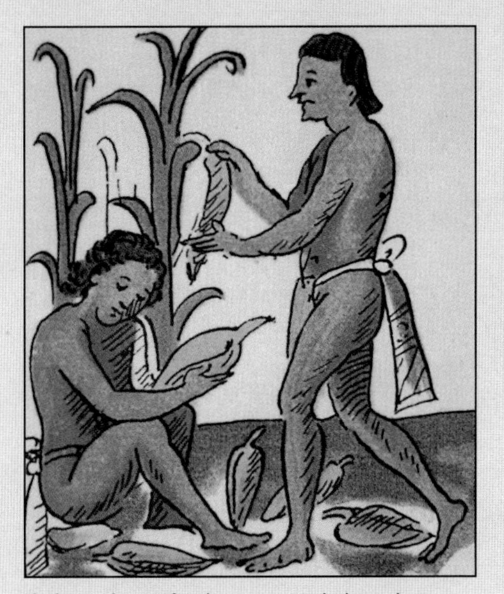

The harvest began after the rainy season had ceased, and went on for some time.

A variety of storage bins were used; shown here is an Aztec version.

Foods

Griddle-toasted tortillas were the staff of life anciently in central Mexico and areas influenced from there. Raised bread like ours was unknown. In southern Mesoamerica the tamale (ground cornmeal wrapped in a leaf and cooked in hot water) was the preferred form for corn cookery. The only ovens were stone-lined underground pits, and there was no frying (fats were scarce and metal was not used for cooking utensils). Boiled beans were typically mashed into a paste. Squash of several sorts was roasted or toasted. Many varieties of chilis were used to season all staple foods. A number of other grains, especially amaranth, were extensively used, as far as they could be grown in particular localities.

Different kinds of root vegetables—manioc, sweet potatoes, jicama—were also in use, although they were not preferred at the level of the beloved, even worshipped, maize. Tree fruits, such as the guava and a type of cherry, were also enjoyed, though only during the seasons when they matured, for techniques for preserving them were unknown.

Fish were consumed where it was convenient to obtain them. Especially because of the need for protein, a great variety of other strange foods gathered from nature were also utilized, including varieties of insects and fungi. In fact, virtually every edible substance was consumed by some part of the population, including many things that we now consider inedible.

The commoners' cuisine consisted mainly of the fundamental food triad—corn, beans, and squash[34]—but there were hundreds of regional and community variations in recipes and supplementary dishes. The whole array was far too varied according to regional tastes, products, and customs to be lumped together accurately as though there had been just one pattern. (The invading Spaniards were told that the Aztec emperor Montezuma dined from a choice of two thousand dishes that his cooks were capable of preparing.)

Mesoamerican and Andean farmers between them had domesticated a large number of American plants before 1492. These were welcomed and adopted in most parts of the Old World where they were carried by European travelers after Columbus. Nowadays those foods help feed our teeming world on every continent, and cultivators in places like China and tropical Africa have no historical recollection of when and from where they received their borrowed-from-America crops. Among the most useful food gifts to the world were corn (including popcorn), potatoes, chili peppers, peanuts, avocados, and tomatoes.

These carved fish were found in excavations in the Aztec Great Temple beneath present-day Mexico City.

Several major races (a term used by botanists) of corn, encompassing hundreds of varieties, were grown and eaten.

Visualizing Book of Mormon Life

The Book of Mormon speaks only in general about food (see, for example, Mosiah 4:17), as we might expect in a preponderantly religious text. The most comprehensive list of Nephite crops emphasizes grains (see Mosiah 9:9). Corn is there implied to be a, if not the, mainstay (compare Mosiah 7:22 and 9:9). The term *bread* referred to a cereal food that was functionally equivalent to modern bread (see, for instance, Alma 8:21–2). That could be the tortilla, since nowhere in the text is there a hint that the leavening process was known. Fruit too was grown and consumed routinely, the book tells us (see Enos 1:21 and Mosiah 10:4). Meat is also mentioned as part of the diet.

Various kinds of beans were grown in nearly every zone.

Many varieties of mushrooms were gathered and eaten. A few types were used by some groups for their hallucinogenic effects.

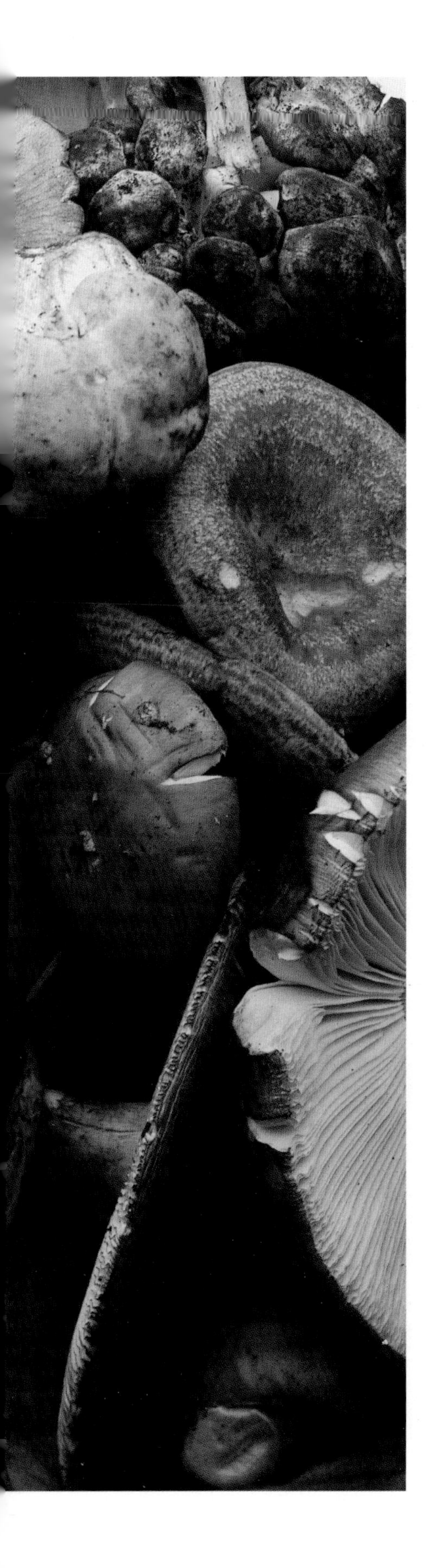

Chilis put spice in an otherwise bland diet, and they were vitamin rich.

A variety of squashes had been staples in the Mesoamerican diet for thousands of years by the time this Aztec stone sculpture was made in the fifteenth century.

Avocados provided a nutritional rarity in the diet—fat—comparable to the olive in Mediterranean cuisine. Mexican tomatoes were small but tasty garnishes to go with plainer food.

One of the most popular ways of cooking maize was in the form of a tortilla, the hand-flattened, unleavened cake now familiar worldwide.

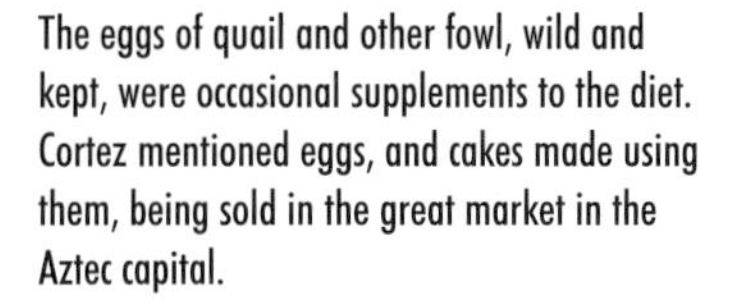

The eggs of quail and other fowl, wild and kept, were occasional supplements to the diet. Cortez mentioned eggs, and cakes made using them, being sold in the great market in the Aztec capital.

Vegetables were not staples but provided variety. All the foods shown on these pages are consumed by some Mexicans still today.

Roots (such as the sweet potato), tubers (like the small variety of potato included here), and fruits were important in the diet in some areas.

Luxury Consumption

There were luxury foods too, of course. The most valued was the cacao bean from which the chocolate or cocoa drink was made (our word *chocolate* comes from the Nahuatl word *chocolatl*). Since the cacao bean was also used as a form of currency, consumption of chocolate was mainly limited to people of wealth. The tree grew mainly in a few moist, foothill zones, especially in southern Chiapas and near the Gulf Coast in Tabasco. Honey was gathered from the wild, but stingless bees were also domesticated and kept in log hives. Sweetened popcorn in the form of balls or squares was also enjoyed. Sugar was made from the agave plant, with some difficulty and expense; its use was not common.

Fermented alcoholic drinks made from various plants were in wide use. The Spaniards labeled these beverages wine (technically they were closer to beer). There seems to have been no knowledge of distilled (hard) liquors anywhere in the Americas until the Europeans conferred that dubious gift on the Native Americans. Most of the consumption of these wines took place in connection with religious celebrations (of which there were many!). Certain moral restrictions on drinking restrained people's consumption at other times. The aged were seldom restricted from drinking as much and as often as they wished.

VISUALIZING BOOK OF MORMON LIFE

Wine is mentioned quite often in the Book of Mormon from Jaredite times on. It was used both routinely and to excess (see Mosiah 22:7; Ether 15:22; Alma 55:31; and 3 Nephi 18:2). Apparently they made more than one type (see Alma 55:32). The only other beverage mentioned is water (see Alma 5:34).

The Jaredites kept bees, though nothing is said about honey. Nothing is said in the Nephite record of sweets or treats, but we may suppose from comparison with other peoples of the world that they must have made and enjoyed some kinds despite the fact that the mass of people would have had little chance to consume such relatively expensive products on a routine basis.

Chocolate comes from seeds of the cacao fruit that were ground to powder. The seeds are shown at the top. The beverage made from ground chocolate was whipped to produce thick foam on the top. At the bottom of the photograph is vanilla, a valued condiment that was sometimes added to the drink.

This elaborately carved container in Izapan style dates to around the middle of the Nephite period; the style is diagnostic of the area and period that the main narrative of the Book of Mormon covers. One can imagine drinkers of the higher social class (such as are described among Noah's people) taking their wine from such a beautiful vessel, while commoners settled for a plain gourd or shell container.

The most popular fermented drink in modern times is pulque, made from fermented juice of the agave plant. In central Mexico its use was very ancient, although other wines were also made. Incidentally, the Spaniards spoke of the plantings of the agave cactus as vineyards (recalling Mosiah 11:15).[35]

The lack of a source for making abundant sugar, combined with the relative difficulty of getting honey, meant that, at least in some areas, a majority were too poor to indulge a sweet tooth very often.

Peanuts, amaranth seeds, or popped corn were combined with honey to make these delicacies—peanut brittle or popcorn treats—for special occasions.

Animal Use

The practical uses of animals in Mesoamerica were somewhat limited. The number of potentially valuable species was fairly small, and then for unknown reasons the people failed to show much interest in their utility. A few species were kept for food (domesticated, or at least tamed). Flocks of turkeys were common, and occasionally quail, doves, one kind of duck, a kind of pheasant, and grouse were maintained in flocks. A small hairless dog was fattened and eaten; the Spaniards referred to these dogs as being kept in herds.[36] Certain other animals were kept somewhat incidentally without their meat ever more than lightly supplementing the vital vegetable foods. Several types of wild fowl were hunted and their eggs were gathered to be eaten. Game animals, particularly deer, were hunted regularly, but of course whenever the human population increased and cultivated areas became extensive, it disrupted wild habitats, so the yield from hunting near population centers declined.

Among certain groups, attention to animal husbandry was common enough to show that overall, Mesoamericans could have done more had they chosen to. Animals occasionally tamed included the tapir, the peccary (wild pig), the guinea pig, the paca (a large rodent), rabbits, and deer; they even kept some of these in penned enclosures. Yet these societies chose to make a point about not exploiting nature practically. This reluctance was somewhat like their determined refusal to use complex technology, as noted earlier; they managed well enough without going to the trouble of elaborating their tools or doing much with the fauna.

"Impractical" uses of animals were numerous. For instance, a wide variety of fowls were kept tied or penned so that their feathers, which were valued decoratively and ceremonially and were widely traded, could be collected. Many animal species—coatimundi, deer, and pigs, for instance—were kept as pets, especially by women and children, and pets were not eaten. Animals were also important in ritual and myth. All the common species were considered sacred in some context or other, which may have been a reason that they were infrequently exploited as mere meat. Several types were sacrificed. An Asiatic type of chicken was present that was used only in divination ceremonies. Furthermore, there was curiosity about animals; the Aztec emperor had a large zoo, aviary, and aquarium adjacent to his palace, where three hundred men worked full-time caring for the caged birds alone; others tended jaguars and other wild felines, deer, wolves, foxes, and even a buffalo.[37]

There was an incidental benefit of great significance in the fact that these people did not dwell amidst large numbers of animals, as was the case in many Old World communities. Scholars concerned with medical history in America now believe that this lack of animal hosts for diseases was an important reason for the relative lack of epidemic disease here as compared with the central Old World.[38]

Visualizing Book of Mormon Life

The flocks and herds of the Nephites (only sheep are mentioned for the Lamanites) presumably included several sorts of fowls. Turkeys are native to the New World, and flocks of them would have been valuable possessions. The Book of Mormon account refers to people who "tend," "raise," and "have" useful animals, but the words *domesticated* or *tame* are not used (see Enos 1:21; Mosiah 10:21; Helaman 6:12; Ether 9:17–9). Some of the names applied by the Nephite record keepers to the native beasts they found on the land when they arrived (they brought none themselves) probably were applied to broadly similar species, just as the Spaniards did when they arrived (for example, the Spaniards called the bison or buffalo a cow). Deer were the most numerous large mammals in Mesoamerica. Artists depicted deer in sacred scenes and even being ridden. The failure of the Book of Mormon to mention deer may mean that it was one of the animals for which the record in English uses a name of what we consider some domestic beast, perhaps the Nephite "horse." All told, the record of the Nephites is notable for its emphasis on crop agriculture rather than animal husbandry as central to their culture, considering that their tradition originated in Palestine where animals had been so vital.[39]

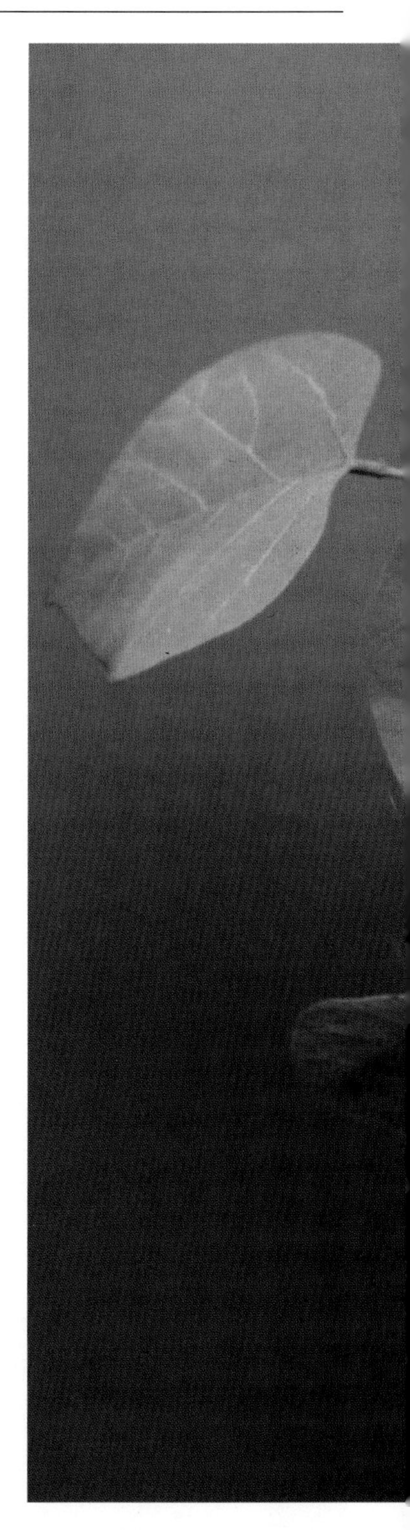

This is one of dozens of types of kept birds from which prized feathers were plucked.

Quail were taken from the wild and sometimes kept in semidomesticated flocks. They were sacrificial as well as practical objects.

Several kinds of ducks are represented in the work of Mesoamerican artists, such as in this fine modeled pair from Colima, west Mexico, dating to the period A.D. 200–600. At least one species, the Muscovy duck, was domesticated.

American gobblers had been kept in flocks for many centuries before the Spaniards came, as shown by this ceramic effigy (dated before 500 B.C.) Their flesh, eggs, and feathers served obvious ends, but the whole fowl was also often sacrificed.

The peccary is a close relative of the Old World pig. It usually ran wild in the forests, but in a few places in America it was tamed.

Barkless dogs were fattened and eaten, as some people do with rabbits today. The Spanish conquerors considered them good eating when fed them by the Aztecs.

The tapir was one of the largest animals in the area (up to 650 pounds), although it generally shied away from settled areas.

The tepeixcuintli, this pig-sized rodent, has tasty flesh, although it has not been demonstrated to tolerate very well living in the vicinity of humans.

Crafts and Tools

One of the key craft activities in ancient Mesoamerica was making ceramic pots. Archaeologists are fascinated by these ancient vessels because fragments of them are so abundantly preserved at many archaeological sites. Millions of the vessels were used anciently, but after a fairly short time, those in use would shatter or crack. When replacements were made, small changes in style would be inevitable, hence a continuous series of variant fashions over time can be identified if we have a sufficiently large sample of potsherds in hand. The sequence of style details in each region has been worked out with considerable exactitude, so the variations become a guide to chronology. Looking at any pot, or a major fragment from one, a well-informed archaeologist can tell within a century or so (and sometimes less) when it was made.

Almost as common as pots for carrying or storing supplies were perishable containers: baskets, gourd shells, and vessels carved from wood. Unfortunately, few such items have survived decay in the damp soil of the tropics for archaeologists to recover.

A subtle decorative design is evident on this pot. It is from Cuicuilco in the Valley of Mexico in late B.C. times.

This vessel in the Usulutan style features wavy, "combed" lines that were produced by the use of wax to protect certain areas in the decorating process (like batik dyeing of cloth). Usulutan was popular on vessels from El Salvador, Guatemala, and Chiapas in the final centuries B.C. It may prove to be something of a marker of the early presence of Nephites and Lamanites.

We are even more impressed by the sight of an entire set of ceramic vessels that a culture's potters produced than by any single specimen. Here is an artist's reconstruction of the entire suite of pieces by craftsmen of the Barra phase on the Pacific coast of Chiapas around 1400 B.C. Since this, the earliest pottery known in the area, is already very sophisticated decoratively and technologically, the craft had obviously had a long history already.

The intricate Izapan style, exemplified by this stone bowl from the Pacific coast near the Guatemala-Chiapas border, characterized the period when Nephites lived in or influenced the area, around 1 B.C. "The city . . . in the borders by the seashore" likely was in this area (Alma 56:31; see 56:32).

Knowledge about minerals was extensive, but smelted metal was not of as much concern to them as it was to Europeans or Asians. A majority of the metal products that have survived are decorative, not practical. Relatively few practical implements of metal have been discovered in the ruins, and probably few were used.

Obsidian was crucial in Mesoamerican technology. Extremely hard (though brittle), the edge on a fragment of this volcanic glass is sharper than most metal knives. This substance was the fundamental raw material from which cutting tools were manufactured. Weapons, knives, points, woodworking tools, razors, and other implements were all made of it. Trade in obsidian was carried on through networks of merchants that extended up to a thousand miles. That trade was as vital to the Mesoamericans as oil commerce is to the modern world.

Equivalents of our hammers, saws, chisels, and axes were made from obsidian or from polished stone. Some stones were fastened by glue or wrappings to wooden handles. In certain ancient sites archaeologists have found workshops where artisans specialized in producing particular implement forms. The waste products are still found lying about. Finished products were traded to other places.

Wood also served for making certain implements, such as digging sticks for planting and paddles for boats. Bone, antler, and leather were other materials turned into utensils—needles, awls, scrapers, straps, and the like.

Wide-edged bowls like this one clearly mark the last two centuries B.C. in highland Guatemala. This specific type contained gifts of food or incense placed with the dead in a tomb (compare the "sepulchre" in Alma 19:1, 5) and dated about 100 B.C.

These examples of everyday baskets from the state of Tabasco are similar in style and function to containers from two thousand years ago.

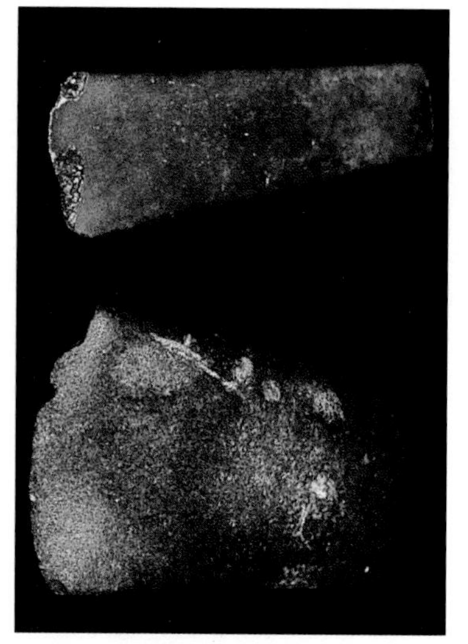

The practical quality of metal tools like these, mainly of copper, left much to be desired. They did not retain a good cutting edge for long. A stone axe was cheaper and about as effective as one with a metal head.[40]

Custom-finished obsidian tools were sometimes made from large, semiprepared chunks of the raw material at or near markets, where customer needs could be matched more easily than at the obsidian source.

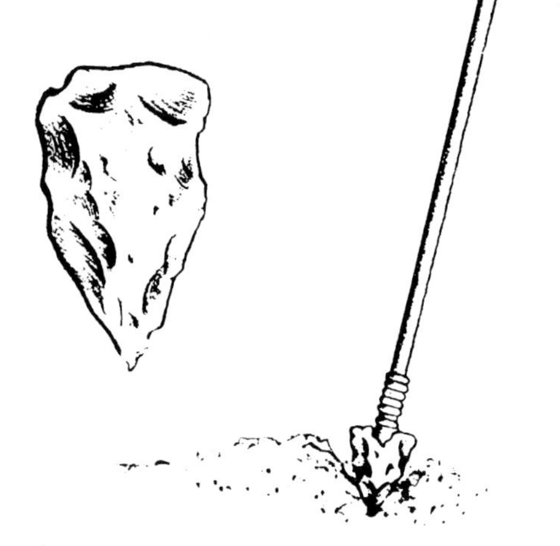

Either a stone-tipped stick or a pole with its wooden end hardened by fire served for digging.

Skilled men used an antler tip or a bone point to press at key points on chunks of the volcanic glass, splitting off thin fragments one after another.

Ancient tools and their modern equivalents are shown paired.

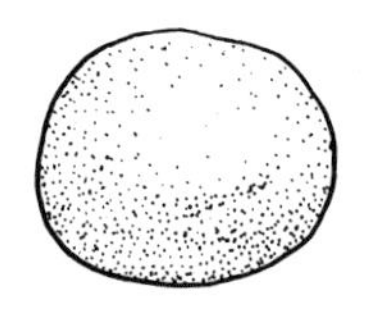

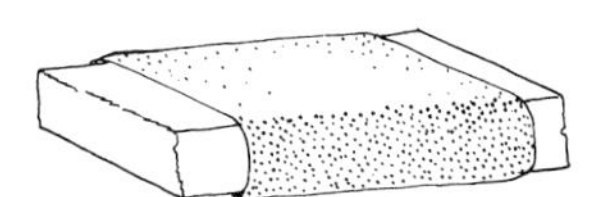

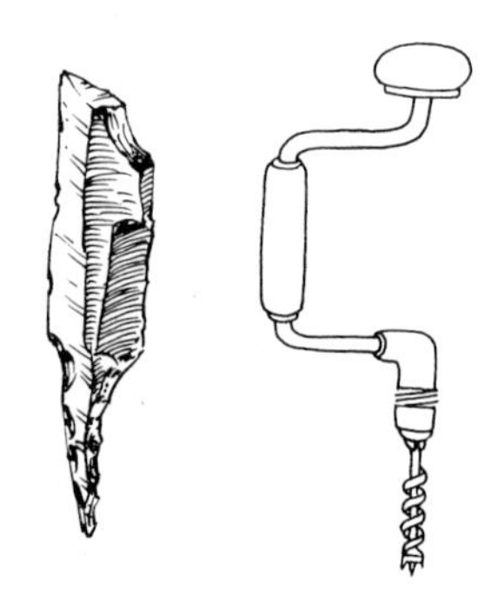

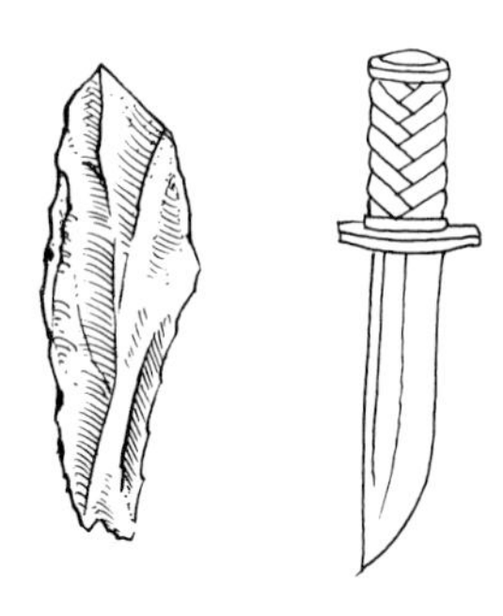

One type of drill was rotated by the back-and-forth motion of a bowstring

Examples of superb ancient wood carving have been preserved on only a few specimens, like this Aztec drum from the period of first Spanish contact. There must have been many such masterpieces.

Sahagun's Florentine Codex pictures an Aztec metalworker plying his craft with a very simple but effective apparatus. Molten copper pours from the crucible into a mold to form an axe head.

VISUALIZING BOOK OF MORMON LIFE

Most practical objects were too workaday to be mentioned in the sacred Book of Mormon. Tools are mentioned in general (see, for example, Jarom 1:8 and Helaman 13:34), but nothing more specific is said about equipment that the Nephites and others must have had, like pots, baskets, or hoes. Cups (see 3 Nephi 18:8) and cords (see 1 Nephi 7:16) do happen to be mentioned.

Weapons, of course, are often mentioned. They include the axe, which could have served for everyday tasks as well as for war. In a Mesoamerican context, it seems probable that "Onidah, . . . the place of arms," (Alma 47:5) to which certain Lamanites fled to defend themselves against their ruler's oppression, refers to an obsidian outcrop where they would have at hand all the crude weaponry they could want.

The ceramic containers illustrated in this section are among a wide repertoire that was characteristic for Mesoamerica during the main period of Nephite history. The Nephites might have used similar pots for preparing or serving food or conveying "the last tribute of wine" (Mosiah 22:7) to the Lamanite guards. Not shown are plain, grubby, undecorated vessels that were used to carry or heat water and store raw foods. Only minor changes ever took place in their forms.

A scene from the Florentine Codex signifies that the Aztec merchant, like those before him for thousands of years, was considered to live a hard, dangerous life on the road. Yet the prospect of wealth made the profession attractive to some types of men.

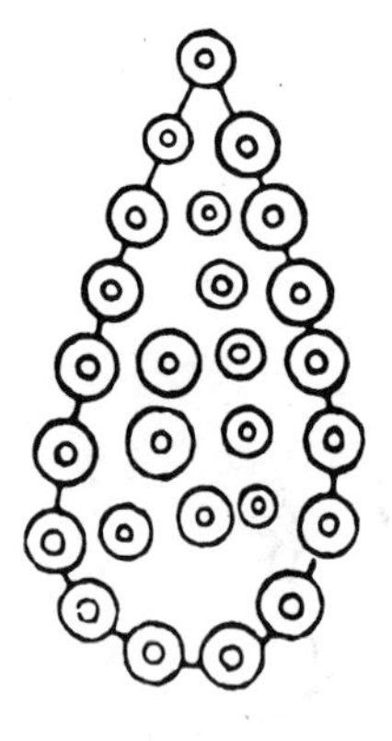

Above: The Aztec glyph sign for marketplace uses footprints to convey the idea of a bustling crowd. Below: T[illegible]stellation known to us as the Ple[illegible]the Marketplace by the A[illegible] is obvious from a

Markets and Commerce

Trade was a vital process in Mesoamerican civilization. For thousands of years both long- and short-range commerce was carried on, archaeological studies demonstrate. Variation in terrain, soils, and climates meant that people in any one area needed or wanted products they could not obtain except from somewhere else. For instance, cotton was the preferred fiber for clothing everywhere, but the plant only grew at the lower, hotter elevations. For highlanders to obtain a supply, they had to exchange products they had available. Outcrops of good obsidian occurred only in a few localities, while the demand was universal, and salt, an essential in the diet, was rarely available except on the coast. So specialization in the production of food, fiber, animal products, and minerals tended to develop from place to place.

The control of crucial resources was probably key in the development and maintenance of early governments. Only rulers were in a position to control the wealth that was required to outfit an expedition headed off to seek distant products and negotiate trade with local rulers or merchants. In some periods a special class of full-time merchants existed who were given unusual privileges. Among the Aztecs the merchants also acted as spies for the military.

Every administrative center (town or city) of any consequence had a regular market, usually held at a plaza adjacent to a key temple or other religious installation. Visitors usually combined trade with worship. At such "downtown" scenes, important social interaction and news sharing took place. No doubt the market experience provided many with relief from the relative boredom of rural life.

Native markets continue today in parts of Mexico and Guatemala that still convey the color and excitement that characterized such places anciently. The best description of an elaborate pre-Columbian-style market comes from Cortez's first visit to the Aztec capital. He was told that over twenty thousand people daily visited the plaza in the Tlatelolco portion of the metropolis. (There were smaller markets—"shopping centers," as it were—in other parts of the city.) He wrote

> There are all sorts of vegetables, and . . . many kinds of fruits, amongst others cherries, and prunes, like the Spanish ones . . . , honey made of a plant called maguey . . . ; from these same plants they make sugar and wine. . . . They also sell skeins of different kinds of spun cotton, in all colors, so that it seems quite like one of the silk markets of Granada [Spain], although it is on a greater scale [here]. . . . They sell maize, both in the grain and made into bread, which is very superior . . . ; pies [tamales] of birds, and fish, also much fish, fresh, salted, cooked and raw; eggs of hens [turkeys], and geese, and other birds in great quantity, and cakes made of eggs.
>
> Finally . . . they sell in the city markets everything . . . which is found in the whole country. . . . Each kind of merchandise is sold in its respective street, and they do not mix their kinds of merchandise . . . thus they preserve perfect order.[41]

The occupation of merchant could bring big rewards, although it was a hard life. The most profitable trips were long and often dangerous. Even if a party of servants helped carry goods (no animals were used to haul loads), the total cargo borne had to be small, so high-value goods were the ones sought—feathers, jewelry, cocoa beans, cloth, obsidian, and salt. Natural hazards on the trail, like storms, wild beasts, and snakes, combined with the threat of

bandits. Moreover, the people at the far end of the journey might be enemies of the merchant's tribe, so diplomacy or even disguises might be needed. Yet the commerce that merchants carried on was so vital to all concerned that the travelers normally went about without much political hassle.

Some of the color and liveliness of the huge marketplace that Cortez described is caught in this museum reconstruction of that scene.

This market at Chichicastenango, Guatemala, has changed from its pre-Spanish status mainly in some of the merchandise, the use of coins, and the costumes of the participants. The basic social and economic functions are unchanged, as are the color and bustle.

VISUALIZING BOOK OF MORMON LIFE

The Book of Mormon emphasizes the significance of trade to the prosperity of the people it tells about some nineteen centuries ago. "The Nephites did go into whatsoever part of the land they would, whether among the Nephites or the Lamanites. And . . . thus they did have free intercourse one with another, to buy and to sell, and to get gain, according to their desire. And . . . they became exceedingly rich" (Helaman 6:7–9). Note the link between trade and literacy on the one hand and wealth on the other in the rise of civilization among the Lamanites, as reported in Mosiah 24:6–7.

Transport

Most goods were moved on human backs. The rest went by boat. For over four hundred years after the Spaniards made large animals available—actually until only decades ago in some regions—carriage of merchandise by men was typical. It was simply more efficient for humans to do the work. Modern experience has shown that it takes longer and costs more to move goods using animals because of the time and trouble it takes to care for and rest them. In any case, the ancient Mesoamericans had a poor selection of beasts available that might have carried a load.

Where a network of waterways allowed, fleets of canoes swarmed, carrying all kinds of goods as well as people. Most were simple dugouts that went only a short distance before the load was moved to another vessel, yet the size of some boats ranged upward to sea-going vessels. One reported during a voyage by Columbus near Yucatan was eight feet wide ("as large as a galley," the report said)[42] and carried over fifty people plus cargo.

Along the Pacific Coast, large, navigable log rafts (of the type built by Thor Heyerdahl), and sizable boats also, traveled from Ecuador via Panama to as far as west Mexico. The prime attraction for this trade was to acquire the Spondylus shell (used as a sacred trumpet), which certain Ecuadorian groups valued highly. Such trips were apparently made periodically for thousands of years, right up to the time of the Spanish Conquest.[43] But Mesoamericans did limited sea voyaging themselves, in part because there were few good harbors along their coasts and in part because the most populous areas were usually located some distance inland.

In recent years, hundreds of miles of roads have been found radiating outward from major population centers throughout much of Mesoamerica. Built-up roads (the Mayan language term was *sacbe*, "white road") like this remnant at the site of Labna in Yucatan were not primarily for travelers but were routes for ceremonial processions, although they were used for routine transport where they were available. Mostly, however, well-worn trails served the surefooted human burden bearers.

Human bearers routinely carried from sixty to one hundred pounds of all sorts of goods on their bent backs. The load was held in place by a band across the forehead. They often traveled at a near trot and for up to ten hours a day.

This 1820s drawing shows the type of raft from Ecuador that sailed along the coast as far as Mexico. Notice the kitchen garden growing at one end of the raft and cooking facilities at the other. Almost identical rafts were used in southern China and Vietnam for thousands of years. Some Europeans who saw these craft thought them primitive, but we now know they were actually highly developed, steerable, safe ships.

An artist has reconstructed what a visit by Maya traders to Tulum, on the east coast of the Yucatan peninsula, would have looked like around A.D. 1500. Tulum is the spectacularly situated site on the coast near Cancun that has been visited by millions of tourists. Significant commercial travel in boats like these was a feature of life in the peninsula area.

VISUALIZING BOOK OF MORMON LIFE

Practically nothing is said in the Book of Mormon about modes of routine travel. All cases of overland movement that are mentioned are phrased consistent with the idea that human carriers were utilized. We read specifically of Alma and his people under their Lamanite and Amulonite masters who "put heavy burdens upon their backs" (Mosiah 21:3). It seems noteworthy that the emphasis in this statement is the heaviness of the loads. Lighter loads probably would have been seen as routine rather than harsh treatment.

In only one very brief period throughout the millennium of Nephite history (and never among the Jaredites or Lamanites) do we hear of their use of ships. The first were built by the inventive Hagoth (see Alma 63:5–8 and compare Helaman 3:10). But only one route is indicated, northward up the Pacific coast from the "narrow neck of land" (Ether 10:20), apparently Tehuantepec, and even then the risk or cost involved seems to have discouraged further maritime ventures, for after the master builder disappeared on a voyage, most migrants to the land northward went by land, as they had done before (see Alma 63:4, 9; Helaman 3:3–5, 8, 12).

Lacandon Maya of eastern Chiapas make and use a traditional dugout canoe. Thousands of these were once used to fish, to cross streams, or to be poled along waterways to destinations no great distance away. Some merchants also used them on legs of longer journeys.

THE LITTER

Cultural preference throughout Mesoamerica called for a person of social prestige to be transported by litter. The system was sensible enough in practical terms—in whatever remote spot a group of travelers might stop, fresh carriers could be found so long as carriage depended on human muscles. Furthermore prestige entered in; this form of transport was reserved for nobility and others of the upper social levels. To have used any other mode would have been to give up privilege and demean oneself. Privileged and sacred leaders were similarly carried in the stretch of the Old World from the eastern Mediterranean through Southeast Asia in earlier times.

This drawing from a Maya painted vase from around A.D. 750 shows a priest or dignitary being borne in a litter. Bishop Landa reported from Yucatan that dogs bearing spots that resembled a cacao bean, like the one shown here, were seasonally sacrificed amidst the cacao trees to implore the deities to bless the yield of seeds from which prized chocolate was made. Maybe this hound would not have been wagging his tail if he had known what awaited him.

The higher the prestige of the person being carried, the fancier the litter. This is an artist's representation of the Aztec ruler's plush "vehicle."

THE WHEEL

It once was supposed that ancient American peoples did not even know the principle of the wheel, but discoveries by archaeologists of many small, wheeled "toys" has changed that view. The "toys" are now understood to have been miniature ceremonial objects connected with ideas about death, burial, and, probably, the sun. Mexican specimens date from as early as the first century A.D. In the Near East similar wheeled models were in use from before 3000 B.C. into medieval times, having spread as far as western Europe and China.[44]

The usual interpretation of these objects by Mesoamericanist scholars is that while the prehistoric peoples obviously knew the principle of the wheel, for unknown reasons they never translated the idea into practical vehicles. Yet these same scholars celebrate the inventive capabilities of the early Americans. Would they have been familiar with these miniatures for at least fifteen hundred years without trying to make a practical vehicle? In fact, the vehicle concept was known. When the Spaniards invaded Guatemala, they reported that the Quiché Indians used "military machines" consisting of wooden platforms mounted on "little rollers" to haul weapons around one battlefield to resupply their soldiers.[45] But on the broken terrain so common throughout Mesoamerica, wheeled vehicles may rarely have seemed worth the trouble. (One interesting suggestion is that Mesoamericans lacked lubricants that would have made full-sized wheels practical.)

Archaeologists have not found direct evidence of any useful wheeled vehicle. This lack in Mesoamerica is made less surprising when we learn that no fragment of a chariot has ever been uncovered in the Holy Land, despite the fact that thousands of them are reported by the Bible to have been used.[46]

This object in a private collection probably was looted from a tomb in west Mexico.[48] That the craftsmen who constructed the device knew what a vehicle was is beyond question. Perhaps a wheeled platform like this was used ritually in a funeral procession.

Some of the so-called toys had wheels attached to an axle running directly through the feet of a modeled animal. Most often these were dogs or deer, both of which had a mythical connection to death. But this example from Veracruz, of unknown meaning but probably from between A.D. 600 and 800, is unmistakably constructed on the principle of a wheeled vehicle. A monkey (or perhaps only a monkey skin) is draped over a wagonlike platform.

VISUALIZING BOOK OF MORMON LIFE

In two situations reported in the Book of Mormon, a word is used that might be supposed to refer to wheeled vehicles, once among the Lamanites and once among the Nephites. Yet what is said is so brief that we are left unclear about the nature of their "chariots."

In the story of Ammon in the land of King Lamoni, "horses and chariots" were made ready to "conduct" the king to the land of Middoni (Alma 18:9; see 18:10, 12; 20:6). Because nothing is said or hinted about mounting, riding, or dismounting from a vehicle, we cannot confidently conclude that vehicles were used to carry people, although this may have happened. Later, according to 3 Nephi 3:22, the Nephites who gathered at a refuge zone where robbers would besiege them had "taken their horses, and their chariots." Yet in 3 Nephi 4:4 the "horses" are considered along with "cattle" as "provisions." So it remains a mystery what "chariot" means in these texts. The word might have been used in a nonliteral sense. Nonliteral language abounds in the record. For instance, the Savior speaking to the Nephites applied the words of Isaiah to a future day when Israel was to be gathered, prophesying, "I will destroy thy chariots" (3 Nephi 21:14) as well as modern "graven images" (3 Nephi 21:17) and "groves" (3 Nephi 21:18), whatever they might be. Clearly some analogy, not literality, was intended in these cases.

The text of the Bible also leaves the word ambiguous. Hebrew roots translated to English as "chariot" include the dictionary meaning of "wagon or chariot" but also "litter, portable couch" or human-borne "sedan" chair (in the Talmud the same expression even meant nuptial bed).[47]

"Chariots" aside, nothing else in the Book of Mormon indicates that the people it describes used vehicles.

Houses and Furnishings

People in ancient Mesoamerica generally spent as much time outdoors as they could (most inhabitants of the tropics do the same). Socially prominent families in towns and cities constructed substantial houses, sometimes of adobe bricks or more rarely of stone blocks. Typically, however, walls were of small, straight sticks (or even reeds or cornstalks) aligned vertically and tied to the house frame. The spaces between the sticks might be left open, allowing smoke from the cooking fire to disperse, but if cold temperatures or frequent storminess called for better protection in a particular locality, mud would be smoothed over the sticks and then the wall would be whitewashed. Most roofs were of thatch.

Dwellings most often stood apart from other buildings. Multistory structures were very rare. In some large cities, side-by-side "apartments" were constructed. Houses for related groups of nuclear families were sometimes arranged around a courtyard where there was a shared shrine. Except in the most densely populated cities, fruit trees and a kitchen garden often sat near the house complex; wealthy homes might have more elaborate, even decorative gardens.

Furniture familiar to us was virtually absent. Meals were eaten seated or squatting on a mat on the floor. There were no tables, although a workbench in some houses held the hearth, a flat stone for grinding maize, and a clay griddle. Beds normally consisted of mats placed on the floor for the night, although a hammock or a mat-covered pole platform was sometimes used. No nighttime bedcover was used except one's own garment, such as a cloak. The possessions of a common family were so few that a shelf or a few baskets would provide enough storage space. Chairs were unknown, although stools, or in fancy houses a stuccoed platform built against a wall, could serve as seats for senior males. Window coverings and fitted doors are other features familiar to us that the ancients did without.

Thatched-roof huts are still the norm in Mexico and Central America. With the exception of the extension built on this house, which has been constructed of sawed boards, this hut near Izapa, Chiapas, would be nearly identical to a commoner's house two millennia or more ago.

Multiplying the size or number of rooms, as in the case of this set of connected buildings in the state of Tabasco, anciently could have turned a village headman's residence into a public building as a community grew.

VISUALIZING BOOK OF MORMON LIFE

Nothing is said directly in the Book of Mormon about the houses of the Nephites, but a few inferences shed some light. That the city of Zarahemla "did take fire" (3 Nephi 8:8) from lightning (see 3 Nephi 8:7) confirms their perishable nature, especially of the roofs, no doubt made of thatch.[49] Most people would have had houses only large enough to contain their immediate family (consider "the poor" in Mosiah 4:24, Alma 5:55, etc.) But upper-class people must have had larger units into which guests could be received. Amulek, a man of means (see Alma 10:4), had a sizable household; his establishment included "my women, and my children," and, perhaps in the same household, "my father and my kinsfolk" (Alma 10:11). The hospitality he offered $Alma_2$ was returned to him when, destitute and exiled from his home community (see Alma 15:16), Amulek was taken into $Alma_2$'s own house (see Alma 15:18). But of course his host was the high priest and former chief judge over the Nephites, so no doubt he dwelt in a substantial house that could accommodate guests, including at a later time the princely sons of $Mosiah_2$ (see Alma 27:20). The text is also appropriate in reporting that $Nephi_2$, another upper-class person and former chief judge, had a house and garden with a tower in it for worship involving, probably, his extended family (see Helaman 7:10).

Archaeologists find remnants of simple pole-frame houses from earliest times. This sculpted representation of such a house is on a stone arch at the Maya site of Labna, dating almost fourteen hundred years ago. It shows what the prototype temple structure looked like—little more than a common house.

Three structures under construction in the Maya area display the steps still followed in constructing rural housing. The biggest investment consists of labor, which was shared among kin or neighbors.

A sketch of a house built in Yucatan sixty years ago shows the inside, with the roof omitted by the artist for the sake of visibility. It also demonstrates that the ancient custom of using little furniture has persisted even through centuries of Spanish influence.

Hundreds of miles northward, in a much cooler spot (Tlaxcala state), the same basic house form was also used. Materials are a little different, but the basic form varies only slightly throughout Mesoamerica.

URBAN HOUSING

The desire to have green nature close at hand was strong. Only under extreme political and economic conditions did people crowd their housing together side by side. Even then the desire for family autonomy favored isolating complexes from one another behind walls, each group building around a courtyard with the dwellings of close relatives adjacent.

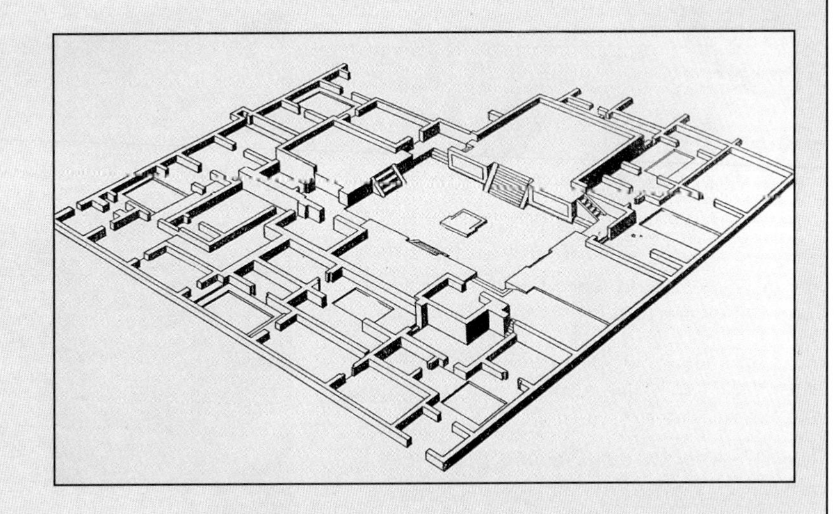

In relatively dry central Mexico, flat-roofed apartment-style units were utilized. Adobe brick and cement were common materials in an area with limited forests. This housing form was developed in response to what seems to have been a political plan to resettle people in as small a space as possible; the reason for this plan is not clear. This complex at Teotihuacan dates to about A.D. 500.

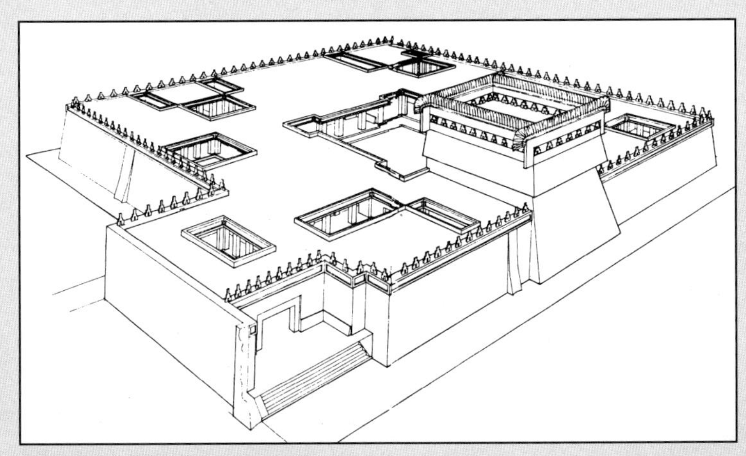

An architect's reconstruction of an excavated palace (?) at Teotihuacan shows how these urban units were roofed. Notice the openings at various points to let in light and allow smoke to escape.

In A.D. 1500 the Aztec capital, Tenochtitlan, utilized housing units somewhat like those from nearby Teotihuacan a thousand years earlier. This artist's reconstruction is said to show a "middle-class" Aztec house, but that may be an overstatement in terms of today's connotation. A typical home probably was less consciously decorated and somewhat more shopworn.

Society

Overview

We saw earlier that the fragmentation of Mesoamerica into a mosaic of culturally, linguistically, and ecologically diverse areas is striking. The ways for organizing societal relations were correspondingly varied. Almost any rule that one might propose as *the* Mesoamerican way for organizing and managing social matters had many local exceptions. Nevertheless, three general categories of social concern stand out. One is family and kinship, another is community or locality, and the third is social rank or class.

In certain areas of the world, intricate networks of kinship were maintained and complex institutions and labeling systems based on descent resulted. That was not so in Mesoamerica. Kinship factors were relatively straightforward. There were large-scale kin linkages that resulted in lineages or clans (scholars differ in their definitions of such terms in this area), but the mass of people probably did not identify themselves with particular ancestors beyond a few generations. The social elite—leaders—on the other hand, clung to knowledge of their descent lines because their privileges or rights to rule and enjoy benefits depended on their ability to establish connections to the elite of previous generations, that is, to validate their social standing by "blood."

A second significant aspect of social organization was community. If an ancient Mesoamerican had been asked, "What group do you belong to?" he or she may well have responded with the name of their local land (roughly the equivalent of a county in the United States—after the Spanish Conquest, these local lands are called *municipios* throughout Mexico and Guatemala). At least outside the cities, the people who lived together in one land usually shared similar customs and most knowledge about the world. Similar ecological conditions prevailed within these units. Throughout each, the same tongue or dialect was likely to be spoken, and an integrated pattern of economic activity,

A beautiful wall plaque from a Late Classic site in the mountains of Chiapas displays the power and confidence leaders possessed by virtue of their elite standing.

political governance, and worship usually prevailed. (In urban areas the variations could be much greater.) Such broad, vague concepts as "nation" or "tribe" meant little if anything to commoners. Easily 90% of what was of direct significance in the lives of most persons was referable to close kin and this local scene.

These two social dimensions, kinship bonds and links with the community, played against each other. If several kin groups happened to live in close proximity, the necessity for social cooperation to form livable relationships with nonkin neighbors would push community forward as an integrating mechanism. On the other hand, some settlements consisted of essentially a single extended kin group, so relationships based on ancestry played a greater role in tying the people together.

Above this fundamental fabric of society, there was a superstratum of institutions. Higher-order links tied families, kin units, and communities into the larger entities we call by such terms as *tribe, nation,* and *civilization.* These ties included the social class structure, government, shared cults, and associations one chose to join, similar to the guilds of medieval Europe.

Political and economic relationships were key shapers of society on this higher level of integration. There were kingdoms and even empires, of a sort, in Mesoamerica. Sharing the rulership of a particular leader or leading family was an obvious way to stitch together the diverse interests of localities, kin groups, and individuals. But, we shall see later, political institutions as we think of them today were inherently weak in ancient Mesoamerica.

Not surprisingly, economic ties also effectively served to meld local units into networks of mutual dependence. For example, relationships and expectations between buyers and sellers, between craftsmen and patrons, and between merchants and other merchants formed a pattern through which much of life in large-scale social gatherings was ordered. Merchants required the cooperation of political leaders, and those leaders benefited from the enterprise and wealth of the traders. Merchants everywhere tended to look out for the interests of other merchants, even forming cooperative guilds or secret associations to support one another and facilitate their wealth-gaining activities. Rulers and their relatives in one region made alliances, sometimes through intermarriage, with their equivalents in other regions.

Virtual churches or cults also existed—that is, sets of persons and families who practiced the same rituals and shared certain religious beliefs. We are uncertain what relationships resulted from religious diversity, but there are indications that it could have been a significant issue.[50] The social significance of differing belief systems was made visible by the priesthood structures. People looked to the priests as leaders in many important matters, especially where tradition and written records were involved, for the priesthood held the important key of full literacy. In turn the religious leaders lived off the offerings contributed via the political leaders by adherents to their beliefs and practices. Priestly power-holders were aligned with political and economic power groups in an establishment that shaped such aspects of culture and society as concerned them. Differences in access to privileges marked the social classes. The upper crust—the political, economic, and religious elite—was small in number compared with the mass of farmers and craftsmen on whose productive backs fell the burden of supporting the whole show.

The presence of a dominant class at the top of the social pyramid had the merit of giving focus and direction to regional culture. Within such a unit, the inevitable disputes that arose between neighbors, localities, communities, or rival kin groups could be mediated or quashed by the exercise of the combined powers of governmental sanctions, religious belief and tradition, and economic interests. Meanwhile, beyond the local area or group, the elites in their interrelationships from area to area and regional culture to regional culture formed a unifying tapestry of power and custom. Their network facilitated handling the issues of peace, war, and trade.

Family and Kin

Kin or quasi-kin relationships were fundamental in Mesoamerican society, as in all other ancient societies. The nuclear family (husband, wife, and immature children) constituted the basic residential unit, but it was at a disadvantage in agrarian society. Only extended kin groups or networks could muster people and wealth on the scale necessary to hope for security in that uncertain world, so the small family's dwelling tended to be adjacent to or near those of kin. Competition was high, as it is among us, but it tended to be between larger family units rather than between individuals or nuclear families as is the case today. Yet even extended families could prove vulnerable. Amid the mix of ethnic and other units that prevailed in Mesoamerica, no kin-based entity could control enough resources to guarantee its continuance. Consequently, extended families hedged their bets by forming bonds with other players in the society—other families linked with them as lineages and tribes, friends, merchant associates, the folks in the neighborhood, a powerful political leader and his supporters—rather than depending entirely on their own family group. Thus the mosaic nature of the Mesoamerican physical scene had its counterpart in social relations, which featured variety and interdependence.

Besides the benign side to kinship, which provided economic, political, social, and emotional support for participants, there was a dark side. In many ways individuals were not free to choose their own course of action because they were bound so tightly to kin.

Where it counted, attention was paid to genealogical descent (records were kept by priests). Lines of ancestry determined membership in the larger kin groups ("lineages," in a generic sense). Among the Maya, for instance, tracing descent "provide[d] an effective basis for individuals to assert claims to one another's protection and hospitality in their movements from one locality to another."[51] Patrilineal (father-to-son) descent was the most common form, although certain rights could also descend through the mother's line, particularly among the nobility. Yet no one system could serve equally well everywhere when circumstances differed from place to place. In cities it would have been especially difficult to maintain traditional kinship ties and forms, because people settled there from a number of regions and traditions, and urban life by its scale and nature tends to break down the force of kinship bonds.

One man typically married only one wife, although having multiple wives was not uncommon for those able to afford it. The keeping of concubines was also a practice tolerated among some groups, and prostitution was known. Again, in certain groups, divorce and remarriage were not all that difficult to arrange, for men.

Rarely in Mesoamerican society was there much to smile about. More often life was serious, fated, almost desperate, as nature and society combined to make uncertainty the one certainty. These three portraits of figurine groups representing nuclear families (on these pages), plus one of a modern family from highland Chiapas (above right), show a common characteristic—that "aloof dignity that stands for good manners" in Mesoamerican society.[52] The bit of playing-with-the-baby in the figurine set shown on the right (unfortunately, it was partly damaged when found) is the rare exception that proves the rule. Relationships between parents and children were seldom warm; distant respect and obedience were the norm. Nor did husbands and wives demonstrate much warmth in their relationships, even in private, judging by surviving descendant cultures and personalitity types.

Visualizing Book of Mormon Life

The Book of Mormon is full of resonating examples of family and kin relations. For instance, when the central structure of Nephite government collapsed, around the Christian era, most arrangements that provided order in Nephite society reverted to a kinship basis. "The people . . . did separate one from another into tribes, every man according to his family and his kindred and friends" (3 Nephi 7:2). "There was no man among them save he had much family and many kindreds and friends" (3 Nephi 7:4). Power and position also depended on networking. Leaders gained and maintained their positions because they mustered the requisite support through extensive kin and friendship networks; the "judges had many friends and kindreds" (3 Nephi 6:27).

The story of Amulek illustrates that an individual's actions were sometimes constrained due to obligations to his social network. At first Amulek boasted to his fellow citizens in Ammonihah of his prominence and wealth: "I am . . . a man of no small reputation. . . . I have many kindreds and friends, and . . . much riches" (Alma 10:4); and he used that network of relatives to advance the cause of Alma$_2$ whom he befriended. But when he got mixed up in Alma$_2$'s politically sensitive church, he was "rejected by those who were once his friends, and also by his father and his kindred" (Alma 15:16) so he ended up driven out of town penniless (see Alma 15:17–9). Similarly, when rebellious Korihor lost his friends and supporters, he became an outcast from Nephite society, being forced to go "about from house to house, begging food for his support" (Alma 30:58).

The tribes and kindreds referred to in the Book of Mormon record, like those known to exist in most Mesoamerican societies, were defined by descent through the male line (see Jacob 1:13; Omni 1:18; Alma 10:1–3; Helaman 1:2; Mormon 1:5). The most senior living descendant of the founding male ancestor spoke for his lineage, the same pattern as in ancient Israel. (Mormon's being chosen leader of the Nephites while a mere fifteen years of age and with no experience probably reflected his standing as the senior descendant in the Nephi line; see 3 Nephi 5:20 and Mormon 1:5; 2:1.) In order to retain their positions as representatives and spokesmen for their units, group leaders had to keep a finger on the opinion pulse of their group (note "the minds of the people" in Alma 17:6 and 35:5). A kin-group spokesman made sure by internal discussion and consensus building that the corporate vote he cast in community affairs represented the real feelings of the kin he represented. So if the Nephites followed the general Mesoamerican pattern, when they assembled "to cast in their voices" (Alma 2:6), the political process would not have been a "one man, one vote" referendum but an expression by kin leaders of how their blocs felt about an issue or a candidacy (see Helaman 1:2–5). And when Captain Moroni$_1$ was building an armed defense coalition for the land, his support "did increase daily because of the assurance of protection that his works" (see Alma 50:12) gave to play-it-safe kindreds who concluded that his policy would be a winner.

A Teotihuacan couple and their baby, about A.D. 500.

Nephi$_1$'s brother Jacob$_1$ rebuked the men of the founding generation of the Nephite colony for their desire to take multiple wives and concubines (see Jacob 2:22–35), but in the long run the practice may have continued among the Nephites, just as it had persisted in ancient Israel (compare Mosiah 11:4; Alma 10:11, "my women"; Helaman 1:4, many sons).

THE IMPORTANCE OF ANCESTORS

Genealogy was crucial to the holders of power and leadership in ancient Mesoamerican societies. It served to validate elite rights. Oral transmission and recitation of genealogy was frequently sufficient in pre-Spanish times. For some of the nobility, among the Classic Maya and the later Mixtec peoples for example, stone monuments or entries in painted books reported and supported specific relationships (such as, ruler A was the son of B), but systematic summaries in chart form have not survived, if they existed in writing.

The European invaders wanted documentary proof of noble ancestry before they would allow some Amerindian rulers to continue their right to impose tribute payments on their subjects. A variety of visual forms for documenting nobility sprang up in the sixteenth century under Spanish literary influence to meet the conquistadors' demand. So while the presentation formats may have come from Spanish mentors, the factual information and the general sense of the importance of descent records were older.

The "Genealogía . . . de Patzcuaro" from Michoacán in west Mexico visualizes one of the metaphors of descent, the tree, which the Tarascans had previously conveyed by oral means. (Note the use of the tree metaphor in the Book of Mormon in Jacob 5 and elsewhere.)[53]

Despite their simple living facilities, Mesoamericans were meticulous about personal hygiene. Frequent bathing of both children (shown here from the Florentine Codex) and adults caused admiring comment among some Spanish observers.[54]

Childhood

A child's first immersion in ritual came soon after birth. Ritual continued to be vital throughout his or her life. In most late Mesoamerican cultures, a belief prevailed that the calendrical position of the day of one's birth determined one's fate, and it is likely that a similar belief was held in earlier times. The parents consulted a priest or diviner to learn whether their infant would have good luck, ill health, or some other defined fate. It was thought that cautionary measures could redirect some of fate's problems and thus allow one to cope without actually negating the destined effects. There may have been exceptional groups or individuals who took this sense of calendar-decreed fate less seriously than the norm, but overall a powerful sense of fatalism was built into an individual's life from his or her earliest days. Still, in general young children were indulged and treated warmly by all around them.

Both boys and girls associated primarily with the mother in the home in the toddler years. Sometimes an older sister was assigned to care for them while the mother performed tasks away from the house. A few toys were sometimes provided, usually miniatures of tools or other artifacts familiar to their parents, such as tiny dishes or a small bow and arrow. But there was much less elaboration of children's imagination, play, and toys than in cultures of the western European tradition. Life for the young was preparation for their life as adults. They were to learn practical skills, absorb formal and traditional cultural knowledge, and gain the social skills appropriate to the strictly defined roles they would play in years to come. Hence play and training inculcated the emphases on ritual, restraint, and fatalistic acceptance of one's place in society that were so important for adults. Modern individualistic concepts such as having fun or developing the child's potential were completely foreign.

Children were highly valued as projections of the parents into the future. Care was given to provide advantages for them within the circumstances of the family and society.

Male children gained practical knowledge by associating with their fathers in daily activities, but such contact was limited until they had grown big enough (around ten years old) to be somewhat helpful in the field or workshop. Girls, on the other hand, were useful at home from a younger age, at least as caregivers for

The child-rearing practices reported and illustrated in Sahagun's masterful compendium of material on Aztec lifeways were broadly paralleled elsewhere in Mesoamerica. An infant is here shown being put to sleep with a soothing admonition or lullaby, indicated by the scrolls from the mother's mouth, while grandmother supervises.

This Tzotzil Maya child of highland Chiapas has already started learning part of her adult role while "playing."

siblings. Being with their mothers more of the time, they learned about their future responsibilities earlier than males did.

Conscious teaching of moral and cultural standards heavily emphasized admonition. Mesoamerican peoples greatly respected oratorical skills; the formal, poetic manipulation of words was highly valued in general, and it all began with constant repetition of counsel to the young. Even before a child could speak the language, elders and parents told them via standardized exhortations that they ought to follow certain ideals of behavior (see page 77 for an example of a text of admonition).

Midwives presided at childbirth and commonly received a gift or fee for their service. They not only called on their considerable practical knowledge of obstetrics and herbs but also talked the mother through the birth process with a stream of instruction, ritual blessings, and exhortations.

Continuity of social and cultural life was ensured by the transmission of knowledge and values, particularly through women to their children. Alma 43:45–47 recognized that in the case of the "sons of Helaman," whose faith was molded by their mothers. The importance of this relationship continues today among these people of Santiago Atitlan, Guatemala.

Infants were carried most of the time, in arms or on the hip or tied onto the back with a cloth garment. Since house floors were usually of earth, and the hot, ashy hearth was at floor level, only fully mobile children were turned loose. (Classic, south-central Veracruz)

An Aztec mother warns her children to be especially careful as she sends them outside on a day predicted by the astrological calendar to be unlucky. (Florentine Codex)

VISUALIZING BOOK OF MORMON LIFE

The Book of Mormon discusses the proper training of children so that they might bring joy and credit to their parents. Strong efforts were necessary because, it was believed, men and women become "carnal and devilish" (Mosiah 16:3; see Helaman 12:4) despite the initial innocence of infants (see Moroni 8). The Book of Mormon emphasizes both good and bad examples of adult influence on children. Lehi's and Sariah's concern for their children at the beginning of the account sets the tone (see, for example, 1 Nephi 2:8–19 and 18:17–9). Benjamin was immensely concerned that his sons have advantages (see Mosiah 1:2–8). A Nephite man's care for the welfare of his children was considered to be as important as his support of liberty and of his wife (see Alma 48:10). Teaching children was systematically enjoined as a duty to be pursued with diligence (see, for example, 4 Nephi 1:38). Conversely, the negative examples of Laman and Lemuel, the priests of Noah, and other flawed parents on their descendants are pointed out over and over (see, for example, Mosiah 19:11–2; 20:3; 25:12).

The Nephite record also communicates a fatalistic, melancholy sense that sounds virtually Mesoamerican. Jacob tells us that "the time passed away with us, and also our lives passed away like as it were unto us a dream, we being a lonesome and a solemn people . . . [and] we did mourn out our days" (Jacob 7:26). Many prophecies carried the sense of an inescapable, decreed fate awaiting the people because of their desire for evil (see 1 Nephi 12:1–5, 15, 19–23; Enos 1:23; Alma 45:9–14; Helaman 13:6–38). Alma counseled his sons, "Be sober" (Alma 37:47; 38:15); Benjamin urged parents to teach their children "to walk in . . . soberness" (Mosiah 4:15). The child Mormon was praised for being "a sober child" (Mormon 1:2). It is no surprise that no humor or lightness is manifested anywhere in the Nephite record.

Exhortation as a teaching method was prevalent among the Nephites. Both the volume of it in the text itself and the general commandment that it should be a routine teaching practice show the emphasis (see 1 Nephi 16:4; Mosiah 2:40; Alma 21:23; Alma 39–42; Helaman 6:4; Moroni 6:9). The frequent observation of ritual was another form of instruction, in a sense, that was engrained in both Mesoamerican and Nephite life.[55]

Youth

A Maya father exhorts a son thirteen hundred years ago much as Benjamin did his sons nine hundred years before that (see Mosiah 1:2–8). Notice what appears to be a book next to the young man, which reminds us of Benjamin's emphasis to his princes on the importance and significance of mastering the records.

From age ten to about twenty, young people were pressed hard by society to fit into the cultural mold of a responsible adult. The hard realities of economic life did not permit any teenage interval of freedom from responsibility such as many of today's young people enjoy, or endure. The aim in Mesoamerican society was to move the immature as quickly as they could qualify to the duties, privileges, and dignity of adulthood. Age, not youth, was considered desirable; shouldering mature responsibilities, not postponing them, was the ideal. Young men could claim no power, had few resources, and drew little respect or privilege. Young women were even less significant socially, except for their potential as mothers.

As soon as youths of either gender were capable of performing chores, they were pressed to carry them out. Most families needed every hand to work. Boys carried water and firewood by age five, and their responsibilities increased until by age thirteen or fourteen they could help clear a field, plant and harvest, or fish alone. Girls gathered herbs, brought water and wood, swept the floor and yard, and tended younger children. An Aztec girl was expected to have mastered the art of making perfect tortillas by age thirteen and of weaving by fourteen. With all these activities there were sacred and social meanings, taboos, and rules to be observed about how, how not, and why to do everything.

The children tended to model their behavior on their mothers' or fathers' actions; this was also reinforced verbally. Demonstrations and instructions were bracketed with oral urgings, not only regarding the work as such but also on the morality it involved. Other older persons—relatives, teachers, priests—also made a practice of instructing the young. Key values instilled were obedience, respect for one's elders, diligence, and discretion. Stubborn or rebellious youth could be punished harshly by such measures as whipping or forcing them to sleep on hard, wet ground.

Parents who filled special roles in society trained their children in those specialties. Thus the son of a priest started along the way to literacy and participation in that role unless he seemed unfit for the calling, or a girl learned the marketplace sales skills of her mother. By their wealth and position, the social elite obviously had greater resources (for example, teachers hired to help a son learn about the society's books) than commoners to educate their children.

Young men were typically instructed in military matters. In some groups males between sixteen and twenty lived in a village men's house apart from their families, where they were trained in war and other matters.

Centers of substantial population often

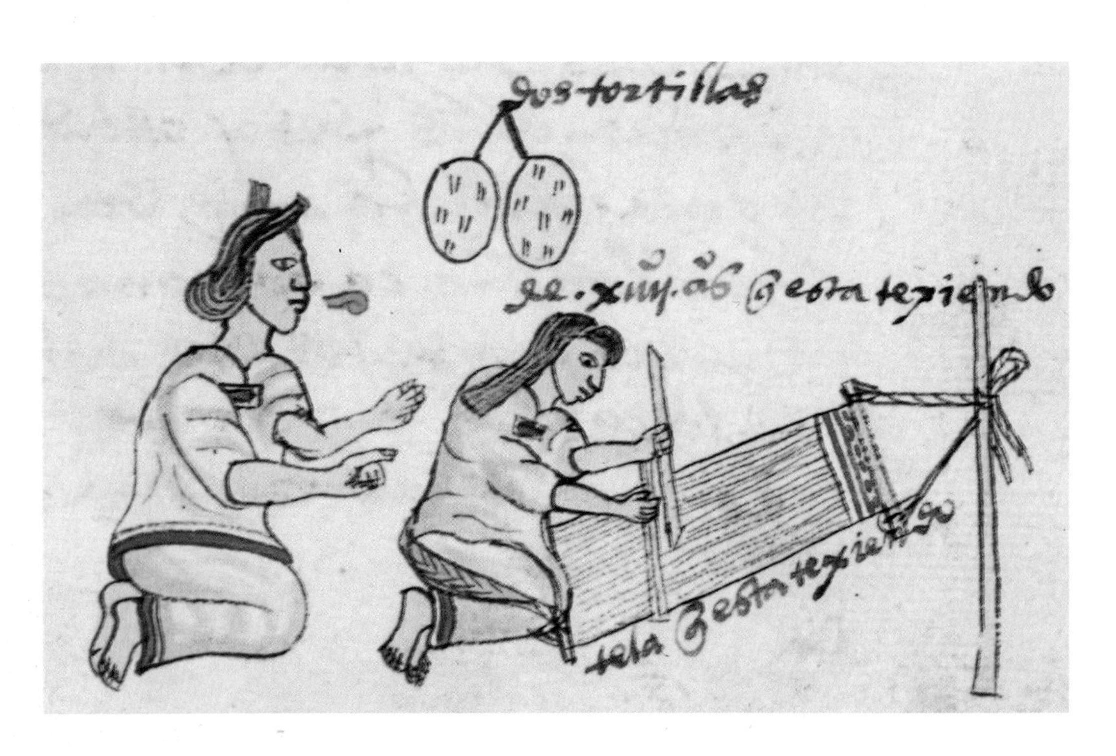

An Aztec mother teaches weaving to her daughter at home. (Codex Mendoza)

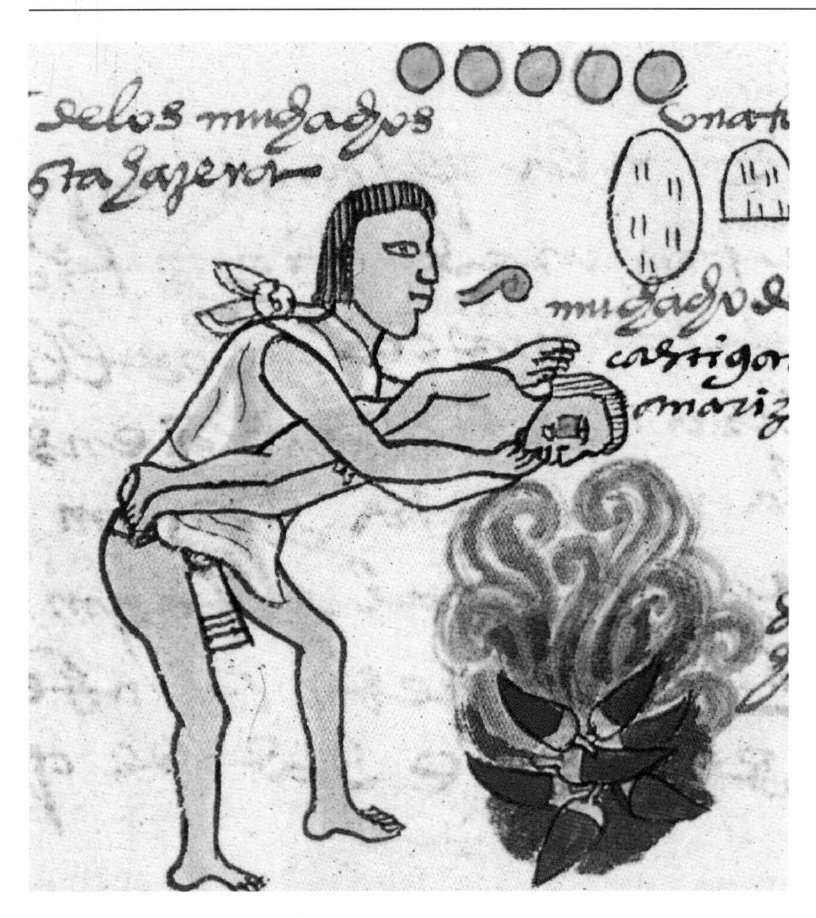

A determinedly rebellious Aztec boy was taught in vigorous fashion to conform to the demands of parents and society. One creative mode of discipline was to hold the rebel's head above a fire into which a handful of chili peppers had been thrown (from the Codex Mendoza).

Boys are delivered by their father to the priest in charge of the Aztec community school (from Sahagun).

had schools that were operated by priests in conjunction with a temple. Boys in their early teen years were instructed in serious aspects of the culture, especially the lore, mythology, and speaking skills that a man of influence was expected to master. Both young men and women were likely to get some formal training also in singing and dancing, but the material they learned was always related to sacred, traditional matters; little merely popular music or entertainment existed. After early childhood there was little "fun" for youths of either gender; nevertheless, given human nature, we suppose there were inevitably certain moments of laughter and light talk among the youth.

In smaller communities, greater informality in teaching and learning and even less literacy were the norm. But even farmers had a great body of lore to learn, such as knowledge about plants and cultivation, techniques for building and repairing devices, and getting along in the forest. Conscientious fathers instructed their sons as far as ability and time permitted, but men in small settlements could only pass on their knowledge orally. It was the priests and specialists who controlled the vast store of botanical, medical, astronomical, and sacred information accumulated at the upper social levels of the cultures.

Marrying and becoming a parent were keys to attaining social standing as a full-fledged man or woman. Military action was also a key qualifier for manhood in the more militant groups. But individual youths could not speed up becoming an adult by precociously going off on their own. There was nowhere to go; nobody could exist on their own, for only within networks of kin and allies could anyone survive in a society where group, not individual, was the key.

In Aztec society a wedding involved a long sermon (or sermons) followed by literally tying the knot. The union was not formalized until the pair had separately completed several days of religious penance following the ceremony.

VISUALIZING BOOK OF MORMON LIFE

Nothing in the Book of Mormon suggests the presence of formal schools, although the fact that King Benjamin "caused" that his sons be taught hints that priests or other skilled persons did the instructing (Mosiah 1:2), but then that was in the royal court. Mormon's childhood also sounds very exceptional; by "about ten years of age" he "began to be learned somewhat after the manner of the learning of my people" (nothing is said of his father's role), but by age twenty-four he was considered mature (Mormon 1:2; see 1:3). Enos's pattern of learning from his father personally may have been more the norm (see Enos 1:1).

How long the social category *youth* lasted is not clear. The case of Alma$_2$'s sons suggests (as does Mormon's maturity at age twenty-four) that youth might have extended into a man's twenties, perhaps until his marriage. Shiblon was considered by his father still to be "in thy youth" (Alma 37:35), yet he was older than, and was held up as an example to, his brother Corianton, who was mature enough to travel alone on religious business (see Alma 31:37) and had gone by himself to another land in pursuit of a sexual liaison (see Alma 39:10). From the norms of ancient civilized society, just as in Old World Israel, it would be more plausible that the "youth," Shiblon, was twenty-three and Corianton was twenty-one than that they were each, say, three years younger.

What Alma$_2$ set as values for his sons sounds characteristic of Mesoamerican values: be diligent, temperate, and humble; bridle your passions; and do not be idle (see Alma 38:10–2). On the opposite hand, values and behaviors condemned by the prophet Samuel, and that would have been taught as negative ideals to the youth, are also what we might expect to find condemned in Mesoamerican culture: great pride, boasting, strifes, persecutions, and envyings (see Helaman 13:22, 27).

AN AZTEC SPEECH URGING A YOUNG MAN TO PREPARE FOR ADULT LIFE

ven though you may long for women,
hold back, hold back with your heart
until you are a grown man,
strong and robust.
Look at the maguey plant.
If it is opened before it has grown
and its liquid is taken out,
it has no substance.
It does not produce liquid; it is useless.
Before it is opened
to withdraw its water,
it should be allowed to grow and attain full size.
Then its sweet water is removed
all in good time.

This is how you must act:
before you know woman
you must grow and be a complete man.
And then you will be ready for marriage;
you will beget children of good stature,
healthy, agile, and comely.[5b]

Elaborate symbolic headdresses and fancy garb distinguish the standing row of men as high-ranking gentlemen, no doubt nobles by descent. Their captives, from a neighboring city, are probably doomed to bondage, if allowed to live. These appear on a mural at the ruined site of Bonampak, Chiapas, dating around A.D. 800.

Social Rank

In all civilizations until recently, a hierarchy of prestige or rank existed in which one's social position at birth largely determined one's life chances. The ladder of rank typically had a small proportion of greatly privileged people at the top and a large mass of commoners below. Slaves or serfs were still lower. Relatively few were in a situation comparable to the modern world's middle class or had any prospects of moving up to a higher level. That was the case in Mesoamerica.

A hereditary nobility stood at the top. Sometimes exploits in war or other unusual situations might thrust a new leader upward on the heap who was not a noble, but he would as quickly as possible imitate the elite ways in order to wipe out any memory of his humbler origin. He would marry an upper-class woman, try to purge and skew the historical and genealogical records to make himself look better, and take on manners appropriate to his newly privileged position.

It is important when reading ancient traditions or interpreting ancient art on stone or paper to realize that the record keepers and artists were of the social elite—kings, prominent priests, officials, or their families—or else worked at their direction. Their position in society affected what they represented or wrote about. On the other hand, it is much more difficult to learn how simple people lived. No doubt their lives were mainly concerned with immediate survival—bread-and-butter and life-and-death issues—rather than politics, war, theology, or theory.

Commoners accepted this social arrangement in part because they knew no alternative. There had to be leaders—to organize defense, to glorify community or tribe and build morale, to negotiate with foreigners, and to judge and quell disputes. Those possessing the abilities to carry out those tasks passed on their power to family members where possible;

Rich clothing and adornments on another Maya Late Classic figurine combine with an arrogant facial expression to suggest a person like those who "turn[ed] their backs on the poor" (Helaman 6:39).

The topmost rank in Aztec society, and no doubt in others that preceded it, enjoyed the choicest perquisites and highest prestige that could be provided. This sumptuous palace garden (as reconstructed by an artist on the basis of Spanish descriptions) was in the palace area of the Aztec emperor.

thus a class of favored nobles was maintained. The "taxpayers" were saddled with the responsibility to support not only the ruler himself and his immediate family but also a whole class of minor nobles who were descended from earlier rulers.

Priests or religious teachers as well as staff functionaries, such as officers, clerks, and archivists attached to the royal court, were also inevitable. By and large, all those in positions of any power were recruited from or were closely linked with the nobility. However, being of the nobility was not a guarantee of wealth, for lands or fortunes could be lost because of natural disasters, squandered by foolish living, or dispersed by having to be divided among many descendants. And nonnobles could find ways of their own to accumulate wealth. Being a merchant was one way. Another avenue for climbing in rank was to become a distinguished military man.

The mass of common people were somewhat protected against the impositions and ambitions of the elite by their kinship organization. Tribes, lineages, or extended family networks had their own standing apart from the government.

Several legal categories of slaves and bond servants were known. A very poor family without adequate lands or supporting kin might enter a bond relationship with a wealthy person in order to maintain themselves in a disastrous economic time. Others could become slaves by virtue of being war captives or refugees. However, given agricultural conditions in Mesoamerica, it rarely made economic sense for a master to utilize slaves en masse to labor in his fields (the equivalent of "picking cotton").

A series of figurines made in the Gulf Coast area of the Mexican state of Campeche and dating to about A.D. 700 shows this "dirty-old-man" theme. The man and woman are thought to represent a particular god and goddess, but the behavior pictured suggests practices open to the top social rank, such as the priests of Noah and their "harlots" (Mosiah 11:14).

VISUALIZING BOOK OF MORMON LIFE

Social structure in Book of Mormon lands, according to the record, agrees with this Mesoamerican characterization. Overall, not only rank differences but a tendency to fall into a formalized class structure was noted (see Alma 32:2; 3 Nephi 6:12, where "class" would be more accurate than "rank" in today's terminology; 4 Nephi 1:26). Virtually no information is provided in the Nephite account concerning commoners (the freemen of Alma 51, presumably), since the record keepers were of the elite. The Book of Mormon mentions or implies an underclass of bond servants or slaves at some points. King Benjamin forbade slavery, which would have been unnecessary had it not formerly been prevalent (see Mosiah 2:13; 7:15; Alma 27:8–9; 61:12; etc.), and servants in a socially fixed sense continued through most of Book of Mormon history. For the Lamanites, see Mosiah 24:8–18; and Alma 17:23, 25, 28.

Claims to noble, or at least elite, privileges were a constant problem in Nephite society; "those of high birth" mentioned in Alma 51:8 are an example of the claimants. Their demand to be supported in the manner they desired would have caused a burden for the common folks. Consider several other cases: the frustration of "the poor class of people" expressed in Alma 32:2–3, in conjunction with the picture of the elite in 31:27–8; see also Mosiah 11:2–6 on the cost of supporting Noah's priests; note the implied condemnation of the usual pattern of exploitative support in Alma 1:26 and compare 4 Nephi 1:26; and, finally, at Alma 30:27–8 consider whether the charges by Korihor of priestly economic abuse would have rung true to "many" (Alma 30:18, echoed in Helaman 16:21) if such abuse by the elite was unknown. Notice further how the Amulonites parlayed their priestly and literacy skills into social and political advantages, and ultimately into a "piece of the action" in the commerce they promoted (see Mosiah 23:35–9; 24:1–8; Alma 21:4; compare 3 Nephi 6:11–2).[57] Moreover, the breakdown of central government reported in 3 Nephi 7 can be seen as a revolt by the mass of people against exorbitant demands by the elite (see 3 Nephi 6:10–2, 15).

Military service could enhance one's social and economic position in Nephite society. Apparently because of Gideon's service as defense chief for King Limhi, a land was later named after him, and he would likely have been its local ruler had he lived (see Mosiah 20:17–22 and Alma 1:7–9). Further, Moroni$_1$, chief captain of the Nephite armies for many years, enhanced his prestige and power by the success of his management of military affairs. He obviously was from a powerful and wealthy family to start with (note "the place of his inheritance" in Alma 62:42), so we are not surprised at his appointment as military chief at only twenty-five. But by the time he successfully concluded the long war, he retired to "his own house that he might spend the remainder of his days in peace" and, presumably, prosperity while basking in public approval (Alma 62:43; see 62:42; 48:11–7).

Far left: Another drawing in the Florentine Codex accompanies a moralistic warning to feasters during an Aztec festival not to ignore charity to the poor.

Left: In the Aztec state, slaves such as these, who had had to sell themselves in order to eat during a time of famine, were marked by a collar device that proclaimed their restricted standing, as shown by Father Sahagun.

CLASS STRUCTURE

We have a fairly detailed description of the social structure of the Cuicatecs, a people who lived in the northern highlands of Mexico's Oaxaca state at the time the Spaniards arrived.[58] Their class structure is representative of the scheme in many other parts of Mesoamerica. The top two levels consisted of categories of persons with different powers and privileges. Royalty included the actual ruler of the state as well as his aides and counselors, who held a measure of quasi-independent administrative power. Below them in rank were army officers, priests, and other noble hangers-on. The mass of the populace were common peasant farmers and craftsmen.

SOCIAL STRATA AMONG THE CUICATECS

ROYALTY	Traditional patrimonial ruler, overlord of the state
	Counselor or "consultant" to the overlord
	Administrative staff of elders, kin to the lord
ARISTOCRACY	Minor lords, magistrates, with rights to tax certain settlements
	Army officers
	Priests
	Other "unemployed" members of the aristocracy
	Administrative assistants to the overlord stationed in local communities
COMMONERS	Female curers or medics, and traders (social status ambiguous)
	Free commoners—the bulk of the peasantry. Also servants, and army recruits in time of war
SLAVES	Slaves; prisoners of war; sacrificial victims

An artist's display of social strata in Maya society, around A.D. 600–700, uses a pyramid format to show the ranks or classes. Except for details, the social structure of the Cuicatec was about the same.

A young commoner woman is here sculpted in the very early Xochipala style of west-central Mexico (ca. 1500 B.C.).

Women

Everyone knows that women were in a disadvantaged social and economic position in the ancient civilized world. Men always had much more privilege to come and go as they pleased and to make decisions without regard to their spouses. Social standards and cultural patterns severely limited what women were allowed to do, short of their outright defiance. Among other reasons, this differentiation by gender resulted from women's need to care for their children. Furthermore, their living skills usually centered on domestic matters.

When dealing with the world away from home they were heavily dependent on males. On the other hand, as mothers or potential mothers they were given a certain measure of honor. Broadly speaking, Mesoamerican women fell near the world norm in that they received a significant measure of respect yet were unquestionably subordinate to males.

Some public activities were open to women. For example, ritual and herbal curing and divination were done by females in some cultural situations. They were not expected to participate in warfare, although women and even their children sometimes accompanied warriors on longer expeditions where duties of cooking and foraging for food and shelter, or of course garrison duty, demanded such support.

But in the commercial sphere, women commonly participated in the town market. In some regions, the power and independence females could attain were substantial.

Typically, men and women performed different economic tasks. Cooking and weaving were almost entirely carried out by women. Men did the heavier work, especially in field preparation, although gardens near the residence of the family could be worked by either sex as opportunity allowed.

As suggested above, what we know about the personalities of Mesoamerican peoples leads us to believe that typically men and women were relatively unexpressive toward mates or other family members.

Foremost among a woman's concerns was her family. It appears that a wife's relation to her husband was governed strongly by a sense of duty, but her connection to her children was based more on love and hope for their future. This striking Maya Late Classic pair illustrate the latter.

The primary task of a wife and mother was to prepare food, especially maize. Over her lifetime a woman might spend fifty thousand hours grinding corn for, shaping, and cooking up to one million tortillas! At meals she first served older males, then she ate with the children. There were no family meals as such, nor was there much conversation while dining (eating, especially eating corn items, had an atmosphere of sacredness about it).

While they were not visible movers and shakers in public life, certain women were esteemed and had power in their own right. This dowager wife of a Maya lord is sculpted in the Jaina style and comes from the state of Campeche around A.D. 650. This illustrates how an upper-class Maya female might have borne herself. Earlier nobility would have maintained a similar demeanor.

Visualizing Book of Mormon Life

The Book of Mormon provides no examples of Nephite women who were powerful in government. (Among the Lamanites, respected queens are twice mentioned, although they did not possess independent power, judging by Alma 19, 22, and 47.) In desperate circumstances females could be armed for battle (for example, see Alma 54:12), but for normal warfare they are not mentioned, so they either stayed home or were camp helpers (note Alma 58:31).

The Nephite ideal saw women in the role of mother (see Alma 56:47–8), where success was considered to consist of bearing and rearing valiant sons. Aside from Lehi's wife, Sariah, or the antiheroine, the daughter of Jared (see Ether 8), daughters or wives are never presented as personalities. They were expected to be good workers in domestic tasks, with emphasis on weaving (see Mosiah 10:5 and Helaman 6:13). Still, alternate roles, such as selling at the market, would have been available to them, judging by conditions among their probable descendants.

The mentions or hints of harlots, concubines, and multiple wives in the scriptural record imply that those lesser social positions existed because of the impositions of men upon the women. Proper females were expected to be chaste, and one man ideally had one wife, although that rule had exceptions.

The Book of Mormon pictures male-female relationships as quite formal; there are only a few points where the text hints that emotions stronger than respect played a part in how mates treated each other. Parent-child relationships too come across as rather stiff.

Young unmarried women normally had clear, if limited, expectations. The fact that most of them stayed in the home to learn directly from their mothers meant that the girls had some time to share with nearby friends, while boys spent more time in the scattered fields or at other work scenes.

Several types of disease are depicted on ancient figurines. This one showing an ulcerous growth on the face dates before 600 B.C., but no doubt the condition continued into later times.

Health

Sickness was a constant problem anciently. Some scholars have mistakenly considered the New World a virtual paradise for its lack of some of the serious Old World diseases. It is true that epidemic diseases were limited in occurrence in America, and certain illnesses introduced by the conquering Europeans did cause sudden, widespread deaths when first introduced. However, recent research has shown that the factors behind these conditions were complicated. Many of the same diseases known in the Old World were already present in pre-Columbian America, but their effects were restrained. In Europe, Asia, and Africa, cities were breeding places of the most deadly illnesses, and the large numbers of domestic animals kept were reservoirs for various infections. Mesoamerican cities were healthier because they were less crowded and because few animals were kept there. When the Spaniards forced the native people into crowded settlements (to control and Christianize them), their relatively healthy situation tended to weaken.[59]

Illnesses on this side of the ocean tended to be more endemic and probably were connected with nutritional stress in many cases. The basic foods—corn, beans, and squash—provided for most needs when supplemented adequately by a wide array of other items, but those desirable additions came into short supply whenever population density increased enough so that even the basic foods might run short. When the amount of cultivated land per family was reduced due to a growing population, the soil could not stay idle long enough to rejuvenate before necessity demanded that it be cultivated again. The result was not only reduced crop production but also lessened nutritional quality. Furthermore, nonstaple and wild animal foods and plant supplements were more difficult to obtain. For example, when the acreage anciently exploited was compared to indicators of ill health in skeletons of the ninth century A.D., when the city of Copan in Honduras suffered serious decline, a clear correlation was found.[60]

The diet of the elite population on the one hand and of common folk on the other differed, of course. The Aztec king Montezuma daily ate from a huge array of foods, including fresh fish carried more than 150 miles by runners from the Gulf of Mexico. Yet poor people sometimes wondered how they could get anything to eat at all.

Some of the manifestations of illness shown in art have not been definitely identified with clinical diseases known today, although they probably could be with more systematic study. This specimen is from Nayarit in western Mexico, thought to date in the period A.D. 200–800.

There were, of course, periodic famines due to climatic irregularities, yet perhaps more telling on health in general was the shortage of food that occurred annually during the months between exhausting the old maize crop and the ripening of the new supply.

Mesoamericans treated ailments mainly through herbal remedies[61] and ritual healing at the hands of several sorts of curers. One cause of illness was thought to be violating the proper use of foods classified as "hot" or "cold" (without any reference to their actual temperature); imprudent mixing of those categories in the diet was believed to result in specific symptoms. (The Spaniards brought a similar set of notions that was Greek in origin, while the Chinese used still another scheme that was quite similar.)

Among health maintenance practices, the steam bath (resembling the sauna of northern Eurasia) was prominent.

One cure attempted was skull surgery; an opening was cut through the bone in some cases, perhaps releasing pressure resulting from some trauma. Healing of the bone is evidence that sometimes recovery resulted.

Virtually all beliefs about health—causes, diagnoses, treatments, good health—involved sacredness. Illness was never simply something that happened in a mechanically operating world. Astrological luck, breaking of social or religious rules, or bad magic by an enemy were supposed to be at fault. The solutions invariably demanded following certain rituals, even if taking an herbal concoction was also involved.

THE DENTIST

This sketch, copied from a mural showing Tlalocan (paradise) in the Temple of Agriculture at Teotihuacan, seems to show a dentist doing something with a patient's mouth or teeth employing a stone knife. One dental "beautification" practice among the Maya involved inlaying front teeth with a design in delicately cut semiprecious stone. Perhaps that is what is represented here.

Famines were recorded in traditions preserved among a number of Mesoamerican peoples. Malnourishment may always have been a health problem, but children and the elderly must have been the hardest hit. (See Alma 62:39, for example.)

This modeled scene from west Mexico seems to show a shaman (spiritual healer) giving a caring treatment. Shamans, generally like counterparts known particularly well in Siberia, still diagnose and treat patients by relying on guidance from a guardian spirit who is accessed by going into a trance.

Old age (however many years that might have meant) could be considered one of the "illnesses" of the ancients. Most people lived hard, draining lives with few comforts to enjoy. It is doubtful that more than a small proportion survived to enjoy "the golden years," as we now euphemistically refer to advanced age.

The true doctor.
He is a wise man (tlamatini);
he imparts life.
A tried specialist,
he has worked with herbs, stones, trees, and roots.
His remedies have been tested;
he examines, he experiments,
he alleviates sickness.
He massages aches and sets broken bones.
he administers purges and potions;
he bleeds his patients;
he cuts and he sews the wound;
he brings about reactions;
he stanches the bleeding with ashes.
The false physician.
He ridicules and deceives the people . . . .

As this characterization shows, the Aztecs had the same problem of distinguishing good from bad practitioners that modern people have.

Visualizing Book of Mormon Life

In Mormon's record there is no evidence that Book of Mormon peoples suffered from epidemic diseases, but there is mention of less serious illness. Specifically, "there were some who died with fevers" that were very frequent "by the nature of the climate," but the herbal remedies known were said to be generally effective against those maladies (Alma 46:40). Otherwise, reference is made only to "all manner of diseases" (Mosiah 17:16; Alma 9:22).

Warfare likely took a serious toll in death and disablement (see, for example, Alma 28:2–3; 57:25; Moroni 9:16, 19), yet civilian casualties incidental to war, due especially to malnutrition, must also have been a serious problem. At the time of the final Nephite wars, a grim picture is painted by Mormon of "widows and their daughters" being left "to wander whithersoever they can for food" (Moroni 9:16). The tenuousness of the food situation at a much earlier date is illustrated in the account of an Amlicite/Lamanite attack on Zarahemla. As a result of the Nephite army's pursuit of the aggressors, "many of their fields of grain were destroyed, . . . trodden down by the hosts of men" (Alma 3:2). As a consequence, the following year "the people were . . . greatly afflicted . . . for the loss of their fields of grain" (Alma 4:2).

A favorite health-enhancing practice was the steam bath. It is not clear whether women had access to this facility (from Sahagun).

Clothing

It may seem strange to consider clothing under the heading of society rather than of daily life, but in fact the primary function of garments in ancient Mesoamerica was to communicate social position. "Dress was identity." "An individual's clothing immediately designated not only cultural affiliation but rank and status as well."[62] To cover the body against the elements was secondary. These people in the tropics did not need nor want as many garments as, for example, my Scandinavian ancestors in northern Europe.

A set of five or six basic costume elements for each gender was shared throughout Mesoamerica for millennia. (Comparable elements of modern costume are, for example, shirt and pants for men and blouse and skirt for women.) In a particular region of ancient Mexico or Guatemala, some of the normal repertoire of garments were used or avoided in certain local situations according to climatic conditions and traditions, but all the core garments were familiar and would have been used in some situations everywhere in Mesoamerica.

The wealthy used sumptuous fabrics and inventive decoration to place themselves visually atop a hierarchy of prestige and privilege and to display icons that signaled their social roles. Which men were rulers, warriors, merchants, or priests could be detected at a glance by anybody sophisticated in the culture. Women's positions were correspondingly made visible. Some materials, like the feathers from certain birds, were prohibited to those not socially entitled to them.[63]

Even the masses observed clothing distinctions. Inhabitants of each local land were marked by wearing its unique variations in garb and ornament. To the practiced eye those details set apart both commoners and higher ranks living in that place from people from all other hometowns.

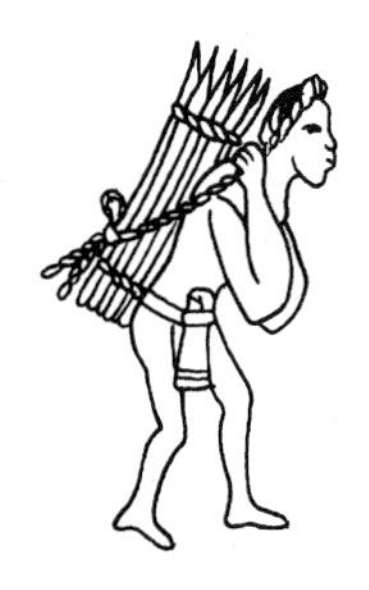

A famous Mixtec noblewoman of about a thousand years ago, Lady 3 Flint, is pictured in the Codex Zouche-Nuttall dressed in three elaborate costumes appropriate to three events or contexts in her life story.

A mural shows how socially significant costume was around A.D. 800 among the Maya elite at Bonampak, Chiapas. These proud gentlemen all wear the same three garments (except for one fellow whose social role obviously differs), but design details individualize the effect for each one. Headdresses were clearly required, but sandals were optional. (Notice how wearing a long cloak like these men do could have given away the murderer detected by Nephi$_2$, according to Helaman 9–10.)

This figurine in what is called the Jaina style illustrates what an upper-class Maya woman could have looked like wearing "costly apparel" (Alma 31:28 applies the phrase to the Zoramites. By coincidence, this figurine was made in southern Campeche state, not very distant from where the Zoramites may have dwelt eight centuries earlier.)

Visualizing Book of Mormon Life

The Book of Mormon is explicit about clothing serving as social insignia. For example, in Alma's day dissonance among "the people of the church" was signaled by their beginning to wear "very costly apparel" (Alma 4:6; see 4:7), and the prophet Samuel condemned the Nephites because they considered "costly apparel" (see Helaman 13:28; see 13:27) a key to a man's status as a prophet. Commoners, on the contrary, relied on "good homely cloth," as well as perhaps possessing a certain amount of "silk and fine-twined linen" (Alma 1:29).

Naturally, style changes occurred in clothing over time. The styles seen by the Spaniards when they conquered the area, or those seen on Classic-era monuments from a millennium earlier, are not exactly what either the Nephites or Lamanites wore during the Book of Mormon period. Yet continuity in the essential elements is evident over thousands of years of the archaeological and artistic record, so that when Book of Mormon people inhabited Mesoamerica, they surely wore some of the basic garment forms characteristic of that area.

At least there is no question that Mesoamerican art shows nothing like the flowing robes of Arabia that some LDS artists have supposed the Book of Mormon peoples wore. Moreover, both Nephites and Lamanites probably left more skin uncovered than Latter-day Saints feel comfortable with today.

This dresslike garment shows off a spectacular design probably made by the batik tie-dye method. It suggests how much social detail we would miss if we had to rely entirely on what archaeologists can dig up, for no such cloth would have been preserved in the earth. This Maya painted vase dating around A.D. 700 was brought to light by modern tomb looters.

Weaving and Textiles

Both plain and elaborate weaving were done in ancient Mesoamerica. Illustrations in native books (codices) combine with some sculptures and modeled ceramic figurines to show tremendous variety and skill in the textile arts.

The Aztecs, for whom we have much information from documents about the period when the Spaniards arrived, made and used huge numbers of garments. Lists of tribute or taxation demanded of certain communities called for large annual shipments of cloth and garments to the capital city. Those objects were given as rewards of privilege to nobles and other upper-level groups in the society or were sold in the markets.

Women were the weavers. For the Aztecs, "The life of a woman from birth to death centered around the production of beautiful, well-made textiles. A newborn baby girl, at her bathing ceremony, was presented all the equipment of women [for weaving]." When a woman died, her weaving implements were destroyed to make them available to her for her journey after death. A woman who wove poorly was held in the lowest regard, being described as lazy, indolent, nonchalant, sullen, and a deceiver.[64]

The highly developed weaving tradition continued among the descendants of the peoples conquered by the Europeans. Today, particularly in highland Guatemala, there is a thriving manifestation of that heritage. Colorful fabrics from there are sold to connoisseurs of fine textiles worldwide.

The thread of choice was cotton. The plants were grown wherever the climate was suitable. Higher elevations were too cool, but the trade and tribute system supplied the needs of people living in those

Most garments were not sewn, although certain pieces were. Archaeologists find needles like this one of bone that dates from B.C. times. Mesoamerican garment makers could have tailored their clothes more often than they did in fact, but they preferred the looser fit, perhaps for climatic reasons.

Only rarely do we get glimpses of actual cloth preserved from the past, like this undated fragment now in the regional museum in Tuxtla Gutierrez, Chiapas.

A weaver from thirteen hundred years ago, shown in a Jaina clay sculpture, uses a type of freestanding loom that was no longer used by the time of the Spanish Conquest. (There may well have been other cultural losses too.)

areas. Hand spinning of cotton thread was done by women in many areas as a normal domestic task. On the completed fabrics, elaborate tie-dye techniques were sometimes used, and fancy weaves like brocade and tapestry were produced.

Some vegetable fibers other than cotton were also used, particularly henequen, made from the leaf of the agave plant (the same plant from which the drink pulque was derived). Henequen cloth and other bast (vegetable fiber) threads were woven into fabrics that resembled linen in stiffness. People of rank wore cotton; commoners often made do with the coarser, cheaper fibers. Bark cloth (made from soaked and pounded sheets of bark stripped from the trunks of fig trees) was also used.

Buttons or pin fasteners were not utilized, as far as we know. Sewn or fitted garments were relatively uncommon. A cape was often worn by tying the upper corners into a knot or wrapping a kiltlike piece around the body then tucking in a corner or the end at the belt line.

Turning lint cotton into thread with a hand spindle consumed a great deal of time for those who, like this Guatemalan woman, lived in cotton-producing areas.

Visualizing Book of Mormon Life

The Book of Mormon mentions weaving and textile work in many places. It indicates that considerable skill was involved in their production. For example, Helaman 6:13 reports, "Their women did toil and spin, and did make all manner of cloth, of fine-twined linen and cloth of every kind, to clothe their nakedness." Given the importance of a Mesoamerican woman's weaving in judging her character, the statement in verse 13 may connote, "so the Nephite women were of high character."

A woman weaves on a typical pre-Columbian-style back-strap loom, with Lake Atitlan, Guatemala, in the background.

Ornamentation and Insignia

Mesoamerican peoples were very partial to vivid ornamentation. Nearly all of it had symbolic significance, some social, some political, some religious. We have already noted symbolism exhibited in clothing. Accessories to complete the effect were equally important. Elaborate headdresses often outshone the clothing, and face and body paint added to the effect of one's headdress. Everyday headdresses were often of cloth in the form of a turban wound around the head in various manners. For formal occasions, more elaborate devices were made of intricately worked flowers, feathers, and cloth on a wooden frame. Jewelry added still another dimension to dressing up.

To modern tastes the effect of such exaggerated decor seems garish, but in the Mesoamerican view, at least among some groups, there could never be too much of a good thing. Especially in the later cultures, baroque extravagance was considered superior to modest simplicity or quiet elegance. Farther back in time, cultures such as the Olmec displayed more restraint. That is one of the reasons their art pieces please moderns more than, say, the busy art of the Aztecs.

Rich symbolic elements in the dress-up outfits make it difficult nowadays to distinguish between the concepts of decoration and insignia. Many of the representations or characteristics (such as green stones or green feathers, which betokened "water," hence "life") were there as badges or identifiers of the powers of nature or of the supernatural. They communicated something like, "the bearer is a devotee under the special protection of the supernatural power whose insignia is displayed." Some version of truth, rather than of beauty, was being proclaimed.

Unfortunately, the Spaniards winnowed the supply of ornaments that were preserved. They were interested in native items only for the gold or silver they might incorporate; any decorative materials or costumes that came into their possession had the precious metals stripped from them immediately. Gold and silver objects

This Jaina-style ceramic figure of a Maya dancer, dating around A.D. 700, shows how ornaments finished a spectacular outfit. Decorative devices inserted in the ear lobes (could this be what the scriptures refer to as ringlets?), the necklace, the fancy breastplate, the bracelets, and an imposing headdress of wicker and cloth are integral to the outfit.

The deep green of jadeite stone was one of the most revered colors. It recalled still waters, the crucial maize plant, and all life-giving vegetation. No wonder beads of the material were put into the mouth of the dead at burial, in token of hoped-for rebirth (this was also done in China). These Olmec-style ear ornaments (inserted through holes in the lobes) date long before 500 B.C., but the popularity of jadeite continued right up to the Spanish Conquest.

Scarring the skin as a form of decoration was not common, but this example shows how far some Mesoamericans went to complete the total effect of a costume. Some tattooing was also done. (Classic Veracruz)

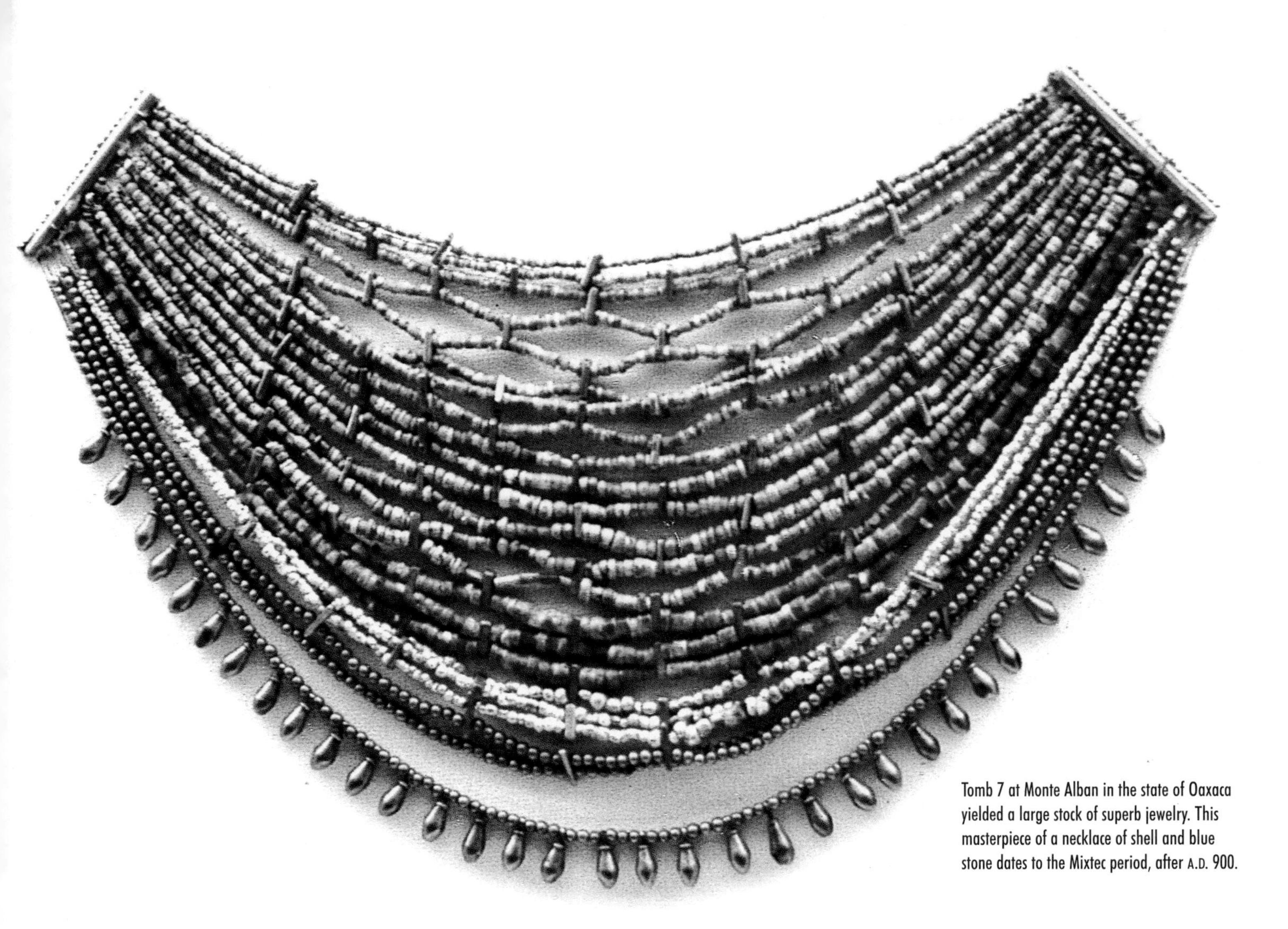

Tomb 7 at Monte Alban in the state of Oaxaca yielded a large stock of superb jewelry. This masterpiece of a necklace of shell and blue stone dates to the Mixtec period, after A.D. 900.

Other lovely materials were also used to decorate the earlobes, like the gold and the varicolored stones in these Maya items (after A.D. 800).

Metals were used primarily for decoration, not for practical objects. A favorite form was the copper or tumbaga (copper-gold alloy) bell like this one. Cast by the lost-wax method, it contained a tinkling stone inside, so that dancing or just walking produced musical accompaniment. Known bells are nearly all dated after A.D. 800, but earlier monuments picture them being worn. (Almost identical bells were made and worn in the Mediterranean area.)

were abundant at the time of the Spanish Conquest, and some of them amazed the Europeans with their technical cleverness or spectacular appearance. But thousands of those objects were melted down by the conquistadors, who were interested only in how many pounds of precious metal they could lay hands on. Some decorative items were sent off to Europe as curiosities, but many of those were lost en route and few were preserved once they got there. Anyway, a large majority of Mesoamerican ornaments were made of perishable materials; not many passed down to descendant peoples, and even fewer were preserved in the ruins to be found by archaeologists. Today we have only a few spectacular pieces to eke out a picture of the ornaments used in pre-Columbian times.

Visualizing Book of Mormon Life

The Book of Mormon says little on this topic. Alma condemned the ornaments worn by the elite among the Zoramite rebels: "Behold, O my God, their costly apparel, and their ringlets, and their bracelets, and their ornaments of gold, and all their precious things that they are ornamented with; and behold, their hearts are set upon them" (Alma 31:28). Precious things are mentioned quite often, but usually in connection with building decoration rather than personal ornamentation. But 4 Nephi 1:24 mentions "all manner of fine pearls" together with "costly apparel" among the features connected to social class distinctions that arose about A.D. 200. If decorative items generally had symbolic significance connected with cult matters, that would agree with the Mesoamerican cultural situation, and it would not surprise us that the strict-minded prophets in the Israelite tradition who kept the Nephite record either condemned or ignored them.

A woman's hairdo was another means for signifying status and enhancing beauty. This striking coiffure is of Olmec age from the Valley of Mexico.

In many communities of modern Mesoamerica, American Indian populations still parade Catholic images from the community's church around town on certain calendared days in the same manner as sacred representations (idols) were treated in pre-Hispanic times. Drinking typically accompanies these celebrations and probably did anciently too.

Routine, nonceremonial drinking was generally frowned upon, but the aged were given more leeway in that regard. This fine ceramic sculpture in Jaina style depicts a drunkard in a manner intended to condemn excessive drinking.

Diversions and Holidays

Entertainment and diversion as we think of them today were concepts of little relevance to ancient Mesoamericans. Life for most people focused on humdrum work and nose kept to the grindstone. Naturally there were occasions to relieve the tedium. The category we think of as religion was so pervasive in Mesoamerican life that we look first to that aspect of culture for clues on what constituted diversions.

A calendar heavy with ceremonial events has deep roots in tradition in this area. When the Spaniards forcibly converted the native peoples to Christianity in the sixteenth century, their local pre-Columbian calendars and events were combined with Spanish saints' days. Images or relics standing for the Catholic saints or the Virgin took on a heavy load of meaning from the native cultures. Processions, feasting, and other worship activities carried on in honor of the hybrid deities continue still today to follow forms and have meanings once associated with pre-Columbian supernaturals. But those activities also served functions we think of as recreational.

The colonial-era Spaniards lamented how much money and time the Indians "wasted" in their frequent religious holidays. They only partially realized that those activities were tied to the old belief system and to the social system of the community. We now see that the so-called waste provided temporary relief from the harshness of a life that demanded much and gave back little (as was true also of medieval European fairs and saints' days). A common feature of such occasions was the considerable consumption of alcoholic beverages; the periodic release of inhibitions that this drinking triggered apparently helped people cope with the formality and solemnity that characterized everyday relationships and routines.

Mesoamerican market days also provided diversion. Buying or selling in those nominally commercial settings yielded more than the exchange of goods. The lively market scene allowed locals contact with stimulating strangers in the form of merchants from nearby zones and often even people from enemy lands, under a kind of commercial truce. Participating in the color, bustle, and novelty of the marketplace must have been one of the highlights of an otherwise routine life, especially for children. People might also enjoy watching sleight-of-hand magicians, jugglers, dancers, and musicians.

Strange as it might seem, war too could have served a function of social diversion for men, as did the Crusades for Europeans in the Middle Ages.

We know that certain games were played among the ancient Mesoamericans. Most of our information comes from the elite sector of society. It is uncertain whether commoners played the same games, but at least the young could hardly have been stopped from imitating them in simplified versions.

The best known game was a contest with a rubber ball; the game was called by the Aztecs *tlachtli*. Two opponents faced each other on an elongated court. The ball was struck using only elbows and hips. The object was to drive the ball past the defender into the goal area at the opposite end of the playing space. The movement of the ball was considered symbolic of the sun moving across the heavens and into and out of the underworld, and winning or losing a game was considered a forecast of one's future. For the Aztecs, sacrifices sometimes preceded a game in order to gain approval of and support from the gods. Gambling accompanied the action; at times a player even bet his life on winning a ball game and was sacrificed if he lost. Variant forms of this game are evidenced back to at least 1300 B.C.[65]

Another game, called *patolli* by the Aztecs, was widely played beyond their territory. It too was old, having been around since at least A.D. 500. It was similar to the modern board game Parcheesi (which was adapted from an ancient game of India, *pachisi*). Markers were moved space by space around a cross-shaped board until the winner's piece reached a finish spot. A number of scholars have concluded that the Mesoamerican game was imported anciently directly from Asia because of the startling number of similarities with the Indian form.[66] Again sacred elements were crucial, for the four divisions on the Aztec playing board represented the four quarters of the world, and the squares on which the pieces moved represented the days of the calendar.

A few basic toys were made for the use of children, and animal pets were also popular, especially among women and children. Reportedly there was verbal humor, although little or none of that has been preserved (perhaps "you had to be there," culturally, to appreciate it).

Humor and Whimsy

Dr. Munro Edmonson writes of the "brooding religiosity, the aloof dignity that stands for good manners, the formalism that converts games into ceremonies and sports into sacrifices—all the values . . . that set the tone of Middle American cultures."[67] Yet showing through the grimness of life in Mesoamerica at certiain points is what Edmonson refers to as occasional "spontaneous gaiety" and "the normal eventful absurdities" of human life.[68]

At the time of the Spanish Conquest, a celebration for the god Kukulcan (equivalent to Quetzalcoatl) in Yucatan involved "clowns" or "comedians." They performed "farces . . . and comedies for the pleasure of the public."[69] This character, drawn from a scene on a painted Classic Maya pot, reminds us of a clown.

Visualizing Book of Mormon Life

The same would have been true of Book of Mormon peoples. Of course, we expect little lightheartedness to filter through Mormon, the editor of the Nephite account. His entire life was spent in military leadership, and he finally died in the war of his people's extinction.

This creation (from the Maya Classic period) stems from some artist's unusual sense of the whimsical side of life.

Related to humor is a sense of keen and innocent observation of nature. This large Aztec-age ceramic sculpture of a spider lightens the heart even today.

Children's Fun

Children would have found ways to have pleasant, amusing moments of their own, however solemn the world of the adults around them. Simple games and toys (for example, miniature dishes), play with other children their age, and the comfort of a pet would have been available to children, until their increasing involvement in the adult world crowded out the childhood frivolity.

This pair seem to be ritually painted and engaged in serious business (the piece, from Veracruz, dates to around A.D. 300–600). But since swings were known, some children surely took advantage of them for sheer pleasure.

Figures with movable arms and legs are considered to have been used in ceremonies by shamans or priests, who may have used ventriloquism to make them speak on behalf of spirits. But with the idea around, it is hard to believe that children did not use movable dolls for play. This one is in Teotihuacan style, dated perhaps A.D. 400–500.

A child with a pet acts about the same worldwide. This boy enjoys his *tejón*, or coatimundi, still a favorite pet among children and women in the Maya area. Rabbits, dogs, and birds were also kept as pets. These little dogs were favorite subjects of the ceramic artists of west Mexico for centuries, starting A.D. 200 or earlier.

Even in small villages the basic ball game was played but under more informal conditions than in cities. This west Mexico ceramic model (about A.D. 200–700) conveys some of the atmosphere—perhaps something like a small town baseball contest in the USA a century ago.

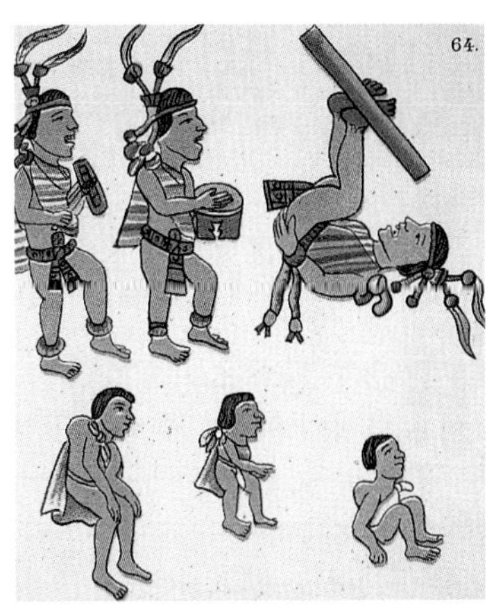

Aztec performers inherited a very old tradition of juggling (Olmec-age figures more than two thousand years earlier show the same thing). Sahagun's Florentine Codex displays this "combo" of Aztec dancer-musicians accompanying a juggler. Perhaps they represent a full-time company of entertainers at work before a group of nobles or in a spot near the marketplace before the public.

Boards for playing the patolli game have been found painted or scratched on ancient floors. It seems to have been a less formally ritualized activity than the ball game, though still sacred in tone.

VISUALIZING BOOK OF MORMON LIFE

Under Mosaic law the Israelites assembled frequently to celebrate certain Sabbaths with sacrifices and feasting. The Nephites also observed that law (see Mosiah 2:3 and Alma 30:3), so they too would probably have combined formal ritual events with festivities and a market. Furthermore, there would have been celebrations in connection with political happenings, like the ritually important new year anniversary and coronations. The Lamanite king referred to making "a feast unto my sons [i.e., subordinate kings], and unto my people" (Alma 20:9); it is likely that there was some calendrical, sacred element in such a feast. All early societies at the same level of civilization as the Nephites and Lamanites participated in similar events. Mesoamerican descendants of Book of Mormon peoples still today follow an entrenched tradition of scheduling ritual holidays that serve several functions simultaneously. Of course we cannot know how many of the Mesoamerican games or other diversions were known to the Nephites.

Cities, Towns, and Villages

Most of Mesoamerica's inhabitants lived in villages ranging in size from fifty to several hundred inhabitants. Village life was considered the ideal pattern.

What we call cities in ancient Mesoamerica were like our cities today in certain ways but very different in others. Experts still quarrel over the definition of a city as well as whether particular sites deserve to be called cities. Yet the fact remains that when the major settlements in Mexico or Central America are compared with those in, say, the Near East, the name *city* clearly deserves to be applied as much to Mesoamerica as to the Old World.

The Hebrew term translated in the Old Testament as "city" *('ir)* was applied to administrative centers over regions regardless of the size of the center. The fundamental meaning of the word may have been "fortress." Even tiny posts for armed garrisons were sometimes called by the term for *cities* in the Bible.[70] In Mesoamerica the concept was roughly the same. As long as a settlement was constructed according to a plan and was not just a product of slow historical accident, and if it had its own temple structure at its center—a sign of administrative dominance over neighboring places—it probably deserves to be classified as a city.

Some major settlements deserve to be called cities by any standard. Teotihuacan in central Mexico was one of the most notable (its peak population of probably over one hundred thousand was reached by around A.D. 300), but many others as well, such as tourist attractions Monte Alban, Tikal, and Copan, unquestionably fit in the category of cities by either their sheer size or the intricacy of their plans. In addition, there was an abundance of sites that could well be called towns, judging by their size. Yet even a noted capital city need not be large in population; the historical capitals of the famed Tarascan kingdom on the Aztecs' west side "were not towns of any great consequence"[71] despite the fact that overall the land had a high population density.

This tiny hamlet on the Pacific coast of Chiapas, Mexico, today illustrates the sort of rural hometown that was the point of reference for many of the common people, whether called Mesoamericans, Nephites, or Lamanites.

A land was usually conceived as a territory bounded by specific physical boundaries—a valley would constitute a land, for example—and governed from a common administrative center. Naturally, a land was also an economic entity; the chief community hosted a regular market that drew buyers from throughout the land and merchants from farther away. Los Trigales, in the Cunén area of Guatemala, shown here, might have qualified as a local land in ancient times.

El Mirador, near the northern border of Guatemala, may have been the largest and most spectacular city ever in Mesoamerica. Its peak glory lasted for only a couple of hundred years, in the vicinity of 200 B.C. This artist's reconstruction is based on excavations led by BYU archaeologist Ray T. Matheny.[74]

VISUALIZING BOOK OF MORMON LIFE

The Book of Mormon distinguishes five levels of settlement size: great cities, cities, towns, villages, and small villages.[72] Book of Mormon cities are often named, but their size clearly varied greatly. Perhaps on the small end of the scale was Helam, built by Alma's people. It was designated a city almost from the moment it was settled—by fewer than five hundred people (see Mosiah 18:35; 23:20). Only four of the more than forty Nephite and Lamanite cities whose names are given in the record are termed "great cities," although others, unnamed, were conceived as having the same rank (see Helaman 7:22; 3 Nephi 8:14). But we should be cautious about overestimating the actual population size of even the largest of those, for Mormon's record also refers to Jerusalem in Palestine as a "great city" (1 Nephi 1:4) even though its population down to Lehi's time may never have exceeded twenty-five thousand inhabitants (in Solomon's fabled day it had only around three thousand).[73]

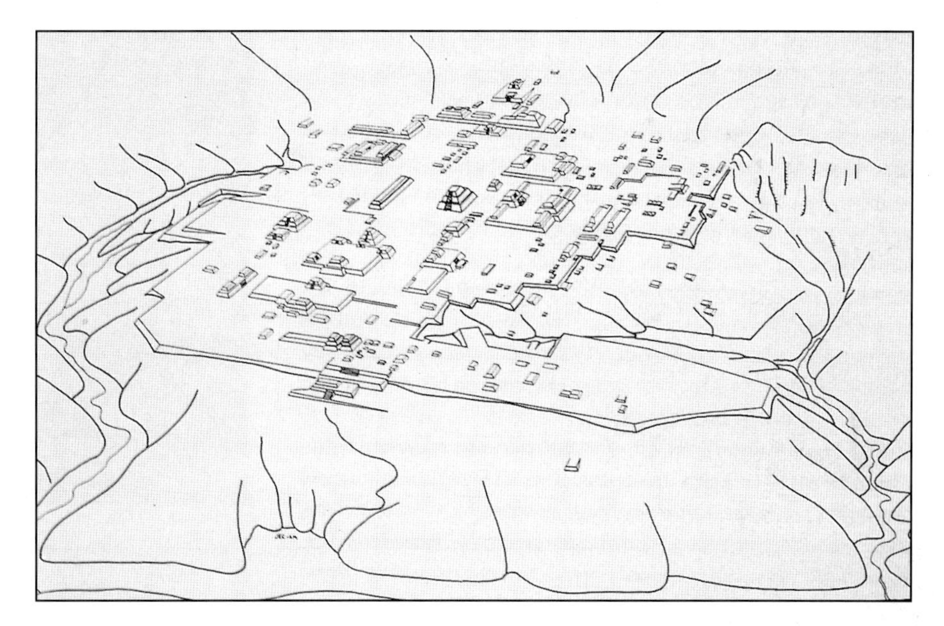

This sketch of the site known as Finca Acapulco in central Chiapas, dating to late Olmec times, shows how a settlement could be placed to take advantage of natural terrain.

Public Architecture

In a civilization so thoroughly infused with sacred matters, the most imposing structures all had religious significance. Archaeologists routinely refer to certain of the ruins today as temples, often without defining very carefully what that term might signify, but we are usually on sound ground in supposing them to have been religious in nature. Not only the size but also the central position and visual dominance of buildings devoted to the divinities were features of all major settlements.

A second component of public architecture was those structures where the rulers resided or carried out their civic functions. However, their activities were in turn so intermingled with religion that it would be arbitrary for us to distinguish neatly residence from temple from civic center. The quarters of the governing, and perhaps the priestly, elite were set apart from the housing for commoners, and they were built on a scale that was correspondingly distinct. Yet the mass of people were used to such differences; perhaps they would have had it no other way, for the impressive appearance of the buildings devoted to the use of their leaders would have been a matter for community pride. Again, however, we should remember that a majority of the population lived in more or less rural settings, and probably had little to do directly with elite persons.

Just as in ancient Egypt and Mesopotamia, for example, architectural forms were shaped by three influences: tradition, function, and materials. Over generations each people developed notions of what they thought were the appropriate forms and styles for public structures. Those cultural rules were often explained by referring to myths about deities or ancestors. For instance, the basic concept behind a divine center, in Mesoamerica as much as in the Near East, was of a mountain or hill upon which sacred power from heaven descended; contact with the upper, and under, worlds was most likely at that hill, termed the "navel of the earth."[75] A mound of earth, often covered with a stone sheathing to protect against weathering, was erected there, and atop it the temple proper or

A prominent feature of some of the largest cities was an acropolis or massive platform atop which various public buildings were erected. This famous example at Palenque illustrates the concept.

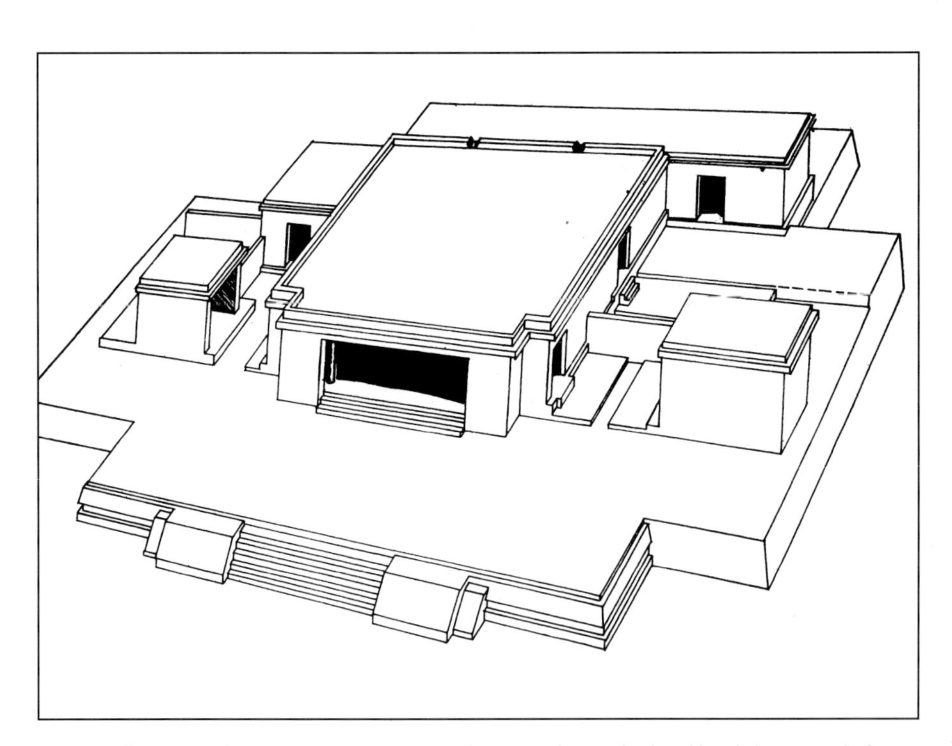

People in different cultural and ecological areas developed their own architectural styles, although there was wide sharing of concepts throughout Mesoamerica. This flat-roofed style functioned well at the relatively dry site of Chiapa de Corzo on the Grijalva River in the Central Depression, but it would have been unsuitable nearer the Gulf Coast where rainfall might be as much as five times as great. This structure (designated 5-H1 by archaeologists of the BYU New World Archaeological Foundation) is at a site that some Latter-day Saints consider to be the Sidom of the Book of Mormon. It dates to the beginning of the Christian era.

While the essential techniques of construction used by the people of Mesoamerica to make major structures were relatively simple, the plans were grandiose and the completed works were impressive. Here an artist accurately shows the construction methods used for one of the huge structures at El Mirador, Guatemala.

god's house was erected. By extension, a surrounding zone, often walled off from the everyday world, was also thought of as constituting part of the temple.

Variations on the theme of a divine contact point were played out to accommodate various activities. For example, sacrificial altars, spaces for acting out ceremonies, an archive for priestly records, and a place for a market near the sacred mound and plaza were defined according to local emphases and traditions. Moreover, the natural resources accessible in a given spot also affected the architecture. On the central and southern Yucatan peninsula both massive hardwood trees and plenty of limestone for stonework and plaster helped determine how cities were constructed and how they looked. In more arid areas timber was scarce and convenient building stone hard to procure.

Relatively little attention has been paid by scholars to the engineering practices used anciently, but increasingly it is evident that considerable expertise and some mathematical knowledge must have been involved. Some settlements were placed according to lines of sight to sacred mountaintops or to rising or setting points of the sun, moon, or stars on a certain day in the calendar. Some of these alignments even crossed over intervening hill barriers to extend perhaps hundreds of miles. Roads also were laid out that extended in straight segments for scores of miles. Water drains, dams, canals, and even aqueducts were built. One recent discovery identified the stone abutments for a hanging bridge over a major river.[76]

Astronomy was one factor in settlement planning and architectural placement. The structure in the foreground, Mound J at Monte Alban, is generally considered a type of observatory, because angles of view through the holes and doorways are toward key positions of the heavenly bodies.

The subfield of research called archaeoastronomy has developed to deal with the complex relations between ancient astronomy and the symbolic uses to which that knowledge was put in construction. From Uaxactun, lowland Guatemala, this architectural group illustrates one of the first alignments to be recognized by archaeologists. The sight lines to the right and left indicate where the sun was visible at the horizon when it reached its northernmost and southernmost points.

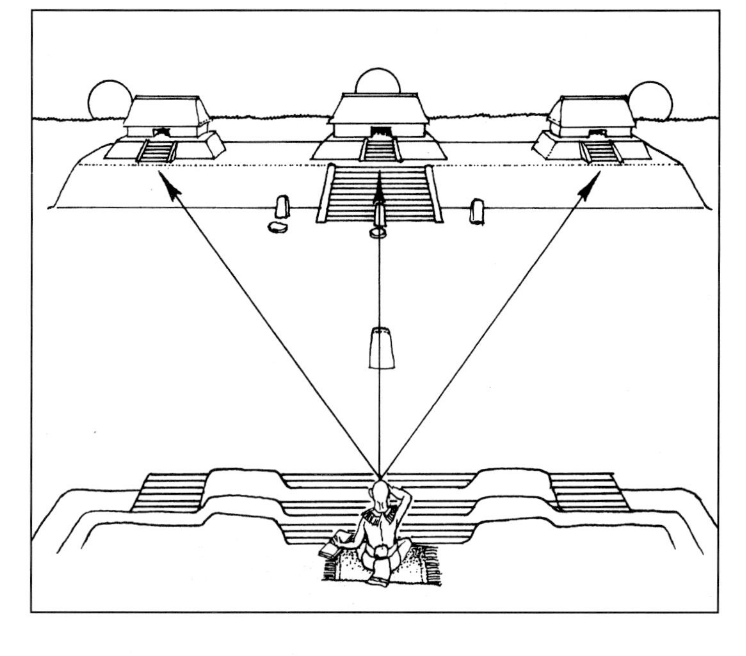

That ancient Mesoamericans possessed significant engineering knowledge is becoming evident as archaeologists look beyond buildings to examine other works of the ancient people. This stone drain was in use at San Lorenzo in the Isthmus of Tehuantepec, a site considered by some Latter-day Saints to correspond to the city built by Jaredite King Lib at the narrow neck of land.

VISUALIZING BOOK OF MORMON LIFE

In the Book of Mormon account, frequent mention is made of the construction of towers (meaning artificial mounds), temples, other public buildings, and cities (for example, see Helaman 3:11, 14). Highways were also constructed ("cast up," 3 Nephi 6:8). No more specific engineering or construction activities are mentioned. However, significant knowledge of astronomy was part of Nephite culture (see, for example, Helaman 12:15; 14:5; 3 Nephi 1:21), which implies systematic observations and the possibility of sight-line placements. (Israelite sites sometimes were so aligned in ancient Judah.)

Government

Overview

Government in ancient times resembled very little what modern people experience under that heading. Most activities involved in administering civil authority and law took place at the community level. The people involved there were all rather familiar with each other, at least culturally if not personally. There was little in the way of an apparatus or bureaucracy of officials, and what officers there were did not act as impersonally as modern bureaucrats must.

Rudimentary executive offices developed in some situations to facilitate decision-making and enforcement, but most political or administrative mechanisms—a legislature, a police force, a professional civil service—had not yet been invented in this civilization. Most often the strength of government lay in charisma—the awe or charm induced in subjects by the personality of the leader.

The ruler in ancient societies was the linchpin that held government together. He was supposed to exemplify the cultural virtues and moral values. The sacred sphere of the culture, represented publicly by priests and their rituals, validated the ruler's power and vouched for his fitness to rule. But were he to challenge prevailing cultural beliefs, myths, or moral standards by too much, or should he lose the affection or respect of his people, his rule could be on shaky ground; he might even be slain.

The Aztecs provide our best-documented Mesoamerican example of how government operated, although the governments of other peoples varied significantly in some of their ways. When the Spaniards arrived, the Aztec state directly administered perhaps a million people in and near the valley of Mexico. The dominant tribe among the ethnic mixture involved called themselves the Mexica (pronounced meh-shee-kah); the term *Aztec* refers more comprehensively to the state and the culture. Perhaps a million or more other inhabitants of vassal kingdoms beyond the actual Aztec state were controlled by the Aztec rulers through a system of tribute payments and threats.

Governing was partly aided by the use of written records, but literate people were in short supply, thus the extensive record keeping on individuals that is so vital to modern governments was impossible. Oral communication via messenger was common. Full, consistent control of peoples distant from the political center, particularly across geographical, cultural, and language barriers, was such a problem that it was rarely even attempted.

Ultimately, coercive force was relied upon to keep troublesome groups under control. The lack of a systematic information system that routinely reported to the ruler at the capital meant that issues of control might not be picked up on until they had become sizable. When some group's disobedience finally became evident, then the ruler's fist in the form of an armed expedition would smite them. The temple in the defeated community would be looted and set afire, whereupon both sides usually accepted that the game was over and the rebels would surrender. Another local ruler was then appointed who promised to toe the mark better.

VISUALIZING BOOK OF MORMON LIFE

The same system prevailed in the ancient Near East, where the level of civilizational development was roughly the same as in Mesoamerica. The Babylonians, for example, put a puppet ruler, Zedekiah (the father of Mulek of the Book of Mormon), on the throne of Judah in Nephi's day when his predecessor failed to measure up to the Babylonian standard of loyalty. But it was beyond the overlords' power or desire to maintain hands-on rule over a distant, minor place like the kingdom of Judah in the same way they could within their close-knit Babylonian heartland. So when Zedekiah in turn refused to follow the rules laid down by the administration of Nebuchadnezzar, another army was sent to punish the renewed impertinence. Jerusalem was besieged again, and upon its fall and destruction in 586 B.C., stubborn Zedekiah had his eyes put out and was carried to Babylon a prisoner (see 2 Kings 24–5). Book of Mormon governments operated similarly. For example, note Lamanite expeditions against rebellious subject Zeniffite rulers (see Mosiah 19:6–29; chapters 20 and 21) and Moroni$_1$'s subjection of the insurgent king-men who were "hewn down" (Alma 51:19) or forced to "hoist the title of liberty [flag] upon their towers" (Alma 51:20; see 51:17–9).

This magnificent monument from the lowland Maya area (dating about A.D. 700) captures the essence of Mesoamerican rulership. An officer (a virtual "lawyer") of the royal court informs the ruler, who is acting as high judge seated on a sumptuous throne (compare Alma 60:7, 11), about a matter involving three bound prisoners. They are of some social significance, judging by their costumes and the fan or book in the hand of one. They might be foreigners, or they might be subjects charged with political defiance (or dissent, in Book of Mormon terms).

Oaths were major mechanisms for constructing loyalty networks. Their force stemmed from drawing sacred power into the political realm. This striking scene is from the Alvarado area in the southern Veracruz state, only a few miles from the probable final battleground of the Nephites, their hill Cumorah. Dating to about the first century B.C., the scene shows a lord apparently giving an oath to a pleading prisoner (compare Alma 44:15).

Rulers and Their Methods

Most Mesoamerican societies operated at the chiefdom level of rule much of the time.[77] Tribal chiefs had to walk a careful line. They lacked sure control over effective instruments of coercion, so they had to play on persuasion in order to fend off rivals. Adroit speech-making helped cement a leader's position. It also helped for him to be of a descent group that had supplied rulers in the past. Close connections with and approval from the priests of course supported his power. Another way for a leader to bolster his position was to gain supporters by dealing out privileges, ranging from making special luxury goods accessible, to assigning friends to subordinate positions yielding their own payoffs (i.e., tribute payments), and even to furnishing noble wives.

Still, rulers were vulnerable to loss of support and eventual overthrow. A revolution could be couched in the name of the gods. A king who was cowardly or inept, or who taxed excessively, or who too flagrantly lived contrary to traditional morals could be defined as abandoned by the gods and thus become subject to assassination or whatever other course of drastic replacement was necessary. A dramatic example was the case of the Aztec ruler Montezuma (Motecuzoma II). At first he impressed Cortez as an absolute ruler, but before long he was being jeered and stoned by his own subjects as his weakness in handling the Spaniards became evident to the Mexica people.

Periodically in Mesoamerica in the Pre-Classic period, as populations grew or control was exercised over wider territories, attempts were made to firm up governance to the level of a state. That more sophisticated pattern of government provided more mechanisms for control of the people by broadening the government's right and ability to use force. Early Mesoamerican attempts to operate at the state level usually failed, not only because the necessary economic and administrative tools were undeveloped, but also because local ways were too divisive for stable government—the potential citizenry of the state would not pay the price in discipline and wealth. Governmental forms in Mesoamerica never reached the sophistication or stability that came to be commonplace much earlier in the central Old World area or in China.

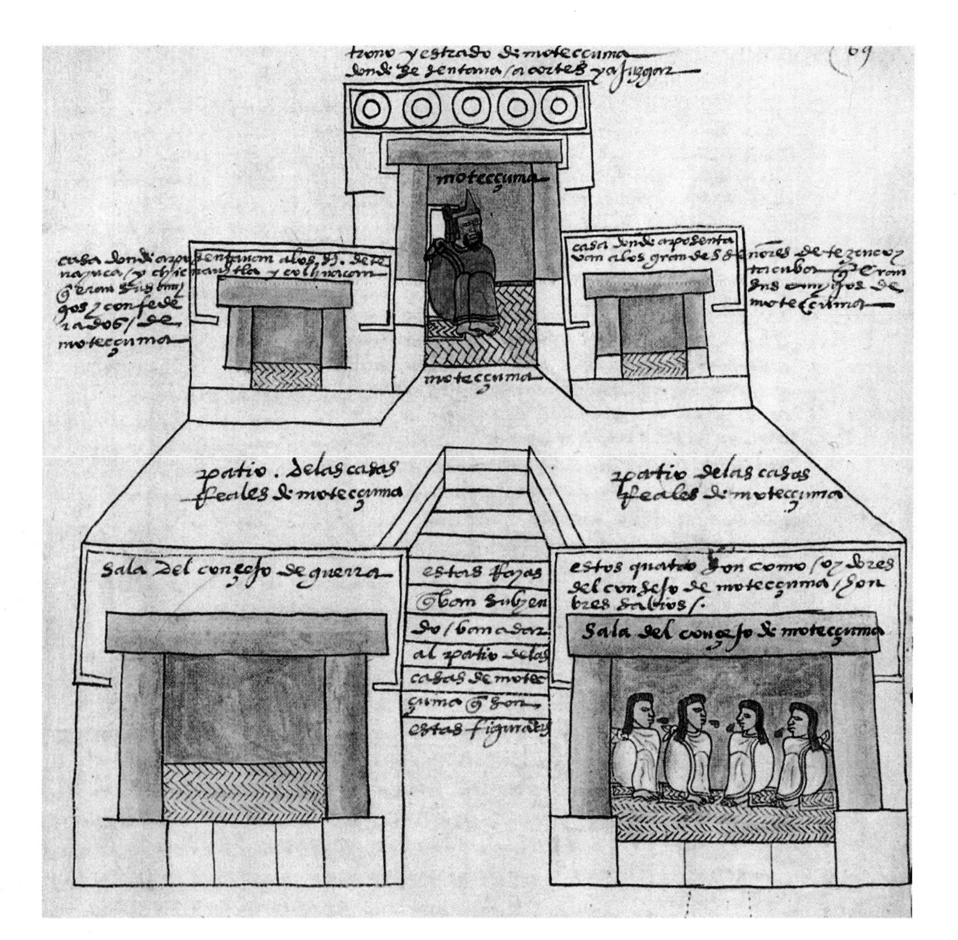

A sketch of Montezuma's palace (in the Codex Mendoza) emphasizes the public view of his dominance. This is shown by his quarters being on the highest level at the center of the complex. But all around him were other powerful people and kin—counselors, judges, military leaders—whom he was obliged to involve in decisions.

Maya and other rulers made a big show of their sanctity and power by sitting on ornate thrones like that shown with this Late Classic figurine. However, the newly deciphered inscriptions make clear that their power constantly had to be justified in the eyes of the public.

An artist's portrayal conveys the delicate problem of an "absolute" ruler. Aztec monarch Montezuma was rejected by his people when they concluded that he had acted foolishly in giving in to Cortez and his Spaniards.

Visualizing Book of Mormon Life

The Book of Mormon reports instance after instance that fit with what we know about ancient rulership in general and Mesoamerican patterns specifically. For instance, the failure of central government to maintain itself against secession and defiance by local and special groups is repeatedly manifested. Amlici got control over an entire rebellious region not far from the Nephite capital apparently before the governing officers got wind of it, and then they could only snuff it out by armed violence (see Alma 2:1–10). The situation was repeated in the case of the king-men (see Alma 51:1–8, 13–20). The Nephite government could not keep the secessionist Zoramites within the Nephite nation (see Alma 31:1–5; 43:4). Among the Lamanites, when Lamoni's father, king over all the Lamanites, wished to know why his son, the local subking over the land of Ishmael, had failed to show up for an appointed festival in the capital, he did not send a functionary to find out but had to come personally, illustrating the limitations on the very form of his government. Eventually his apparatus of rule proved incapable of dealing with the problems of control once he renounced militarism (see Alma 24–5).

This is not to say that there were no secondary roles or institutions for administration. Limhi, king of the Zeniffite group, had "guards" (Mosiah 7:7), and later there were "many lawyers, and many officers" (3 Nephi 6:11) involved at the central headquarters of the short-lived Nephite state. But the tools of government that they had were too limited to govern an extensive territory or diverse peoples. In a real emergency, captain Moroni$_1$ could only get authority to deal with the recalcitrant king-men by the awkward process of sending out for community or regional or lineage leaders to ratify his proposal (see Alma 51:14–20). He later felt that the Nephite political system was almost incapable of functioning effectively (see Alma 60).

Kings, or their successors in the case of the Nephites, the judges (who also "reigned"), exercised rule mainly by charisma or force of personality. Note King Benjamin's careful language in Mosiah 2:9–19 about his noncoercive relationship to his people, Limhi's being made king "by the voice of the people" in Mosiah 7:9, and the flattery mechanism necessary according to Alma 20:4. Fear could also be involved in a ruler's power, as shown by Lamoni's arbitrary executions (see Alma 18:6, 13, 21; 19:20); Moroni$_1$ also invoked fear in trying to control the Nephites (see Alma 60:27–31 and 51:22). How people viewed their ruler was the chief component in successful governance (note Alma 50:12). The role of ruler was set apart by customs intended to elevate

At modern-day Zinacantan, a Tzotzil Maya community in highland Chiapas, elder leaders, who function as judges and constitute the village's decision-making body, sit before the civic center. Except for a few elements of the costumes and minor customs of Spanish origin, this scene might have been repeated in a sizable village a millennium or two ago.

him above day-to-day issues (for example, see Alma 18:12–4; 22:2–3; 26:4–12); being above the fray meant that, ideally, he reserved his full power to judge matters that he considered crucial.

A ruler collected tribute, that is, taxes, yet cultural standards inhibited him from using official resources merely according to his whims. He indeed had a higher standard of living than his people. Lamoni, a lesser king, had only a "house," which could still accommodate quite a crowd in it, but his father, the king over the entire land, dwelt in a "palace" (Alma 22:2; see 19:18 and 22:1). If he was charismatic enough, the ruler could somewhat stretch the rules governing his role, but eventually he was subject to what his people felt about him; note the strong condemnation voiced in the Zeniffite record about King Noah for going too far past the norm (see Mosiah 11:1–15). The Lamanite king discussed in Alma 24 and his son, Anti-Nephi-Lehi, lost the respect, and thus the support, of a majority of their people by displeasing them. Alma 47:2–7 reports another revolt against a Lamanite king. Clearly, a successful leader had to want what the cultural definition of his role allowed him legitimately to want. Meanwhile, rebellions too were built around attractive, charismatic leaders, as in the cases of Amlici, Nehor, and Amalickiah.

A ruler's position was defined and supported by religion. He himself was likely some type of priest, at least in name, and he was sustained by a circle of official priests (consider Mosiah and his priests in Mosiah 27:1). In fact, government and religion ran together so fully that they were not considered to be distinct categories of thought or behavior (see Alma 43:47).

Given this background, it is apparent how difficult—and ultimately how temporary—was the enlightened concept of governing through democratically chosen judges, which King Mosiah$_2$ got the Nephites to adopt. The rise of a whole string of dissidents shows that the old pattern of putting public problems on the shoulders of a single ruler remained a strong current in Nephite thinking.

Nothing about any of these situations is surprising in ancient Mesoamerican terms.

Taxes and Tribute

Anciently there was no meaningful distinction between taxes and tribute. The men in charge of any unit of governance have always received resources from their subjects to provide for their needs. At a very local level, the measure of prestige derived from public service may have been sufficient compensation for the modest commitment of time and expense incurred by purely local leaders, who served at their own expense. In fact, the actual costs of serving in grassroots government probably took more from those who occupied office than they gained from that service, even if they collected some payments.

The larger the political unit, however, the costlier the process. Rulers over a region served full-time or nearly so, and they might have to support aides. With population growth and resulting political elaboration, there had to be a stronger system of support. That was usually phrased in terms of tribute, which could take many forms. A ruling family, for example, might have the cultivation of its lands taken care of by "voluntary" community labor assessed from each kin group. Certain privileges might also be granted a ruler, like a proportion of booty taken in war. Annual contributions of precious materials or clothing or fuel, nominally for the public glorification of the community, could also enter the picture. Supplies for military forces and the construction of public structures also had to be produced by a version of tribute.

A major codex (native book), the Mendoza, written immediately after the Conquest, gives detailed data on the vast quantities of all sorts of materials—both common and precious—that were collected to fund and fuel Aztec government. Thousands of people were supported out of the tribute—clerks, archivists, priests, architects, engineers, military leaders, servants for the lords, and so on.

Assessments were levied according to each region's ability to produce—gold dust from some areas, cotton from the warmer agricultural territories where it was grown, and liquor from where the agave plant flourished. Local and then regional authorities had to obtain from the people and send up the tribute chain whatever the central seat of government demanded, in addition to a percentage taken to support the local apparatus of rule. The tax collector was no doubt as dreaded then as now, especially by the common people on whom the final burden of payment rested.

The *Matricula de Tributos*, another Aztec list, illustrates the political symbolism involved in the ritualized payment of tribute. Every item ticked off signaled submission to superior power, just as must have been the case when the Zeniffites turned over their tribute to the Lamanite king.

Keith Henderson's drawing that shows the arrival of Aztec tax collectors on the Gulf Coast catches both the deference that had to be shown to them and the fear of incurring their displeasure.

VISUALIZING BOOK OF MORMON LIFE

The Book of Mormon speaks of a similar system of payments. Mosiah 19:15 (see also 19:22) describes the Lamanite overlords demanding of the Zeniffites "one half of all they possessed, one half of their gold, and their silver, and all their precious things" as "tribute to the king of the Lamanites from year to year." Their own king, Noah, had already put a heavy tax on his own people to support himself and his courtiers and priests, and to build "many elegant and spacious buildings" (Mosiah 11:8; see 11:6–7). Mosiah 22:7 and 10 mention paying a regular tribute of wine, plus an extra amount as a present to the Lamanite garrison outside the city of Lehi-Nephi at the time when Limhi and his people escaped. Note too King Benjamin's emphasis that in his kingly role he had not taxed his people, implying that he was not like typical kings in that regard.

Nephite rulers were thought to have "possessed" (see Alma 8:7) their villages and cities, and no doubt the same concept prevailed among the Lamanites. King Benjamin's concept was that the Lord had given his people to him (see Mosiah 1:10). Surely the possessor would be justified in being reimbursed for his costs from those given to him by deity. Such taxes would have been used to support, at one point in time, the "thousands of those, yea, and tens of thousands, who do . . . sit in idleness" at the center of government at Zarahemla (Alma 60:22), according to the charge by Captain Moroni$_1$. Giddianhi, the head of the Gadianton secret society, was blunt about wanting a piece of the action, as modern parlance would put it. He wrote to the Nephite ruler, Lachoneus, that "I hope that ye will deliver up your lands and your possessions, without the shedding of blood, that . . . my people may recover their rights and government" (3 Nephi 3:10). Those rights obviously included control of the possessions mentioned and involved the receipt of tribute.[78]

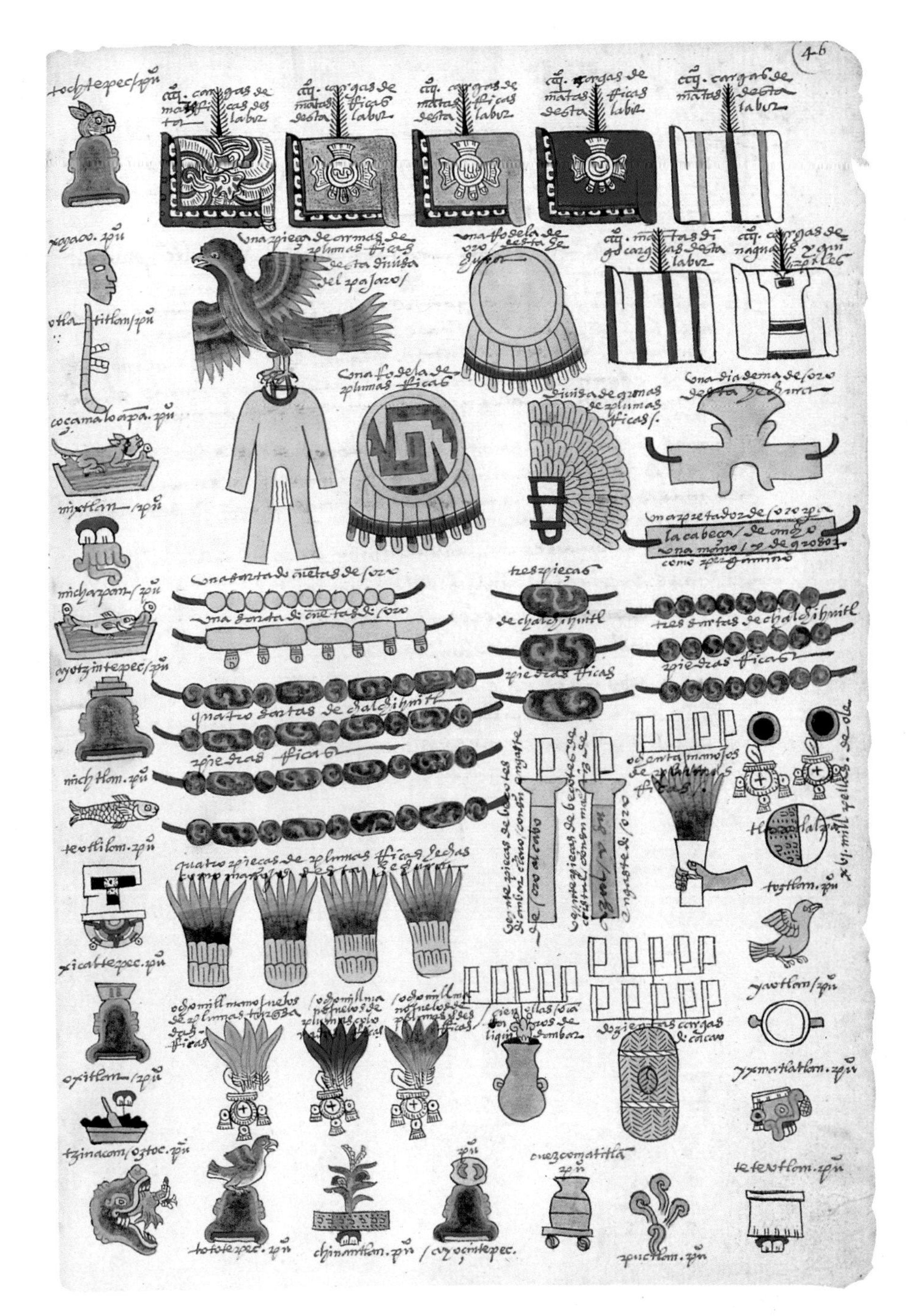

Types and amounts of tribute are listed in this tabulation from the Codex Mendoza. One province, for example, had to submit annually to the capital 12,800 cloaks, 1600 loin cloths, 1600 women's tunics, 32,000 bundles of paper, 8000 bowls, and four bins of maize and beans.

When the Spaniards conquered the Aztecs, as far as commoners were concerned little changed politically. Collectors still extracted goods from the producers and those materials disappeared upward in the governmental pyramid. The only difference was that Cortez now sat on the throne. This scene shows the Tlaxcalan lineage heads greeting and submitting to the conqueror, an act confirmed by the material goods offered.

This unusual method of confinement among the Maya could recall the situation of Abinadi, the Book of Mormon prophet who was slain by burning. Perhaps he was restrained like this when "they took him and bound him, and scourged his skin with faggots" (Mosiah 17:13).

Jail in Zinacantan, Chiapas, a generation ago had not changed significantly from sixteenth century practice as shown in the Aztec representation. Larger prison structures were probably used in large centers of population.

Courts, Justice, and Punishment

One of the primary duties of a ruler was to settle disputes among his people. Sometimes that could be done by him personally, but in a population of much size, he would not have time to deal with every conflict. Judges were delegated to carry out that duty.

Cortez, for example, described the situation at the great market in the Aztec capital: "There is in this square a very large building, like a Court of Justice, where there are always ten or twelve persons, sitting as judges, and delivering their decisions upon all cases which arise in the markets."[79] In public assemblies, the Spaniards observed native police officers with pine cudgels who enforced order if required to do so by the authorities.

In modern times, at Zinacantan, a Maya center in highland Chiapas that has been extensively studied and where much of the ancient pattern of thought and living continues, a rather similar judicial pattern prevails. Four judges sit during each day on a bench in front of the civic building making themselves available to plaintiffs, who arrive bearing a gift of rum. If the officials consider a plea worthy, they send their police (the *mayores*) to bring in the defendant. There follows a trial that goes like this: "The defendant appears, also with a bottle of rum, bows to the officials, and presents his defense. Usually, both parties, accompanied by relatives that are known to be 'good talkers' who serve as 'lawyers,' all talk at once and one wonders how in the ensuing pandemonium a judgment is ever reached."[80]

The task of judges in Mesoamerican communities was and is, if possible, to restore harmony to the community.[81] In clear-cut cases, repayment of damages to the injured party might be a sufficient solution. The punishment turns out to be a social, not just an individual, matter, for any fine would actually be paid by the offender's kin group and would be distributed to the kin of the plaintiff. If the judges could not reach a decision, they might resort to exhortation or verbal chastisement to both parties in an effort to calm the situation down. A variety of harsher punishments, ranging from jail to execution (in pre-Spanish days) were also available. Moral crimes as well as civil offenses were dealt with. Adultery, for example, called for the death penalty in certain cases or a fine under other conditions.

It is not clear whether there were professional lawyers in ancient times. The Spaniards did not let the native courts continue, so little is known about their actual operations. But judges very likely were appointed for given terms, not for life, so they must have relied upon some sorts of legal experts who might be thought of as lawyers.

Scenes showing bound prisoners are plentiful in Mesoamerican art. Some were clearly war prisoners, but others were criminals detained for trial.

Visualizing Book of Mormon Life

Judges were, of course, preeminent figures in Nephite government. The aim of Nephite jurisprudence was more often to produce renewed harmony than to execute vengeance, which is similar to what we know of Mesoamerican cultures. In the disputes that are described in detail, the authority figure could offer to accept a compromise by which punishment could be avoided (see, for instance, Mosiah 7:10–1). In policy disagreements, the same desire for compromise is shown more often than not (consider the Morianton-Lehi conflict in Alma 50:25–36). Book of Mormon discussions of trials are incomplete, but correspondences to Jewish legal thinking and procedures are displayed.[82] Religion, as we might expect, played more of a role than in modern, secular jurisprudence. (See, for example, Mosiah 17–8; Alma 1:10–5; 10:13–6.)

Prisons and prisoners (both civil and military) are mentioned (for example, see Alma 14:17 and 3 Nephi 5:4). Routine executions were carried out by unspecified means (see, for example, Alma 2:1; 62:9), but ritual executions were done in bizarre ways: (1) on top of a hill "between the heavens and the earth" (Alma 1:15); (2) by burning malefactors (see, for example, Alma 14:8; 17:13; 25:5); (3) by hanging from the top of a tree, whereupon the tree was cut down (see 3 Nephi 4:28); and (4) by casting into wild animal dens (see 4 Nephi 1:33).

Aztec punishments included stoning, a form of public participatory execution called for in the law of Moses, said to be followed by the Nephites.

In an Aztec court a panel of four judges is shown observing different modes of execution, as seen in sketches made by Father Sahagun's informants.

Masks like this from the south coast of the Mexican state of Guerrero have been interpreted by some as evidence for a jaguar cult, or perhaps a military order with the jaguar as guardian spirit. In Olmec times, corresponding with the Jaredite period of the Book of Mormon, the power of the jaguar was widely admired, yet feared. The imagery continued to Aztec times. Cecilia Klein has observed, "Most Aztec masks must be understood as advertisements of and tools to maintain and augment the material advantages of the ruling classes."[84]

Secret Groups

Historical sources indicate that secret organizations have existed in many parts of the world. They have taken many forms, but their shared intent has been to provide participants with assistance in undertakings at odds with public norms of conduct. Mesoamerica had its share.

The internal social structure of long-distance merchants among the Aztecs at the time of the Spanish Conquest provides an example. They had their own deities and rites to comfort and support them on the road; they mutually protected their economic secrets and contacts, in the fashion of the medieval guilds of Europe; and they passed secret intelligence to each other about exotic lands that they penetrated and to a degree shared the same with the Aztec war machine.

Military orders were another type of quasi-secret society; their members—dedicated super-warriors, so to speak—fought together as a unit in battle but in peace supported each others' ambitions for power and influence. There is also evidence for the existence of little-known secret cults associated with the night, perhaps jaguars, and caves or lairs in isolated wilderness spots. In central Mexico the god Tezcatlipoca, the arch-sorceror who was associated with darkness, the night, and the jaguar, may have had a particular link to culturally subversive groups. The pattern seems to go back a very long time. Some of these elements in society were manifest in colonial times and right up until recently, but by their clandestine nature it is now impossible to learn much about them.[83]

Visualizing Book of Mormon Life

Nephites and Lamanites went through periods when secret groups were powerful and subversive of the regular political order (see Helaman 7:4). Their prototype was a secret order among the Jaredites that dated as far back as the second millennium B.C. and claimed Near Eastern inspiration. From soon after the Christian era, for example, the Nephite account quotes a communication from the chief "capo" of "the secret society of Gadianton" who claimed that his "society and the works thereof I know to be good; and they are of ancient date and they have been handed down unto us" (3 Nephi 3:9). At the very end of Nephite history, this revived secret order, called the robbers of Gadianton, became so influential that they occupied their own lands and mounted their own armies on a par with those of the Nephites and Lamanites (see 4 Nephi 1:46; Mormon 2:8, 28).

A remarkable photographic record of underground cultic activity in modern Yucatan was made a generation ago. This picture hints at some of the ritual long ago practiced in secret or sacred cave sites. Underground was associated with the jaguar in pre-Hispanic times.

Bandits would seek out for their bases inaccessible locations where they could be free from control measures by conventional society. The relation is illustrated in this picture from hills at the northerly end of the Central Depression of Chiapas. Major settlements lie in the river valley seen in the middle distance.

Secrecy was heavily ingrained in Mesoamerican life. Witchcraft and sorcery were, and still are, common ingredients in the social and ritual life of certain groups. The remarkable piece of ceramic sculpture shown here dates to the Maya Late Classic. It recalls Mormon 1:19, written in the fourth century A.D.: "There were sorceries, and witchcrafts, and magics . . . upon all the face of the land."

Foreign Relations

Rarely were there extensive political structures in Mesoamerica that could justifiably be called empires or even geographically extensive kingdoms. A city-state dominating its region was the more frequent political arrangement. With competing polities in close proximity, what we think of as foreign relations were frequent concerns.

Even large political blocs like the Aztec so-called empire actually was composed of distinct political systems that had once existed as independent governments. When subsidiary units were conquered, the overlords simply left the existing government in place, after obtaining a pledge of subservience from the top local chief. Thus such imperial government as there was consisted of the central city dealing with lesser kingdoms in a sort of foreign relations mode.

Where two societies were formally independent of each other (no matter that one might be dramatically bigger than the other), relationships were governed by two considerations—war or the threat of war, and trade access. The Tlaxcalans, located only a few miles east of the Aztec heartland, successfully defended their autonomy for centuries against their formidable rivals. The two dealt only in terms of current or potential warfare. (It was Cortez's ability to tap into that old rivalry that availed him of the native Tlaxcalan manpower and cultural knowledge that allowed him ultimately to defeat Montezuma's Aztecs.)

Treaties, alliances, truces, ambassadors, spies, and appointments for war were all known cultural forms for relations between societies. In some cases, marriages were consummated between ruling families in separate societies to help cement peaceful relations.

Typically, societies were happy to leave their neighbors alone politically and militarily so long as they could count on not being attacked and so long as their merchants had freedom to circulate across boundaries.

Sometimes, nevertheless, ambition for greater tribute payments would combine with the sheer desire to exercise dominance and lead to wars of conquest. Ethnic prejudice also contributed.

The sketch on the left is an artist's speculation as to what the scene on La Venta Stela 3 may have shown originally. Persons from two distinct ethnic groups are seen in some sort of ceremonial meeting. Some have supposed that the Jewish-looking man on the right represents a people who had gained control over the other folk. The date of the stela, in the vicinity of 600 B.C., makes some Latter-day Saints wonder if this representation involves the arrival of Mulek from the land of Israel (see Omni 1:15–6 and Helaman 6:10; compare the faces on the Alvarado stela on page 110).

Rulers or their representatives regularly made diplomatic visits, during which terms of dominance, subservience, or cooperation were negotiated. These visits usually involved a fair amount of ritual, and presents were often given. Maya vases, like this one from Nebaj, Guatemala, dating to the Late Classic period, sometimes picture these visits.

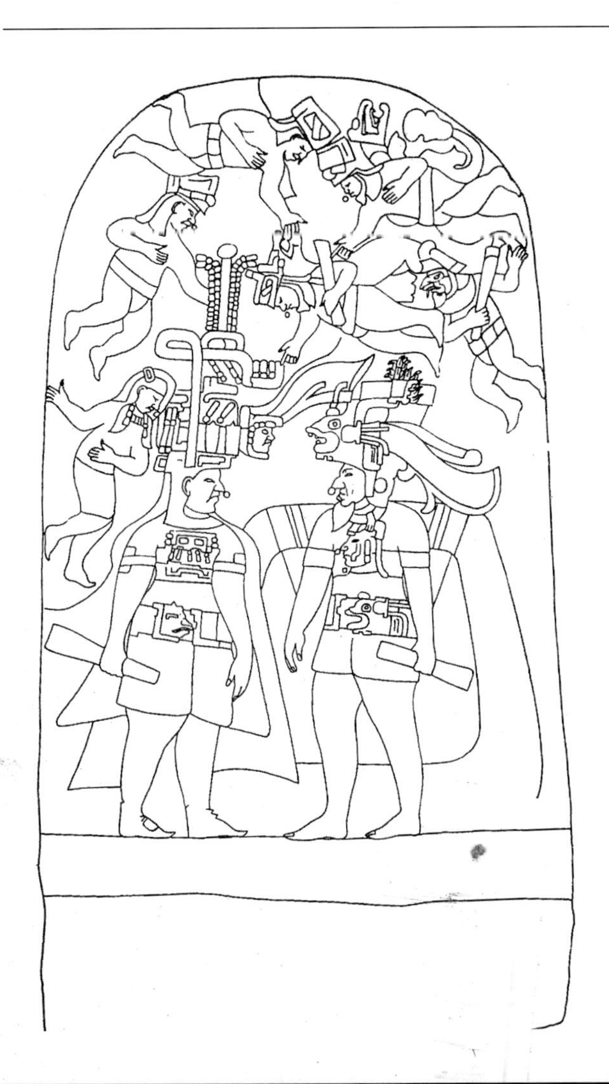

This artist's drawing of Totonac representatives welcoming Cortez as he arrived on the Gulf Coast conveys how even strange or unknown dignitaries were treated if they appeared strong—with a measure of respect and signs of peace.

A failure of the usual foreign policy of negotiation could, of course, result in harsh measures against a rival ruler. That may be what is shown on this monument from Izapa, on the Mexico-Guatemala border; it dates to the first century B.C. (Or it might represent some event in an ancient tale; note Ether 8:11–2.)

A codex shows a native ambassador sent by Cortez to meet with Tlaxcalan lords as his conquering army advanced toward the Aztec capital. A similar concept is represented above on an Olmec monument from La Venta that is two thousand years older.

Visualizing Book of Mormon Life

In the Book of Mormon, relationships among the Lamanite kings are varied and instructive. What is said is compatible with Mesoamerican patterns. The head king of the Lamanites sent "a proclamation throughout all the land, amongst all his people who were in all his land," (Alma 22:27) consisting of many subordinate kingdoms, that Nephite missionaries could go where they wished and not be harmed nor hindered (see Alma 28:1–2). In a direct encounter with his son Lamoni, king in the land of Ishmael, the great king first commanded his son to slay Ammon, Lamoni's Nephite mentor, but later, when forced to it, he granted that his son be completely independent (see Alma 20:14, 26). When Lamoni had to deal with the king of the land of Middoni, another subordinate kingdom, his approach was flattery on the one hand (see Alma 20:4) and pleading on the other (see Alma 20:7). Obviously there were a number of patterned possibilities in dealings between kingdoms.

Between Lamanites and their long-term rivals, the Nephites, several diplomatic mechanisms are seen. Oaths were considered binding across the boundaries of societies (see Mosiah 20:14; Alma 44:8). Activities of ambassadors and negotiations are pictured in the Book of Mormon account (for example, see Alma 52:20). Treaties were also made (see Mosiah 7:21; Mormon 2:28). Appointment for battle is illustrated in Mormon 6:2–3. Intermarriage as a possible instrument of statesmanship is illustrated in Alma 17:24 and 47:35. Conquerors might also slay an opposing leader and ravage his city (see Helaman 1:20–2; Alma 47:33, note "spare the people of the city").

War

Overview

More often than not, war was a matter of ritual more than of combat. Conflict was carried on so consistently that it, rather than peace, was viewed as the basic condition for society and about as inevitable as planting crops or engaging in sex. Each of the three activities was fraught with danger, but more threatening than fighting or planting or sex as such was the possibility of acting inappropriately in those processes. Doing any of the three improperly could upset the sacred balance in the universe. So war was approached as a delicate emergency in which the role of sacred powers must be carefully planned for and, if possible, controlled. That required ritual.

As among many other American Indian cultures, and in fact throughout ancient civilizations generally, most military engagements tended to boil down to individual contests. There were rudimentary general staffs and a bit of strategic planning, training exercises, and propaganda, but the army as a corporate entity was secondary. In the final analysis, war was not so much a series of battles between organized societies as it was a summation of the struggles of single men against other lone combatants. It was considered that if enough personal confrontations were won by one side, then they had won the battle. Still it was not mere individual strength, skill, and zeal that were decisive. Each two-person engagement was seen as a vehicle for the expression of divine will; if the gods wished to give victory to one man, and thus to one side, then so it would be. The combatants were working out the determination of the supernatural powers, one personal clash at a time.

It was crucial to learn the gods' intentions when planning war. Several modes of contacting the supernatural could be tried. Astrological indicators were often consulted to set a date for an attack, a prophet or seer might have been consulted to learn where and how to deploy forces, holy images or icons were carried onto the battlefield, priests accompanied each expedition to implore sacred favor even during battle, and a battle leader or his honorific representative—a person chosen by deity to lead his favored people—was the head of government. Sacrificial thanks to divinity necessarily followed a victory; ritual sorrow and apology for whatever sins had been at fault sprang from defeat.

Obtaining slaves made little economic sense, but taking captives to humiliate, execute, or sacrifice them was routine.[85] It was not common for a conqueror to force his detailed religious system on a subject people; there may have been no religious wars in the medieval European sense, although the possibility remains.[86] Societies in mainstream Mesoamerican civilization did, however, have the cultural decency, if defeated, to add key gods of the conquerors to their local pantheon as a sign of their subservience. In the worst of circumstances, the conquerors slaughtered the people and burned and looted their property, but conquest's usual outcome was little more than the conquered people's promising not to rebel anew and to pay tribute assessments faithfully.

Part of the pattern is illustrated in the Old Testament. In 2 Chronicles 36:2–3, for instance, we read that "Jehoahaz was twenty and three years old when he began to reign, and he reigned three months in Jerusalem [and presumably made trouble]. And the king of Egypt put him down at Jerusalem, and condemned the land in [i.e., to payment of] an hundred talents of silver and a talent of gold [as punitive tribute]."

This pair of west Mexico figurines set in a combat posture epitomizes Mesoamerican warfare. Neither fancy formations of warriors nor efficient weapons were thought to determine the outcome of the conflict so much as the will of the gods. For that reason, the decorative emblems that a warrior donned were not just to show off, nor to inspire fear, nor simply for practical protection. They were a demonstration of, or appeal for, divine protection and strength.

Visualizing Book of Mormon Life

Nearly everything the Book of Mormon tells us about warfare agrees with the picture just sketched. The sacred element in war is made especially clear. It was the Nephites' custom to appoint as military leaders those who "had the spirit of revelation and also prophecy" (3 Nephi 3:19); and prophets were asked for specific military guidance (see Alma 43:23–4; 48:16). Combatants credited their God for success in battle (see Alma 44:3–4; Alma 43:50; 46:16–21). Human sacrifice and even cannibalism were associated with warfare (see Mormon 4:14 and Moroni 9:7–10). Personal combat, particularly between leaders, was crucial (see Ether 14:30; 15:27–32; Words of Mormon 1:13; Alma 2:16, 29–33). Meanwhile, strategy as a means to winning battles was looked down on or seldom employed (see Alma 43:30; 52:21). Battles were sometimes scheduled, probably based on calendrical or astrological considerations (see Alma 2:15–6; Mormon 6:2–5; compare Alma 52:1–2).[87]

Military Organization

The vast majority of warriors in Mesoamerican units were militiamen. That is, they were common citizens who left their homes and regular activities to go off to war with their neighbors in hometown units. Among the militaristic Aztecs and others of the most warlike peoples near the time of the Spanish Conquest, certain special units were composed of essentially full-time professional soldiers, but that was not generally the case. However, some militia leaders no doubt spent much more time and energy in preparation for military campaigns than common soldiers did.

Uniforms, particularly colorful headgear, distinguished each unit (or at least the leaders). Just as at home, some features of everyday costumes worn by soldiers probably distinguished the inhabitants of one community or region from those living elsewhere. Of course all the men in a given unit spoke the same dialect. Leaders may have been more resourceful linguistically in order to interact with unit leaders from other areas, but then at home they likely dealt with a wider range of people in the marketplace or politically already.

Given the mass public source of manpower, most units were essentially duplicates of each other in function, although there were some units specialized by weaponry, such as slingers and bowmen. Amassing a larger army meant mainly bringing together more bodies, not wider expertise. Overall command was in the hands of officers appointed by the central, overall ruler. Their aims and viewpoint were not as localized as those of the militia leaders. Motivation and experience as political leaders, not practiced combat abilities or special skills, probably were what distinguished leaders from those they led.

When approaching a battle, no doubt a general strategy of action was laid out to govern battlefield eventualities, but in the heat of attack or defense, changes in plans probably could not be communicated very effectively from the overall commander to his units. Weakness in the technology of communications hindered any attempt to send signals to units in battle beyond flags or standards, shouting, and hand signals.

Supplies were obtained in two ways. Some necessities, such as extra weapons, were brought from the home base. A support camp moved along with the armed units. It consisted of less able warriors, servants, or slaves as bearers, plus the families of some of the soldiers. Their women prepared food in the field for the troops much as they would have done at home. Food carried along was supplemented by requiring local leaders of the unfortunate populace through whose area the troops moved to provide whatever was needed, as a kind of war tax on the locals.

Typically an Aztec expeditionary army numbered approximately eight thousand men. Special military orders were on permanent service and served as the shock troops; men qualified for them by the number of captives they had taken and the valor of their deeds. Each city had its own army, which marched under a common banner. Men from the same ward or sector in a city formed subunits in a municipal army. A squad was made up of four tactical units, each with four or five men in it.[88]

AZTEC MILITARY ORGANIZATION

UNIT	LEADER ROLE
Combined Aztec Army	King–Commander in Chief Commanding General
Army of City	?Chief Captain
Army of "Ward"	?Captain
Unit of 400	Veteran Warrior
Unit of 200	Veteran Warrior
Unit of 100	Veteran Warrior
Squad	Veteran Warrior
Tactical Unit	Veteran Warrior

Great Aztec leaders shown in this scene from the Codex Mendoza are dressed in their distinctive garb, which distinguished their hometown, ethnic affiliation, and individual honors won in battle.

Visualizing Book of Mormon Life

The Book of Mormon mentions features of military organization that sound Mesoamerican: (1) the strength and skill of individual warriors are the key to victory (see, for example, Alma 52:31) rather than overall numbers, organization, or strategy; (2) using the plural word *armies* as well as the singular *army* (for example, compare Alma 52:20 and 51:30) indicates in some cases the combining of regional groups, each constituting an army, to form a complex host of armies; (3) the lack of extensive training and the brittle nature of military leadership comes through in places in the text like Alma 48:5 and 49:25, where the slaying of leaders produced chaos in the ranks; (4) the camp accompanying an army is mentioned several times (for example, see Alma 49:12); (5) dependence on supply columns from the home area is also indicated (see Alma 55:34; 57:8–10).

Of particular note regarding organization is Mormon's account of the final Nephite battle. He refers to twenty-three different units of ten thousand that were destroyed: "And Lamah had fallen with his ten thousand; and Gilgal had fallen with his ten thousand," and so on (Mormon 6:14). In later Mexico, similar language was used about leaders and their units of ten thousand.[89] Furthermore, among the Tlaxcalan forces at the time of Cortez, a commander often tied his "great standard" or identifying banner to his own back, so that his men could visually follow him. That custom recalls Captain Moroni$_1$'s use of the title of liberty flag to rally his followers (see Alma 46:12, 19–21).[90]

Glyphs on an observatory known as Mound J at Monte Alban, Oaxaca, (after 200 B.C.) show human heads upside down to denote towns conquered by the rulers of Monte Alban. Some scholars see those rulers as having originated in Chiapas.[93] Their expansion from south of the isthmus into the more northerly portion of Mesoamerica recalls the migration documented in Helaman 3:3–5, which occurred a little before the Christian era.

Battle and Conquest

As already indicated, Mesoamerican warfare generally was characterized by what appears to modern observers to be disorganized confusion. An enemy attack was often more what we might call a raid than planned, pitched combat. There was esteem to be gained by exhibiting individual acts of valor; to help win a battle was of secondary significance.

Heavy vegetation and broken terrain, at least in many parts of Mesoamerica, contributed to confusion on the battlefield. What was happening to units other than one's own probably couldn't be observed very well. In any case, a commander's place was at the front, in the middle of the action, literally leading his men. So without close coordination, once a battle began, the outcome was a summation of what happened in personal conflicts.

The strategic aim of battle was not to destroy the enemy force but to compel them to abandon the fight. Of course there may have been men involved who enjoyed slaying for itself, but the cultural norm was to stop the destruction as soon as both sides recognized the victory of one over the other. At that point, victors as well as vanquished pulled back and tried to restore peace. The victorious army then took key prisoners or perhaps killed a few symbolic leaders, especially if they had a record of rebellion. They burned one or more temples as a means of demonstrating the superiority of the winners' gods and then retired from the field after ensuring that a hefty tribute would be delivered.

Despite this pattern of ritual combat and posturing that characterized most Mesoamerican fighting, systematic slaughter with heavy casualties was not unknown. Ixtlilxochitl, the Aztec chronicler, claimed that the Tultecas under Topiltzin lost 5,600,000 slain over a three-year period.[91] Although small-scale tactics dominated battle action, large-scale strategy was significant in certain cases. The careful planning of defensive fortifications and cultivation of allies, for instance, allowed both the Tarascans and Tlaxcalans to avoid for generations falling to Aztec conquest.

A scene from the Cuicatec Codex Fernandez-Leal depicts different aspects of a minor battle. A fortified hill is being attacked as reinforcements arrive by back trails. They are probably militiamen reporting directly from their homes.

From the Codex Mendoza we see the torching of temples, the culminating act of conquest in pre-Hispanic Mexico.

The throbbing confusion of hand-to-hand battle is shown dramatically in this mural at Bonampak near the border of Mexico and Guatemala. It dates to about A.D. 800.

Visualizing Book of Mormon Life

A majority of the military actions reported in the Book of Mormon involved little or no combat but rather threats and acting out.[92] Very typical of Mesoamerica is the pattern reported in Mosiah 19:12–5. In the face of a raid in force by the Lamanites, the outnumbered Zeniffites put up little resistance. Some of their men fled but were finally forced to surrender and pay an extortionate tribute. Alma$_1$'s people likewise had to take a pacifying stance when a Lamanite-Amulonite force stumbled upon their land of Helam (see Mosiah 23:25–6). The same phenomenon, on a much larger scale, was evident when the Lamanites led by Coriantumr$_2$ caught the defenders of Zarahemla off balance and conquered them quickly (see Helaman 1:14–22). The Lamanite attacks on Ammonihah were of the same ilk (see Alma 16:2–3 and 49:1–25).

In contrast, Amalickiah's ambitious plan for conquest of the narrow neck of land and Moroni$_1$'s thoughtful defensive scheme involved grand strategy, contrary to the general rule (see Alma 51:22–30). And, obviously, the final slaughter of hundreds of thousands of Nephites in the fourth century was out of character, although not without parallel in the Mesoamerican tradition.

The political importance of towers in the Book of Mormon made them an obvious military target. The prototype for the Jaredites was the "great tower" in Mesopotamia (Ether 1:3, 33; compare Genesis 11:4). Not surprisingly, when Moroni$_1$'s army smashed the forces of the king-men, the rebel leaders "were compelled to hoist the title of liberty upon their towers" (Alma 51:20; compare 46:36), perhaps after the sacred houses atop the towers were burned.

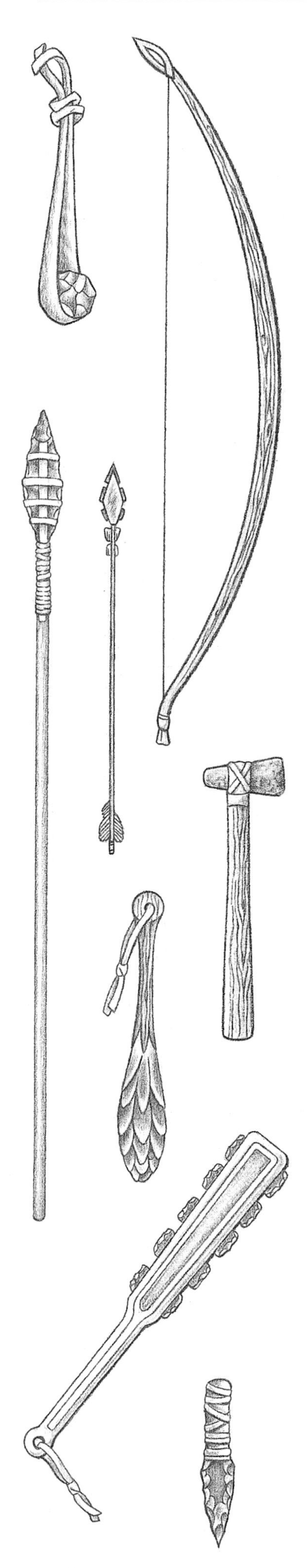

Weapons and Armor

Mesoamerican weaponry gives the appearance of being less efficient than that of, say, the Romans with their abundant metal armaments. But the appearance is deceptive, for death was as effectively dealt out in the one place as in the other. When it came to butchery, simple technology seems to have been sufficient if not efficient.

The most fearsome piece in the armory was the obsidian-edged sword. This device was used for over twenty-five hundred years. It consisted of a flat hardwood club with grooves in the edges into which razor-sharp fragments of obsidian or volcanic glass were inserted and glued. The Spaniards were horrified by its power. They learned to their dismay that a single blow with one of these weapons could sever the head of a horse or, of course, a man. Being both effective and quite cheap to make, this *macuahuitl* (the Aztec name; the Spaniards called it simply "sword") was the instrument most often wielded in Mesoamerican fighting.

In close combat, knives whose blades were chipped from obsidian came into play. Some of those were almost big enough to qualify as swords. There were also axes of several shapes and a variety of clubs. Several types of spears—one also lined at the point with obsidian chips—or javelins were included in the repertoire of weapons.

The bow and arrow were in use too, although the Mesoamerican bow was not as sophisticated as the best ones in the Old World. For long-distance firepower, the *atlatl,* or spear-thrower, was used. It functioned as an extension of the user's arm. The end of a long arrow or small spear was butted against a carved projection at the end of this stick, and the arrow was propelled as the device was swung forward. It achieved greater velocity and range because the thrower's arm was, in effect, eighteen inches or so longer than the man's arm alone. While the spear-thrower was known very anciently in both the Old and New Worlds as a hunting device, it was in Mesoamerica where it came to be used most widely in warfare.

There was some use of metal, mainly in axes, but it was not a frequently used and certainly not a decisive material. One reason may be that the Mesoamericans' knowledge of metallurgy could not produce long-lasting cutting edges. Or the difficulty or cost of preparing metal weapons may have prevented their wide use.

Armor was also in widespread use. The most common type seems to have been a garment composed of two layers of cloth, quilted, between which salt, kapok, or some other buffering substance had been placed. Various other devices were also used—shields, breastplates, and headgear including helmets.[94] The Spaniards found a few native chiefs who possessed certain items of armor made with metal plates, but since that seemed to have been of gold (alloy?), perhaps it was for mainly ceremonial, not practical, purposes.

VISUALIZING BOOK OF MORMON LIFE

All the weapons employed in native Mesoamerica may be referred to in the Book of Mormon. Often the connections are obvious (for example, "spears," Alma 17:7). Certain other names of weapons in that text (for example, "axe" and "sword") leave us unclear in both the Nephite record, as in Spanish descriptions of native weapons that speak, vaguely, about the appearance and function of the mentioned weapons. Yet enough plausible matchups are apparent that seeing Mesoamerican weapons gives us valuable clues to understand those of the Nephites.[95]

Given the generally tropical climate of this land (see Alma 51:33), more often than not the warriors described in the Book of Mormon went on their campaigns with little clothing (note Alma 3:5 and 44:18). However, armor was donned when combat was imminent. Noteworthy in comparison with Mesoamerica are the "very thick garments" worn as armor by the Lamanites and Nephites (Alma 49:6; see 43:19–20).

An interesting statement is found in Alma 49:19 where the Nephites are said to have been "casting over . . . arrows" at the enemy on the other side of a fortification (see also Alma 49:4). The arrows used with bows would not have been "cast," but the verb would be correct if applied to the larger projectiles propelled by Mesoamerican spear-throwers.

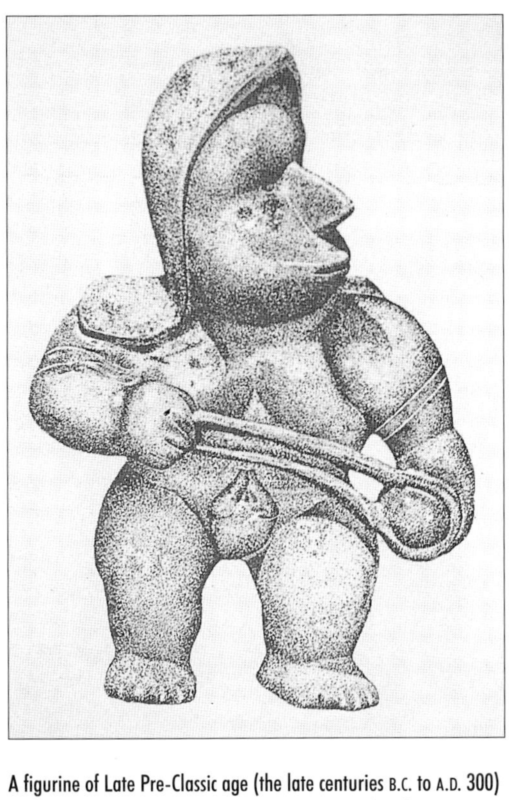

A figurine of Late Pre-Classic age (the late centuries B.C. to A.D. 300) from west Mexico pictures a man preparing to use his sling to cast a stone. Of course the sling was spun in a circle over the warrior's head before one side of the leather holder was released to allow the projectile to sail toward its mark.

A beautiful museum specimen of an Aztec warrior's spear-thrower is seen in one photograph, and the other shows the intricate detail of the hook against which the butt of the arrow or spear rested. Most atlatls would have looked much more workaday, of course.

An artist's sketch of a hunter about to throw an atlatl dart illustrates how that instrument functioned.

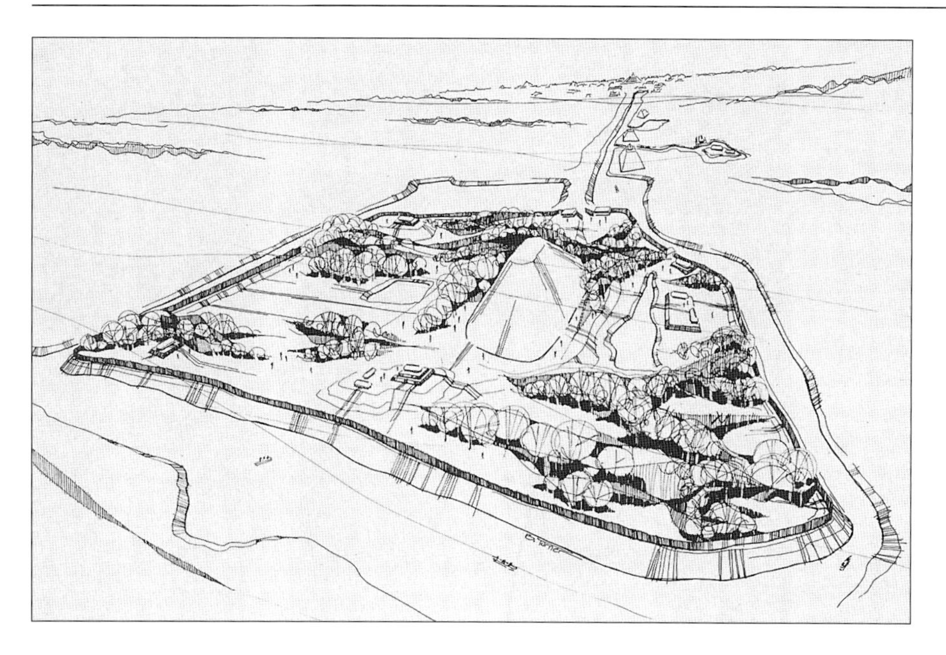

An artist's perspective drawing displays how a drainage system was turned into a moat that enclosed a fortress at the site of Edzna in the state of Campeche. It dates to about the time of the final Nephite wars, although surely not a Nephite construction.

Fortifications

Not many years ago archaeologists were confident that very rarely were sites in pre-Spanish Mesoamerica fortified. The last twenty-five years have seen a huge body of data come to light to the contrary. We now know of over three hundred places that were fortified or sited in relation to protective terrain, and they date from no later than 1000 B.C. up to the Spanish Conquest.[96] Instead of being the rarity it was considered a few years back, military fortification now appears to have been a normal cultural pattern for Mesoamerica with many interesting variations.

The most basic form was begun by digging a dry moat. The earth from the excavation was thrown up to form an inner embankment. Atop that a palisade of tree trunks was erected. The combined moat and bank provided defenders a downward sloping field of fire for their weapons that gave them substantial advantage over attackers. When Cortez crossed southern Mexico on his way to conquer Honduras, he discovered constructions just like this on the southern Gulf Coast of Mexico. In the 1970s, work by David Webster for Tulane University showed examples of precisely the same setup in the interior Yucatan Peninsula that were built between A.D. 250 and 450. Other, still earlier, examples have since shown that this is both an old and presumably an effective mode of site defense.

A number of other types of fortification also existed. Vertical stone-faced walls sometimes exceeded the height of a man. A defensive garrison or whole settlement might be placed atop a steep hill, on a dry spot in a swamp, or on a site partially protected by the steep bank of a stream. Walls of thorny brush or cactus plants could also be employed.

VISUALIZING BOOK OF MORMON LIFE

The Book of Mormon describes some of the same forms of fortifications. In the simplest type, the Nephites "cast up dirt around about to shield them" (Alma 49:2; see 49:4). "The highness of the bank which had been thrown up, and the depth of the ditch which had been dug round about" prevented the Lamanite enemy from climbing over or digging away the ridge without being exposed to deadly fire from above (Alma 49:18; 49:22). A refined form had "works of timbers built up to the height of a man" (Alma 50:2) atop the earthen ridge. Protected towers were erected overlooking those palisades from which defenders could gain even more height to rain down weapons against attackers (see Alma 50:3–5). The original city of Nephi had a stone wall around it, apparently modeled upon the wall at Jerusalem in Israel (Nephi, the city's founder, had firsthand knowledge of Jerusalem) (see Mosiah 22:6), and the Nephite armies also constructed small stone-walled redoubts to protect garrisons (see Alma 48:8).

Excavations at Becán, a Maya site in the middle of the Yucatan peninsula, provides the basis for this artist's reconstruction of the appearance of a dry moat and wall that dates back before the end of the Nephite era.

From Tlaxcala in highland central Mexico we see how an effective defensive barrier could be grown by appropriate plantings of the very thorny agave plant.

Belief and Worship

Overview

Belief and worship were extremely complex and varied in ancient Mesoamerica. Study by scholars of the material on these topics still has a long way to go. One reason for the obscurity is that sources on the subject are limited. Even where Spanish writers—usually Catholic priests—tried to understand and record features of native beliefs and practices, we may doubt that they got everything clear that they were told. In fact, they must have got a lot wrong, not to mention whole topics of which they were told nothing. For one thing, there obviously were different cults—patterns of worship and belief—that served different purposes for different people in different areas. Such variations are still far from straightened out, although some progress is being made.

A subtle danger faces us when we analyze ancient life using ideas from modern times. The conceptual category *religion* is a product of western European thinking. The ancient civilizations, however—the Egyptians, the Hebrews, the Chinese, the Maya—did not separate out a category of human experience nor use a term equivalent to our term *religion.* For them, all of life involved religion, or vice versa. The powers of supernatural beings, beliefs about the origin of the world and of humans, moral and ethical standards, and certain ceremonial conduct—what we mean by religion—were so intertwined with the rest of life that such a formal and restricted category as we employ would have struck them as odd, if not incomprehensible. But because readers of this volume follow the Western tradition, for convenience we lump together here information about the assortment of topics that we consider to constitute religion.

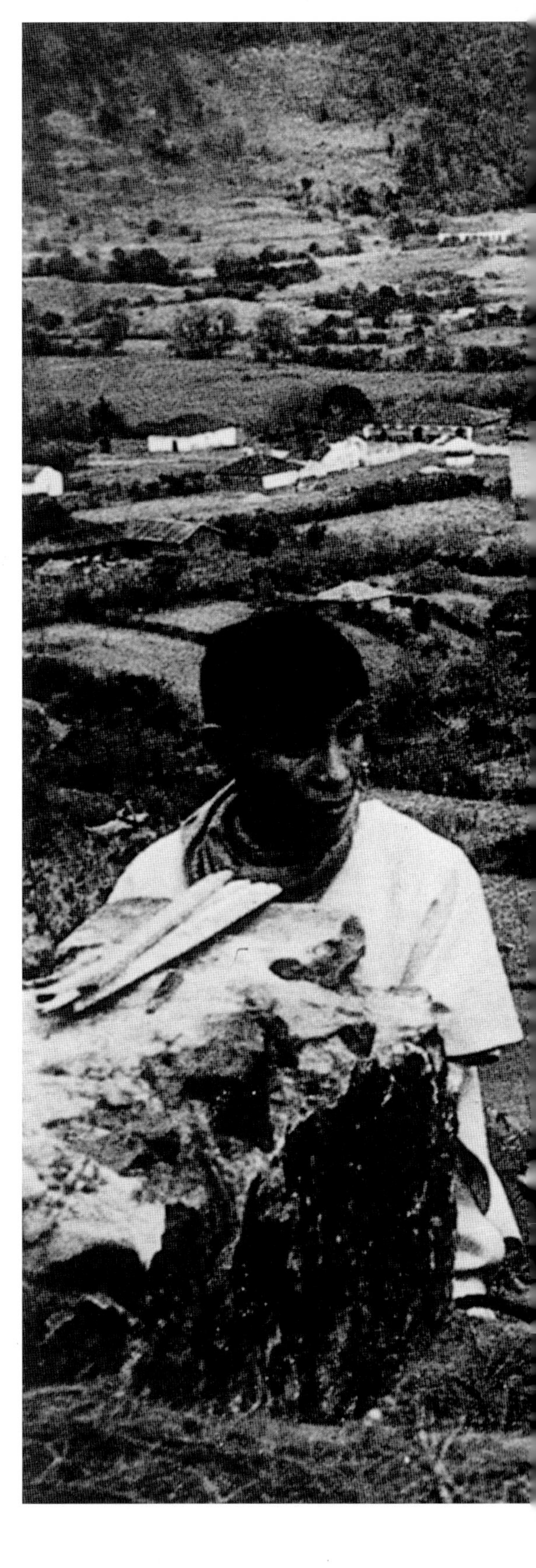

The communal nature of ancient worship continued to be typical among modern Mesoamericans in the villages until very recently and still is in places. A few leaders bore the burden of addressing the invisible powers on behalf of the whole community. Only those with strong interest or with the prestige, learning, and wealth to allow them to participate according to the prescribed standards would normally take part. Many commoners were likely to leave such matters in the hands of the elite, satisfied that the ritual necessities were being taken care of on behalf of all, as by these three representatives in Zinacantan, Chiapas.

When we examine the cultures of central and southern Mexico and northern Central America, one key point stands out. H. B. Nicholson has said the following about the Aztecs, and the statement applies as well to peoples throughout Mesoamerica: "The native societies of late pre-Hispanic central Mexico were among the most highly ritualized of all time. Religion permeated every facet of the culture. No important area of human activity was entirely free from its pervasive influence, and some were almost completely dominated by it. . . . The power and influence of the priesthood was truly remarkable."[97] Every routine activity took on a sacred sense for them. For instance, among the Aztecs maize, the mainstay of their diet,

was considered holy, and if kernels were found lying on the ground, the finder was supposed to pick them up and make a verbal apology for giving insufficient respect to this gift from the gods.[98] Sacred matters were of concern always and everywhere.

Modern descendants continue this extreme emphasis on ceremony and the sacred side of life. For instance, from the ethnographic field work of Evon Z. Vogt and colleagues, we learn that for the Tzotzil Indians who inhabit Zinacantan, a village in highland Chiapas, "every step in life . . . is ceremonialized: being pregnant, giving birth, courting, borrowing and repaying money, taking religious office, being cured of illness, and being buried. There are thirty-four religious fiesta days each year, but these account for only a small portion of [the total] time spent in ceremonial activity."[99]

Historically, Mesoamerican society's concern with religion has been expressed through different complexes of belief and ritual that have spread from place to place over time or have sprung up repeatedly out of basic human needs. One extremely old and widespread complex dealt with healing or finding the cause of good or bad luck; it is called shamanism. A shaman is a person, typically with unusual personality qualities, who believes he or she has received a calling from supernatural powers to be an intermediary between them and common mortals. To make contact, the shaman goes into a trance, with or without the aid of a drug like tobacco. While in the trance, the shaman communicates key information to bystanders, such as a diagnosis for an illness and its magical treatment. (The modern term *shaman* and the fullest descriptions of the practice of shamanism come from studies of tribal groups in Siberia.) These practitioners are known also as, or at least overlap in their role with, curers, witch doctors, and medicine men. Several sorts of shamans continue to function among the least modern peoples in the Mesoamerican area and among American Indian remnants generally, where they coexist with other historical layers of religion.

Alongside shamanism, or sometimes blended with it, were priest-led cults that acknowledged the control of supernatural beings over the powers of nature. Offerings were commonly made by these priests, acting on behalf of the community, to deities who were thought to control the sprouting and harvesting of crops and the reproductive powers of animals and humans. (In the Israel of the Old Testament, this type of cult was called baalism.) Avoiding nature's uncertainties was the most obvious focus of these cults, yet the idea of devotion and sacrifice also extended to other matters, such as pleas for health (as a preventive alternative to the shaman's cures), success in war, and so on. At its most basic, this type of belief system was closely connected with magic in its attempt to control natural events. (Magic supposes that rites carried out in imitation of a desired natural state will lead, or perhaps even compel, nature to follow suit. For example, if crops needed rain, the priest poured out a liquid offering as a metaphor for rain, or he made puffs of tobacco smoke that imitated and so "produced" actual clouds.) Appeals to the deities might overlap with prayers and respect to the ancestors. Their postmortal spirits were supposed to have power to shape events to the good (or harm) of their descendants.

Whether organized systems of belief and worship existed in Mesoamerica that were comparable to the churches known in later Europe and western Asia is a matter of dispute. A few researchers have suggested the possibility, but information is slim for settling the matter, even after the difficult problem of definition has been struggled with.

One key point that moderns need to keep in mind is that in Mesoamerican civilization, as in the ancient Old World, ritual and spiritual concerns were mainly a social, not an individual, matter. Any person's ritual behavior and beliefs were of secondary concern compared with the group's conformity to sacred norms. There was a strong tendency toward family, kin, community, and tribal unity in religious matters. Just as there was little room in society for an individual to act strictly for self in the economic or political realms, so it was in matters of belief; only rarely could an individual afford the luxury of isolation from his primary support group by worshipping differently. Of course there were always a few individuals who did their own thinking and worshipping, but people generally were unable to withstand the demands for unified action made by those who held crucial social, economic, and political power to ruin their lives if they turned nonconformist.

ou are in the innermost regions
of the heavens

giving origin to your word . . .

You, who are God.

What is it that you determine there?

Is it that for us on earth

you have been overcome with weariness?

Must you hide from us your glory and your splendor?

What is it that you determine on this earth?

CANTARES MEXICANOS

Ultimately every religious system addresses all the crucial questions that cultures raise about life's puzzles, although forms and emphases differ from place to place in the way the queries are phrased. This Aztec cry to deity shows the profundity that could spring from minds engaged in what the European conquerors considered barbaric religious beliefs and practices.

VISUALIZING BOOK OF MORMON LIFE

We have already noted how Amulek in the Book of Mormon had a large network of family, kin, and friends (see Alma 10:2–4). When he challenged community religious standards, and thereby those of his kin, by allying with the unpopular prophet Alma$_2$, he was first imprisoned and finally expelled by his cohorts (see Alma 14:1–15:1). For another illustration of the pressure toward group conformity, consider how Alma$_2$'s converts were soon exiled by their Zoramite community (see Alma 35:6).

The Book of Mormon makes clear at other points too the corporate nature of most religious life. For instance, we are told that those of the Lamanites who were converted by the sons of Mosiah and their companion missionaries consisted of all the people in land after land and city after city (see Alma 23:9–13). On the other hand, "the Amalekites were not converted, save only one; neither were any of the Amulonites" (Alma 23:14). Individual thinking and action were clearly not encouraged. Dissenters, whether to or from the Nephite or Lamanite traditions, rarely managed to dwell among a hostile majority of contrary believers. The difficulty of trying to live a distinct pattern of worship in the midst of opponents is emphasized in Alma 1:19–22.

Most LDS readings of the Book of Mormon have focused on the religious ideals preached by its prophetic leaders and historians—the spiritual cream of the cream, as it were. What actually was going on among the people at large has received little attention. We would do well to study carefully the popular version of religion as it was by seeing what the prophets *condemned* in the Book of Mormon. Moreover, most modern readers quite naturally read the ancient text by projecting current religious ideas back upon it, as though the Nephites had thought like twentieth-century Mormons. That would not have been true, of course. The historical and cultural contexts of the two traditions are drastically different, even though interesting similarities can be seen.

Deities and Other Supernaturals

Some Mesoamerican peoples frequently represented their deities in art. Others did not do so routinely. Tlaloc was one of the great gods of the Aztec era in central Mexico and is visible in the art of predecessor peoples for centuries earlier. He was considered primarily responsible for the rain. This striking vase with his face painted on it comes from the Templo Mayor, the Aztec "downtown" sacred center.

Our sources about ancient Mesoamerican divinities (remember that almost all the information was filtered through the Spaniards) seem to show that there were many gods. However, scholars have not agreed on just what that means.[100] At one extreme some (like J. E. S. Thompson)[101] have detected a basic early belief in a single god at least for some groups. Critics maintain that this is a misreading.

Whatever today's scholars think about the issue of one or many gods, they still tend to assume that each people had one consistent set of beliefs shared by everyone in the group. A very different way of looking at ancient Mesoamerican religion is hardly considered—that even a single people did not agree among themselves on a single set of beliefs. Perhaps some argued about dogma and deities as Renaissance Christians did

Most Mesoamerican deities were believed to be in human or animal form. In general the gods were thought to be invisible but could choose to appear to humans through dreams and visions. Many of the supernaturals were said to dwell in a realm above the earth. (Three, or seven, or thirteen levels or heavens were supposed to be piled atop one another above the earth's surface. Other divinities were assigned to corresponding levels beneath the earth.)

An important concept was that a given people had a special relationship, in name and loyalty, with a particular god. "The erection of a shrine for the patron deity usually constituted the first official act of settlement of a new community."[102] This temple structure became the symbol of the town's independence and integrity.

No doubt elite religious thinkers had a more complicated set of beliefs than did common people. It has always been so. For instance, ancient Egyptian commoners certainly did not bother themselves with niceties about how the god Seth related to the deity Horus. Very likely, plain folks everywhere tried to stay out of trouble with the gods by following the lowest common denominator of rituals. Figures higher up the social and economic ladder had more time and schooling to split theological hairs, but the mass probably paid attention largely to the few notions or powers that they thought controlled everyday life, like the growth of crops.

Idols is another problematic label. Interestingly, when the Spaniards arrived, some native Mesoamerican priests scorned them for what looked to their eyes like Catholic "idolatry," for that is what the adoration of the cross seemed. One person's sacred emblem may be another person's idol. In any case, some scholars have observed that carved figures that might have been idols were relatively rare until the Late Classic period, say, from A.D. 600 on. Many of the figures we see on carved monuments are now recognized not as gods at all but as public celebrities or ancestors, sometimes decked out with insignia of a god. So it is hard to know how many idols or gods may have been used anciently, because we don't know

This effigy incense burner from Tapijulapa, Chiapas, may represent what Catholic priests called a "demon" in the native belief system.

The Old Fire God was connected to fire in general and also to volcanoes. This characteristic symbol of him as an old man with a brazier on his back comes from Teotihuacan and is dated around A.D. 500. Similar forms occur from as early as 200 B.C. up to the Spanish Conquest.

Ehecatl was considered by the Aztecs a specialized, wind-connected aspect of the god Quetzalcoatl. (That famous god is pictured later in this book.) This fine representation of Ehecatl (or whatever he was called at that time) came from excavations by the BYU New World Archaeological Foundation at Izapa dating from about the first century B.C.

The sun god was sculpted in plaster on the sides of temples at El Mirador and elsewhere in the lowlands of the Yucatan Peninsula before the Christian era. This thirteen-foot-high version at the site of Uaxactun was repeated a number of times on the faces of structure E-VII-sub. An artist's reconstruction fleshes out the partially destroyed original.

how people in those day defined or worshipped their deities.

Ancient peoples and some of their modern descendants in Mexico and Central America believed in other supernatural figures besides deities. A miscellany of equivalents to leprechauns, angels, demons, and other supernormal entities representing good or evil powers were recognized, but we know little about their natures and functions.

VISUALIZING BOOK OF MORMON LIFE

"The God of Israel" (1 Nephi 5:9, 10) who was worshipped by the Nephite prophets had rivals throughout most of that people's history, we learn upon close examination of their record.[103] The Lamanites had idols and, presumably, beliefs and practices related to gods other than the God of Israel, almost from their beginning (see Enos 1:20). The "Mulekites" can hardly have had anything like a conventional version of Judaism (they "denied the being of their Creator," Omni 1:17). Other divergent patterns and objects of worship are frequently noted as well, except for parts of the first and second centuries A.D. (see, for example, Mosiah 26:1–2; Alma 31; 14:18; 4 Nephi 1:41).

The highly ritualized and priest-led nature of Nephite society is also apparent (see, for example, Enos 1:22; Jarom 1:10–1; 4 Nephi 1:1–2). Especially interesting is the ceremonialism evident in Mosiah 19:20 and 24 and Alma 1:15, where the text mentions but does not explain the strange rites involved, no doubt because it was so obvious anciently that rites were essential. Furthermore, all major events in Nephite history were interpreted as the result of divine interventions (see, for example, Mosiah 5:7–8 and Alma 44:3–5).

According to the Book of Mormon, a variety of lesser sacred beings or powers and rites connected with them were recognized among the Nephites and Lamanites, although only hinted at by the orthodox record keepers. We read of "demons" (Helaman 13:37), "devils and unclean spirits" (1 Nephi 11:31), "the evil spirit" (Mosiah 4:14), "idol gods" (Mormon 4:14; see 4:21), and "sorceries, and witchcrafts, and magics" (Mormon 1:19). Clearly the Nephite record gives us only glimpses of their ritual life and associated beliefs about the supernatural.

THE NAWAL

A very old and basic belief, whose essentials were shared in parts of North America and East Asia, is labeled tonalism or nawalism. Some groups, particularly in northern Mesoamerica, emphasized this belief more than others. Its essential concept is related to shamanism. Each person was supposed to have a guardian spirit, usually an animal. This was one's *nawal* (the Aztecs' term). This spirit being gave support and protection, if one could get in touch with it on the right ritual terms and treated it right. Much of the fancy headdress ornamentation shown on human figures in Mesoamerica apparently depicts guardian nawals. Sometimes a nawal figure is even shown with its own nawal on top of it!

A superb example of a nawal representation is this Zapotec piece (about A.D. 600–900) showing a jaguar guardian. Animals other than the jaguar were also nawals.

This bearded old man with his jaguar protector on his shoulder comes from Tamahu, Guatemala, during the time of the Nephites.

JUDAISM AND CHRISTIANITY IN MESOAMERICA

Some early Spanish priests believed they were observing in native Mesoamerican rituals and beliefs evidence for the prior presence of Jews and of Christianity in the New World. Versions of the cross, baptism, circumcision, and other practices and symbols common in the ancient Near East or eastern Mediterranean were taken to argue for the arrival of the Ten Tribes or of some Christian missionary in Mexico many centuries ago. Other observers were more critical and doubted that any such influences reached America. The opposing views are summarized in Tozzer's great edition of Bishop Diego de Landa's volume on Yucatan.[104]

Despite the naïveté of much of that early argument, the issue has never been fully resolved. A minority of writers in the last hundred years have mustered a good deal more evidence for a connection in culture and religion between the central Old World and Mesoamerica.[105] (See more information on this topic below.) Most experts do not accept any such connection, although the arguments in favor of people from the Mediterranean area arriving in Mesoamerica centuries ago are not trivial.[106]

A fowl, sometimes a quail but here a turkey, was a routine live offering (comparable to the use of a dove in Israelite rites), as shown in this scene of a priest represented in the Codex Nuttall at the time of the Spanish Conquest.

Many observers, beginning with the early Spanish priests, have been struck by similarities in concept between this type of "crucifixion," from the Codex Zouche-Nuttall, and that which Jesus Christ suffered.

Sacrifices

Offerings were part of every ceremony. Incense (the offering was actually the sweet aroma) was burned at practically all rituals. The most common sacrifices were food, flowers, and clothing. Blood sacrifices were also typical; the animal most commonly offered was probably the quail, but deer and other large mammals were also dispatched at altars. Human blood, often spattered on paper, was another frequent offering.

In general concept and practice, and even in many details, the sacrifice complex of Mesoamerica recalls similar practices in the ancient Near East. A. V. Kidder, a famous Mesoamerican archaeologist, wrote about ancient Guatemalan cultures: "The belief that pungent smoke is sweet in the nostrils of the gods is one of the many extraordinary likenesses between Old and New World religions."[107] A sacrifice might be made by a priest on behalf of ruling officials or of the entire community, or the act might be more democratic, performed at the request of a common person for him- or herself or for family.

Just as some offerings were made to deities above the earth, symbolized by the ascending smoke of incense or of a burning object, others were made to supernaturals beneath the earth. For instance, caches were put beneath the corner posts of temples or houses when built. The most spectacular examples involved ornaments of jade or other stones like those that excavators Drucker, Heizer, and Squier consider to be "deeply buried treasures" at Olmec La Venta.[108] The custom of burying offerings continued among successor peoples long after the Olmecs.

VISUALIZING BOOK OF MORMON LIFE

Sacrifice was integral to the law of Moses, which the Book of Mormon puts at the center of Nephite religious life for the first six centuries (for instance, see Alma 30:3). A wide variety of animals and other materials were offered in myriad ways in that system of ritual practice, as in other Near Eastern cultures, and for virtually all of them we find parallels in Mesoamerica.[109]

There is mention of "sacrifice(s)," alone or with "burnt offerings," at 1 Nephi 7:22, Mosiah 2:3, and 3 Nephi 9:19. Human sacrifice is alluded to twice, once in a hypothetical way (see Alma 34:10) and once in a barbaric, derivative form (see Mormon 4:14–5, 21). The possibility of sacrificing one's own blood is cited in Alma 34:11. And does the statement in Helaman 13:18–20 ("hide up their treasures" in the earth) recall the Mesoamerican pattern of caching beautiful and sacred objects?

The practice of animal sacrifice early turned to the sacrifice of humans, it appears. The custom was widespread in Mesoamerica and finally was carried on by the Aztecs "on a scale not even approached by any other ritual system in the history of the world."[110] Was this part of the "abominations" (1 Nephi 12:23) that Nephi prophesied would be present among his brothers' descendants after his own people had become extinct?

An artist's reconstruction shows the massive offering at La Venta (ca. 700 B.C.) of one thousand tons of carefully shaped green serpentine stones imported from many miles away. It was deposited in a pit thirteen feet deep. Colored sands and clays—olive-blue, white, yellow, pink, and red—were selected and dumped on successive layers of stone. The design that appears when viewed from above is of a stylized jaguar face, a favorite emblem in Olmec belief for the god of the underworld and the night.

A typical village sacred center in the Late Pre-Classic period (the centuries immediately before and after the Christian era) looked like this small sacred platform and building at San Agustin, Chiapas, as drawn by an artist on the basis of excavation findings.

Sacred Places

The pervasiveness of things sacred in the thought of the ancient Mesoamericans is evident in their thinking about the physical world. Geographical features were rarely, and perhaps never, merely objective parts of nature. In certain cultures every hill and dale was assigned sacred meaning. Some spots were thought of as more significant than others, such as caves, springs, lakes, and hills. Since sacred beings inhabited the multiple layers of heaven or the underworld, one's approach to those beings was favored at elevated or sunken spots. Caves and bodies of water were considered points of potential access to the underworld; hilltops were places to contact the upper levels of the cosmos. Those places were considered holy and somewhat dangerous (see Jacob's reaction reported in Genesis 28:16–7). If no natural hill was convenient to a settlement, an artificial hill, or "pyramid," was erected to substitute.

No settlement had any standing if it lacked a sacred center. Shrines were scattered here or there—at the mouth of a cave or at a pond or a strange geological formation—places where unscheduled worship could be made, but a worship point of real social efficacy and prestige demanded the presence of an elevated temple structure within a community. The elevation was produced by piling up soil and rock to form a platform upon which a sacred house of god was constructed. In addition to a temple on such a hill that served the entire community, kin groups or sections of a settlement (wards) might erect structures for local use that had less prestige than the community's main edifices. When Cortez and his cohorts reached the city of Cholula on the way to the Aztec capital city, they climbed atop the huge central pyramid temple (the bulkiest construction in central Mexico) from where they counted some four hundred temple pyramids.[111] The scale and number of sacred structures a community could boast was probably an important measure of its prestige in the settlement hierarchy (rather like high-rise buildings in a modern city).

Not just the elevated structure, but a dedicated space around it constituted the temple. Only key priests entered the sacred house on top. For minor priests and public worshippers, the walled enclosure around the temple constituted the scene of their temple experience. The famous temples of Solomon and of Herod at Jerusalem were built in a similar way; only selected priests ever went into the holy building itself. To be "in the temple" (for example, as in Acts 2:46) usually meant to be in the extensive courtyard, where sacrifices and nearly all other activities were carried out. Likely when Benjamin, the Nephite king, called his people to "go up to the temple" (Mosiah 2:1; see 2:6) to hear him, their tents were pitched in the walled-in zone. A modern parallel is Temple Square in Salt Lake City.

In addition to the most formal temple complexes, various smaller holy places were recognized, as suggested above. On

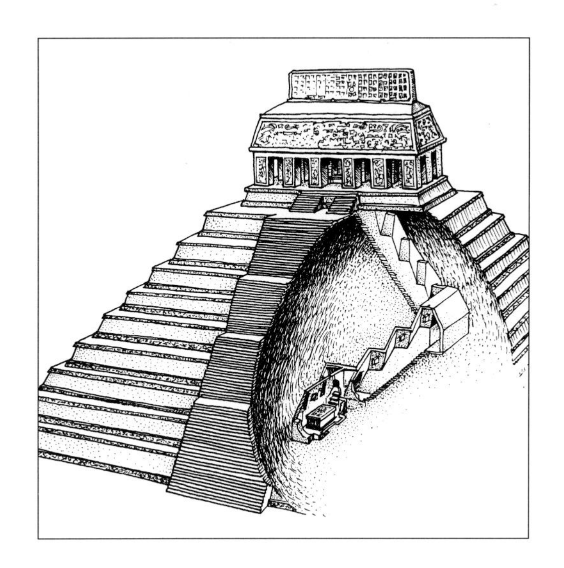

Burials were, of course, most appropriate at or near a sacred pyramid platform, the supposed connection point with the layered overworld and underworld. Here at Palenque's Temple of Inscriptions, the famous tomb discovered by Alberto Ruz was directly beneath the temple structure on top. Many people have commented on the conceptual parallel between this structure and Egyptian pyramids with their tombs.

The great central temple precinct of Tenochtitlan, the capital city of the Aztecs, is seen in this artist's reconstruction. Note the wall that enclosed the entire holy zone.

certain scheduled days, a community ceremonial procession visited particular holy points within the settlement while bearing sacred emblems (nowadays it is the image of the local Catholic saint). In such a sequence of visits, music, dancing, prayers, and other oratorical formulas were presented and offerings were left at the holy spots. Offerings might also be left at mountaintop shrines or beside or in lakes, pools, and springs by individual worshippers. Some of the native peoples of Mexico and Central America still consider ancient ruins and standing monuments sacred and no doubt always have. Unscheduled offerings and prayers, particularly for favors like healing, are deemed appropriate at such places.

Today's shrines or altars within private homes or yards had parallels in pre-Columbian times, which often signified the spot of land where the extended family was thought to be planted or, in other words, the land of their inheritance.[112] Even fields were considered sacred places; prayers and sacrifices were made there upon initiating cultivation or in connection with the harvest.

The sense of a temple being an artificial mountain is clear in the looming presence of the Pyramid of the Sun at Teotihuacan near Mexico City. The Spaniards called these structures "towers." The identical concept applied to the ziggurat or temple platform of ancient Mesopotamia, which was called a tower in the Book of Mormon.

VISUALIZING BOOK OF MORMON LIFE

Temples were central in various Nephite and Lamanite cities (see 2 Nephi 5:16; Mosiah 1:8; Alma 16:13; 26:29; Helaman 3:14). Sacrificial rites and instructional gatherings were carried on at the temple area (see Mosiah 2:1, 3, 5–7). Other sacred structures were called by terms translated "churches" and "synagogues" and were used for exhortation and instruction (see 4 Nephi 1:41; Alma 21:4).

In the Nephite tradition, altars are mentioned in 1 Nephi 2:7 and Alma 15:17 and 17:4; presumably they were normally located at the temples (see Mosiah 2:1, 3). In addition to the political aspect of towers, mentioned above, they were also used as worship sites, as shown by $Nephi_2$'s praying from the top of his own tower (see Helaman 7:10). The equivalence of such structures to mountains is made clear; $Nephi_1$ and the brother of Jared ascended mountains to pray (see 1 Nephi 17:7; Alma 31:13; Ether 3:1; 4:1). Not surprisingly, bodies of water also had supernatural connotations, both positive and negative (see 1 Nephi 12:16; Mosiah 18:5–14, 30; Alma 7:15; 42:27). The "sanctuaries" mentioned in the text were distinct from temples and synagogues (see the distinction in Alma 23:2 and Helaman 3:14). They might have been shrines, such as mountaintops, caves, or pools, where a natural feature or special artifact marked a spot where devotion was considered appropriate.

Caves and cenotes (water holes) like this one at Dzitnup, Yucatan, were thought by the Maya and other peoples to give access to the underworld. The earth was supposed to rest on top of a giant aquatic creature which in turn floated on the primal underworld ocean. The notion of a great subterranean sea creature (or dragon) was shared with the Hebrews and in south Asia.

Altars (this one is at Teotihuacan) were themselves replicas of mountains, often terraced in imitation of the grand pyramid structures. The altar before the Temple of Solomon was similarly stepped, and it and the base of the temple at Jerusalem were conceived as artificial sacred mountains by the Jews.

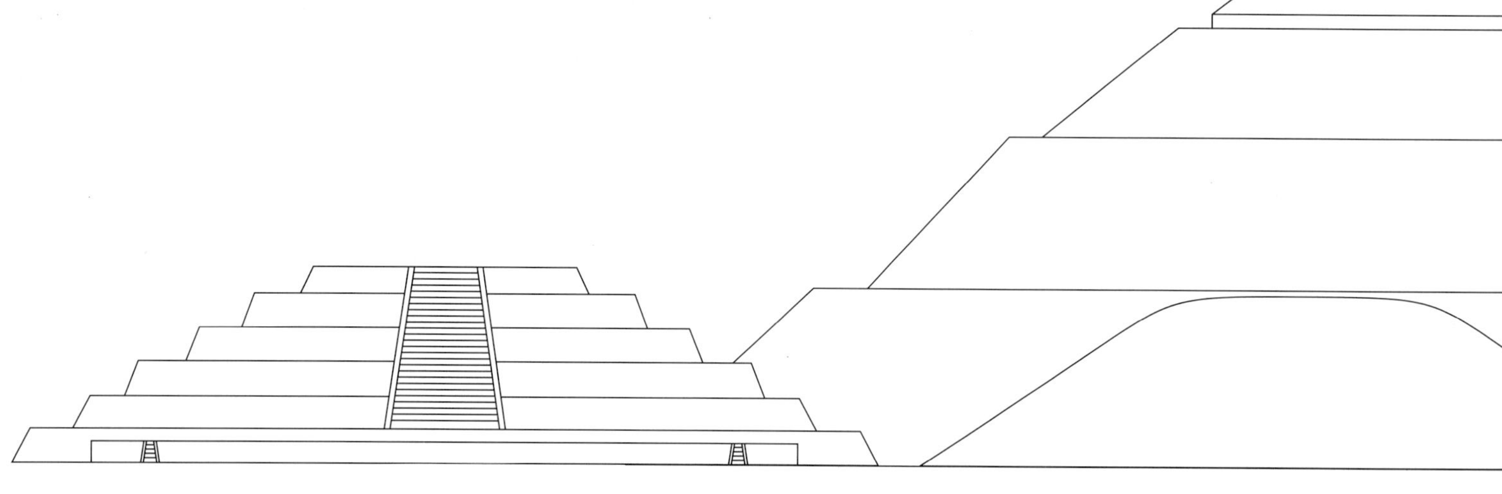

Izapa Mound 60

Kaminaljuyu, Structure E-III–3

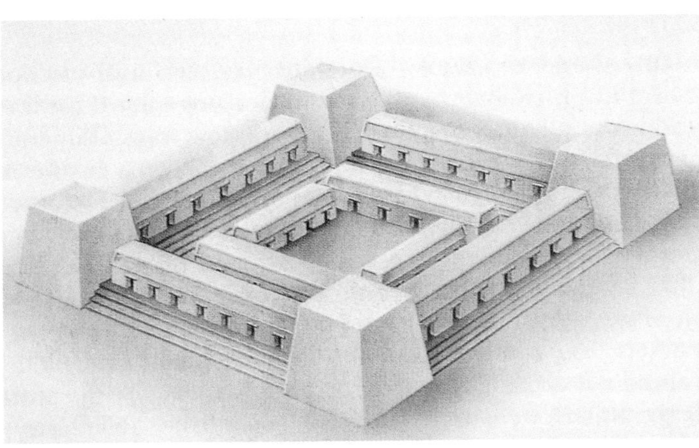

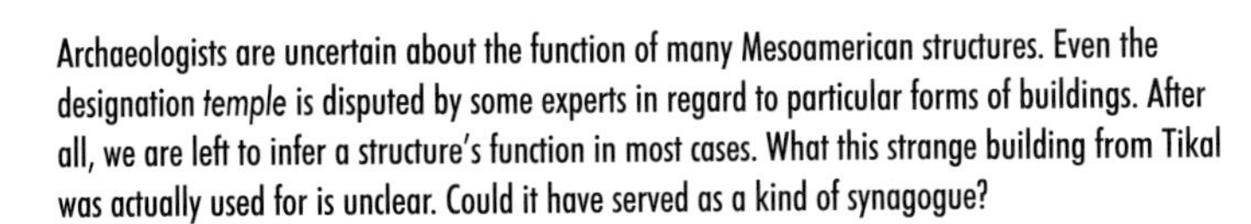

Archaeologists are uncertain about the function of many Mesoamerican structures. Even the designation *temple* is disputed by some experts in regard to particular forms of buildings. After all, we are left to infer a structure's function in most cases. What this strange building from Tikal was actually used for is unclear. Could it have served as a kind of synagogue?

A shaman acting as a priest prays with a couple at a shrine at Zinacantan, Chiapas, for the wife's healing. Ancient shrines were probably scenes for similar rites of a personal nature. (What appear to be crosses are not Christian artifacts but are thought to represent doorways through which to reach ancestral spirits.)

Only in the last twenty years has it become clear that what is still called the Pre-Classic period, which extended to about A.D. 300, saw cultural developments as sophisticated as those in the so-called Classic period that followed. These sacred structures were built during the Nephite period of the Book of Mormon, mainly before the Classic period. (See also the structures at El Mirador on page 103, which are also from the early era.) All of the platform mounds had "house" structures on top, but only for Lamanai do we have the form preserved.

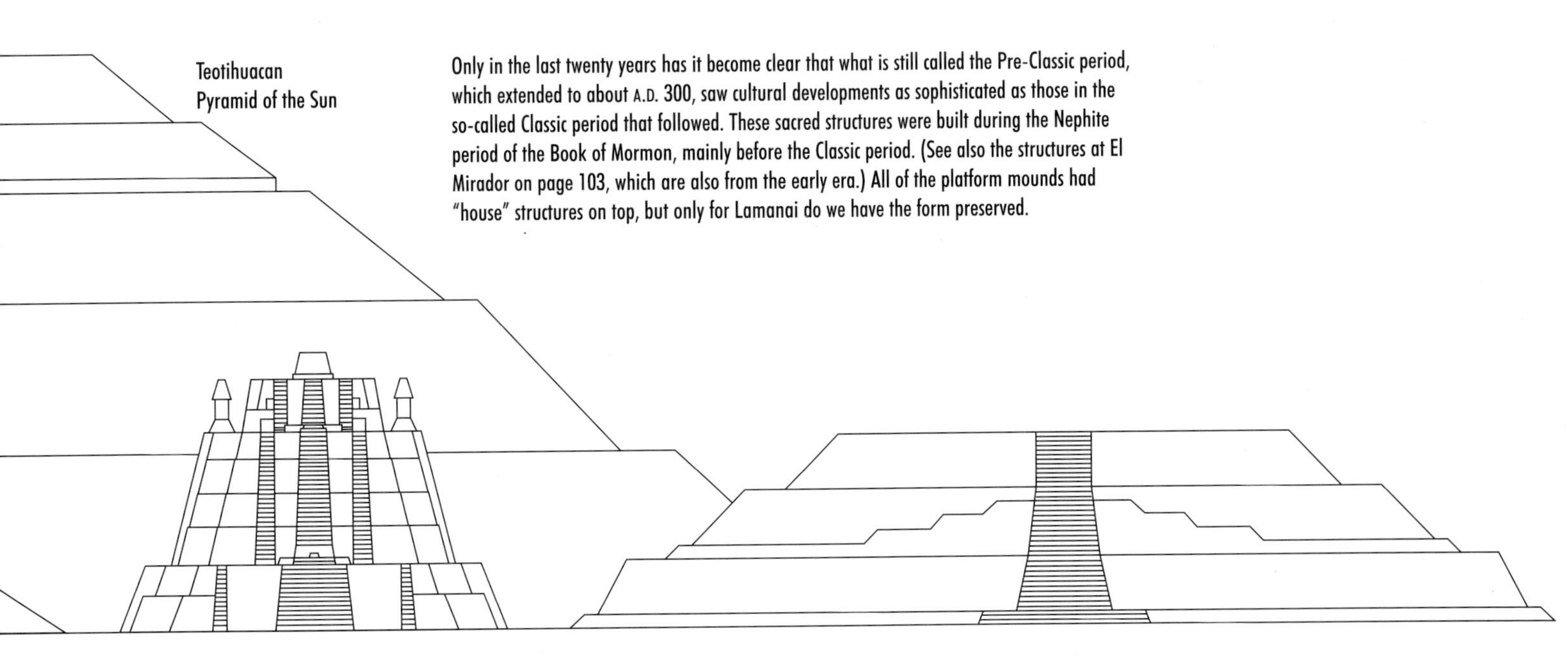

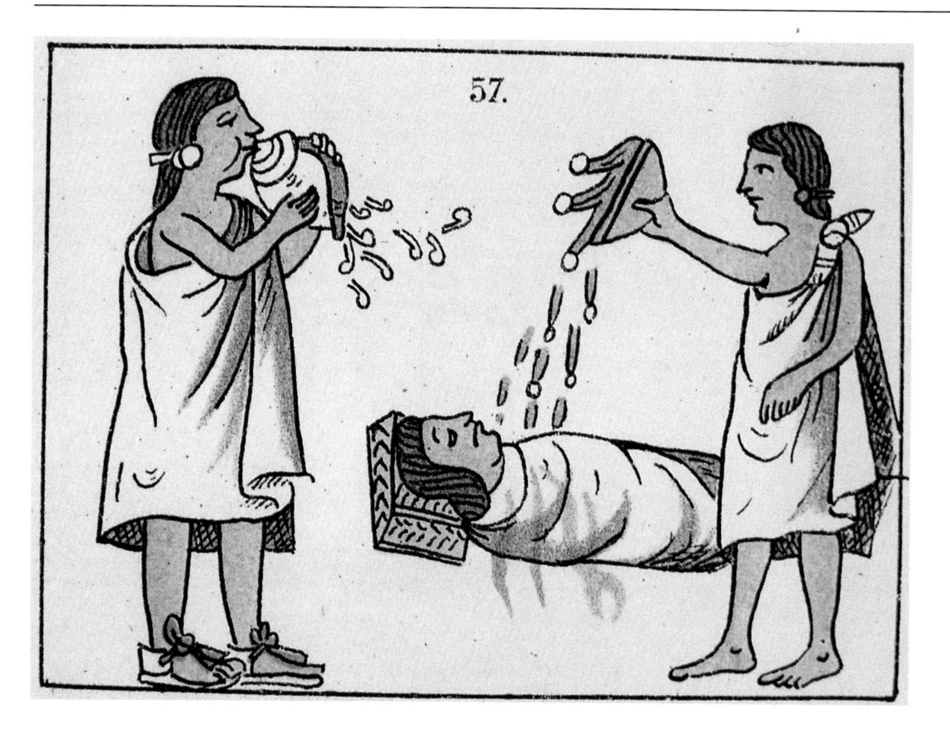

Priestly power was woven into the fabric of all Mesoamerican cultures. Here a sketch prepared for Father Sahagun's Florentine Codex shows two Aztec priests conducting a rite over a man.

Priests, Prophets, and Shamans

In the most advanced centers of the civilization there was an elaborate priesthood. At least three levels of authorities existed—the equivalent of high priest, supervisory priests, and regular priests. No doubt there were also novices still learning the ropes. The priesthood was formally under the dominance of the ruler; he designated whom he wished to fill the key roles, for he himself was a sacred figure who performed occasional core ritual duties. Priests were supported by offerings from the citizenry, particularly in the form of labor that went to cultivate lands held by the priestly body of a community or region. The religious men's prime duty was to see that the elaborate calendar of ceremonies was carried out. They made the sacrifices, prayed, fasted, and—although this is less clear—served as moral teachers and ethical conscience to the community or tribe. What schools there were were taught by priests, and a good deal of music and dancing may have operated under their direction, since most ritual involved those activities.

As one of the few social groups supported for full-time public service (in rural areas priests may have served on only a part-time basis), priests provided much of the continuity for advanced aspects of the culture. They were the custodians of records, probably the astronomers, perhaps the engineers and artists, and so on across the board in the skills crucial to public life.

In areas of limited population a shaman sometimes carried out priestly duties too, but more often shamans were specialists in healing, divination, witchcraft (both "white" and "black"), and other sacred arts of significance mainly to individuals or families. While priests held public offices of a sort, shamans and their ilk had private "practices" like modern medical doctors, psychiatrists, or fortune-tellers.

Prophets are also described in some of the native traditional sources. It is unclear how often they served also as priests, but they were considered to have power to see and announce the future, although their prophecies usually were issued in obscure, metaphoric terms.

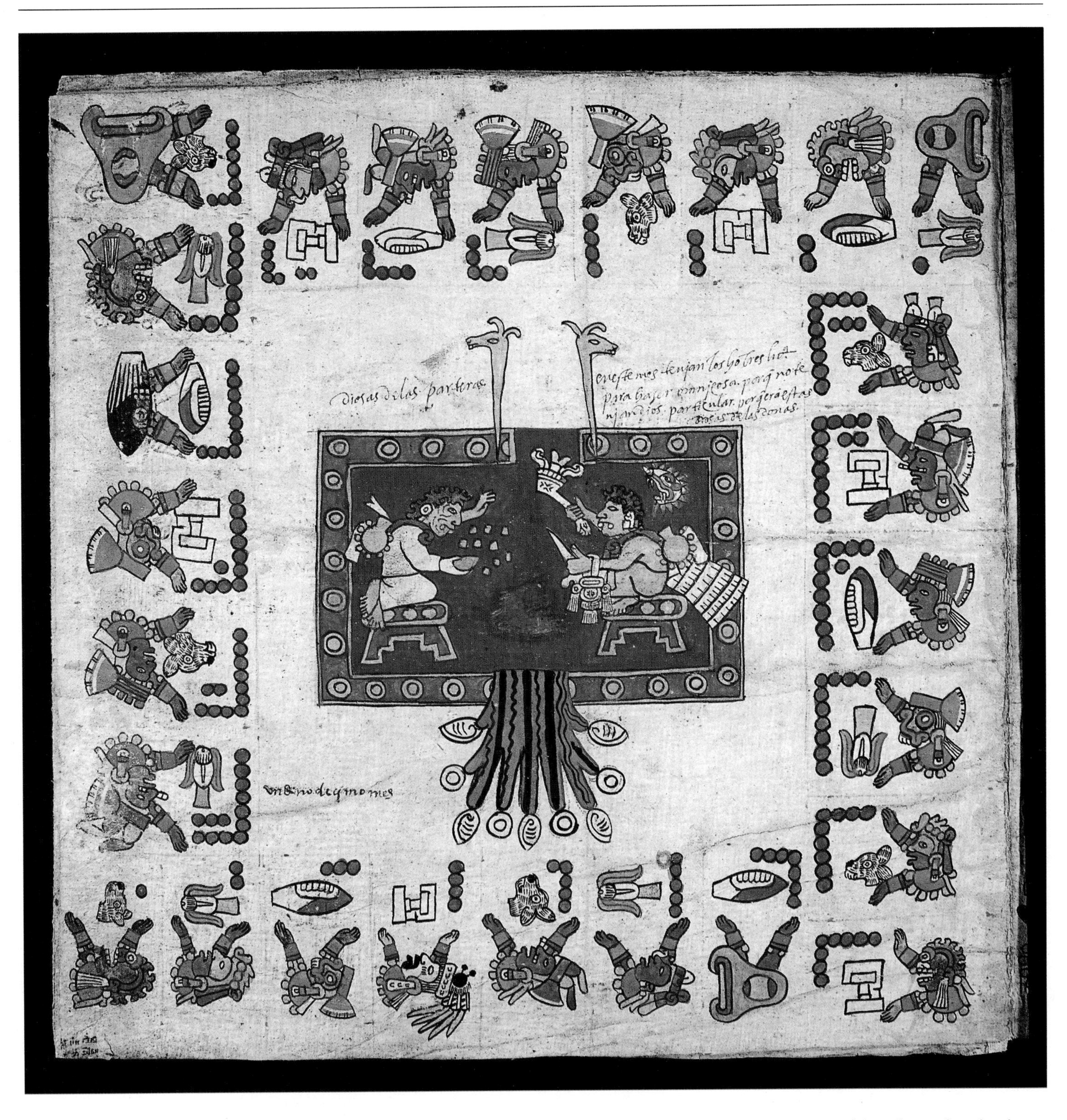

One form of prophecy of great importance at the time of the Spaniards' arrival was astrology—divining the future of individuals and society from the calendar. The moment of one's birth in relation to lucky or unlucky days and cycles was taken very seriously. The resulting sense of fatalism tended to paralyze at least the Aztecs from challenging their supposed fate. Other peoples held similar ideas, though perhaps not to the Aztec extreme. This is a section of astrological prophecy from the Mayan Dresden Codex.

Diviners (who might or might not have been shamans) were specialists in various modes of telling the future by reading omens—observing the movements of birds, for example. In this scene in the Codex Borbonicus, the original ancestors, gods in the Aztec pantheon, who lived in the highest, or thirteenth, heaven, are divining by tossing kernels of corn and interpreting how they land.

VISUALIZING BOOK OF MORMON LIFE

Among the early Nephites, "there were exceedingly many prophets. . . . And there was nothing save it was exceeding harshness, preaching and prophesying . . . and continually reminding" the people of potential doom that could keep them on track ritually and morally (Enos 1:22–3). Those "prophets, and the priests, and the teachers, did labor diligently, . . . teaching the law of Moses" (Jarom 1:11). By the first century A.D., after the appearance of Jesus Christ among them, "they did not walk any more after the performances and ordinances of the law of Moses; but they did walk after the commandments . . . from their Lord" (4 Nephi 1:12). At that time the whole people were led in a theocracy by "the disciples of Jesus" (4 Nephi 1:13). Two centuries later there had arisen "many priests and false prophets" (4 Nephi 1:34). Thus the social role of holy men was central in Nephite life throughout their history.

Among the duties of the Nephite religious teachers was participation in the legal (see, for example, Mosiah 26:6–12) and military systems (see 3 Nephi 3:19), divination (see Alma 16:5–8), moral critique (see Alma 5), the keeping of sacred paraphernalia and maintenance of the key records (see Alma 37:2; 3 Nephi 1:2; Mormon 1:2–3), and chronological and astronomical reckoning (see 3 Nephi 8:1–2).

The Nephite priesthood was structured in at least three levels and involved some specialization in functions (keeping the calendar was one specialty, judging by 3 Nephi 8:1–2).

MAYA PROPHECIES OF THE COMING OF THE CHRISTIANS

Several Maya prophecies about the coming of the Christians were reported to the Spanish priests after the Conquest. One was spoken by Ah Cambal, who held the office of Chilan among the Tutul Xiu group of Yucatan Mayas. Some years before they were conquered he "announced to them publicly that they would soon be subjected by a foreign race, and that they would preach to them one God and the power of a tree, which . . . means 'a tree erected with great virtue against the evil spirit.'" The Spaniards considered this tree to be the cross.

Another prophecy from the same place was uttered by famed Chilam Balam, "whom they considered a great prophet and soothsayer." He told them that "within a short time a white and bearded race would come from where the sun rises and they would bear on high a sign like this + which their gods could not approach and before which they would flee, and that this people would rule the land and would do no harm to those who would receive them peacefully. . . . And afterwards when the Spaniards came and they knew that they brought the symbol of the holy cross which was like that which their prophet Chilam Balam had drawn, they believed what he had told them to be true."

Landa's Relación de las Cosas de Yucatan

Shamans were socially marginal, both esteemed and somewhat feared because of their strange powers. They also had powers of showmanship, including a repertoire of magic tricks to impress their clients. A mask was sometimes part of their paraphernalia. (From Tlatilco, before 500 B.C.)

STRANGE BODY STATES

Bits of information from early Spanish sources fit together with modern investigation to shed light on the use of hallucinogenic and other psychoactive drugs in an area of human experience that overlaps with religion. Certain shamans in central Mexico a generation ago were still ritually consuming intoxicating mushrooms that produced visions. Other substances were also ingested for similar effects and probably have been for thousands of years.[114] Some features of this mushroom cult may connect to the Old World, particularly with Siberia. But tobacco was used in ritual on a wider scale than hallucinogens; it too was considered to evoke a connection with the divine powers. Generally it was priests or shamans who used these substances. There is no evidence of nonsacred usage, for pleasure.

Fasting had the power to produce somewhat similar effects. Again it was mostly priests who fasted, in a sense on behalf of their community congregation. They sometimes fasted for as long as a year, their deprivation consisting of eating only one meal per day with no spices or salt, as well as not bathing. For example, Sahagun's informants referred to those "who had fasted twenty days and those who had fasted a whole year" as having a vital role in ensuring the success of a ritual.[115]

VISUALIZING BOOK OF MORMON LIFE

Visions were considered legitimate spiritual phenomena among orthodox Nephite religious leaders. Not all accepted their reality or significance (see Alma 30:28). There is no hint in the Book of Mormon of chemically induced visionary experiences among the peoples it describes, although perhaps those things might be included among the reported "sorceries, and witchcrafts, and magics" of the third century A.D. (Mormon 1:19; compare 2:10). Fasting was practiced among the devout, especially the priests (see Mosiah 27:22–3; Alma 17:9).

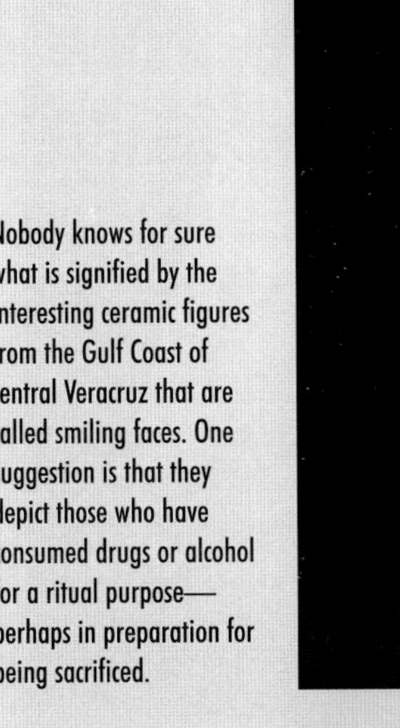

Nobody knows for sure what is signified by the interesting ceramic figures from the Gulf Coast of central Veracruz that are called smiling faces. One suggestion is that they depict those who have consumed drugs or alcohol for a ritual purpose—perhaps in preparation for being sacrificed.

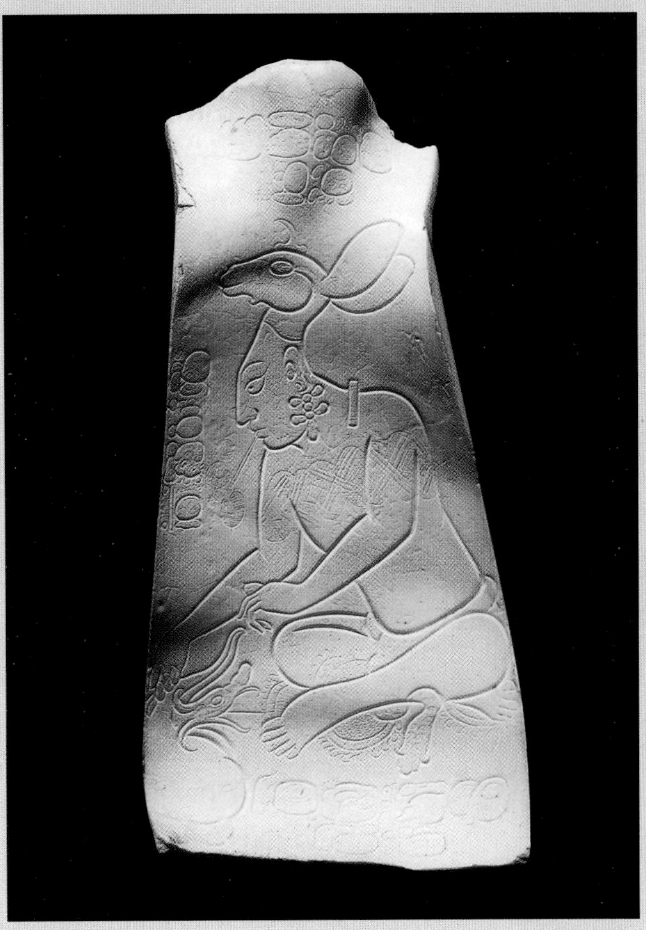

Priests consumed tobacco in the form of cigars, clay pipes (rarely), or cigarettes (in segments of cane) in connection with certain rites. This inscribed shell from Mexico or Guatemala of about A.D. 600 to 800 shows such usage. Other groups throughout Mesoamerica grew and used the plant as well.

From about A.D. 600 in Veracruz comes this powerful image of a worshipper who obviously feels deeply a personal relation with the supernatural.

Personal Worship

Amid the abundant communal rites that so characterized religious life in Mesoamerica, we occasionally detect the struggling of individuals to find meaning for their personal lives. The writings of the Mexica (Aztecs), which have been preserved for us in records written in European script after the Conquest and now translated to European tongues, reveal some of the probing that went on. At places in the Spanish records also, comments and excerpts of native thought are encountered that show the desire of individuals to penetrate beyond the everyday. Some ancient artists captured scenes of this struggle for personal spirituality. Some of these representations may dismay us because their struggles took cultural forms that are different than what our European tradition categorizes as spiritual, yet nobody seeing the intensity they exhibit can question the profound desire of the supplicants for enlightenment or relief.

Visualizing Book of Mormon Life

Careful study of the Book of Mormon shows that, while individual spiritual quests are documented among both Nephites and Lamanites, relatively little is said of that aspect of religion compared with the emphasis on formal, community worship. Enos's "wrestle . . . before God" (Enos 1:2) is an example. The remarkable conversion of the king of the Lamanites, Lamoni's father (see Alma 22), and of a "Lamanitish" woman and her father are other cases (Alma 19:16–7). At the end of Nephite history the lonely persistence of Mormon and Moroni$_2$ in their personal religious convictions stands out (see Mormon 1:2–3, 15–7; Moroni 9:3–6, 20–2). But the small proportion of the individual seekers, as perhaps is the case in most ages, is epitomized in Jarom 1:3–4; there we are told that most of the early Nephite populace were hard of heart, deaf of ear, and blind of mind—yet not all, for some had frequent "communion with the Holy Spirit" (Jarom 1:4). They would have been the type of individual to whom "Helaman and his brethren . . . did declare the word of God . . . unto the convincing of many people of their wickedness, which did cause them to repent"(Alma 62:45). Much more often, however, the behavior documented in the Nephite record emphasizes the group dimension: "And the people of Nephi began to prosper again. . . . But notwithstanding their riches . . . they were not lifted up in the pride of their eyes; neither were they slow to remember the Lord their God" (Alma 62:48–9).

The minority Mesoamerican tradition of seeking reconciliation with the world beyond continues among modern natives. Here a man from highland Chiapas exerts himself in rapt struggle.

A Remarkable Indian Individual

In 1622 two missionaries, a Catholic priest and a lay brother, were put ashore on the coast of Honduras accompanied by four Indian interpreters. No Spanish political, military, or ecclesiastical force had succeeded in penetrating the area by then, a century after Cortez's conquest of Aztec Mexico far to the north. On the morning of their third day they were approached by a band of people wearing mainly feather and flower ornaments. They accompanied a venerable old man with long, white hair.

He greeted them with a profound bow and asked what had taken them so long to arrive. Puzzled, they asked why he had expected them. He explained that "being one day at work in his plantation, there appeared to him a white child, more beautiful than any thing he had ever before seen or could imagine; it looked at him with great tenderness, and said, 'Know that you will not die before you become a Christian; there will come here some white men, with robes of the color of this ground, reaching to their feet; when they arrive, receive them kindly . . . for they are ministers of God, who has granted thee this signal mark of his mercy, because thou hast done well, and hast supported those who wanted assistance!" They then learned that the old gentleman, "*even in his idolatry*, had employed himself in acts of kindness; he cultivated maize to distribute among those who were in distress; he composed strifes, and settled all disputes among his neighbors." (Emphasis in original.)

The missionaries began to instruct their new friends. They baptized the old man, who died shortly afterward, and all his family. Many others of the Indians also received Catholic baptism "from the great respect they bore towards the old man."

A ceramic model from west Mexico displays one form of funeral procession. The death of a person prominent in the community involved the extended kin group with other groups, as relations were reinforced or revised in the aftermath. So the funeral was sometimes an important social event involving multiday feasting and drinking and the exchange of gifts.

Burial and Afterlife

Deceased members of society continued to influence their descendants. Death removed them to another sphere, but they were still considered to be accessible by means of memory and ritual. They were loved, respected, or feared according to cultural forms peculiar to each local group, although these all fit into a broad pattern of beliefs and practices found throughout Mesoamerica.

Important differences surrounded death depending upon the social standing of the deceased. A person of high rank was honored and praised, while the death of one of little social consequence was treated more casually. The belief was general that most of the dead underwent a lengthy journey after death, past assorted perils. A dog was their guide; an actual dog might be slain to be the companion, but the little wheeled toy dogs and other canine effigies of baked clay that have been found in burials could have served as inanimate substitutes. (At times objects thought to be useful on the journey or in the next life were also placed with a corpse.)

Some adults were given a respectful burial in the earth in a grave or tomb. Tombs could be very elaborate in construction and decoration. In a few cultures the dead were cremated. Many tombs apparently were reused, probably to bury kin, as was the case in Old World civilizations. Archaeologists fail to find nearly enough human remains to account for much of a proportion of the ancient dead. This could be due to the practice of cremation but is more likely because the dead were buried at some distance from the community.

The subject of the afterlife in Mesoamerican beliefs has been handled confusedly by scholars. A common interpretation, heavily based on the Aztec material, has it that all who died set out on the road to the underworld mentioned above. Some classes of the dead (for the Aztecs, warriors slain in battle and mothers who died in childbirth) were at length transported to a pleasant realm. The mass of the dead, however, remained in an underworld limbo until they decayed away. A favored few rose to glory in the east out of the underworld on the model of the rising sun, moon, and stars. (On major and certain minor points this scheme was very similar to Egyptian beliefs about death.) Other scholars have interpreted the fragmentary literature on Mesoamerican beliefs as showing a more widespread anticipation of a resurrection whose quality was to be based on the individual's moral state.[116]

Ancestry was an important social dimension in all Mesoamerican cultures (see page 66). At least for the higher social classes, genealogies were kept and social relationships were claimed and cemented on the basis of the prestige of one's ancestors. Most of those connections were probably documented only orally, however. Respect for and commemoration of the ancestors as an element of religious practice was correspondingly varied. For common people, ritual observances in honor of and deference to the departed ancestors were far less significant than for nobility.

Masks were sometimes used to remember an ancestor. This striking wooden mask was preserved amazingly well—including part of the original paint—in a tomb whose location in the Maya lowlands is unknown.

VISUALIZING BOOK OF MORMON LIFE

Book of Mormon peoples were much concerned with their ancestors and with the disposition of the dead. In the Nephite record, the deceased were thought to go to the underworld, apparently the dim, eventless place known to their Israelite forebears as *sheol.* $Nephi_1$ believed an "awful monster," symbolic of the "devil," death, and "hell," held a person in his "grasp,"[117] Those who believed in the Holy One of Israel were delivered via resurrection from the monster into the heavens to enjoy a blessed state. This salvation was symbolized by reaching the tree of life and eating its fruit (see 2 Nephi 9, especially verses 9–10, 13, 19; and Alma 5:34, 62).

Burial was the typical mode of disposal of corpses for both Nephites and Lamanites (see 2 Nephi 4:12; Mosiah 9:19; Alma 3:1; 30:1; 57:28; Helaman 9:10; Alma 53:3). In exceptional circumstances corpses were thrown in the sea, a "watery grave" (1 Nephi 18:18; see Alma 3:3; 44:21–2). To be left unburied on land was a bad fate (see Alma 2:37–8; 16:10–1). A pattern is suggested by the burial of a Lamanite king, who was to be put in a tomb ("sepulchre," Alma 19:1) that had already been prepared to receive him. Mourning for the dead was characterized by extreme weeping, wailing, prayer, fasting, and possibly self-sacrifice of blood, following a pattern received from the land of Judah (see 1 Nephi 16:35; Mosiah 28:18; Alma 30:2; Helaman 9:10, 22; on the blood, compare Alma 34:11 with Deuteronomy 14:1 and Jeremiah 16:6). How much of this customary pattern applied to the disposal of deceased commoners we cannot tell.

The traditions, desires, or memory of the "fathers" were active considerations in dealing with current issues (for example, Mosiah 1:5–7, 13–6; Alma 9:10; 20:18; Helaman 15:11, 15).[118] Written and oral genealogies were kept (see 1 Nephi 5:14; Jarom 1:1; Omni 1:18; Alma 37:3), going all the way back to the patriarchal founders of Israel (see, for example, Alma 10:2–3).

For the prominent and wealthy, or perhaps for the priestly, burial might be in a sumptuously decorated tomb like this reconstructed one of the Classic period in Oaxaca.

From this mural at Teotihuacan dating to around A.D. 400–500 we see a portion of *Tlalocan*, the delightsome paradise still known to the Aztecs a millennium later. It featured abundant water, vegetation, food, and pleasures that qualified persons could attain.

This is one art form that was used to represent an ancestor. From Pacific coastal Guatemala, it was carved within the last few centuries B.C., when the Lamanite people seem to have been inhabiting that zone.

Stela 50 from Izapa, Chiapas, is interpreted by Norman as symbolically showing resurrection of the skeleton through picturing the umbilical cord.

Knowledge Systems

Overview

Every civilization possesses a vast body of knowledge unique to its view of and experience with its environment. For instance, for at least three millennia Chinese civilization conceived in its own way a vast array of information organized in a unique manner that defined what was Chinese. As recently as a hundred years ago the Chinese had their own unique ways of thinking about all areas of human concern, such as geography, botany, agriculture, cuisine, medicine, art, literature, mathematics, astronomy, technology, government, and ethics. Now modern knowledge systems have either been laid over the top of or have completely replaced many of the old ways in China, as in all other parts of the globe. The modern world and its ways of thinking developed out of one earlier area civilization—the western European tradition—in just the last few hundred years. In the process, the West has come to dominate virtually every former civilization and culture by the force of science, a European invention, and the resulting technological power, economic might, military prowess, and communications capabilities. But if we want to try to understand one of those former civilizations—whether it be Chinese or Mesoamerican—we need to step back from our own frame of reference and see the world through their eyes.

The Spanish Conquest of Mesoamerica was an early stage in the spread of those western European ideas and institutions. In the New World the sudden arrival of the new ways almost totally overwhelmed patterns of living that had been accumulating for thousands of years. Those now-extinct conceptions and behaviors were as different from European manners of thought and action as were traditional Chinese modes.

Within the Mesoamerican culture area we detect local differences in details, yet much key knowledge was held in common throughout the area. For example, while each group's calendar differed slightly from those of their neighbors, the principles used to form them all were essentially the same. Meanwhile, structures were planned and built in all portions of the area on the same architectural principles and, as far as possible, with similar materials, despite obvious variation in styles. Musical instruments and rhythmic forms, disease diagnosis and treatment, and astronomical conceptions were all generally shared across the regional cultures. Thus knowledgeable persons from one region could carry on informed discussion with their peers anywhere else within the Mesoamerican territory.

Here we will consider two key knowledge systems, making written records and the astronomically based calendar.

Visualizing Book of Mormon Life

Does the Book of Mormon indicate the development of broadly shared ways of thinking and doing among its various peoples? Yes, at numerous points. For instance, the people of Zarahemla in the third century B.C., although of different language and cultural heritage at first contact, learned the language of the Nephites and came to follow their governmental scheme and laws (see Omni 1:14–9). The reverse of the process must also have gone on in respect to other knowledge. The system of weights, measures, and money employed by the Nephites had visible similarities to, and apparently was derived from, the Jaredite system, probably through the "Mulekites" as intermediaries (see Alma 11:4).[119] Nephite priestly dissenters, the Amulonites, taught the Nephite writing system among the Lamanites (see Mosiah 24:4), who then produced their own books (see Helaman 3:15).[120] A cult known as the order of Nehor spread throughout Nephite territory and far into Lamanite country in a matter of a few years (see Alma chapter 1; 14:16; 21:4; 24:28). The Jaredite-originated[121] secret society pattern became widespread throughout Nephite and Lamanite lands (see Ether 8:9–19; Helaman 6:26–30; 3 Nephi 3:9; 4 Nephi 1:46).[122] Trade, which was conducted throughout the entire geographical area, was facilitated by, and in turn facilitated, the sharing of common knowledge systems (see Mosiah 24:6–7; Helaman 6:7–9; 4 Nephi 1:46).

The transmission of sophisticated elements of cultural knowledge through the generations in Mesoamerica depended on written records. This fine Jaina-style figurine from around A.D. 700 underlines how the control of books conferred power on the lowland Maya elite, one of whom is shown here, and on the elite in other Mesoamerican societies.

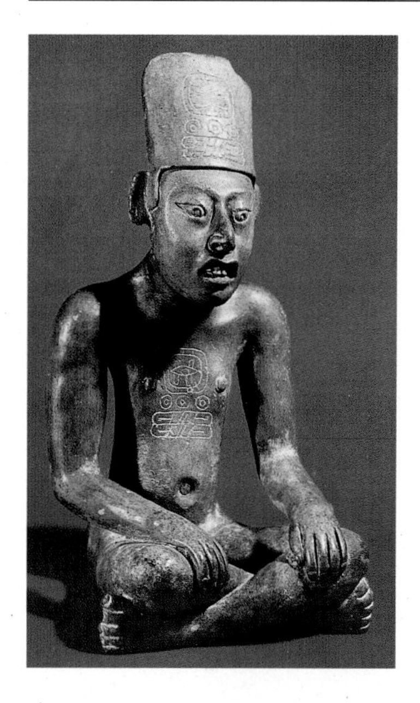

This figure, the "Scribe of Cuilapan," is named after the place in Oaxaca where it was found. It is considered to represent a keeper of records. Observers have noted its general similarity to representations of Egyptian scribes, although it is not clear what that might mean.

Writing and Records

In only one part of the New World was genuine ancient writing in use on a regular, culturally significant basis. That was Mesoamerica. For nearly twenty-five hundred years before the Spaniards arrived we find direct evidence for writing in the form of actual remains of documents (mainly on stone) and indirect evidence through representation in art depicting characters, documents, or scribes. At least fifteen different scripts are known from this area, and their use stretched over millennia.[123] The earliest writing was already quite sophisticated. That implies that still earlier written material awaits archaeological discovery.

Aztec records are the best described. They included "annals of ancient times, contemporary events, year counts, accounts compiled yearly, specific records for each year, books of each day and day-by-day counts or diaries."[124] Some of the records constituted histories of peoples that incorporated accounts of "victories, defeats, the lives of rulers, memorable ceremonial occasions," and even "the adventures of individual heroes, often in intimate and vivid detail."[125] Letters were also exchanged.

We know a good deal about the Mayan writing tradition from four preserved Mayan books or codices, sixteen lineage histories from Yucatan (the Chilam Balam records, written in the European alphabet soon after the Conquest), and inscriptions on many stone monuments. The Maya "used to write their histories, and the ceremonies and method of sacrifices to their idols, and their calendar, in books." Also "they had written records of . . . the prognostications of their prophets and the lives . . . of their lords."[126] Tax and trade records were also kept.[127] Other Mesoamerican peoples had similar types of documents.

Records of the types mentioned were surely kept long before as well, in the Classic and even the Pre-Classic period, before A.D. 300. In fact, many of the documents recorded at the time of the Conquest were "simply transcriptions of the old hieroglyphic manuscripts" put into Spanish characters.[128]

On a large, carved stone that is now part of a wall at Monte Alban is this Zapotec inscription. It dates to the early centuries A.D. Inscribed stelae (large free-standing stones) or panels like this were often used in Mesoamerican architecture and site planning to evoke religious devotion in or communicate political propaganda to the public.

A Classic-era painted plate shows a Maya dignitary (or perhaps a deity) painting a codex with a brush.

One of the most interesting of the obscure writing systems is found only on this roller seal that was uncovered accidentally at the site of Tlatilco, just west of Mexico City. From other materials at the site, the writing appears to date between 400 and 700 B.C. Experts have suggested that it represents writing even more advanced than the hieroglyphic or pictorial writing typical of Mesoamerica.[129]

VISUALIZING BOOK OF MORMON LIFE

According to the Book of Mormon account, the carving of texts on stone was being done at the behest of royalty as early as the sixth century B.C. (see Omni 1:20–2). By the first century B.C., the Nephite history reports that "there are many records kept of the proceedings of this people, by many of this people, which are particular and very large" (Helaman 3:13). Moreover, the tradition of literacy probably continued after the destruction at Cumorah among "robbers" (Mormon 8:9; these were either ex-Nephites or totally other people) and among descendants of former Nephites who had defected to the Lamanites (see Moroni 9:24). Anyway, the Lamanites were earlier said to have copied the Nephite pattern (see Mosiah 24:6), so the tradition of written records would likely have continued among them regardless of what happened to ex-Nephite groups.

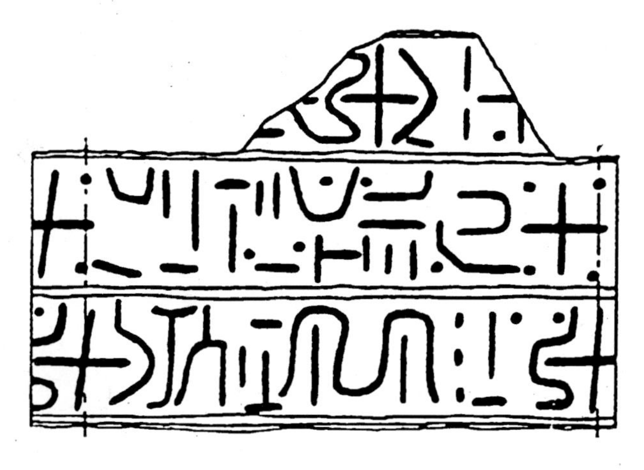

This is how the whole inscription on the Tlatilco roller seal looks when rolled out. Carl Hugh Jones has compared these characters to those on the Anthon transcript, which Joseph Smith copied from the record that he translated. His conclusion was that only a few of the characters were not shared by the two sources.[130]

In a little vignette on a Maya vase, a rabbit busily paints on a codex. A rabbit was thought to be visible on the face of the moon, and the animal was a patron of scribes.

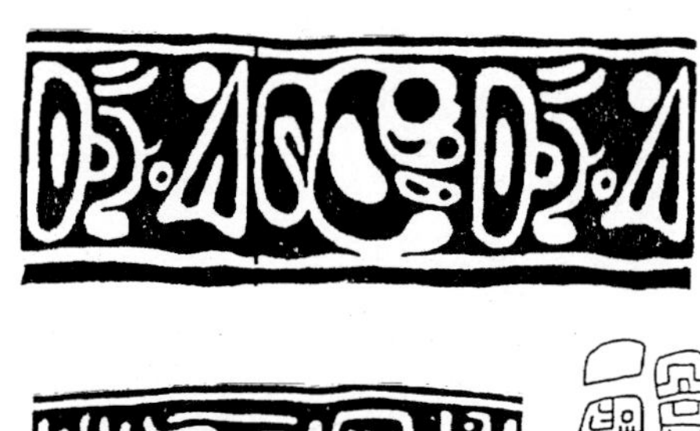

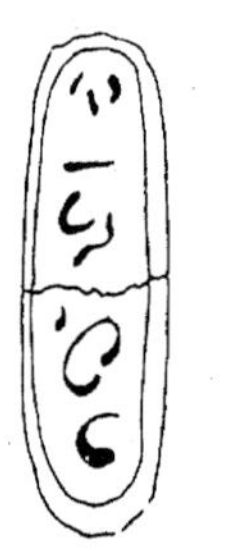

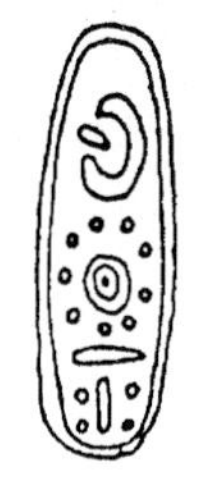

Our understanding of writing in Mesoamerica is far from complete. Here are samples of apparent scripts that have been discovered but for which we have little or no historical or cultural context.

BOOKS

In the sixteenth century the European invaders found large numbers of books in use that the natives held in great respect. Those hand-produced books are called codices (singular, codex). Michael D. Coe supposes that "there must have been thousands of such books in Classic times" (A.D. 300–900).[131] Most records were destroyed by zealous Spanish priests who suspected (correctly) that they were an integral part of the old religious system that they wanted to destroy completely.[132]

The Madrid Codex constituted an almanac of astrological predictions dating around the time of the Spaniards' arrival.

VISUALIZING BOOK OF MORMON LIFE

The Book of Mormon reports that books were used by the Jaredites, Nephites, and Lamanites from perhaps the third millennium B.C. until at least A.D. 400. "Many books" were in use among the Nephites in the first century B.C. (Helaman 3:15; see 3:13). Mormon, the last major writer in the Nephite tradition, buried a whole library of such documents during his people's final days in the late fourth century A.D. (see Mormon 6:6; compare 1:3).

An artist has accurately reconstructed the processes of papermaking, ink preparation, and codex painting among the Maya. The basics were the same throughout much of Mesoamerica.

Details of how Mesoamerican astronomers made their observations are nowhere described, but sketches like this from an Aztec source, the Codex Borbonicus, let us know that sighting devices were used to assist.

Calendar, Astronomy, and Astrology

Every Mesoamerican people considered their calendar to be more than a practical tool for keeping track of time. A calendar was more like a pseudo-scientific model of the unfolding of each individual's and society's history and fate.

There was not just a single calendar but several. One system was built around 13 numbered days (a sort of "week"). A separate cycle of 20 days provided a rough equivalent to a "month." In the 20-day cycle each day was named for a god. The two cycles ran in parallel. Thus a day would be labeled, say, 4 according to the first count but Chuen in the second. Another day 4 Chuen would not come around again in the meshing of the two cycles for 260 days (making one kind of "year"). But there were other counts going on simultaneously. A 360-day "year" and, for different purposes, a 365-day "year" were also counted. Cycles of the moon were also tracked, and there probably was a 7-day "week" (one-fourth of a lunar month) as well. Even the cycle for the appearance of Venus was calculated. Mastering this maze of interlocking counts clearly involved a high degree of expertise, constant attention, and books.

In the best-known regional version, that of the Maya in Yucatan, the most basic year consisted of 360 days (marking one Maya *tun*). Twenty tuns formed a *katun* (20 x 360=7,200 days) or approximately 20 of our years. Each katun period was identified by the name of the day that began it—katun 11 Ahau had its start on the day that was named 11 Ahau. The way the cycles meshed, it would be 260 tuns (256 of our years) before the day 11 Ahau would again begin a katun. To refer to katun 11 Ahau would define a period of history somewhat like our speaking of the fifteenth century.

The Maya believed that each period of this calendrical history would essentially reenact what had gone on during the last era when the same calendar label had been in use.[133] If katun 11 Ahau had proved disastrous before, according to the astrological almanac, then look out the next time 11 Ahau was slated to begin the katun; it too would bring bad news.

Astronomy as the accumulation of a mass of information on the heavenly bodies for its own sake was unknown. The observations were to construct or document astrological models. Thus even though enough data had been collected and conceptualized that certain eclipses could be predicted, the interest of the Mesoamericans was not in the eclipse as such but in the sacred significance that they supposed was behind it.

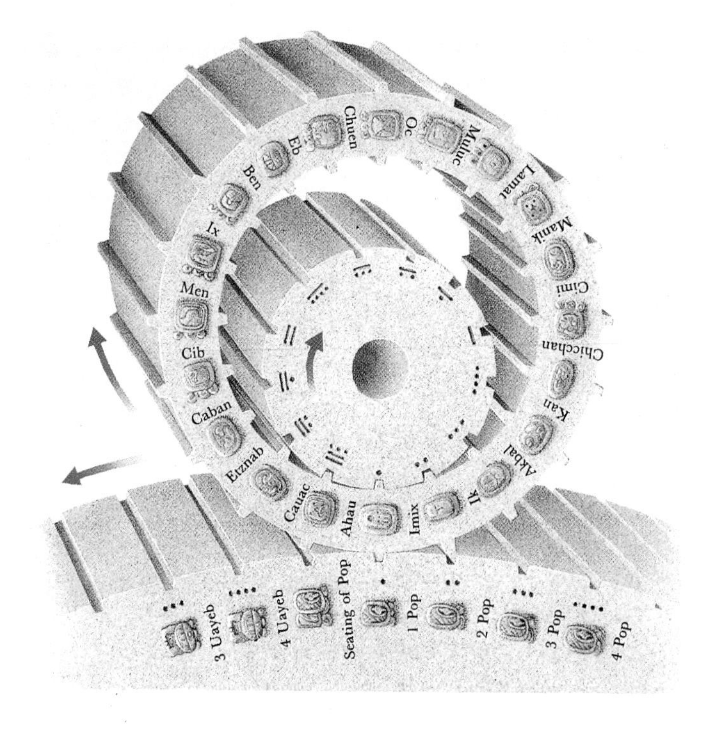

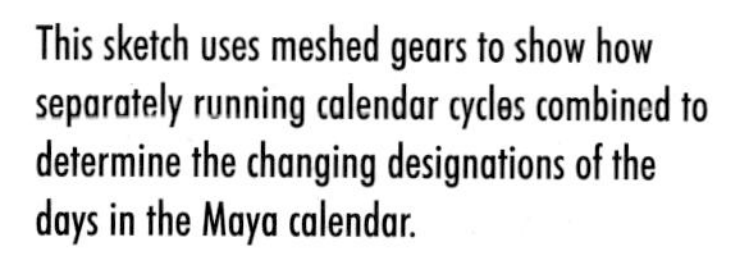

This sketch uses meshed gears to show how separately running calendar cycles combined to determine the changing designations of the days in the Maya calendar.

Architecture sometimes reflected the calendar. This pyramid at the site of El Tajin in northern Veracruz has 365 niches that are meant to represent the days of the solar year. Masonry designs elsewhere use calendar-significant numbers such as 13, 52, and 260 in this same general way. (The idea may have seemed natural for those concerned with astronomy; one old Korean observatory consisted of a tower that contained 366 stones laid up in courses of 28—the number of days in the lunar month.)[135]

VISUALIZING BOOK OF MORMON LIFE

While little is said in the Nephite record about their calendar, the few glimpses we get show us that they took calendrical cycling and its fateful consequences seriously, in general agreement with Mesoamerican thought.

The Nephites used several calendrical systems that ran concurrently. In the first place, as Randall P. Spackman has convincingly argued,[134] their founders must have maintained the moon-based calendar of the Jews after they left Jerusalem (see Omni 1:21). Another count of years was begun with the departure from the land of Judah. Later, at least two other counts were employed, and all four were meshed. How the cycles related was historically very significant.

Third Nephi 1:1 shows the pattern most clearly: the 91st year in the era of the rule of judges over the Nephites coincided with the end of the 600th year since Lehi departed from Jerusalem. Moreover, the year was

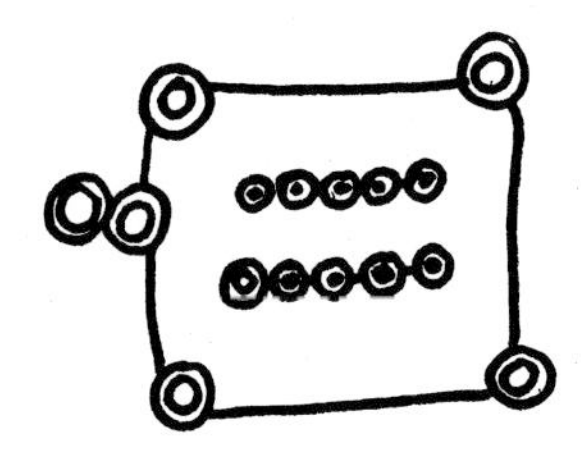

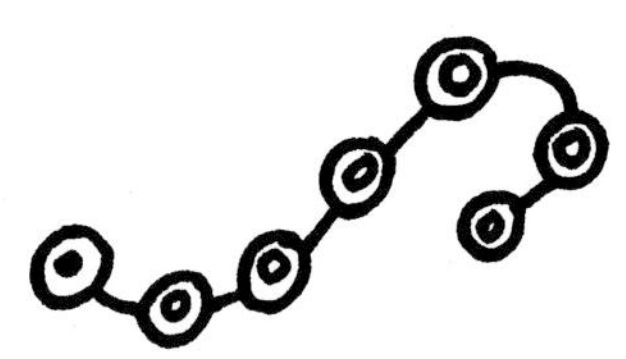

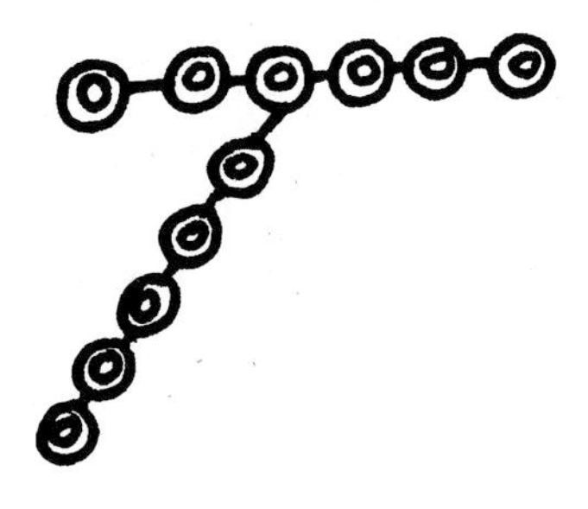

related to astronomical phenomena—"signs" (3 Nephi 1:4; see 1:8, 9), and particularly a sign involving the failure of a regular night of darkness (see 3 Nephi 1:8; Helaman 14:3). The 600-year interval had first been prophesied by founder $Nephi_1$ (see 1 Nephi 10:4; 19:8; 2 Nephi 25:19). Samuel, the Lamanite prophet, reiterated the prediction with greater detail in 10 or 11 B.C. In five more years, he announced, the great sign of the coming of the Messiah would be given. There would occur a night without darkness, a new star would appear, and there would be many signs and wonders in heaven (see Helaman 14:2–6). The signs appeared as scheduled. By the 100th year of the reign of the judges, 609 Nephite years had passed since Lehi's departure (see 3 Nephi 2:5–7). "Now the Nephites began to reckon their time from this period when the sign was given" (3 Nephi 2:8).

The pattern of calendrical, astronomical, and prophetic calculations among the Nephites was confirmed a few years later when the record reports the great physical catastrophe that marked the crucifixion. "And now it came to pass that according to our record, and we know our record to be true, for [it was kept by a prophet] . . . if there was no mistake made by this man in the reckoning of our time, the thirty and third year had passed away; and the people began to look with great earnestness for the sign which had been given by the prophet Samuel, . . . darkness for the space of three days" (3 Nephi 8:1–3).

The sense of inevitability that the Nephites felt about calendrical prophecy is also like that in Mesoamerica. Both $Alma_2$ and Samuel foresaw the destruction of the Nephite people as definitely going to occur some "four hundred years" after the birth of Christ (see Alma 45:10; see 45:11–2; Helaman 13:5; confirmed by $Moroni_2$ in Mormon 8:6). (I have suggested further parallels to patterns of Maya calendrical prophecy in another publication.)[136]

A vignette in the story of Nephite-Lamanite warfare underlines how the calendar could shape their behavior in a Mesoamerican manner. A massive Lamanite expeditionary force was on the verge of gaining control of the narrow neck of land from the Nephites when they camped on the beach near the city Bountiful, their last obstacle (see Alma 51:26–32). The Nephite captain Teancum crept into the enemy camp at night and silently killed the enemy leader (see Alma 51:33–4). The next morning happened to be the astrologically significant (in Mesoamerican terms) first day of the new year. "Behold, when the Lamanites awoke on the first morning of the first month, behold, they found Amalickiah was dead in his own tent. . . . When the Lamanites saw this they were affrighted; and they abandoned their design in marching into the land northward, and retreated with all their army into the city of Mulek" (Alma 52:1–2). The timing of Teancum's act of psychological warfare could not have been better, nor more instructive about the powerful role of calendrical expectations.

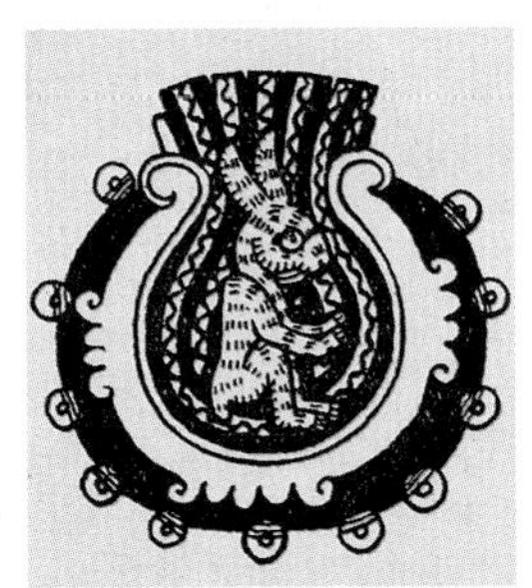

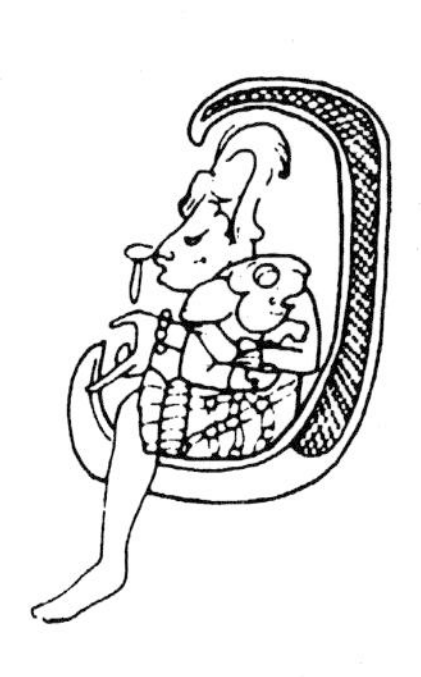

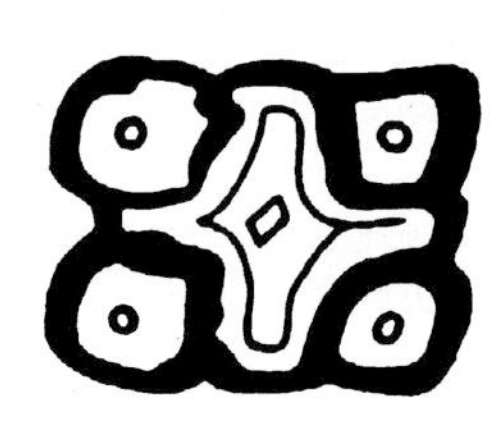

These Aztec symbols (the six symbols in the vertical column above, from Sahagun) were used by astronomers to represent some of the bodies or constellations they observed in the heavens. Incidentally, the practice of connecting circles with lines to represent a constellation was known only in China and in ancient Mesoamerica.[137] The four symbols on the right were used by the Maya. Note the rabbit in the moon motif in both Aztec and Maya symbols

ARCHAEOASTRONOMICAL ALIGNMENTS

Lines of sight to where the sun, moon, and stars appeared on the horizon at key times in the calendar were used in picking sites for settlements and aligning structures thereon (somewhat in the manner of the Chinese with their pseudoscience, geomancy, by which they erected and oriented structures in accord with the supposed flow of forces in the earth). For example, V. Garth Norman has shown that the key structures in the main group at the site of Izapa, near the border between the state of Chiapas and Guatemala, are lined up in relation to each other, to the standing stone monuments, and to mountain peaks on the horizon over which the sun or moon rose or set at crucial calendar dates.[138] The entire site was consciously laid out and built as a kind of cosmic calculator before the Christian era.

Orientations of this sort are found throughout Mesoamerica and must have been begun early, because the original spots on which important sites were founded were chosen with this thinking in mind. This map[139] shows some of the cities that were sited in relation to an adjacent peak that was astronomically significant.

VISUALIZING BOOK OF MORMON LIFE

Latter-day Saint readers may find it interesting that at least three major sites were laid out in relation to sunrise over Cerro El Vigia in the Tuxtlas Mountains of southern Veracruz, since it is the likely site for the hill Cumorah of the Nephites and the hill Ramah of the Jaredites.[140]

CITIES ALIGN WITH PEAKS AT SOLSTICES

▲ Mountain Peaks

● City Sites

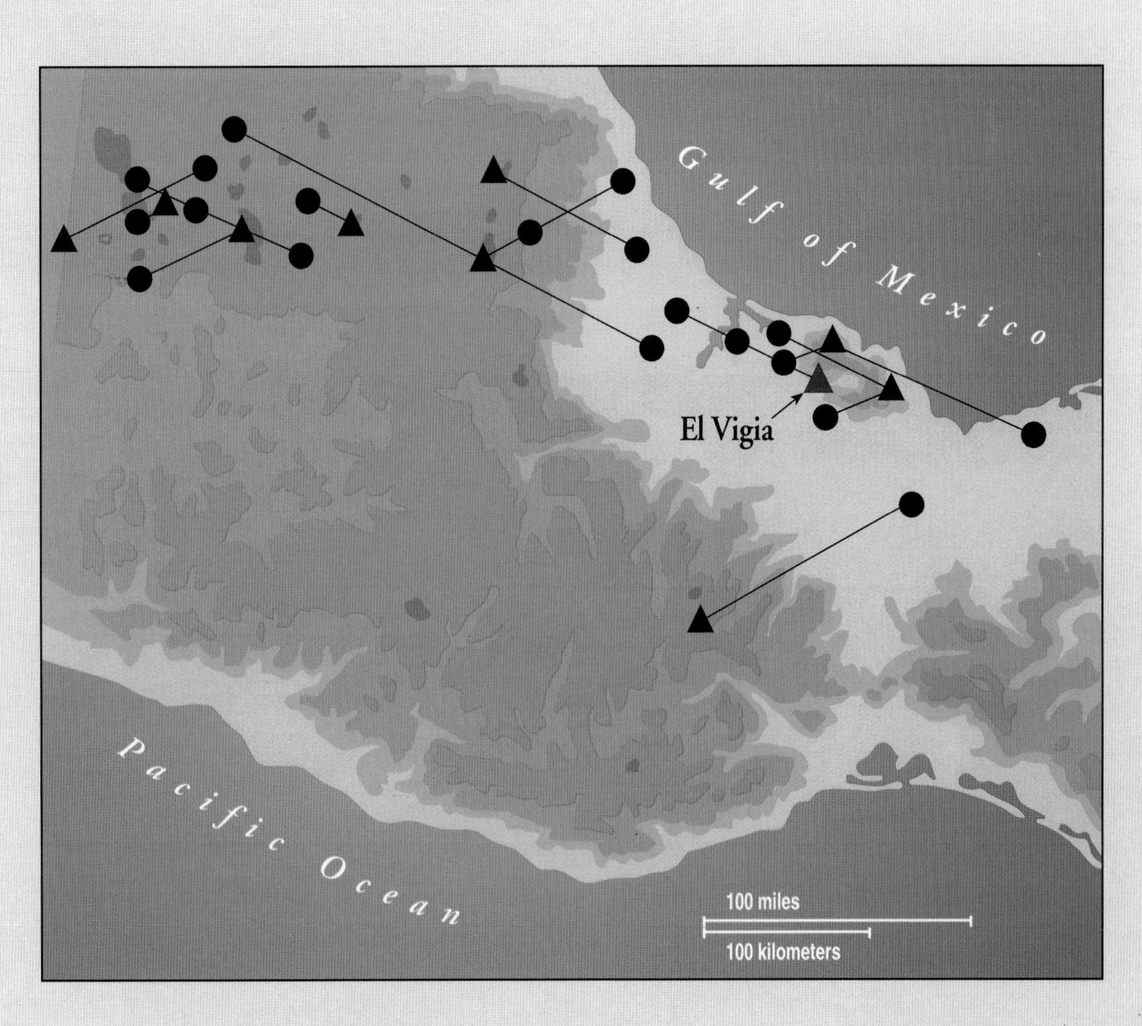

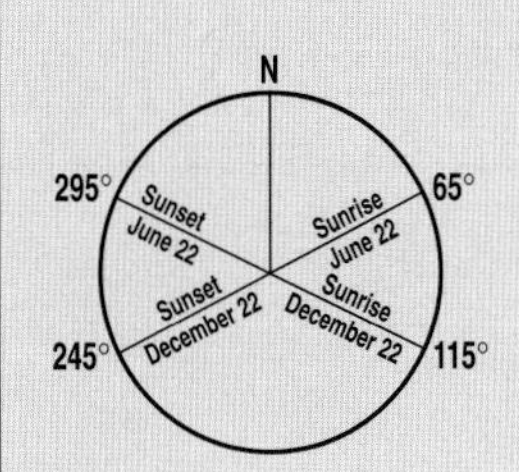

This "Mr. Potato Head" graffito was scrawled on an ancient Maya wall. It gives us a glimpse of informal, popular art that combined humor with fantasy. To see more of these folk sketches would counter some of the formality of the official art.

Art and Beauty

Overview

Beautiful objects were highly prized in Mesoamerica. But what constituted beauty was defined in different ways than by us today. At least four principles or rules appear to have governed Mesoamerican esthetic expression.

One of the principles was that the sacred penetrated and suffused every aspect of life and quite dominated some areas of experience. The shadow of things supernatural hung over all, more often in an ominous than in a reassuring manner. The divine powers were mainly seen as fearsome; a person or a people had to deal carefully with them. Pessimism about life outweighed optimism. Mesoamericans were a solemn people, and much art of the area—on public buildings, in depictions of deity, on funerary vessels, etc.—reflected that solemnity. But in the face of fear, one of the consolations that could be pursued was beauty in nature, ornament, and speech. Fortunately the divinities too were thought to approve of and enjoy beauty.

A second principle was that tradition was a linchpin of society. As far as possible, problems were solved not by thinking new thoughts but by discerning how old notions applied to a current situation. It is striking to observe in Mesoamerican art how many ways—though not all—of thinking, doing, and representing endured for many centuries without fundamental change.

Third, the social elite—mainly the nobility and the top priests—set public standards, very much as in medieval Europe or other premodern societies. Most long-distance commerce was in luxury items that catered to the desires of the upper strata of society, for they alone had the wherewithal to reward merchants for bringing to them natural or cultural treasures from a distance. Their patronage also supported craftsmen and artists, so their upper-class whims modulated the long-term patterns of beauty through which the culture was expressed.

One of the most famous of all sculptures from Mexico, "The Wrestler," as it has been called by some in our day, displays sculptural mastery of a high order in representing the human body. This Olmec piece dates from before 600 B.C.

The intricacy of symbol piled upon symbol that is illustrated by this Zapotec funerary urn (about A.D. 500) is present in much of the orthodox art of the later periods of the Mesoamerican tradition.

The fourth consideration was that the most notable pieces of art that have been preserved were political. That is, they glorified and justified the rulers, their allied priests, and the deities connected in the public mind with the dominant class (just as was the case with Egyptian art). We today give much attention to this ancient propagandistic art because the makers and sponsors saw that it was placed in prominent positions—the great stone monuments, the mural paintings, the temple facades. Yet there were pieces of art that had no apparent political purpose. These items appeal today to our sense of beauty, and they could have appealed to ancients too, beyond any propaganda value.

Did the mass of people have their own esthetic life? That is hard to know, but it seems likely that at least simple expressions of beauty, ranging from seeing the hand of an infant, to observing delicate flowers, to watching a sunset, were appreciated by many of the folk even if they lived in isolation from most high-class art.

Such busy sculptural detail as this on a structure at the site of Kabah in the Yucatan peninsula further illustrates the principle frequently evident in Mesoamerican art that elaboration was considered better than simplicity.

The beauty of the natural world in Mesoamerica, exemplified by this sunset over Lake Atitlan, must have made an impression on many observers. Alma the elder, in the commonest interpretation of Nephite geography, would have seen evening views like this from "the place of Mormon" nearby. So when he rhapsodized about "how beautiful" the spot was (Mosiah 18:30), it may not have been just because of spiritual experiences enjoyed there.

This large "abstract" mural is a reproduction in the Museo Nacional of a scene in the Temple of Agriculture at Teotihuacan in the Valley of Mexico. The original is now destroyed. Shell symbolism (which has parallels in Andean South America and in India) was frequently emphasized at this metropolis.

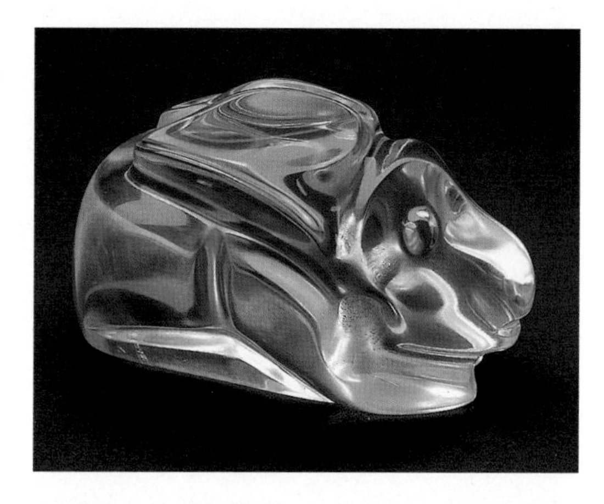

Not all Aztec artists felt obliged to crowd up their sculptures to excess with religious or royal symbols. This rabbit done in rock crystal shows skill and taste that would likely have pleased the sculptor of "The Wrestler," who lived more than two millennia earlier.

Once again, in observing nature rather than representing sacred symbolism, an exceptional Aztec artist has let simplicity triumph in this stone sculpture representing a shell.

Flowers were enjoyed for themselves by some people, who planted them around their homes. Their beauty struck Aztec wise men as embodying the mystery of all artistic expression—oral, musical, graphic, or other. For the entire class of esthetic phenomena, they used the metaphorical label *in xochitl in cuicatl,* which translates to English as "flower and song." More deeply it signifies something like "the mysterious moving power of symbolism." Moreover, these lovely blossoms from the *flor de mayo* tree were sometimes steeped in hot water and made into a delicate preserve to be eaten.

Feather Work

An Unusual Form of Art

Some exotic Mesoamerican artistic media went well beyond what we think of nowadays as art. For example, the Aztecs used seeds to make images of sacred beings and then ate them as part of a ceremony (which they thought of as "eating the flesh of god," a kind of communion). High artistry was also used to construct mosaics of flowers. The products of most such perishable media we cannot concretely visualize, but a small number of specimens of Aztec feather work exist that provide a window for us on one lost esthetic tradition that strikes us still as justly famous. Feather art was highly prized throughout Mesoamerica for centuries. Problems of preservation have destroyed most of those objects, of course. Historical accident has preserved a few specimens that allow us to see the details of this form of art among the Aztecs of sixteenth-century Mexico.

Rare feathers were imported by Aztec merchants (hummingbird and quetzal feathers were most prized), sometimes from distances of more than a thousand miles. Vast quantities of feathers were among the items of tribute brought to the rulers in Tenochtitlan, the capital of the domain (see the Codex Mendoza listing shown on page 115).

This has been traditionally called "Montezuma's Mantle" in the records of the European museum that owns it, but the feathers turn out to have come from Brazilian species of birds. It may have been collected in that area in the last century and mislabeled. Nevertheless this magnificent full-length garment conveys something of the grandeur that would have characterized the best specimens of Mesoamerican feather work.

From Father Sahagún's monumental report on Aztec customs, we see scenes depicting feather craft. Here, the emperor Montezuma praises a merchant arriving with a shipment of feathers from a distant land.

In his workshop a virtuoso designer prepares varied, lovely pieces; probably no two were alike.

This headdress is one of the few featherwork specimens that the early Spaniards sent to Europe and that have been preserved in museum collections.

These multihued delicacies of every size were passed to extended families or guilds of feather experts to be groomed and sorted. Master artists then designed objects intended to strike the fancy of royalty or other wealthy patrons or to be sold in the marketplace. Cane or reed frameworks provided a backing to which feathers were glued or tied in rendering the design. Most designs had some religious significance.

The Aztec feather workers lived in a special district in the capital city where they enjoyed privileged rank. They had their own gods and rites through which they sought protection and inspiration to assure that they would do quality work and not waste the precious, nonrecyclable materials. Among the art objects constructed were tall standards or flags of a sort, each of which identified a particular god, leader, kin group, warrior order, or community. Dancers gestured with specially made feather arrangements held in their hands. Or a person's arms, legs, ears, hair, or waist were decorated with tufts in some special style.

An accomplished dancer at the court required a variety of feather devices as part of his performance.

The pose of this Jaina-style figure from the western Maya area around A.D. 700 suggests the use of priestly or lordly rhetoric to teach, please, and persuade audiences.

Oratory and Poetics

Facility in speech was highly prized in most ancient American cultures. Examples of oratory from Mesoamerica preserved from the time of the Spanish Conquest demonstrate to what a high level this art form had been developed.

Written sacred texts were at the core of much oral performance. The writings contained fundamental information about many subjects—history, famous people, the calendars, astronomy, mythology, characteristics of the gods, and ritual. But in order for the glyphic characters to be fully interpreted, readers of the written text needed or were greatly benefited by extensive oral learning. The Aztec *calmecac* or school demonstrates the pattern of use of the later Mexican documents. Priests and teachers explained and interpreted the painted codices in detail, making their young students memorize extensive commentaries about the texts (comparable in function to Jewish midrashic literature). The commentaries were lectures on moral, religious, historical, and poetic matters. In southern Mesoamerica, the texts themselves, rather than commentaries, were more often studied, but only experts were thought to have a complete knowledge of the texts.

The ability to memorize that resulted allowed those properly schooled to incorporate long oral excerpts when they spoke on public occasions. They were called upon as priestly teachers to exhort, encourage, and critique personal and group behavior, information, and ideas. The test of a wise man or skilled teacher was his mastery of the content of the records and his ability to weave them with skill into an oral performance.

Munro Edmonson has pointed out that much of everyday speech among the Quiché Maya of highland Guatemala even today remains repetitive, poetic, literary, and oratorical, like the texts preserved from earlier times. Nuances of the Quiché language are still used to produce effects that are "comic," "elegant," moving, or "discursive." "Words matter, and formal discourse matters even more."[141] This love of speaking and admiration for effective forms of speech led to deep appreciation for oratory as art. A great, wise, powerful public figure ought to have superb speaking skills, it was felt. One of the titles of the Aztec ruler was Great Orator. We may suppose that some of the lay population also gained substantial oral facility involving some of the formal texts in order to participate in ceremonial events.

Among the forms of oral literature were epic and lyric poems, hymns, songs,

The extensive records of Aztec oral art that were transcribed by Father Sahagun and others in early-sixteenth-century Mexico show how much exhortation was laid upon members of that society. In this example, a father presses his son in powerful language to plan for a successful life with patient preparation.

Even though you may long for women,
hold back, hold back with your heart
until you are a grown man, strong and robust.
Look at the maguey plant.
If it is opened before it has grown
and its liquid is taken out,
it has no substance.
It does not produce liquid; it is useless.
Before it is opened
to withdraw its water,
it should be allowed to grow and attain full size.
Then its sweet water is removed
all in good time.

This is how you must act:
before you know woman
you must grow and be a complete man.
And then you will be ready for marriage;
you will beget children of good stature,
healthy, agile, and comely.

sagas, histories, and dramatic presentations that combined music, symbolic costumes for the characters, recitations, and dance. An Aztec category, which may have been equally common among other Mesoamerican peoples, was called *huehuetlatolli,* or "speeches of the elders." These long discourses of exhortation and warning were given on occasions of important social transition—the coronation of a ruler, birth, reaching adolescence, marriage, even death. They taught the most profound values of society, warning the person to be humble and diligent in the face of the new role and the burdens being assumed.

While we today distinguish poetry from other forms of speech, Mesoamericans did so only to a limited degree. Admired everyday speech verged into formal oratory, and poetic elements infused both. However, the fundamental poetic form, Edmonson reminds us, was semantic;[142] they did not use word rhymes or meter. Rather, successive lines or statements were connected by the repetition of words closely linked in meaning. These forms frequently involving puns or allusions to history and mythology. Couplets—a single concept repeated in two forms—were often used for emphasis and to please the ear, such as in the Aztec characterization of an accomplished oral artist: "he has flowers on his lips . . . flowers come from his mouth."[143]

The power of prayer, chanting, or singing to the heavens is suggested by what may be the earliest (about 400–300 B.C.) carved monument from highland Guatemala. In any case, this kilted man is engaged in serious, probably ritual, activity. This piece was found in the ruin of a sacred structure at the site that some Latter-day Saints consider to have been the city of Nephi (Kaminaljuyu, in suburban Guatemala City).

VISUALIZING BOOK OF MORMON LIFE

Ancient Israelite writers used the same couplet form found among the Quiché, and it occurs in the Book of Mormon too. For example, compare Psalms 47:5, "God is gone up with a shout, the Lord with the sound of a trumpet," with 2 Nephi 25:2, "Their works were works of darkness, and their doings were doings of abominations."[144] A more extended form of parallel phrasing is called chiasmus (see sidebar), and it too occurs in the Bible and the Book of Mormon and among native peoples in southern Mesoamerica.

Other poetic forms are also shared in Old Testament, Nephite, and Mesoamerican literary expression.[145] One of these combines two adjectives with narrow meanings to signify a more general concept. For example, in Job 29:8, the combination of "the young men" plus "the aged" conveys the meaning everybody; Psalms 95:5 uses "the sea" and "the dry land" to stand for all creation. Alma 37:7 means continually when it couples "liest down at night" and "risest in the morning." Among the Aztecs, the expression "skirt and blouse" signified the sexual aspect of a woman, while "face and hear" referred to personality.

The love of and facility with language manifested in the materials from Mexico and Central America recall the Nephite ideal of being "learned [with] a perfect knowledge of the language of the people."

At one extreme such mastery allowed one to "use much flattery, and much power of speech" (Jacob 7:4). But the Mesoamerican love of skilled speech also resonates with Moroni$_2$'s statement that the Lord had "made us mighty in word" (though not in writing). "Thou hast made all this people that they could speak much" (Ether 12:23), indeed, "Thou hast . . . made our words powerful and great" (Ether 12:25).

From the Mayan Dresden Codex, a text and illustration represent an ancient flood, part of a myth cycle widely shared throughout Mesoamerica (as well as in southern and eastern Asia) that tells of the destruction of the world by different catastrophes.

Chiasmus

One of the stylistic devices that aided ancient people in memorizing and recalling long oral texts was chiasmus. It consists of a pattern of word arrangement that presents a subject in stepwise fashion from beginning to a climax statement, then reverses the order, ending with the same concept with which the piece began. It was often used in the Bible and in Near Eastern and Greek literature.[146] John W. Welch first detected this form in the Book of Mormon thirty years ago and has since shown that it was often used and highly developed in Nephite texts.[147] More recently the form has been shown to characterize native Mayan literature that dates before those people were made acquainted with the Bible by the Spaniards. The example here compares a chiasm in the Popol Vuh, the sacred book of the Quiché Maya, with a passage from the Book of Mormon.

Book of Mormon (Mosiah 5:10–12)

And now whosoever shall not take upon them *the name* of Christ
must *be called* by some other name;
therefore he findeth himself *on the left hand of God.*
And I would that ye should remember that this is the *name*
that should never be *blotted out*
except it be through *transgression*; therefore
take heed that ye do not *transgress*
that the name be not *blotted out* of your hearts
I would that ye should remember to retain this *name*
that ye are not found *on the left hand of God*,
but that ye hear and know the voice by which ye shall *be called*
and also *the name* by which he shall call you.

Popol Vuh

"At, *u K'ux Kah*, . . .	"Oh *Heart of Heaven*, . . .
Nabe q'ut *vinaqir*	and once *it had been created*,
Ulev,	*the earth*,
Huyub, tak'ah,	*the mountains* and valleys,
X ch'oboch'ox u be ha	The *paths of the waters were divided*
X biniheyik k'olehe r aquan xol tak huyub.	and they proceeded to twist along among the hills
Xa ch'obol chik x e q'ohe vi *ha*	So the *rivers then became more divided*
Ta x k'utuniheyik nimaq *huyub*.	As *the great mountains* were appearing.
Kehe q'ut u vinaqirik *ulev*	And thus was the creation of *the earth*
Ri ta x *vinaquirik* k umal ri	When it was *created by him*
U K'ux Kah	Who is the *Heart of Heaven*

Music and Dance

As with the oral arts, so with music and dance: long traditions lay behind the forms and cultural standards that were in vogue in Mesoamerica at the time the Europeans arrived. Increasingly, careful looks by scholars at the carved monuments and painted vases of the Classic Maya reveal that dance was common and that probably few if any serious or ceremonial events in public failed to involve both music and dancing. It is from the Aztec culture that we learn the most regarding these arts because of the relatively full descriptions left to us by the first Spanish priests to arrive in central Mexico.

As might be supposed in a civilization as involved with religion as that of Mesoamerica, much of the music and dance was performed on ceremonial occasions. On the basis of the scenes painted on vases found in Maya tombs, Michael D. Coe believes that rites for the interred dead might well have used the text of "a long hymn which could have been sung over the dead or dying person."[148] The Spaniards mentioned compositions that nobles or priests danced to and sung or chanted slowly and seriously on solemn and important occasions. Other types of music and dance were livelier and included songs of love and flirtation. Still another sort scandalized the Catholic fathers as "highly improper" with "wriggling and grimacing and immodest mimicry."[149]

The most common musical instruments

This ninth-century A.D. Maya mural at Bonampak shows long wooden trumpets blown as part of a procession of nobles. One music scholar has claimed that these instruments are similar in form and maybe in function to silver trumpets mentioned in the Bible in Numbers 10:1–10.[150]

were rhythmic (drums, scrapers, rattles), but melodic ones were also heard, including whistles, flutes, panpipes, long single-toned horns, trumpets of hollowed wood, and shell trumpets. No remnants of actual music have been preserved for us to hear today.

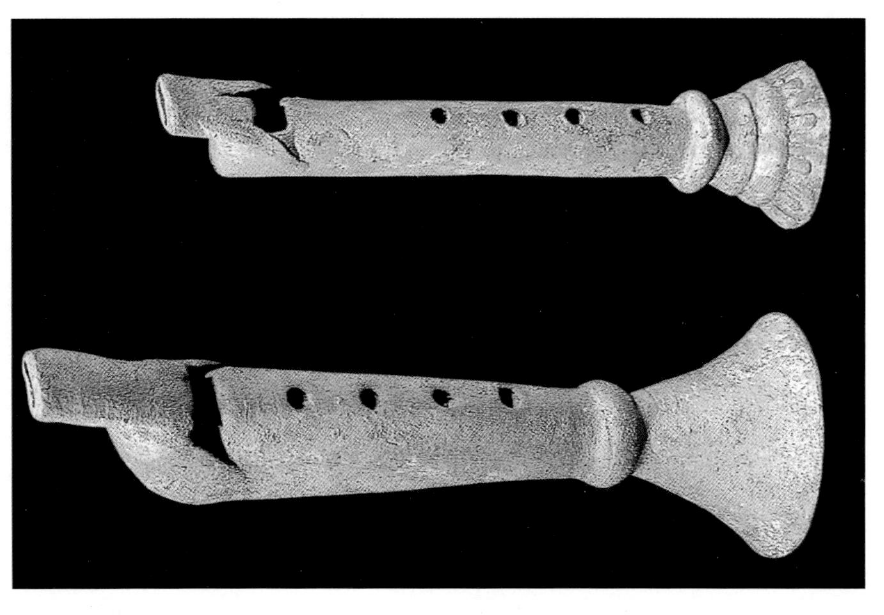

These Aztec flutes or flageolets were excavated in Mexico City at the site of the Great Temple, which the Spanish conquerors destroyed.

VISUALIZING BOOK OF MORMON LIFE

Little is said about music and dance in the Book of Mormon. The use of music in Israelite rites at Jerusalem is reported in the Bible, and we can suppose that elements of that pattern were brought along by the people of Lehi (and the Mulekites) as part of the Mosaic ceremonies. They had musical and dance forms for entertainment too (see 1 Nephi 18:9 and Mosiah 20:1–5).

Men dance near a lord or priest seated on a platform. Many of the people shown on Classic Maya painted vases, like this one, are engaged in serious dance. Social, political, and ritual etiquette clearly demanded that a person of social stature be competent in a variety of dance forms.

A superb figurine in the Jaina style (ca. A.D. 700) has been called "The Troubadour" because it appears to represent a man singing.

This troupe of musicians and dancers are represented in Sahagun's record of Aztec life at the time of the Conquest.

A set of figurines dug up at Zaachila, Oaxaca, obviously represents a musical "combo." For what occasions they played we cannot guess.

The world tree in Maya belief was a ceiba, the tree that yields kapok. The tall, strong trunk lends itself to the idea of reaching into the heavens.

The complex mythological scene on Stela 5 at Izapa, Chiapas, has been interpreted variously. Many Latter-day Saints have considered it a symbolic depiction of Lehi's dream recorded in the Book of Mormon, following the views of M. Wells Jakeman. More recent, better-documented analyses take different positions regarding it.[159] But almost all agree that the tree of life is central in the scene.

Symbolism

Trees

Materials preserved from an ancient people use a profusion of symbols impossible to grasp in full because we cannot fully recover their complex view of the world. In Mesoamerica a host of exotic symbols is evident. To attempt to grasp them involves seeing both their strangeness and their likeness to our meanings.

A first level of understanding is simply to appreciate how great the chasm is between their view of the world and ours. Yet, some meanings seem well-nigh universal, such as the opposition between light (good) and dark (evil), or between right (lucky) and left (unlucky). A few similarities like those let us feel a common humanity with the ancients.

The tree as a symbol is one feature the Mesoamericanas emphasized. The growth and death of trees, their fruit, and the shelter they provide represented individual, social, and divine activity. A common notion in Mesoamerica is the "world tree." A pillarlike tree was said by the Maya to represent the first tree of the world. It was supposed to exist at the center of the world, or navel of the earth, where it grew up through the layered heavens; its trunk served as a route for moving between levels. The tree's root connected the multiple underground levels.[151] Other Mesoamerican peoples had similar ideas. Related conceptions occurred in other parts of the world (for example, the city of Jerusalem was conceived as the navel of the world).[152]

Another meaning spoke of the tree of life. Some Mesoamericans thought that it had nourished the infant founders of their group and had thus, in a sense, given them life. That concept was associated with the representation of a tribe or descent group as a tree, with the founder as the trunk.[153] The tree of life also had the sense of a sacred objective that worshippers sought to attain in order to confer life on the seeker. In the last sense, Mesoamerican beliefs paralleled religious ideas in the Near East and Southeast Asia.[154] It was in this sense that certain trees, and even groves, were considered necessary at temple centers and sacred areas in general. For example, the Maya of Yucatan combined the idea of the world tree and of a sacred grove located at a sacred well at the navel of the world in the center of certain cities,[155] and the same combination characterized Near Eastern sacred centers.[156]

Alfred Maudslay's century-old drawing of this famous sculptured panel at Palenque displays the same basic features as the Assyrian scene shown above it.[160]

In the famous tomb deep beneath the Temple of the Inscriptions at Palenque, a prominent seventh-century ruler of the city, Pacal, is represented on this superbly carved stone cover of his burial sarcophagus as sliding or falling down the world tree axis into the underworld in a metaphor associated with the setting of the sun.

A descent group, the Xiu family of Yucatan, displayed for their colonial Spanish masters their royal descent in the form of a tree, with the current family head at the bottom.

VISUALIZING BOOK OF MORMON LIFE

Tree symbolism pervades the Book of Mormon. $Lehi_1$ and $Nephi_1$ each saw in vision "the tree of life," which was "precious above all" (1 Nephi 11:9) and "whose fruit was desirable to make one happy" (1 Nephi 8:10).[157] $Jacob_1$, the first priest among the Nephites, expounded an involved allegory in which trees represented Israelite tribes (see Jacob 5).[158] $Alma_2$ compared the word of God to a seed planted in the human heart that could be nurtured to become a tree of life (see Alma 32:28–42).

Warriors and priests who wished to emulate the jaguar or who felt under its protection wore skins of the feline to cultivate the link. This man appears in the Tudela Codex from central Mexico.

Symbolism

Felines

Norman refers to the jaguar as "the most impressive zoological motif" in Mesoamerican art, yet it had religious significance beyond being just an art motif. Some of its popularity derived from the animal's standing as "the New World 'king of the beasts' with wide-ranging mystic and shamanistic qualities."[161] This conception of the jaguar is widespread in tropical America. Mainly its associations are malevolent: "The fierce jaguar. Bloody his mouth; bloody his claws. A slayer as well. Devourer of flesh. Killer of men."[162]

Appropriately, the jaguar was a prime symbol of the god of the underworld, where the spirits of the dead had to go. (Thus, in a sense, the god/animal eventually "ate" everybody.) This supreme cat prowled the jungle during the night hours, when it was supposed that the sun was passing through the underworld. The beast's independence of movement and freedom from enemies who could injure him was also admired, though this admiration was tinged with fear. Jaguars were also envied because they were considered to live a lazy life of ease. One can see how these characteristics would be attractive to power-hungry rulers[163] or perhaps secret-society adherents.

A different version of the jaguar was associated with sky, rain, moisture, and fertility.[164] But the dual connection is not far-fetched because the seas, the ultimate source for rain, were thought to be underground, so to speak, and thus connected with the underworld feline. Furthermore, in nature jaguars often live in jungle areas with abundant water and vegetation.

In the Near East, incidentally, the lion represented the Sumerian and Canaanite Nergal, god of the underworld and burial; the lion was also connected to kingship, because he was also considered the sun god who spent the night in the underworld.[165]

The jaguar in the wild is still greatly feared wherever it is found in the lower forestlands of Mesoamerica.

This representation on Relief 4 at Chalcatzingo, Morelos, has been interpreted as the night jaguar capturing the day's light.[166] But it could just as well represent a vicious man under the influence of his jaguar nawal attacking a human victim, actually or politically.

VISUALIZING BOOK OF MORMON LIFE

In the Nephite record, the lion is represented as a predator that was dangerous to domestic animals and who also was an instrument of divine vengeance (see 3 Nephi 20:16; 21:12; Mormon 5:24). The association of the lion with the office of the king of Judah would have been familiar to the Nephites through the brass plates record they brought with them.

HYBRID BEINGS

The neat zoological categories—feline, snake, bird—that we would feel comfortable with in trying to deal with Mesoamerican symbolism refused to stand still in ancient thought and art. After all, these are supernatural, not merely naturalistic, beings, and it is their symbols we are seeing, so why should they be confined by earth's natural forms? So in symbolic form, jaguars sometimes prove to be half serpents, or reptiles may bear feathers and fly about.

Even more striking is the hybridization of animals with humans. One of the most ancient versions of this unity is seen in the Olmec practice of turning images with largely human bodies into effigies with jaguar characteristics, especially by drooping the corners of the mouth. One proposal to account for these distortions of nature is that what we are seeing stems from shamans' experience with trances. Another view is that the use of hallucinogenic substances by artists played a part in generating these unusual concepts.

This classic Olmec sculpture from Las Limas, Veracruz, shows a man holding a passive infant with jaguar facial characteristics. The piece is now in the Museum in Jalapa, Veracruz.

The coyote was an important figure in the mythology of the Nahua-speaking peoples, who included the Toltecs and Aztecs. This feathered coyote[167] from Teotihuacan may be connected to that myth cycle.

Unique hybrid creatures are represented in this artist's copy of a mural called "The Mythological Animals," at Teotihuacan.

The massive, armored crocodile, or cayman, thrives in certain areas of the Mesoamerican lowlands. Known as *cipactli* among the Aztec and the *imix* earth monster in Mayan iconography, this symbol conveys the sense of the interior of the earth and underworld.[171] In Mesoamerican sacred art, features of the jaguar and other animals were at times combined with those of the cayman so the figure turns out a fantastic hybrid.

Symbolism

Reptilian Figures

Reptiles—snakes, crocodiles, and even dragons—constituted another complex category of symbols of divinity. One connotation these creatures convey is obvious—danger! These are beasts not to be toyed with, so a reptile could be a very potent nawal protector. A second symbolic meaning comes from the reptile's connection with water. While not all reptiles are found near water sources, some of the most fearsome, like crocodiles, are, hence there is logic to the linkage. Water is one of the ultimate life-giving realities in Mesoamerica; either too much or too little can be disastrous, so one wants to be on the good side of the powers controlling the moisture. Moreover, reptiles were thought to be connected not just with water but most often with the subterranean world, where Mesoamerican thinking supposed the great supply of waters, and the dead, were located. The earth was considered to rest on the back of a great reptilian creature that floated on the underearth ocean. This monster was modeled on the crocodile, although its appearance could take variant forms. Many sculptured scenes show at their base this subearth creature, often very stylized and hard for the inexpert eye to detect.[168]

Another Mesoamerican reptilian symbol is a dragonlike being connected with the sky and rain; its two-headed symbol is spread widely in east Asia as well as the Americas.[169] Yet sky and earth elements are so often combined that a reptile above and another beneath are hard to separate.

In the Bible, the Israelite myth of Leviathan (mirroring the Babylonian myth of Tiamat) also portrays a dragon in the waters under the earth. Jehovah was considered to have conquered this monster at one point in mythological time.[170]

Snakes are found throughout the art of Mesoamerica, a fact that is not surprising since snakes are common in the tropics. The symbolism conveyed includes both positive and negative aspects. The god Quetzalcoatl (see below) was pictured as a serpent that blessed, but other manifestations, such as this Aztec coiled rattlesnake, were threatening.

RAIN AND THE EARTH MONSTER

The monster/dragon/serpent was associated not only with night and the underworld abode of the dead but also with life-giving rain. Izapa Stela 25 signals this dual nature of reptilians. They can damage or they can bless. A dualistic balance appears, as it does with much Mesoamerican symbolism. Men live by the grace of the life-conferring power of divinity at the same time they are at risk from encountering or managing that power in the wrong way; there is "an opposition in all things" (2 Nephi 2:11).

Norman interprets this scene (enlarged at right) as depicting the action of the god who confers or controls the rains (compare Helaman 11:4–17). In his view, symbolic representations of the evaporation–precipitation cycle, a metaphor for resurrection, are found on this stela.[172]

Stela 25 at Izapa (first century B.C.) shows a cayman with vegetation growing from its body, which ties the creature unmistakably to the earth monster of later Mesoamerican tradition. This scene represents a specific mythic event told in the Popol Vuh in which a crocodile bites off the arm of a hero-god.[173]

VISUALIZING BOOK OF MORMON LIFE

The Book of Mormon uses reptilian imagery in several ways. (1) "That old serpent" in the Garden of Eden was the devil—beguiler, antagonist, destroyer (2 Nephi 2:18; Mosiah 16:3). (2) "That awful monster the devil, and death, and hell" (2 Nephi 9:19; see 9:10, 26; compare 2 Nephi 24:9) was both a metaphorical being and a place associated with the death of the body (see 2 Nephi 9:10). (3) This monster is likely the same as the reptile of chaos, Leviathan in the Bible (see 2 Nephi 8:9; Isaiah 27:1); filthy waters beneath the earth represent hell, the abode of this serpent/dragon (see 1 Nephi 12:16). But water from beneath the earth could also be considered "pure," as shown by Mosiah 18:5, which recalls a Maya practice of entering caves for the purpose of obtaining sacred water for use in some ceremonies. (4) "Like dragons did they fight" (Mosiah 20:11; see Alma 43:44) was an expression used by the Nephites to connote strength and vigor in battle. It could well refer to the Mesoamerican cayman, or crocodile, which is a powerful, fearsome foe.[174] (5) Moses erected the brass image of a benign serpent in order to heal the Israelites who had been bitten by hurtful "fiery flying serpents" (1 Nephi 17:41; compare Numbers 21:6). This image was treated by the Nephites as a symbol of Jesus Christ and his healing power and superiority over mundane evil (see Helaman 8:14; 2 Nephi 25:20; Alma 33:19). The fact that the saving serpent icon was lifted "upon a pole" could remind one of the "flying" aspect of the Mesoamerican feathered hybrid serpent.

Book of Mormon Peoples and History

The first part of this book related information on Book of Mormon peoples and cultures to their Mesoamerican setting, topic by topic. While that approach has value in being systematic, it leaves issues of history and geography in limbo. What follows will connect the Nephite story to the Mesoamerican scene in terms of the broader topics of times and places.

Key to Numbers

1. Waters of Ripliancum
2. Limit of Nephite retreat
3. Shiz's death; plates left
4. Hill Shim
5. Narrow passage
6. Hagoth's ships
7. Moroni's camp
8. Refuge between the land of Bountiful and the land of Zarahemla (see 3 Nephi 3)
9. Hill Onidah
10. Hill Manti
11. Hill Amnihu
12. Hill Riplah
13. Valley of Alma
14. Missionary dispersal point
15. Waters of Mormon
16. Hill north of Shilom
17. Mount Antipas
18. Place Onidah
19. Wilderness west of the land of Zarahemla
20. Wilderness west of the land of Nephi
21. Lamanite king's land
22. Land of first inheritance
23. Wilderness (see Alma 43:22)
24. Mountain pass
25. Hagoth's destination (?)
26. Wilderness of Hermounts

□ Land: no city mentioned
River tributaries illustrative only

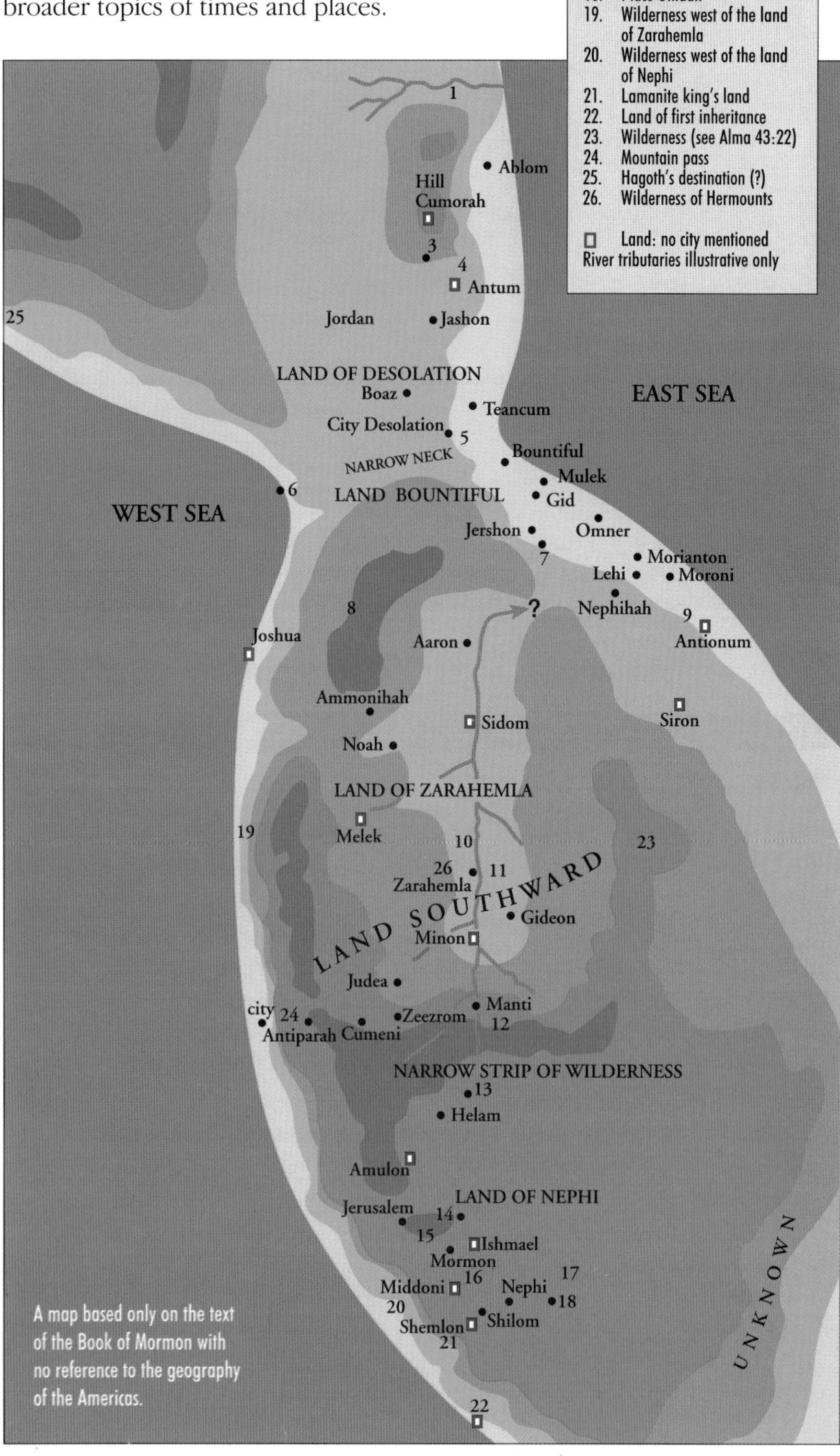

A map based only on the text of the Book of Mormon with no reference to the geography of the Americas.

Mormon's Map in Relation to Mesoamerica

Mesoamerica is the only part of the western hemisphere that qualifies as the Nephites' "land of promise." Just where were the Nephites located within Mesoamerica? Only when we have an idea of that can we know which historical traditions or archaeological sequences can be compared most usefully with Mormon's text. The internal consistency of the geographical statements in the Book of Mormon referred to earlier must be accounted for by assuming that the primary author and editor of the Book of Mormon, the fourth-century A.D. prophet-general Mormon, had a definite mental map in mind. (This consistency cannot be accounted for in terms of Joseph Smith, for his translation of the volume was dictated at such a pace and published with so little revision of content that he could not have accurately crafted the picture of spatial relations involved in the complex story.)[175] The brief biographical material on Mormon included in his account tells us that he personally traveled throughout most of Nephite territory (see Mormon chapters 1–6). The consistency exhibited by his geographical statements must have come primarily from his own experience with the landscape.

The map on this page shows what we can discern of Mormon's picture of spatial relations in what the Nephites called the land of promise.[176] The territory it encompassed, as indicated by statements in the scriptural text, was on the order of five or six hundred miles long and a couple of hundred miles wide. The major contrast was between a "land southward" and a "land northward," (Alma 22:32), which were connected by an isthmus, a narrow neck of land. The southerly territory was in turn divided in two: a general "land of Nephi" consisted of mainly mountainous terrain distinctly set off in topography from the lower-lying "land of Zarahemla," which lay in a northerly direction (Alma 22:32). Only one major river is noted, the Sidon (Alma 22:29), whose basin constituted most of the land of Zarahemla. The climate was tropical or semitropical, although areas of higher elevation would necessarily have been cooler.

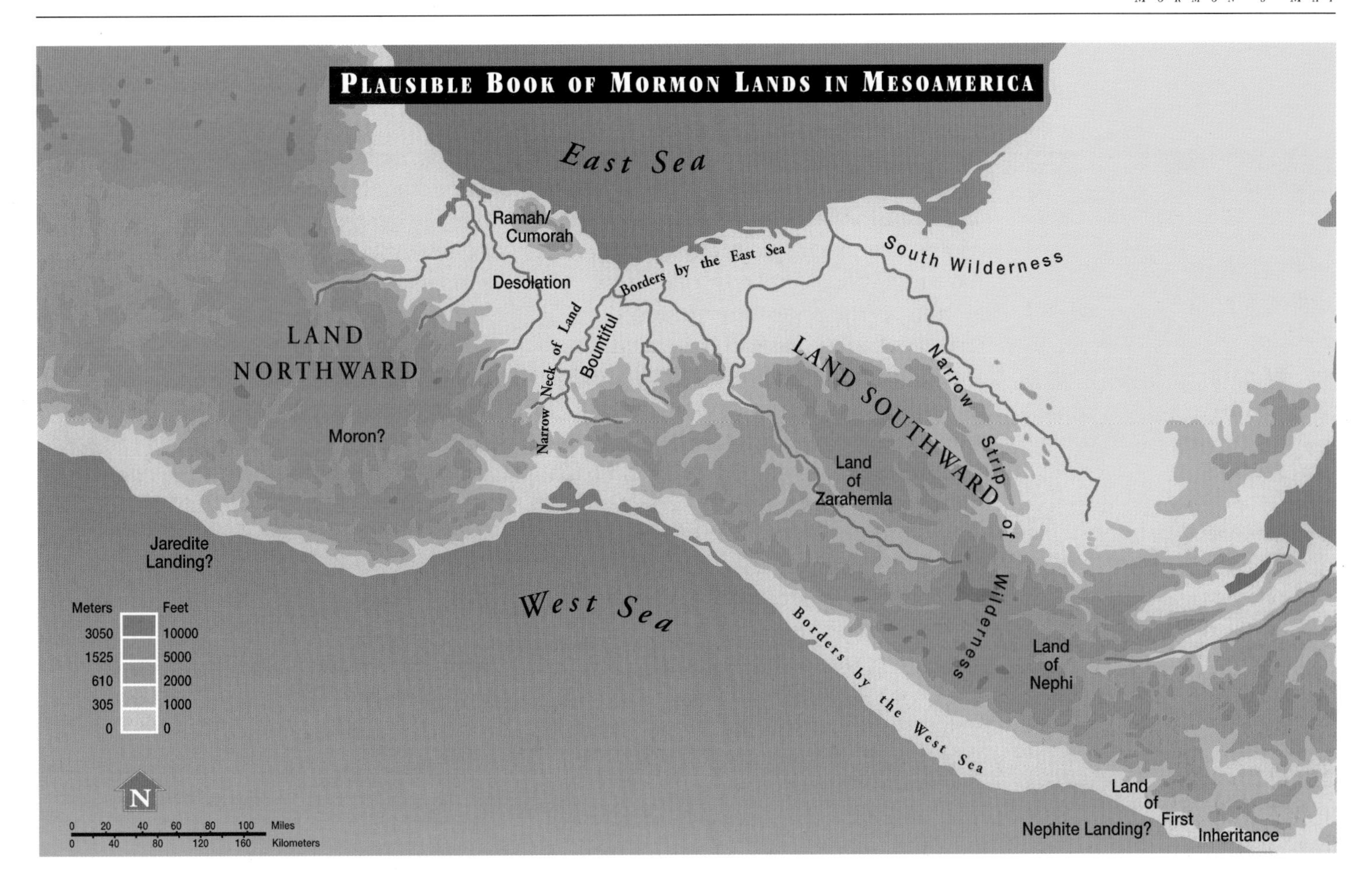

Characteristics of the civilization in which the Nephites participated are often mentioned or implied but are not reported in much specific detail. Mormon's record pictures his people having an agrarian economic base, a population in the millions, many cities, extensive commerce, numerous books written in more than one script, elaborate religious institutions, intensive warfare, and many luxury goods.

When Mormon's geography and the characteristics of the civilization involved are compared with possible scenes in the Americas, only one area fits consistently: Mesoamerica, that is, central and southern Mexico and northern Central America. Only in this one area do we find the required combination of uplands and lowlands, an isthmus and river system, a warm climate, and an advanced, literate civilization.

The map on this page displays the most likely specific correlation between "Mormon's map" and Mesoamerican territory. The lands of the Nephites, it turns out, probably comprised highland Guatemala (although that land was possessed much of the time by the Lamanite faction), Chiapas, and areas to the north and west of Chiapas extending to central Veracruz. (Some Latter-day Saint students of Nephite geography have differed from this schema on important details.)[177]

Identifying on today's map where the Nephites and other peoples of the Book of Mormon story lived opens up important new sources of information on them. On the basis of this correlation, we can tap into the information that scientists and scholars have been accumulating about Mesoamerica for a hundred years.

The conjunction of scriptural information with the facts from scholarly study of Mesoamerica sheds new light on the Book of Mormon in two ways. First, obscure portions of the Book of Mormon text may be clarified. For example, Mosiah 19:24 speaks of a "ceremony" in connection with the slaying of king Noah by his rebellious subjects, but there is no hint of the nature or pupose of that ceremony. Much information is available on Mesoamerican ceremonial practices involving death and sacrifice, and it may clarify the mystery of the strange ritual. Second, identification of the area as the scene of Book of Mormon events can bring to readers a sense of realism hitherto missing in their studies.

But before Nephite events can be compared usefully and accurately with Mesoamerican history, qualifications about the data on both sides of the prospective equation need to be recognized.

Nephite History

NEPHI LINEAGE RECORD KEEPERS

Nephi
*Jacob**
Enos
Jarom
Omni
*Chemish**
Abinadom
Amaleki
Mosiah*
Benjamin
Mosiah
Alma*
Alma
Helaman
Nephi
Nephi
Nephi
Amos
Amos
Ammaron*
Mormon*
Moroni

* record not passed from father to son
italic sacred record
bold king

Readers have often erred in expecting the Book of Mormon to be a history in the sense of that word common among us nowadays. Nowhere in the writings of Mormon or of his son, $Moroni_2$, is the book they produced termed a history; instead it is called "an abridgement of the record of the people of Nephi" and an "account" (see title page). *History* is a label that comes from modern thought; we typically suppose that a history presents a more or less continuous and thorough account of what happened—of all the important events—within a certain area over a certain period. With rare, partial exceptions, the ancients had neither the access to adequate information nor the desire to produce such a systematic discussion. We should not expect of their record what it does not intend. What Mormon meant to do was teach readers certain moral lessons by citing selected episodes from events that occurred among his people, not to tell their whole story.

In ancient cultures a people was most often defined in terms of descent from a claimed ancestor. On the title page of the Book of Mormon, $Moroni_2$, its last custodian, spoke of "the people of Nephi." It is not clear what he meant in regard to ancestry and descent when he used this expression. The phrases *the people of Nephi* and *the Nephites* are used in the book with more than one meaning. On the face of it, we might think they referred to those literally descended from $Nephi_1$, the son of $Lehi_1$. That proves an oversimplification. Most often the label *Nephites* is applied to all those who acknowledged the sovereignty of $Nephi_1$'s descendants, even though the subjects had no genetic connection with the founding ancestor, $Nephi_1$, or his family. Legitimate rulers came from $Nephi_1$'s direct descendants, but diverse groups came under their political umbrella by a kind of adoption process well-known in the ancient world. Meanwhile dissenters—although sometimes literal descendants of $Nephi_1$—opted out of the political system and were no longer counted as Nephites. Examples demonstrate the pattern: certain Lamanites "took upon themselves the name of Nephi, that they might be called the children of Nephi and be numbered among those who were called Nephites" (Mosiah 25:12); however, the Zoramite faction went the other direction—they changed from the sociopolitical category of Nephite to that of Lamanite by secession (see Alma 43:4). Other cases could be cited. Furthermore, the Book of Mormon quietly lets us know that other people, not just those from Lehi's initial party, were on the scene.[178] Those inhabitants willing to be subject to the ruler, the descendant of $Nephi_1$, were also included among the Nephites.

The Book of Mormon proves to be a record of only selected events that particularly affected the royal line. Much that went on among the diverse groups under the Nephite rulers is given short shrift or no mention at all. Moreover, ethnic, linguistic, and cultural variety could also be expected among those under Lamanite rulers. Thus the book is not a history in the modern sense. This is to be expected in the light of ancient record-keeping practices. For example, the Old Testament, a version of which the Nephites possessed and which served them as a model for recording their past, relates only a limited range of events about the patriarch Jacob's descendants, with strong emphasis on the royal line through Judah. In short, Mormon's record is a lineage history, the typical kind of account of the past that was produced in most societies before European historians developed a broadened view of their task a few centuries ago. Many events that we moderns may be curious about were omitted because a lineage's writers did not consider them relevant to their aims.

In Mesoamerica virtually all traditional histories were by and about lineages (using the term broadly),[179] as was true in the Near East. The records were about the ruling groups, not the commoners. For instance, the historical portions of the Popol Vuh tell of a small group of foreigners (of Mexican extraction) who invaded Guatemala a few centuries before the Spaniards and gained military control over the resident Mayan-speaking population. In the course of a number of generations, those elite intruders were culturally absorbed by their subjects, but the document fails to make that clear.

What we know about the record from which the Book of Mormon was translated by Joseph Smith indicates that it was one of the class of Mesoamerican lineage histories recorded in the form of a codex.[180] The Book of Mormon talks chiefly about the elite stratum of society, and it was rulers or their kin who kept the Nephite records. Naturally enough, they give us little information about the commoner majority whom they ruled. The scribes themselves emphasize how selective they had to be in deciding what to include (see, for example, Jacob 3:13; Words of Mormon 1:5; and Helaman 3:14). Because the record is silent on whole topics, it, like the Popol Vuh, can be compared only with difficulty with the archaeological and inscriptional record of ancient Mesoamerican life.

Did the Mesoamericans Write Real History?

Questions are sometimes raised whether the Mesoamerican scribes had developed historical writing in anything like our modern sense. Some scholars suspect that myth or ideological interpretations played such a big role that we do not really get any reliable reports of historical events in the ancient sources. Despite some coloring of accounts, it appears that it was possible, in some cases at least, for native historians to report events in an informative, sequential manner. That is illustrated in an excerpt from the *Annals of the Cakchiquels,* a sixteenth-century account from highland Guatemala of an event that happened not long before the Spanish Conquest and that had no doubt been transmitted via a hieroglyphic text down to Colonial times, when it was written in Spanish script.

When the sun appeared on the horizon and its light fell on the mountain, the outcry and shouts of war broke forth, banners were unfurled, and the big flutes, drums, and conch shells resounded. It was indeed terrible when the Quichés arrived. But with great speed they [the Cakchiquels] went down to surround them, concealing themselves so as to form a circle; and arriving at the foot of the hill, they went close to the banks of the river, cutting off the river houses from the servants of the kings Tepépul and Ixtáyul who were accompanying their god. Immediately was the enounter. Truly the contest was terrible. The outcries resounded, the shouts of war, the flutes, the drums, and the conch shells; then the warriors performed their acts of magic. Quickly the Quichés were defeated; they ceased to fight and were dispersed, annihilated and dead. It was impossible to count the dead. . . .

Recinos 1950

Book of Mormon Peoples in Terms of Mesoamerica

The peoples, cultures, or ruling lineages known to scholars who study Mesoamerica are called, especially in popular books, by names like *Aztecs, Zapotecs, Mayas,* and *Olmecs.* None of them are known to have been called Nephites. (Keep in mind that since "none other people knoweth our language," according to $Moroni_2$ in Mormon 9:34, we have no linguistic clue to what the term translated to English as "Nephites" might have been in any Mesoamerican language.) Were the Nephites in any sense ancestors of the Aztecs? Were the Toltecs of Mesoamerican tradition descended from the Nephites? Were the Mayas Lamanites in Mormon's terms? To provide useful answers to questions like these, we must be aware that archaeologists cannot directly answer questions about the identity of the peoples whose remains they investigate. New World excavators never find inscriptions that proclaim, "We are the people named such and such."

The whole topic of ethnic identification is a confused one in scholarly studies on Mesoamerica. Rarely is a people's own name for themselves used in either scholarly or popular literature. Well-known terms like *Toltec* have no settled historical meaning but are unclear catchalls. Other ethnic labels like *Aztec* and *Chichimec,* let alone *Olmec,* are equally murky.[181] In many cases archaeologists use labels they have coined to denote mere pottery complexes as if they represented peoples, which they surely do not.

In the absence of crucial information as just indicated, any attempt to compare Mormon's account with the findings of archaeology and related fields is bound to be ambiguous. Nobody can say at this time who the scriptural Nephites were in Mesoamerican terms. Yet we may approximate a relationship if we can correctly identify the time and place where they lived.

The probability is that the Nephite and Lamanite ruling lineages whom we read about in Mormon's book represented portions of societies that were found in highland Guatemala and the Mexican state of Chiapas during at least the first and second centuries B.C. From that time to the middle of the fourth century A.D., there is evidence that these possible Nephites expanded into the states of Veracruz and perhaps parts of Oaxaca, Mexico. They probably gathered in southern Veracruz to make their last stand near A.D. 380.

A striking bowl from the state of Campeche dating to the Late Classic period shows an old man with a Jewish-looking profile. We catch only occasional glimpses like this of a Near Eastern component in the Mesoamerican peoples, who are typically called, oversimply, Maya or the like.

CHRONOLOGY OF NEPHITE EVENTS COMPARED WITH MESOAMERICAN CULTURAL HISTORY

Date	Book of Mormon: Land Northward	Book of Mormon: Land Southward	Mesoamerica: North of Isthmus	Mesoamerica: South of Isthmus	Period
			Various States	"Classic Maya"	LATE CLASSIC
600	Prophetic view: wars, "abominations"		Teotihuacan influence declines	Maya stelae cease	
500					EARLY CLASSIC
	Wars continue among non-Nephites		Teotihuacan groups spread widely Militarism increasing; cults abound		
400	Nephites exterminated Nephites retreat north			Chiapas abandoned	
300	War, turmoil spread Widespread trade Cults, priests flourish Dynamic, prosperous society Classes reappear		Peak in cultural creativity Priests flourish Surge in class symbols, trade		
200			Stable socioeconomic growth		PROTO-CLASSIC
100	Classless, theocratic-led society				
			Hesitation in growth Volcanic action		
A.D. 1	Great natural, social catastrophe Class distinctions, state rule Migrations northward Expansion of Nephite & Lamanite lineages and influence		Precursors of Classic at Tikal, Monte Alban, Cuicuilco, etc. Izapan influences go north		LATE PRE-CLASSIC
100 B.C.					
200					
300					
400		Small tribes	Small sociopolitical chiefdoms		
500					MIDDLE PRE-CLASSIC
600	Approximate extermination of Jaredite lineages		Approximate end of Olmec civilization		

The Early Nephites in the Land of Nephi

The party led by Lehi$_1$ and his son Nephi$_1$ arrived by boat on the Pacific coast of Guatemala or El Salvador around 575 B.C. The aged father died soon afterward. Before long the antagonisms between Nephi$_1$ on the one hand and his older brothers Laman$_1$ and Lemuel on the other caused the little colony to split. Nephi$_1$ and a handful of followers moved inland to the highlands, which thereafter were always said to be "up" in relation to surrounding areas. In what must have been an extensive mountain valley, they laid out a small city named after their leader, and he became their first king. They called themselves Nephites or the people of Nephi. They immediately constructed a temple, said to be modeled after the temple that Nephi$_1$ had known in Jerusalem. Before long, their rivals, the Lamanites, reencountered them and armed conflict began between them that continued through most of the next six hundred years.

Topographical and other information in the Book of Mormon record neatly supports the proposition that the city of Nephi was located in the Valley of Guatemala. The preeminent archaeological site in that area, located in a suburb of the capital, Guatemala City, was one of the most important in Mesoamerica in the centuries just before the advent of Christ. It has been named Kaminaljuyu (pronounced kah-mee-nahl-hu-yu, often called KJ for short) by archaeologists, but they have no idea what the name was anciently. The first substantial inhabitation of the site has been found to date between 600 and 500 B.C. Meanwhile, the people whom the Nephites called the Lamanites dwelt in the coastal lowlands and foothill zone a few miles away to the south of Nephi$_1$'s settlement. Quite surely, descendants of Jaredite-era groups were then occupying portions of that lowland wilderness, and it looks as if some of them were incorporated under the rule of the Lamanite immigrants.

The highlands of Guatemala enjoyed a temperate climate and vegetation; the area has been called the land of eternal spring. In contrast, the coastal territory was oppressively hot and humid and much of it was covered with tropical forest.

The historical information covering the first three centuries in the Nephite record is exceptionally fragmentary (see the books of Jacob, Enos, and Jarom). There is no hint that their occupation extended outside the valley first settled and named by founder Nephi$_1$, and their numbers would have been limited to no more than a few thousand.

The valley seen here, where Guatemala City lies, has been identified by a number of students of Book of Mormon geography as the immediate land of Nephi, the first area settled by Nephi$_1$ and his party after separating from the Lamanite faction. The view from the vantage point of the photographer of this scene is the same as that Ammon$_1$ and his group would have had when they came into the land and paused "at a hill, which is north of the land of Shilom" (Mosiah 7:5). From there "they went down into the land of Nephi," where they met King Limhi (Mosiah 7:6).

From any part of the strip of wilderness near the Pacific coast, the lands along the west sea in southern Guatemala, the mountains are visible, beckoning with a promise of cooler climate.

This view is of the lower portion of the Valley of Guatemala. It meets the textual requirements to have been the land of Shilom of the Nephites. This section occupies several square miles and lies only about ten miles from Nephi, thought to have been at Kaminaljuyu. At the city of Nephi, King Noah climbed on a tower or pyramid where he could "overlook the land of Shilom" (Mosiah 11:12).

The Land of Zarahemla

In the third century B.C., Mosiah$_1$ was divinely instructed to lead a party out of the decadent Nephite society in the land of Nephi to a settlement called Zarahemla. Those left behind disappear from the history, presumably being exterminated or incorporated by the Lamanites. The account speaks of the course the refugees took as "down" (Omni 1:13), that is, out of the highlands of Nephi, across the narrow strip of wilderness, which seems to have been a mountainous watershed, and into the basin of the Sidon River. There they discovered a people more numerous than they, and Mosiah$_1$ became king over the combined Nephite migrants and the resident "people of Zarahemla" (Omni 1:19; see 1:12–4, 17; compare Alma 2:27–8).

The people of Zarahemla, or at least their leaders, were of Jewish extraction, but they apparently included in their culture customs and knowledge transmitted down through time among remnant groups left after the earlier Jaredite dynasties had destroyed themselves.

The most plausible geographical scene for Zarahemla is on the Grijalva River in the Central Depression of Chiapas, probably centered at what is known as the archaeological site of Santa Rosa.

The Central Depression is a major geological feature of southern Mexico. At its southern end the land rises abruptly to a towering strip of mountains along the present border between Guatemala and Mexico. The great valley constitutes the upper drainage area of the Grijalva. Rimmed by mountains on three sides and a great plateau on the fourth, the depression is something of a world unto itself. Shielded from sea winds by mountains, it receives far less rain than surrounding zones; land within the basin is not forested heavily as in the wetter portions of Mesoamerica. This valley constitutes the "heart" of isthmian Mesoamerica, "surrounded by security" (Alma 60:19). It is relatively hot compared with the highlands but not oppressive like the nearby areas close to sea level.

No marked regional style of art or culture has yet been identified that uniquely distinguishes the culture of the Central Depression in Book of Mormon times. Rather the area was something of a mixing zone or crossroads (as was Palestine, incidentally). Maya people and culture from both the lowlands and Guatemalan highlands intruded into the area at various times without ever clearly dominating it. It occupied a central position within the broader area encompassed by the Izapan style of art, which ranged from coastal southern Guatemala through Chiapas into southern and central Veracruz state. The peak Izapan development dated between the second century B.C. and the fourth century A.D. This Izapan style is, so far, the best hint of the presence of Nephites, although the association is based on inference from time and space factors. The exact relationship of a Nephite presence to the Izapan area remains unclear and uncertain. Beginning in the late fourth century A.D., when the Nephite demise came, most cities in Chiapas were abandoned and the population dropped markedly. The area never again became a significant player in the ongoing course of Mesoamerican civilization.

From the extreme southerly limit of the Central Depression (or Zarahemla area) the great strip of mountainous wilderness looms; beyond it lay the highland zone of southern Guatemala—the likely land of Nephi.

The site of Santa Rosa, in the upper Central Depression, qualifies in important ways as the city of Zarahemla. Part of the archaeological site is seen in the foreground of this aerial view, with the Grijalva River adjacent. $Alma_2$ and his Nephites likely fought their way across this river at a ford not far upstream from this spot as they battled against Amlicites and Lamanites (see Alma 2:26–37).

An area a few miles from Santa Rosa shows the relatively open, unforested landscape, in contrast to the jungle-type vegetation of many lowland areas. These two photos at the top of the page are over forty years old. For the past quarter century the area has been covered by the waters of a lake impounded by a major dam built thirty miles downstream.

The barrier hemming in the Central Depression on the north and east is formed by the Chiapas highlands, a forested wilderness zone that was only lightly populated in ancient times. When Lamanite armies were foiled at Jershon, toward the east sea, or Gulf of Mexico, they "took their journey round about in the wilderness" (Alma 43:22) to attack the Manti area. In their strategic redeployment, they likely skirted or cut through the far part of the vast tangle of jungled mountains shown here.

The Lamanite Land of Nephi

A good deal of detail about the highland area known as the land of Nephi is included in Mormon's account thanks to two historical episodes on which he dwells. The first concerns the Zeniffites, a party of Nephites who returned to Nephi after $Mosiah_1$ had fled from there with his group. They dwelt in the land of Nephi under Lamanite dominance in the early half of the second century B.C. The second account relates the activities and movements of the sons of $Mosiah_2$ when they and companions missionized among the Lamanites in the land of Nephi between about 80 and 65 B.C.

The geographical centerpiece of the area was always the original valley where three distinct local lands, Nephi, Shilom, and Shemlon, lay adjacent to each other. From Nephi, the highest in elevation, one could "overlook" the other two lands (Mosiah 11:12.) Other named lands were "round about" (Alma 24:1; see 23:1–12;), chiefly in a northward direction. One place, the city of Jerusalem, lay beside a sizable lake (see Alma 21:1–2; 3 Nephi 9:7), and the Mormon area probably lay next to the same body of water. Extensive uninhabited areas separated the settled lands; groups could become lost trying to move between lands (see Mosiah 23:30–7). All this scene is "up" (Mosiah 10:8) in the highland zone. The primary settlements must have been in valleys amidst hills or mountains (compare Mosiah 7:5; 10:7–8).

The relationships of the lands to each other and to natural features that are mentioned in the record fit nicely with the actual geography of highland Guatemala. Archaeological materials of appropriate age (the Late Pre-Classic period) and type also appear in these indicated areas.

The near shore of Lake Amatitlan seen in this photograph qualifies as the Lamanite land of Shemlon. What could be the land of Shilom lies above the bluffs across the lake. According to Mosiah chapters 11 and 19 through 22, Lamanite forces consistently went "up" (roughly five hundred feet in elevation here) from Shemlon through Shilom to attack Nephi.

The beauty of "the waters of Mormon" deeply impressed $Alma_1$ and his companions (Mosiah 18:30). Lake Atitlan, west of Guatemala City, fits the scriptural text's characterization of the "fountain of pure water" (Mosiah 18:5) adjacent to Mormon.

This delta of the little Panajachel River at the northeast corner of Lake Atitlan could be where $Alma_1$ hid from the armies of King Noah in a "thicket of small trees" (Mosiah 18:5).

The great city at Kaminaljuyu was once at least a mile square and contained hundreds of major buildings. This photograph only hints at the former extent and the density of public structures. Encroaching suburban growth has by now destroyed all but a small portion of the site, which is preserved as a park.

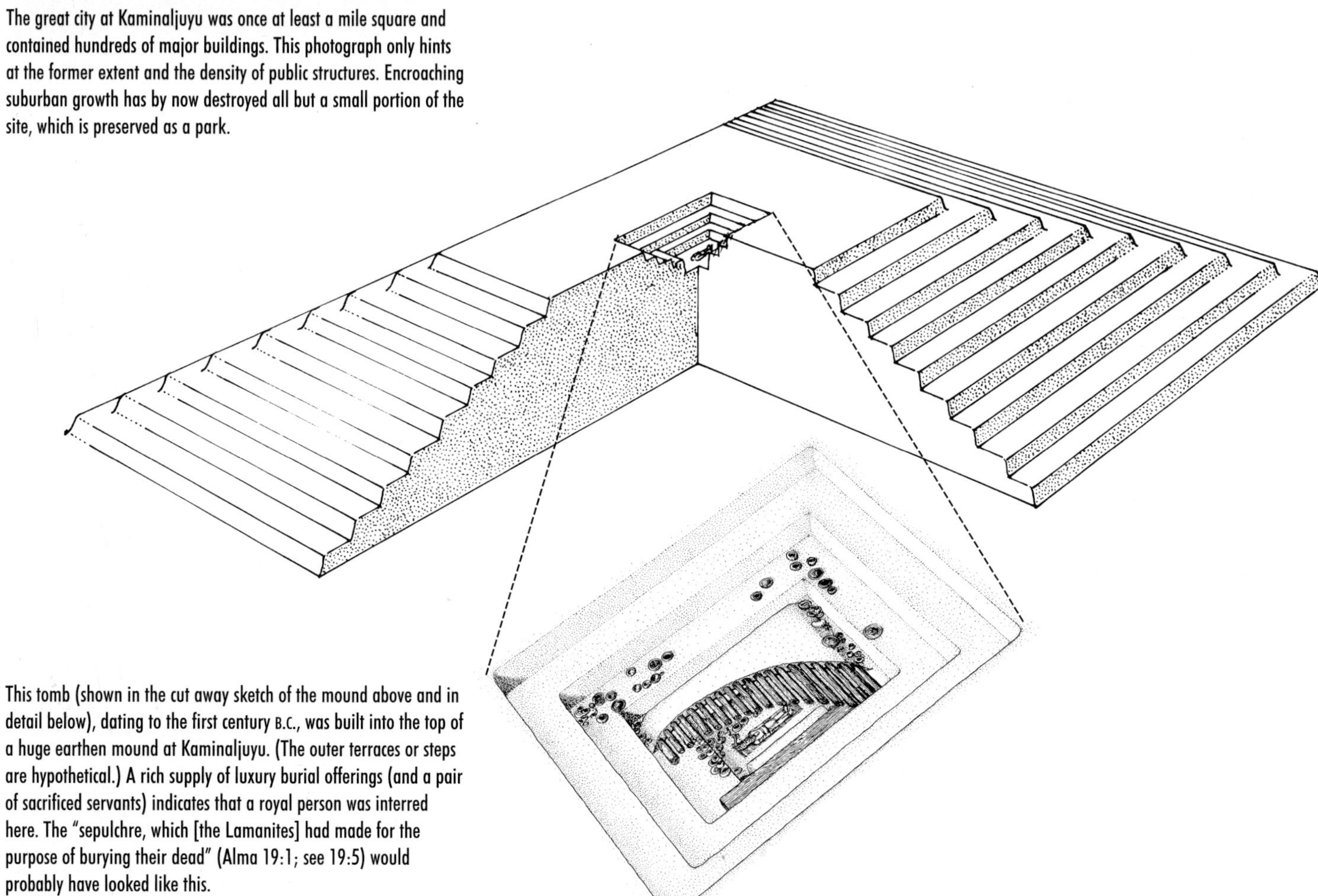

This tomb (shown in the cut away sketch of the mound above and in detail below), dating to the first century B.C., was built into the top of a huge earthen mound at Kaminaljuyu. (The outer terraces or steps are hypothetical.) A rich supply of luxury burial offerings (and a pair of sacrificed servants) indicates that a royal person was interred here. The "sepulchre, which [the Lamanites] had made for the purpose of burying their dead" (Alma 19:1; see 19:5) would probably have looked like this.

The Land Southward at the Time of the Great War

The greatest detail about the land of Zarahemla is given in the books of Alma and Helaman, covering approximately 90 to 30 B.C. The account of wars during that period contains significant details about relationships among landmarks and the movements of individuals and armies.

Nephite political and military control had by this time been extended from the original center, the city of Zarahemla on the upper Sidon River, plausibly identified above with the site of Santa Rosa on the Grijalva, throughout the entire river basin and beyond. That included the lowland "borders by the east sea" (Alma 52:13), a hot plain that would have encompassed the delta of the Sidon, and the adjacent land of Bountiful (see Alma 50:7–11, 32). Bountiful occupied the southerly side of the immediate isthmus zone, or "small neck of land" (Alma 22:32; see 22:27–34) that connected to the land northward.

Nephites and Lamanites—at least the leaders—were broadly aware of the general configuration of the lands south of the narrow neck and even beyond to the north. Amalickiah and other dissident Nephites who had fled to the Lamanite capital in the land of Nephi were planning military strategy on a grand scale that extended all the way into the land northward. Nephite counterstrategy was on an equal scale (see Alma 48–51).

This lord pictured on Kaminaljuyu Stela 11 dates to the first century B.C. His richly symbolic garb could represent approximately how King Amalickiah would have been dressed when in full regalia (compare Alma 49:10).

This key Olmec site, La Venta, is located on a segment of dry land surrounded by swamp in southern Veracruz state. It was an impressive city for centuries until about 600–400 B.C. when it seems to have been abandoned. Archaeologists have found that later a smaller, very different group resettled part of it.

Here is where the great Stela 3 was found (see page 121). It shows, according to a prominent scholar, "figures represent[ing] two racially distinct groups of people," one of whom is Semitic or Jewish in appearance.[182] This is intriguing since in geographical details La Venta meets the requirements to have been the city of Mulek, named for the prince of Judah of the Nephite record who arrived by sea in the sixth century B.C. The city was later occupied by the Nephites, at one point was captured by a Lamanite army, then was recaptured by Moroni$_1$ and Teancum (see Alma 52:22–6).

When Amalickiah's Lamanite invaders "marched to the borders of the land Bountiful" (Alma 51:28) and camped "on the beach by the seashore" (Alma 51:32), the scene would have been like this.

The narrow strip of wilderness consisted chiefly of rugged mountains that appear to coincide with the deeply canyoned chain that forms the headwaters of the Grijalva. These mountains separate Guatemala and Chiapas. An extension of wilderness reached toward the Gulf of Mexico through the Chiapas highland wilderness. Seen here is the western anchor of the narrow strip. It includes Tacaná volcano, Central America's highest peak (extreme left in the picture). Helaman's expedition that lured the Lamanite army out of the garrison city of Antiparah would have headed through a pass (to the left in the picture) down toward a lowland city "in the borders by the seashore" (to the right of the picture) (Alma 56:31; see 56:30–6).

Into the Land Northward

The Nephites had been curious about the land beyond the narrow neck for generations (see Omni 1:20–2 and Mosiah 28:12). Rebel Morianton wanted to set up rule there, and Moroni$_1$ saw how vital the area was to the Nephites' future (see Alma 50:29, 32). No doubt adventurous merchants had already penetrated the land northward for trade, but it was not until the end of the Amalickiahite war that systematic moves were made to control parts of the land by colonizing them (see Alma 63:4–10).

A generation later Nephite presence there was substantial (see Helaman 6:6, 10, 12). By the time the risen Jesus Christ appeared at Bountiful, the Nephite demographic center of gravity had already shifted northward from Zarahemla, for all twelve of the chosen disciples were already residing in the Bountiful area. By the time Mormon opens the curtain of history on events in his own lifetime, after A.D. 300, the official Nephite records had long since been moved to the land northward, and he was a native of that area.

The main lands settled by the migrants from the south lay toward the east sea side of the land northward, the same territory on which we have the most information from the Jaredite account (although neither record gives us geographical information in the depth we should like). In the final Nephite-Lamanite wars, which took place in that area, Mormon's hilly homeland was the source of his people's greatest strength in manpower and provisions.[183]

The position and nature of the Coatzacoalcos River qualifies it to have constituted "the line" that, practically and conceptually, marked the separation between the lands of Bountiful and Desolation (3 Nephi 3:23; see Alma 22:32). Through the wetlands of this river's basin there was only one "narrow pass" by which the journey northward could be made (Alma 50:34).[184]

These mounds in the isthmus area at Tatocapan, Veracruz (age unknown), are typical of many vegetation-covered sites that King Limhi's exploring party could have encountered when they passed through this area on their way to discover the Jaredite record (see Mosiah 8:7–10). Sites like these could not have been dated by them any more than by today's tourists; thus they could conclude logically enough that they had found ruined Zarahemla (see Mosiah 21:25; compare 8:8).

Lago de Catemaco in the Tuxtlas Mountains of southern Veracruz qualifies as part of the complex of "many waters, rivers, and fountains" in the area of Cumorah (Mormon 6:4).

The part of the land northward toward the west sea was evidently drier than the land toward the east. Little is said in the Nephite record about the west sea side. The aridity visible in this scene in southern Oaxaca suggests why colonies planted by Hagoth's voyagers on the west coast lacked timber for building construction (see Alma 63:5–8; Helaman 3:5–10).

This ruined city at Dainzu, Oaxaca, dates to the Monte Alban II period, between 200 B.C. and A.D. 200. In this period there is specific evidence for cultural intrusions from Chiapas in parts of Oaxaca, including Dainzu (possibly reflecting the migrations noted in Helaman 3:8–9).[185] The pair of pillars at the doorway of the temple structure, which are structurally unnecessary, reminds us of the symbolic columns built at the entry to the Temple of Solomon (see 1 Kings 7:21).

The Crucifixion Catastrophe

Unparalleled destruction struck the Nephite land of promise at the time when Jesus Christ was crucified at Jerusalem. The event may be reflected in archaeological remains already discovered in Mesoamerica, but there is uncertainty about this for two reasons. The first is that the scriptural record of the event leaves us unclear about details. It is obvious enough from the descriptions in 3 Nephi 8 and 9 that a major earthquake and volcanism were involved and that there was also an array of intense storms. Similar events have occurred in the area in recent centuries, although not on the scale reported in the Nephite account. But if the rubble of quake-destroyed buildings was later removed and new structures were erected, the destruction might not be obvious to archaeologists. The second problem is that our methods of dating material remains still leave uncertainty about the exact time to be assigned to the excavated remains. Furthermore, relatively little excavation has been done in Mesoamerica that can be approximately set at the Christian era. Still there are a few interesting indicators of what might have been

This dramatic photograph shows the first stage of the 1974 eruption of the Volcan de Fuego, in Guatemala. Simultaneous eruptions from several volcanoes could have produced the "thick darkness" (3 Nephi 8:20) mentioned by the Nephite reporters.

Ash from volcanoes could have smothered crops, animals, and humans over wide areas. The type of desolation resulting is illustrated by this scene near the volcano El Chichón in highland Chiapas in 1982.[186]

this disastrous event (for example, a layer of volcanic ash at the great city of Teotihuacan dates to near A.D. 30), and they may be augmented by future findings.[187]

Certainly the *types* of natural disasters known historically for Mesoamerica fit what the scriptures portray: volcanic eruptions and ashfalls, earthquakes, hurricane winds, landslides, torrential downpours. The question yet to be answered is whether a unique, monumental combination of such forces can be documented for the right historical moment.

Also according to the Book of Mormon, a major consequence of the great disaster was a huge loss of life. Great social changes must have resulted from the changes in nature and the massive casualties, in addition to the new social teachings by the Savior when he appeared among the Nephites (for example, no social classes and having "all things common"; 4 Nephi 1:3). Certain archaeological data gives indications of at least a pause or historical hiccup in populational and social development in about the first century A.D. that might signal a destruction like that reported in 3 Nephi.[188]

The leading geographical correlation of Book of Mormon lands with the modern map puts the city of Jerusalem, built by the Lamanites and Nephite dissenters (see Alma 21:2), at this location in southern Guatemala, near the village of Santiago Atitlan.[189] Third Nephi 9:7 reports that the city was destroyed by waters that did "come up in the stead thereof." Lake Atitlan is prone to sharp rises and falls in its level due to the volcanic geology of its environs.

The site of Copilco in the Valley of Mexico, near Cuicuilco, suffered from a major lava flow that covered remains that probably dated in the first century A.D.

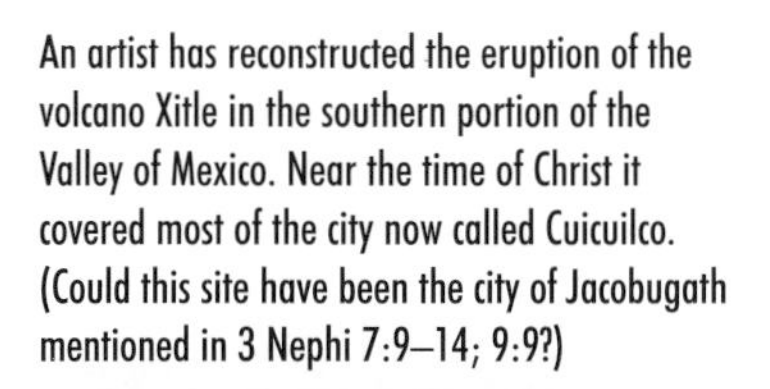

An artist has reconstructed the eruption of the volcano Xitle in the southern portion of the Valley of Mexico. Near the time of Christ it covered most of the city now called Cuicuilco. (Could this site have been the city of Jacobugath mentioned in 3 Nephi 7:9–14; 9:9?)

The god Quetzalcoatl was still important to the Aztecs at the time the Spaniards arrived, although by then his identity had been confounded with later figures. This representation combines feathered and serpentine symbols of him with a humanlike face.

This reconstruction of what the original Temple of Quetzalcoatl at Teotihuacan looked like (in the second century A.D.) is based on information gleaned by a competent archaeologist-architect.

The Golden Age

Many myths and traditions tell about Quetzalcoatl, "precious serpent," one of the most important of all Mesoamerican deities.[190] Some scholarly interpreters of the traditions have claimed that he was not a god at all but just a historical personage who lived at the famous city of Tula in central Mexico in the eleventh century A.D. He departed abruptly from there for the Gulf Coast, where he was said to have disappeared miraculously (incidentally, from precisely the region identified above as the Nephite land Bountiful, where Jesus disappeared into the heavens) after promising to return someday. When Cortez arrived in Mexico in A.D. 1519, Montezuma took him to be this returning Quetzalcoatl and handed power over to him.

However, symbols associated in the traditions with the deity have been found in archaeological materials that date long before the day of the priest from Tula. Confusion has arisen because the name *Quetzalcoatl* was adopted as a personal name or title by various Mexican priests from at least the eighth through the eleventh centuries. Some scholars recognize the "fundamental historicity" of the original man-god behind the traditions, although that status can be discerned only "through a dense screen of mythical, legendary, and folkloristic accretion."[191] The distinguished Mexican scholar Miguel Leon-Portilla confidently calls the first Quetzalcoatl the founder of an "elevated spiritualism, a vision of the world that led to ancient Mexico's greatest cultural achievements" a millennium before his namesake dwelt at Tula.[192]

Some Latter-day Saint writers have assumed, perhaps too confidently, that the Quetzalcoatl god figure is to be identified with the resurrected Jesus Christ reported in the Book of Mormon. The historical and archaeological data are not clear enough to establish that relationship decisively; nevertheless, a reasonable case can be made in support of the proposition.[193]

Following the visit to the Nephites in Bountiful by the risen Jesus, from around A.D. 30 to near A.D. 200, according to the very abbreviated account in 4 Nephi, a classless society existed in the lands occupied by the Nephites and Lamanites.

Ethnic distinctions were erased, and governmental functions were in the hands of local priests.

Features of the cultural history of central Mesoamerica in the first two centuries A.D. fit with this picture.[194] One phenomenon that is of interest is visible at the metropolis of Teotihuacan. The second century A.D. saw construction of the huge Pyramid of the Sun (so called by the later Aztecs), an act that would only have been carried out on the basis of some powerful belief system.[195] In the same period the beautiful Temple of Quetzalcoatl was completed.

Around A.D. 200–300, 4 Nephi reports the renewal of social class differences among the Christians, the creation of rival churches or cults, and the reemergence of a group "called Lamanites" (4 Nephi 1:38). At the same historical moment, the old Temple of Quetzalcoatl was enclosed by a new structure characterized by a strikingly different theology and set of symbols.[196] The coincidence is provocative, although we cannot confidently place Nephite believers at the site.

The reptile on the Teotihuacan temple has feathers, which signify "descending from heaven" or "elevated," as well as a sense of preciousness that beautiful (probably green, for water) feathers connoted. This calls to mind the serpent image that Moses "did raise up" (2 Nephi 25:20) for the Israelites to look upon to be healed. According to Nephite belief, it represented Jesus Christ/Jehovah (see Helaman 8:14–5). The shell symbol on the same facade signified resurrection.[197]

The figure engraved on this bone, which was excavated at Chiapa de Corzo by the BYU New World Archaeological Foundation, shows a feathered serpent thought to represent the god Quetzalcoatl. (The sketch at left clarifies the design.) Its date, probably in the first century B.C., is not much earlier than when $Nephi_2$ prophesied about the coming of the Savior, symbolized by "the brazen serpent" (Helaman 8:14). ($Nephi_1$, in 2 Nephi 25:20, and $Alma_2$, in Alma 33:19, had, of course, used the same symbolism earlier.)

A stela from the Late Classic site of Piedras Negras shows a sacrificial scene that may recall a distorted version of the Book of Mormon image of the gospel seed sprouting from the human heart (see Alma 32:28).

Apostasy

Archaeological and art remains dating from the period A.D. 200–400 in Mesoamerica display a surge of construction and innovation as the area enters the Early Classic period. Priests were the prime movers in this process. Formerly, experts supposed that the Classic (conventionally put at A.D. 300–900) marked a climax in the elaboration of culture unique in the history of Mesoamerica, but in recent decades it has become apparent that most of the characteristics of the Classic had already been developed (previewed, as it were) several centuries before at sites like El Mirador, Tikal, Kaminaljuyu, Teotihuacan, and Monte Alban. Near A.D. 200 there erupted an almost frantic pace in the development of cities, cults, and art. Interchange of ideas was spurred by extensive trade. By A.D. 300 every section of Mesoamerica had followed suit.

This surge coincides remarkably with the characterization that Mormon, who was born around A.D. 300, gave of Nephite society in his day: "The people had . . . spread upon all the face of the land, and . . . had become exceedingly rich. . . . [Some] were lifted up in pride, such as the wearing of costly apparel . . . and of the fine things of the world. . . . And they began to be divided into classes; and they began to build up churches unto themselves" (4 Nephi 1:23–6). These they adorned "with all manner of precious things" (4 Nephi 1:41) while they "did traffic in all manner of traffic [i.e., commerce]" (4 Nephi 1:46).

In subsequent centuries, in the elaborate religious art of Mesoamerican civilization and in customs among surviving peoples, we see beliefs and practices (such as baptism, communion, and confession) that some observers have considered distortions of teachings given to his believers by the resurrected Savior. For example, a form of baptism[198] (with the meaning "to be born again") was widespread at the time the Spaniards arrived.

Archaeologist-artist Pierre Agrinier has given us an imaginative picture of cult practices of the fifth century A.D. at the site of Mirador, Chiapas. (Mirador may have been the city of Ammonihah that was destroyed in Alma's day.) All the objects and activities in the scene are based upon actual finds by archaeologists of the Brigham Young University New World Archaeological Foundation.

Elaborate religious symbolism, like this hybrid eagle, became the rule at later Teotihuacan, in contrast to the relative simplicity of the former Quetzalcoatl belief system.

A magnificent Late Classic sculpture from the Maya city of Yaxchilan on the Usumacinta River shows a noblewoman, Lady Xoc, offering a sacrifice of blood from her tongue. This form of self-mutilation was a very common ritual practice up to the time of the Spanish invasion. Could Alma have been arguing against an early version of this practice in Alma 34:11: "There is not any man that can sacrifice his own blood which will atone for . . . sins"?

The Nephites' Fall

Scholars long claimed that it was only late in Mesoamerican history when warfare began. In the last twenty-five years, however, overwhelming evidence has appeared to the contrary. Conflict, violence, and battle are now believed to have long been a part of life in ancient Mexico and Central America, exactly as they were in Europe and Asia.

For the fourth century A.D., Mormon's and Moroni's day, there is plenty of evidence that conquest and armed violence were commonplace in Mesoamerica. One of the chief evidences is the remains of fortifications.[199] There is less possibility of finding material evidence of actual battles, for their locations could have been on some undistinguished spot of ground that archaeologists might never have reason to examine.

One of the strongest evidences so far for the destruction of the Nephites by the Lamanites comes from the widespread abandonment of cities in the late fourth century in Chiapas, the area consided here to have been the land of Zarahemla. The roughly two centuries after A.D. 200 saw a spectacular flowering of public life and religious or cult structures, as discussed above. But at Mirador in western Chiapas, for example, the period was ended "by an intense fire that totally destroyed" the largest sacred building, set either by those who abandoned it or by invaders who occupied the place around A.D. 400–450. They partly rebuilt the site with "shoddier construction." Furthermore, the new culture was related to highland Guatemala.[200] As we have seen, that was likely the land of Nephi, from which came the Lamanites who expelled the Nephites from their Zarahemla homeland. For the next century and more, most of the old cities in central Chiapas remained abandoned.[201] The picture derived from archaeology thus agrees basically with the Book of Mormon story of the Nephites' retreat.

Archaeological research around the Cumorah area, thought to be in the Tuxtla Mountains of southern Veracruz state, could shed further light on the end of the Nephites. Unfortunately, very little excavation has been done thereabouts for the correct time period.

To visualize an actual battle, we have to depend on the art and historical accounts of later peoples, but likely the basic forms of war had not changed a great deal over the intervening centuries. This well-documented artist's reconstruction of a defeated Aztec army suggests the despair of the doomed Nephites (compare Mormon 6:7–9).

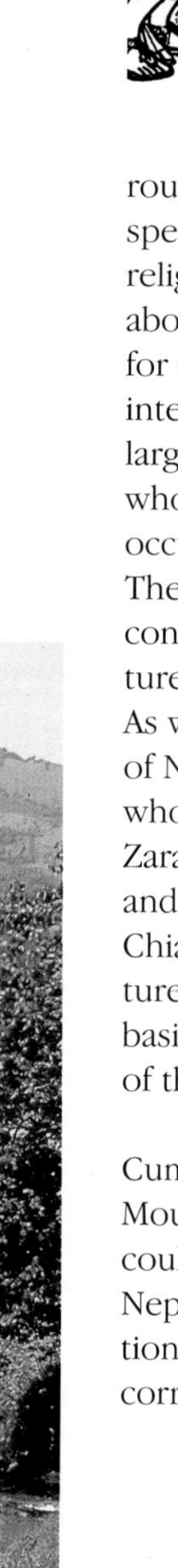

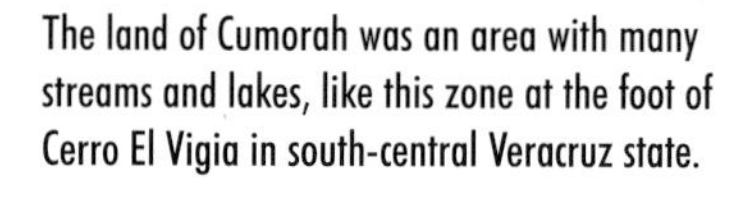

The land of Cumorah was an area with many streams and lakes, like this zone at the foot of Cerro El Vigia in south-central Veracruz state.

The information in Mormon's record about the final battle area matches in detail the characteristics of this hill, Cerro El Vigia, in southern Veracruz state and the region around it. This view of 2600-foot El Vigia is from the plains to its southwest, where the final battle likely took place.

This view from the top of Cerro El Vigia looks down on the plains to the west. If this is the correct hill, Mormon and the handful of survivors with him had this same view on the morning after their climactic battle, with hundreds of thousands of the dead and dying in their view (see Mormon 6:11–5).

Nephites, Lamanites, and Successor Peoples

The Aztecs carried the earlier, occasional rituals of human sacrifice and cannibalism to levels of depravity never equaled. Nephi$_1$ had seen in vision his brother's descendants as a "loathsome, and a filthy people, full of . . . all manner of abominations" (1 Nephi 12:23).

In the eleven centuries that passed between Moroni's termination of the Nephite record and the arrival of the Spaniards in Mexico, rulers and their peoples rose and fell in restless sequence. In the south-central Mexico area that constituted the land northward of the Nephite record, most cultures after A.D. 400 lived off cultural capital from the past. At the huge city of Teotihuacan, far to the north of our Cumorah, for example, no major building projects were carried out after the fourth century.[202] The population at the place remained sizable after A.D. 400, but the creative juice of the culture had dried up. Similarly, at Monte Alban, Oaxaca, the dominant view after about A.D. 400 was toward the past, as jostling regional kings strove to reconstruct the brilliance of earlier centuries.

Sacrificial blood stains the steps at Aztec Malinalco.

Some old cities in Mesoamerica did get reconstructed, brilliantly, and new ones were built. Craftsmen, architects, and other experts went on using and in some cases elaborating on the old cultural ways, as Byzantium did after the fall of Rome. But warfare became endemic. Population may have grown to outpace resources. Exploitation of the underclasses by elites could have become excessive to the point of stirring local social revolts.

The Classic era as characterized a few decades ago was supposed to have been led by noble philosopher types who spent their time peacefully making complicated calendrical calculations and patronizing the arts. Now it turns out that these people were not that admirable and surely not peaceful.[203] Even the Maya culture at impressive sites like Tikal, we see from recently deciphered monuments, was marked by continual cycles of aggression among regional rivals led by lords who were somewhat mafialike in their aims and methods. They also displayed some unusual customs, such as ritual enemas perhaps involving hallucinogenic drugs. Human sacrifice and even cannibalism (compare Mormon 4:14–5, 21; Moroni 9:8–10) came to be practiced in many areas and eventually became dominating themes.

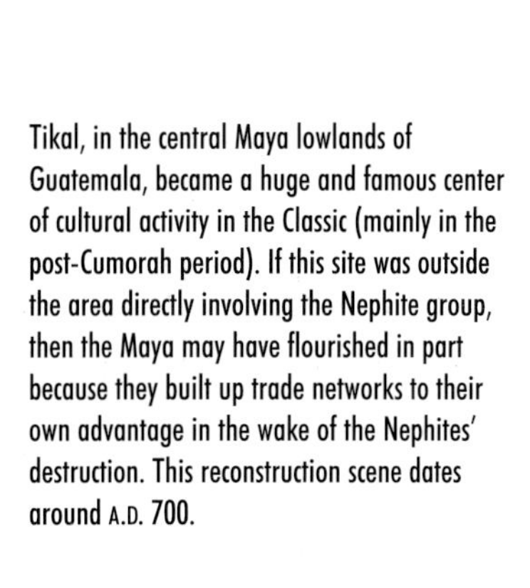

Tikal, in the central Maya lowlands of Guatemala, became a huge and famous center of cultural activity in the Classic (mainly in the post-Cumorah period). If this site was outside the area directly involving the Nephite group, then the Maya may have flourished in part because they built up trade networks to their own advantage in the wake of the Nephites' destruction. This reconstruction scene dates around A.D. 700.

By bravery and audacity, the Spaniards defeated their opponents against vast odds. The Aztecs, used to certain cultural norms for the conduct of war, found they could not cope with the completely foreign Spanish practices and superior technology (especially their horses). After the Aztecs gave up, other Mesoamerican peoples put up relatively light resistance, suspecting that they could not succeed where Montezuma's feared forces had failed.

Diego Rivera's famed mural shows the Spaniards making slaves of Mexican Indians during the colonial era. Recall that $Nephi_1$ had prophetically seen "the seed of my brethren" being "scattered before the Gentiles and . . . smitten" (1 Nephi 13:14).

From a post-Olmec context comes this incense burner at the site of Monte Alban. The telltale drooped corners of the mouth reveal that the Olmec jaguar motif was the distant historical source for this piece.

The Jaredites

The brief historical summary of the earliest Book of Mormon people, the Jaredites, that is reported in the book of Ether appears almost at the end of Mormon's record. The account had been translated by Moroni$_2$, the final Nephite prophet-scribe, and he attached it as an appendix to the record of the people of Nephi that his father left in his custody. The account tells of one Jared and his unnamed brother who led their families and a number of friends and their families from Mesopotamia, the scene of the confusion of tongues and the great tower of Genesis 11:1–9. Traveling across Asia, probably, they reached the ocean (likely the North Pacific) where they embarked on barges they built. They reached America in the area known to the Nephites later as the land northward; the land they settled turns out to have been in south-central Mexico. The date can only be estimated; students of the text have suggested times ranging from 3200 to later than 2000 B.C.; however, in my view an arrival after 2500 B.C. is unlikely on the basis of the genealogies in the record.

Ether's record was a history of the ruling lineage, Jared's kin line, that reigned over the combined descendants of the immigrant party. It was written in about the sixth century B.C. by Ether, the last prophet among them. The story summarily documents the ups and downs of the Jaredite dynasty until they were exterminated in a civil war in the days of Ether; the last ruler lived briefly among the people of the Mulek party.

A limited amount of descriptive information is included in the book of Ether about the culture and society in which the Jaredite lineage participated. Cities, kings, trade, written records, metallurgy, large-scale wars, "spacious buildings" (Ether 10:5), and a population, at the end, in the low millions are among features reported. All of the historical events occurred in the land northward, not far from the narrow neck. In fact the place where the Jaredites were exterminated (the hill Ramah) was the same as for the Nephite finale (their hill Cumorah).

Significant cultural traces of the Jaredite people (for example, crop plants and

Oxtotitlan Cave in the state of Guerrero in southwestern Mexico contains remnants of a fascinating mural of an Olmec-period ruler. An artist has here tried to restore its original appearance. Key features of this lord's regalia and throne are repeated much later in the Maya art style. Could that be due to a revival of the Jaredite-period secret society tradition at the end of Nephite history that continued into post–Book of Mormon times? (Compare 4 Nephi 1:46 and Mormon 8:9 with Ether 10:33; 13:18; and 3 Nephi 3:9.)

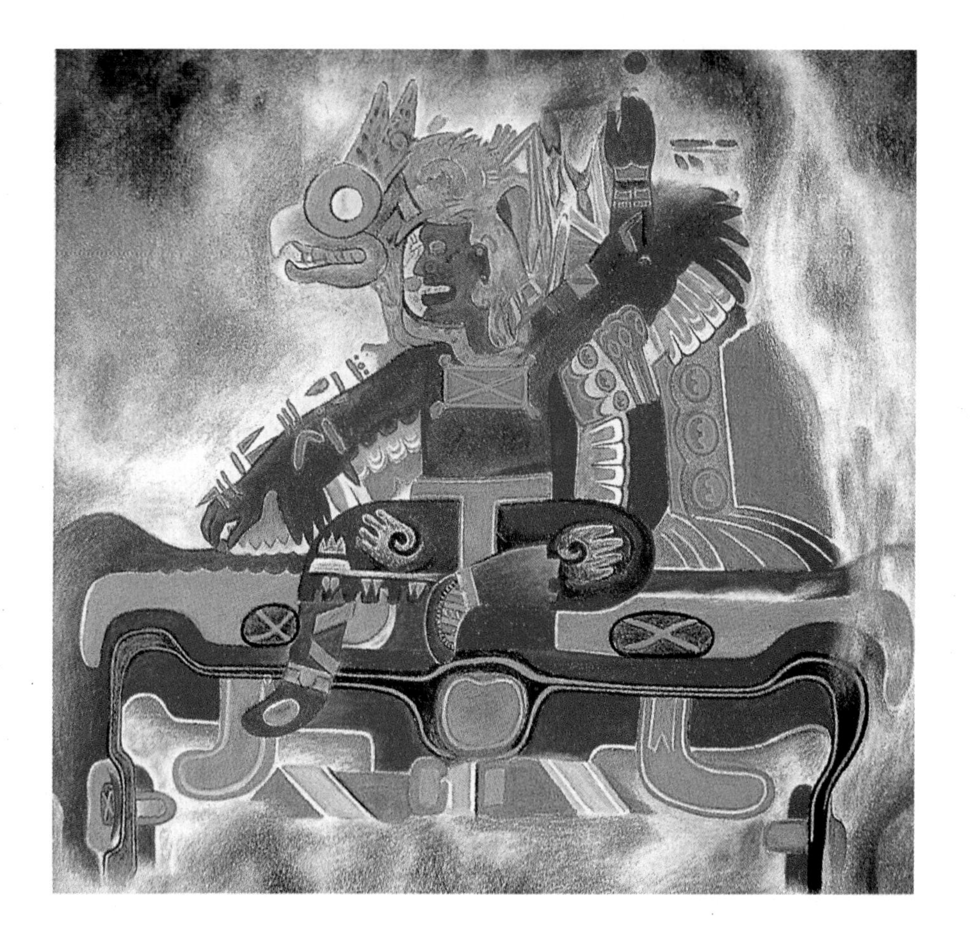

The Jaredites were deeply concerned about the power of snakes in connection with drought (see Ether 9:30–4; 10:19). Some priests or rulers may have considered themselves to be under the protection of serpents. This awesome Olmec rattlesnake is on Monument 19 at La Venta.

Seventeen colossal heads have been discovered so far in the Gulf Coast Olmec heartland. Each is a portrait of an individual, although not necessarily a completely accurate one, considering the problem of sculpting the hard volcanic stone. They are thought to represent chiefs or kings wearing ball-game headgear. Serious effort was expended to deface most of them after they were completed.

personal and place names) cropped up centuries later among the Nephites.[204] The most plausible explanation for this partial continuity is that, while the rulers killed each other off and the elite components of the civilization collapsed, small groups who succeeded in avoiding participation in the final wars of the Jaredite lineage lived on to become involved with the undocumented "Mulekites" and thus came unrecognized within the range of the Nephite record.

The Jaredite story is so brief that only cursory analysis of their geography and history can be made. Because of the overlapping locations pointed out in the Nephite record, we know that the Jaredites inhabited part of the Nephites' territory. Their scene appears to have been central or southern Mexico before and during the time of the Olmecs. But Ether's text implies that, as in the case of the Nephites, other peoples were present in addition to those descended from Jared and his family; presumably those others were "native" groups.[205]

The brief Jaredite history agrees broadly with what we know from archaeologists about Mesoamerica in the Early and Middle Pre-Classic periods (about 2000–500 B.C.). The climax Jaredite phase, which can be estimated on the basis of the genealogies to include the time range 1200–900 B.C., corresponds interestingly with the peak Olmec development in southern Veracruz during the same period. Several centuries of relative cultural turmoil followed, according to the account by Ether, and in the Olmec archaeological sequence a similar phenomenon can be observed. Finally, what had been Olmec-derived high culture in Mesoamerican term essentially terminated around the sixth century B.C., although certain elements of the old pattern continued down into the succeeding Late Pre-Classic era. The textual account of the violent end of the Jaredite line at about the same time as the Olmec demise, followed by Jaredite cultural influences springing up among the Nephites later on, corresponds quite closely with the picture from archaeology about the fate and influence of the Olmec. It is inescapable that a close relationship existed between Olmec civilization and the Jaredites; nevertheless, the text from Ether is too brief to permit saying that the Jaredites actually were the Olmecs.

Given the space limitations of the present book, it is impossible to provide more than brief hints here of how Olmec-era Mesoamerican materials could shed light on the Jaredite record. This short section can give only a glimpse of a few Olmec cultural elements that might have been involved in Jaredite life.

When the famous Olmec sculpture shown in the drawing above (see also page 185) was discovered by farmers at Las Limas, in the Isthmus of Tehuantepec, it quickly became the center of a modern cult. Locals even substituted it for the community's image of the fabled Virgin of Guadalupe "because it is older,"[206] they said, and so was presumably more powerful. We can see from this event why some Olmec-period pieces have been found reused in later archaeological contexts, even dating to Aztec times.

Remarkable artistic sophistication is visible in this piece from the Olmec era. Tattooing seems indicated. Animal characteristics shown on this man suggest the nawal, or guardian spirit, concept.

The specialized, cooperative nature of modern archaeology can be seen from this large team of researchers from a number of specialties and institutions that was assembled in 1996 to restudy the famous murals at the site of Bonampak in southern Mexico under the leadership of Dr. Steven Houston of Brigham Young University.

How We Learn about the Past

Archaeology

Archaeologists make use of the material remains left behind by past peoples in order to describe and interpret their life patterns. Ideally they excavate sites but digging is not always possible or necessary.

Many specialized fields of expertise are represented under the broad term *archaeologist.* Some of them study art styles shown on specimens whether dug up or found above ground, as in rock art. Others use the analytical and comparative methods of physical (biological) anthropologists in order to interpret what skulls and skeletons have to tell about the ethnic affiliation, age, disease, etc. of a people whose remains have been excavated. Certain specialties are even further removed from the process of excavation. For example, sophisticated scientific instruments are used to test the chemical composition of obsidian that was used for ancient tools. No two sources of this volcanic product are quite the same; therefore the tests tell where the stones came from; that is, they reveal patterns of trade.

Sophisticated imaging equipment was used at Bonampak to reveal new information that the naked eye could not detect on these vital Maya paintings, which are badly deteriorated due to atmospheric pollution.

Chemical tests have also been used to determine what types of life activities (for example, food preparation, stone working, or painting) were carried out in particular rooms in a structure.[207] And the climate of an ancient site may be described based on plant pollen retrieved from soil samples.

The wide variety of expert tasks involved in modern archaeology means that teamwork is essential. Generations ago the archaeologist was a lone heroic figure, and he is still celebrated in movies as the professor who knows everything about every ancient group. (The type is classically exemplified by the photograph on page 1, in the introduction, of British archaeologist Alfred Maudslay at work more than a century ago under primitive conditions at the ruins of Chichen Itza.) Today, however, the coordination of a wide variety of skills is essential for doing proper archaeology and may also entail such high-tech tools as internet-linked computers at the dig site. The new mode also means that long periods of laboratory work have to be completed in order for the specialists to have their full say. (Thus archaeology is very expensive.) Finally, an integrated picture of the ancient lifeways is constructed by a team of synthesizing scholars out of the mass of technical data.

At most sites the first and most basic kind of archaeology is collecting specimens from the surface, chiefly pottery fragments because they are often abundant. The position of artifacts must be recorded since nobody can know at the time of the field investigation what facts about ancient life may eventually be revealed by detailed studies of the distribution. Often, surface collecting and mapping are the only studies of a site that researchers can afford to do.

Whether one layer of remains lies above or beneath another (stratigraphy) is a key concern in excavation, because those vertical relationships establish what is earlier and what is later. Eventually the relationships discovered are summarized in diagrams such as this simplified version from the work on the north acropolis at Tikal.

Governments may be concerned that important ruins be restored so that visitors may come to a site and learn about life in the past. This scene shows rebuilding work at Monte Alban under the direction of archaeologists and engineers.

Archaeologists like to discover monuments, especially those with inscriptions on them, like this Maya stela from Ixtutz, Guatemala. Much of the writing can now be deciphered. But most areas in Mesoamerica, and even most Maya sites, do not yield stones with writing on them.

Fragments of pots are the most abundant kind of artifact the archaeologist brings to light. Rarely are whole vessels discovered. When carefully washed, sherds can sometimes be fitted together into a three-dimensional jigsaw puzzle so that we can see the shattered pot reconstructed.

Here an artist shows the full repertoire of the ancient ceramic artists' craft at two moments in history. From the Chiapas-Guatemala border region, a suite of styles (left) made during the Ocós phase (about 1400 B.C.) is compared with those of the Cuadros phase (below) from about three centuries later. Once these styles have been dated, discovering even a single new fragment may tell the expert the approximate date of the layer in which it was found.

Complementary Studies

By our day many ruins and monuments have been destroyed by nature or have been looted for artifacts to sell to rich collectors, so information about ancient ways that the ruins and artifacts might have given to archaeologists had they been properly discovered has often been lost. But early explorers' accounts of ruins, as well as reports from observers of how natives lived before modern ways changed them, tell us things of value about what has disappeared. This drawing by Frederick Catherwood was executed during his exploration with John Lloyd Stephens at Copan, Honduras, in 1839. Joseph Smith and his associates were excited when they saw scenes like this in Stephens's 1841 book, the first substantial information they had access to that showed that there even was an ancient American civilization.

Social anthropologists (or ethnographers) and other observers have lived among surviving Mesoamerican peoples that are descended from the bearers of the ancient civilization. Much of our ability to interpret the remains found by the archaeologists is based on this eyewitness information. Here a Lacandon Indian of Chiapas demonstrates to visitors and his sons the old technique of fire starting still in use among his people.

Comparison of Ugrian Languages of Northwestern Siberia with Penutian Native American Languages of Central California

Ugrian		*Penutian*	
ulu, uli	head	uli, uri	head
tabor	hair	tapor	hair
tai	forehead	tai	forehead
xorox	throat	xorxos	throat
t'iwy	lung	tawe	lung
ngissu	finger joints	'issu	finger
kora	leg, foot	koro	leg, foot
jet	to tattoo	yétkû	tattoo on face

Language comparisons offer another line of information to be researched for history. Conventional linguists consider the comparison of languages between the Old World and the New to be naïve, so they don't attempt such studies. A few qualified scholars, however, have braved professional disapproval to make such comparisons and report interhemispheric links. Dr. Otto Sadovszky, a native speaker of a language belonging to the Ural-Altaic group of central Eurasia, by a strange set of career accidents ended up studying Amerindians of northern California and was shocked to discover direct parallels to Old World tongues familiar to him. He has concluded that a small group of people migrated in a short period of time, three or four thousand years ago, from interior western Siberia along the Arctic coast to Alaska then along the coast to California. His discoveries defy the dogma of no linguistic connection between the hemispheres preached by the majority of linguists. A tiny sample of the thousands of similarities in vocabulary that he has established is shown in this table.[209]

While the languages he has treated do not occur in Mesoamerica, his work should warn scholars that unsuspected but convincing linguistic links may yet be shown for Mexico and the Old World too. In fact, one linguist, Dr. Mary LeCron Foster of the University of California at Berkeley, claims such a connection between Egyptian and Mixe-Zoquean, the language of the Olmecs, although her results are not yet fully published.[210] Brian Stubbs has documented the presence of Hebrew/Arabic elements in tongues of the Uto-Aztecan family.[211]

Linguistic scholars collect information from native language speakers. Their data yield valuable dictionaries that permit reconstructing much of the history of the two hundred or so languages once used in Mesoamerica. The historical data in turn show anthropologists some of the concepts that were used in the ancient cultures. For example, Dr. Lyle Campbell, seen here working with informants in Mexico, and a colleague have shown that the people we now call the Olmecs, of the second and first millennia B.C., apparently had words meaning "dance," "incense," "festival," "tobacco," "to play music," "to buy something," and "to plane wood."[212] Archaeologists are unlikely to discover material remains that would establish the presence of such culture traits in that remote period. (Recall that these people were contemporary with the Jaredites.)

Art historians apply principles derived from studies of art in other parts of the world to interpret pieces from Mesoamerica, place them in orderly sequences, and establish interconnections between styles. This famous ceramic disk, which shows a few Near Eastern features, comes from central Veracruz and dates between the seventh and tenth centuries.

his is the story
the old men used to tell:
In a certain time
which no one can now describe,
which no one can now remember,
those who came here to sow,
our grandfathers and grandmothers
landed here, arrived here,
following the way,
and came at last to govern
here in this land,
which was known by a single name,
as if it were a little world of its own.

They came in ships across the sea
in many companies,
and arrived there on the seashore,
on the northern coast,
and the place where they left their ships
is now called Panutla
which means, "Where one crosses the water."
They followed the coast,
they sought the mountains,
and some of them found
the mountains capped with snow,
and the smoking mountains,
and arrived at Quauhtemalla [Guatemala],
following the coast.
The journey was not made
at their own pleasure:
the priests led them,
and their god showed them the way.
They came at last
to the place called Tamoanchan,
which means, "We seek our house."

Traditions and legends provide information about the past, although it is not easy for the specialists in those matters to sort fact from fancy in the tales. Of particular interest are a series of accounts that report that Mesoamerican ancestors had arrived from across the sea.[214] The text of one such account, from the Codex Matritense obtained by Sahagun, is reproduced here.

Epigraphy, the study of inscriptions, has flourished in recent decades in Mesoamerica. More and more writings on the monuments can now be read. Mayan texts, decipherers now say, quite often use versions of this glyph sequence that means "it came to pass."[213] Of course, similar phrasing is very frequent in the text of the Book of Mormon.

Old World Connections with the New

A nineteenth-century visitor to the Yucatan ruin of Uxmal copied this design. The circular device at the top is, of course, the star of David, a significant symbol among the Jews.

One of the beliefs widely shared among Mesoamerican groups at the time of the Conquest by the Spaniards was that at least some of their ancestors had arrived from across the ocean. Conventional archaeologists and historians, on the contrary, believe that the entire civilization and, indeed, all Amerindian cultures developed independently of the Old World. They handle the traditions about transoceanic voyaging as inexplicable superstitions or ideas borrowed from the Spaniards. But the frequency of the stories of ancestors crossing the sea may indicate that the natives knew more than scientists allow them.

For example, the Aztec ruler Montezuma told Cortez, "We are foreigners and came here from very remote parts. We possess information that our lineage was led to this land by a lord to whom we all owed allegiance." A different version of the same tradition went this way: "It has been innumerable years since the first settlers arrived in these parts of New Spain, which is almost another world; and they came in ships by sea." A Guatemalan tradition maintained that "they came from the other part of the ocean, from where the sun rises." Many other legends sound much like these.[215]

Modern researchers seeking to clarify the origins of the Mesoamericans have found and published a vast body of information that convinces some observers that the Indian traditions were correct. Much of the data consists of parallels in cultural patterns shared between Mesoamerica and other parts of the Americas, on one hand, and various parts of the Old World, on the other. Of particular interest is a set of over two hundred features found in both Mesoamerica and the ancient Near East. Some of them are highly specific, and it seems unlikely that they were all independently originated by American "indigenous" peoples with no connection to the ancient civilizations in the Old World.[216]

Among the theories offered to explain Old World similarities to Mesoamerica is the proposal that Israelites reached the area by sea from Bible lands. Versions of this notion have been around since the first Spanish priests arrived in the sixteenth century. One of the better-informed recent treatments of this theme is by Dr. Cyrus H. Gordon, a renowned expert on Hebrew and related languages and history.[217]

One version of the Near Eastern theory is recounted in the Book of Mormon. It remains a question for future research to determine, however, what degree of influence the three Book of Mormon voyages had on Mesoamerican cultures, or whether other voyages, say by Polynesians or Chinese, had major, direct influence on New World areas. We cannot tell from the Book of Mormon text exactly how much of Israelite culture was transplanted to the new scene. Nephi$_1$ was explicit in saying that he tried to weed out many Jewish notions in founding his new colony (see 2 Nephi 25:1–5), although a version of the law of Moses was followed. In the less material aspects of culture such as religious beliefs and ceremonies, which are hard to detect through archaeology, the Judaic influence is represented in the Nephite record as important, at least among the leading lineage. But Israelite elements in the life of the more numerous Lamanite group are hard to detect in Mormon's account.

There is a huge body of writings—good and bad—on transoceanic contact between the Americas and many other parts of the Old World. It was recently made accessible for the first time in a massive guide to the literature.[218] The introduction to that study concludes, "It is both plausible and probable on nautical grounds that numerous voyages crossed the oceans at multiple points before the age of modern discovery."[219] Ships from China, Southeast Asia, Japan, the Mediterranean, and Africa, as well as from the Near East, seem to have voyaged across before Columbus, and they left a great deal of evidence of their arrival. This information makes more believable the traditions that ancestors of the Mesoamericans arrived by boat, despite the fact that a majority of scholars still refuse to examine the evidence seriously.

Model ships in a museum in Haifa, Israel, illustrate types of vessels that could have been available to make an early crossing of the ocean to America. On the left is a Phoenician vessel of about 700 B.C. The ship on the right was used by Jews in the eastern Mediterranean in the third century A.D.

Cyrus Gordon, one of the great scholars on the Near East, sees Jewish features in this stela from the state of Veracruz. It dates perhaps a bit before Mormon's day. Gordon claims that the cord wrapped around the forearm of the major figure is arranged precisely like the ritual wrapping of the Judaic phylactery of medieval times. However most Mesoamericanist scholars, unacquainted with the Old World material, consider the scene simply to show preparation for a ritual Mesoamerican ball game.

A well-known series of Egyptian carved relief scenes like this shows a rite known as the "Baptism of Pharaoh." The gods Horus and either Thoth or Seth, who are associated with death, life and health, and the directions, stand on either side of the ruler, pouring a stream of life symbols across him. In a parallel scene, from the Mexican Codex Borgia, the lord and lady of the region of death pour water, a symbol of life in that area, in a similar pattern over the god of healing.[220] A famous archaeological expert on ancient Israel, William F. Albright, considered that this comparison would be convincing evidence of communication between the cultures of the artists had the one scene not been from the distant New World.[221]

We may also wonder about how makers of these ceramic incense burners would independently come up with the concepts and motifs behind such remarkably similar specimens. The one on the right is from Kaminaljuyu, Guatemala, dated about the sixth century B.C. That on the left is from Nuzu, Mesopotamia, a few centuries earlier.[222]

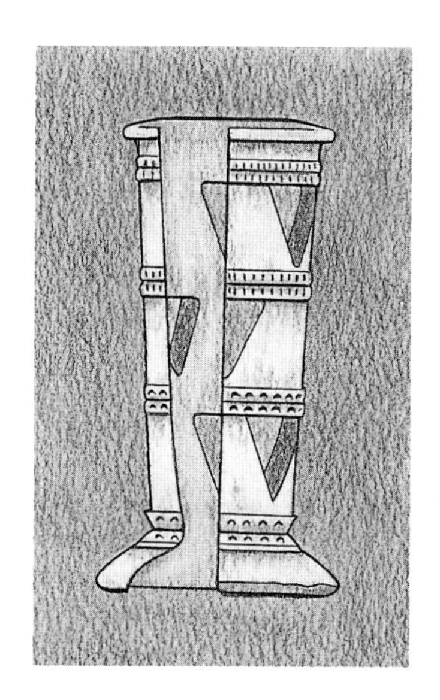

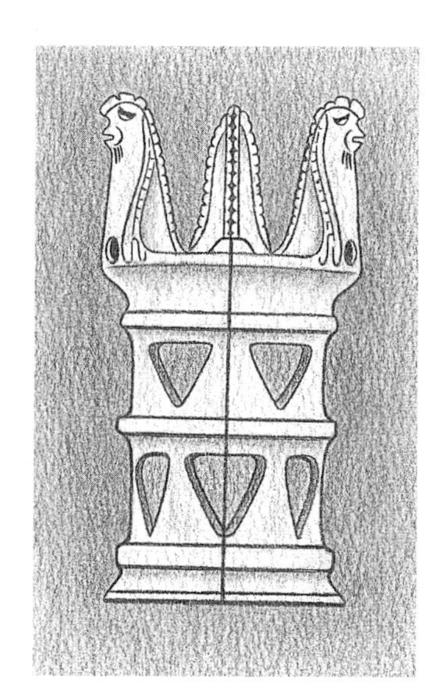

Artists have been intrigued by a variety of similarities between Chinese and Mesoamerican art. The design above is from China before our era, while that on the right is from the southern Maya area in the Late Classic period. Given the time difference, some observers maintain that this comparison is coincidental; however, much more complicated artistic themes show an equal or greater similarity and the notion of coincidence is not very persuasive.[223]

This striking arrangement of jade figures below was found in precisely this position in a carefully prepared cache excavated at La Venta in 1955.[224] The cache is dated to around 700 B.C., although at least some of the objects were clearly older than that. Some profound cultic and social ritual is obviously being represented.

In 1996 H. Mike Xu, a teacher of Chinese at an Oklahoma university, published a short study claiming to identify and translate Chinese writing inscribed on the stone celts in the background of this scene. Xu supposed that refugees from China reached southern Mexico around 1122 B.C. as a result of a historically documented crisis that occurred then in their homeland and that these objects and the inscriptions on them came from the migrants.[225] Prominent Mesoamerican archaeologists immediately disputed his claim, although he backed it up with opinions from eminent mainland Chinese scholars to whom he had shown copies of the inscriptions.

ENDNOTES

1 For example, see James H. Charlesworth, "Messianism in the Pseudepigrapha and the Book of Mormon," and Krister Stendahl, "The Sermon on the Mount and Third Nephi," in *Reflections on Mormonism: Judaeo-Christian Parallels*, ed. Truman G. Madsen (Salt Lake City: Brigham Young University Religious Studies Center, 1978), 99–137, 139–54.

2 The scholarship supporting this statement is sampled very effectively in two volumes edited by Noel B. Reynolds: *Book of Mormon Authorship: New Light on Ancient Origins,* (Provo, Utah: FARMS, 1982); and *Book of Mormon Authorship Revisited: The Evidence for Ancient Origins* (Provo, Utah: FARMS, 1997).

3 See Hugh Nibley, *Lehi in the Desert; The World of the Jaredites; There Were Jaredites* (Salt Lake City: Deseret Book and FARMS, 1988).

4 See, for example, my article, "The Book of Mormon as a Mesoamerican Codex," *Newsletter and Proceedings of the S.E.H.A.* (Society for Early Historic Archaeology) 139 (December 1976): 1–9; and various articles in Stephen D. Ricks and William J. Hamblin, eds., *Warfare in the Book of Mormon* (Salt Lake City: Deseret Book and FARMS, 1990).

5 Some of these results are conveniently summarized in the papers in John L. Sorenson and Melvin J. Thorne, eds., *Rediscovering the Book of Mormon* (Salt Lake City: Deseret Book and FARMS, 1991).

6 See Part 1 of my book, *The Geography of Book of Mormon Events: A Source Book*, rev. ed. (Provo, Utah: FARMS, 1992), for a history of Latter-day Saint thought on this issue.

7 See particularly John L. Sorenson, *An Ancient American Setting for the Book of Mormon* (Salt Lake City: Deseret Book and FARMS, 1985).

8 See Sorenson, "Book of Mormon as a Mesoamerican Codex."

9 See Sorenson, *Ancient American Setting*, 50–6.

10 See Sorenson, "When Lehi's Party Arrived in the Land, Did They Find Others There?" *Journal of Book of Mormon Studies* 1/1 (1992): 1–34.

11 (Salt Lake City: Deseret Book and FARMS, 1985).

12 See Paul Kirchoff, "Mesoamerica, sus límites geográficos, composición étnica y carácteres culturales," *Acta Americana* (1943), 1:92–107. Accessible in English in another work by Paul Kirchoff, "Mesoamerica: Its Geographic Limits, Ethnic Composition, and Cultural Characteristics," in *Heritage of Conquest*, ed. Sol Tax (New York: Macmillan, 1952). H. B. Nicholson's update of Kirchoff's list is actually more useful. See H. B. Nicholson, "The Efflorescence of Mesoamerican Civilization: A Résumé," in *Indian Mexico Past and Present*, ed. Betty Bell (Los Angeles: University of California, Latin American Center, 1967), 64–5.

13 See the following works by John L. Sorenson: "A History of Ideas: The Geography of Book of Mormon Events in Latter-day Saint Thought," chap. 1 in *Geography of Book of Mormon Events*; "Digging into the Book of Mormon," *Ensign* (September 1984): 29–30, 36–7 nn. 6, 8, 11; "The Book of Mormon Mapped," chap. 1 in *Ancient American Setting.*

14 See discussion and references in Sorenson, *Ancient American Setting*, 87–90.

15 See Juan Comas C., "Y eut-il des nègres en Amérique avant Colomb?" *Bulletin de la société suisse d'americanistes* 7/11 (1956): 10–2.

16 V. Morrell, "Research News: Confusion in Earliest America" *Science* 248 (27 April 1990): 440, see pp. 439–41.

17 See, for example, Andrzej Wierçinski, "Inter- and Intrapopulational Racial Differentiation of Tlatilco, Cerro de las Mesas, Teotihuacan, Monte Alban and Yucatan Maya," *Actas, Documentos y Memorias, 36a Congreso Internacional de Americanistas, Lima, 1970* (Lima: Instituto de Estudios Peruanos, 1972), 1:231–48; and other studies cited in Sorenson, *Ancient American Setting,* 365.

18 See, for example, T. Dale Stewart, *The People of America* (New York: Scribner's, 1973).

19 Since the founders of the Nephites and Lamanites originated in Judea and were obviously of the Mediterranean biological group, they would have been a good deal more swarthy and less "white" or "fair" than Scandinavians, for instance. Those adjectives were subjectively defined by the record keepers, as was "dark." The founders could also, by statistical accident, have been atypical of the general Judean population.

20 See Sorenson, "When Lehi's Party Arrived."

21 See ibid., 19–24.

22 See Alma 43:13–4; John L. Sorenson, "Book of Mormon Peoples," in *Encyclopedia of Mormonism*, 1:194.

23 Nibley, *Lehi in the Desert,* 251; see p. 250.

24 For example, see Jacques de Mahieu, "Voici les momies blondes du Pérou," *Kadath: Chroniques des civilisations disparues* 51 (1983): 29–31; compare Pierre-André Gloor, "Blancs et noirs d'amérique avant Christophe Colomb," *Kadath: Chroniques des civilisations disparues* 77 (1991): 4–15.

25 See especially Alexander von Wuthenau's *Unexpected Faces in Ancient America, 1500 B.C.–A.D. 1500* (New York: Crown, 1975); also Luis González Calderón, *Cabecitas Olmecas: origines de la primera civilización de América* (Coatzacoalcos, Veracruz, México: privately published, 1977).

26 Certain noted academic physical anthropologists concur. See, for instance, Eusebio Dávalos Hurtado, "El hombre en Mesoamerica hasta la llegada de los Españoles," *Memorias y Revista de la Academía Nacional de Ciencias* 49 (1964): 411, where that distinguished Mexican expert says that the "falsehood" of the claim of a single northeast Asian ancestry for American Indians has been exposed by the figurines shown in von Wuthenau's *Unexpected Faces in Ancient America.* Moreover, William W. Howells, a noted U.S. physical anthropologist, in "The Origins of American Indian Race Types," in *The Maya and Their Neighbors*, ed. Clarence L. Hay et al. (New York: Dover Publications, 1977), 3–9, stated that there is probably greater variety among Amerindians "than may be found in the White racial stock" (p. 5). An extensive literature on both sides of the question is summarized in John L. Sorenson and Martin H. Raish, *Pre-Columbian Contact with the Americas across the Oceans: An Annotated Bibliography,* 2nd ed., 2 vols. (Provo, Utah: Research Press, 1996).

27 See the following works by Brian Stubbs, "Looking Over vs. Overlooking Native American Languages: Let's Void the Void," *Journal of Book of Mormon Studies* 5/1 (1996): 1–49; *Elements of Hebrew in Uto-Aztecan: A Summary of the Data* (Provo, Utah: FARMS, 1988), which cites additional literature.

28 See my article, "Emergent Systems Analysis," in *First Annual Symposium on LDS Intercultural, Communications, and Language Concerns,* ed. V. Lynn Tyler (Provo, Utah: Brigham Young University Language Research Center, 1972), 159–64.

29 Clifford Geertz, *The Interpretation of Cultures* (New York: Basic Books, 1973).

30 *Fernando Cortés: His Five Letters of Relation to the Emperor Charles V*, ed. and transl. Francis A. MacNutt (Glorieta, N.Mex.: Rio Grande Press, 1977), 1:263.

31 Ibid., 1:220.

32 Fernando Cortez, as cited in Michael D. Coe, *America's First Civilization* (New York: American Heritage Publishing, 1968), 12.

33 "Zarahemla," *Times and Seasons* 3 (1 October 1842): 927. The reference is to John Lloyd Stephens's still-fascinating book, *Incidents of Travel in Central America, Chiapas and Yucatan*, the first substantive work in English reporting on the Maya ruins. It was first published in New York by Harper & Brothers in 1841. After scores of intervening editions, the most recent is by Smithsonian Press, 1993.

34 Regarding the nutritional adequacy of the ancient and modern diet, see Evon. Z. Vogt, *Zinacantan: A Maya Community in the Highlands of Chiapas* (Cambridge, Mass.: Belknap Press of Harvard University Press, 1969), 70, and references there; the diet is considered "highly nutritious."

35 See Sorenson, *Ancient American Setting,* 186.

36 See J. E. S. Thompson, *Mexico Before Cortez: An Account of the Daily Life, Religion, and Ritual of the Aztecs and Kindred Peoples* (New York: Scribner's, 1933), 68.

37 See H. B. Nicholson, "Montezuma's Zoo," *Pacific Discovery* 8/4 (July–August 1955): 3–11.

38 See, for example, Mary Lucas Powell, "Health and Disease in the Late Prehistoric Southeast," in *Disease and Demography in the Americas,* ed. John W. Verano and Douglas H. Ubelaker (Washington: Smithsonian Institution Press, 1992), 41–53.

39 For further information, see Sorenson: "Animals in the Book of Mormon: An Annotated Bibliography," (FARMS, 1992); and *Ancient American Setting,* 288–99.

40 See Paul Sillitoe, "Stone versus

Steel," *Mankind* 12 (December 1979): 151–61. Experiments show that a steel axe "is not decisively superior" to a stone one and that if the comparison were with copper, a softer metal, any advantage for metal probably would disappear.

41 *Fernando Cortés: His Five Letters,* 1:258–9.

42 Hernando Colón, *Vida del Almirante Don Cristóbal Colón* (México: Fondo de Cultura Económica, 1947).

43 See Jorge G. Marcos, "Breve prehistoria del Ecuador," in *Arqueología de la costa ecuatoriana: nuevos enfoques,* ed. Jorge G. Marcos (Guayaquíl, Ecuador: Escuela Politécnica del Litoral, Centro de Estudios Arqueológicos y Antropológicos, 1986), 25–50.

44 See John L. Sorenson, "Wheeled Figurines in the Ancient World" (FARMS, 1981).

45 Domingo Juarros, *A Statistical and Commercial History of the Kingdom of Guatemala, in Spanish America* (New York: AMS Press, 1971), 390.

46 See *Anchor Bible Dictionary,* s.v. "chariots."

47 William Wilson, *Wilson's Old Testament Word Studies* (Grand Rapids, Mich.: Kregel, 1978).

48 See Hasso von Winning, "Further Examples of Figurines on Wheels from Mexico," *Ethnos* 25 (1960): 65–72. Von Winning, who first published this sketch, has told me that the sitting human figure may be a modern fake, but the wheeled portion is pre-Columbian and definitely had some sort of rider shown on it.

49 A famous hurricane noted in Yucatan tradition as occurring in the year 1464 "set on fire" the roofs of the houses so that it "burned up a large part of the people" (Diego de Landa, *Landa's Relación de las Cosas de Yucatan: A Translation,* ed. Alfred M. Tozzer [Cambridge, Mass.: Peabody Museum, 1941], 41).

50 See, for example, comments in Michael D. Coe, "San Lorenzo and the Olmec Civilization," in *Dumbarton Oaks Conference on the Olmec,* ed. Elizabeth P. Benson (Washington, D.C.: Dumbarton Oaks Research Library and Collection, 1968), 75; and Gareth W. Lowe, Thomas A. Lee Jr., and Eduardo Martinez E., *Izapa: An Introduction to the Ruins and Monuments,* (Provo, Utah: New World Archaeological Foundation, Brigham Young University, 1982), 28.

51 William A. Haviland, "Principles of Descent in Sixteenth Century Yucatan," *Katunob* 8/2 (December 1972): 64.

52 See Munro S. Edmonson, "Play: Games, Gossip, and Humor, "in *Handbook of Middle American Indians* (Austin: University of Texas Press, 1967), 6:206.

53 Pablo (Paul) Henning, in his "Apuntes sobre la historia del chalchiuitl en América," *Memorias, Sociedad Científica "Antonio Alzate,"* 31 (1911): 29–46 (México), recapitulates a number of traditions in which Mexican descent groups are represented by tree imagery. Incidentally, Henning was the first Latter-day Saint Mesoamerican archaeologist.

54 See my paper, tentatively titled "The Complex Structure of Religious Groups among the Nephites, 200–1 B.C.," accepted for publication in a festschrift for Richard L. Anderson to be published by FARMS in 1998.

55 See *Landa's Relación,* 125, for example.

56 As cited in Miguel Leon-Portilla, *Aztec Thought and Culture: A Study of the Ancient Nahuatl Mind* (Norman: University of Oklahoma Press, 1963), 148, citing Andres de Olmos.

57 A discussion of this topic is included in my paper entitled "Nephite Political Economy" in *Nephite Culture and Society: Collected Papers* (Salt Lake City: New Sage, 1997).

58 See Eva Hunt, "Irrigation and the Socio-political Organization of the Cuicatec Caçicazgos," in *The Prehistory of the Tehuacan Valley,* ed. Frederick Johnson (Austin: University of Texas Press, 1972), 4:162–259, especially p. 221.

59 The following are good summaries of recent research on this topic: Douglas H. Ubelaker, "Patterns of Demographic Change in the Americas," *Human Biology* 64 (1992): 361–79, and Verano and Ubelaker, eds., *Disease and Demography.*

60 See William L. Fash, *Scribes, Warriors and Kings* (London: Thames and Hudson, 1991), 111, 171, 181.

61 See, for example, John L. Sorenson, "A Bibliography for Yucatan Medicinal Plant Studies by William E. Gates," *Tlalocan* 3/4 (1957): 334–43.

62 Patricia Rieff Anawalt, *Indian Clothing before Cortés: Mesoamerican Costumes from the Codices* (Norman: University of Oklahoma Press, 1981), xiii.

63 A fine treatment of this whole topic is the heavily illustrated book by Anawalt, *Indian Clothing before Cortés.*

64 Anawalt, *Indian Clothing,* 13.

65 For more information, see Vernon L. Scarborough and David R. Wilcox, eds., *The Mesoamerican Ballgame* (Tucson: University of Arizona Press, 1991).

66 Beginning with Edward B. Tylor, "On the Game of Patolli in Ancient Mexico, and Its Probably Asiatic Origin," *The Journal of the Anthropological Institute of Great Britain and Ireland* 8 (1878): 116–31.

67 Edmonson, "Play," 6:206.

68 Ibid.

69 *Landa's Relación,* 158.

70 See Zvi Greenhut, "The City of Salt," *Biblical Archaeology Review* 19 (July–August 1993): 33–43.

71 Robert Chadwick, "Archaeological Synthesis of Michoacan and Adjacent Regions," in *Handbook of Middle American Indians* 11:689; see pp. 657–93.

72 For an extended discussion of this topic, see my article, "The Settlements of Book of Mormon Peoples," in *Nephite Culture.*

73 See *Anchor Bible Dictionary,* s.v. "Jerusalem," which relies on Magen Broshi, "Estimating the Population of Ancient Jerusalem," *Biblical Archaeology Review* 4/2 (1978): 10–5.

74 See Ray T. Matheny, "An Early Maya Metropolis Uncovered: El Mirador," *National Geographic* 172 (3 September 1987): 317–39. This site has no identifiable connection with Book of Mormon lands.

75 For a clear general discussion, see H. G. Quaritch Wales, *The Mountain of God* (London: Bernard Quaritch, 1953). For a comparison of the Near East and Mesoamerica, see Sorenson "The Significance of an Apparent Relationship between the Ancient Near East and Mesoamerica," in *Man across the Sea: Problems of Pre-Columbian Contacts*, ed. Carroll L. Riley et al. (Austin: University of Texas Press, 1971), 235.

76 See Valerie Gladstone, "Archaeologist Discovers Mayan Bridge," *Salt Lake Tribune,* 18 February 1995 (Reuter News Service). The discovery was made at Yaxchilan on the Usumacinta River.

77 For a general discussion and definition, see Elman Rogers Service, *The Origins of the State and Civilizaton* (New York: Norton, 1975).

78 A full discussion of this topic is in my "Nephite Political Economy," in *Nephite Culture.*

79 *Fernando Cortés: His Five Letters,* 1:259.

80 Evon Z. Vogt, *The Zinacantecos of Mexico: A Modern Maya Way of Life* (New York: Holt, Rinehart and Winston, 1970), 23.

81 Much about the process and its intricacies are displayed in a fascinating novel, based on anthropological field experience among the Tzotzil Maya of highland Chiapas, by Carter Wilson, *Crazy February: Death and Life in the Mayan Highlands of Mexico* (Berkeley: University of California Press, 1974).

82 John W. Welch has a book forthcoming on Book of Mormon laws and trials.

83 See the discussion and references in Sorenson, *Ancient American Setting,* 300–9.

84 Cecilia Klein, "Aztec Masks and Economic Gain: A Function of Masking in a Pre-industrial Empire," in *Abstracts of Papers, 44th International Congress of Americanists (Manchester, 1982)* (Manchester, England: School of Geography, Manchester University), 15.

85 Yet there were special circumstances when enslavement was profitable and did occur. For example, at the time of the Spanish Conquest, the town of Sacapulas "served as a jail or prison, where the Quiché kings, to whom these lands belonged, enclosed the captives from the wars which they continually had with their neighbours, because these Quiché kings were very powerful. . . . Every night they put the captives in a kind of rock pen which was very large, and by day they made them go to the salt factory, where they made much salt, and it was of great importance to their king" (W. George Lovell, "The Cuchumatan Highlands of Guatemala on the Eve of the Spanish Conquest," *Katunob* 11/4 [November 1979]: 18, citing Martín Alfonso Tovilla, an early seventeenth century source).

86 For example, see the discussion between Bernal and Proskouriakoff in Coe, "San Lorenzo and the Olmec Civilization," 75–6.

87 See chapter 6 in Sorenson, *Ancient American Setting.* For general and specific comparisons, see Ricks and Hamblin, eds. *Warfare in the Book of Mormon.*

88 See Sorenson, *Ancient American Setting,* 402 n. 56.

89 Hubert Howe Bancroft, *Native Races of the Pacific States of North America* (New York: Appleton, 1875), 2:412.

90 See Ross Hassig, *War and Society in Ancient Mesoamerica* (Berkeley: University of California Press, 1992), 142–3.

91 Accessible in English in Milton R. Hunter and Thomas Stuart Ferguson, *Ancient America and the Book of Mormon* (Oakland, Calif.: Kolob Book, 1950), 385. Samuel Kirkland Lothrop, in his *Atitlan* (Washington, D.C.: Carnegie Institution of Washington, 1933), 10, 13, reports battles in which the Zutugil (Tzutuhil) of highland Guatemala had fourteen thousand slain in one action and eight thousand in another.

92 The appendix in my article, "Seasonality of Warfare in the Book of Mormon and in Mesoamerica," in *Warfare in the Book of Mormon*, ed. Ricks and Hamblin, 462–74, lists all military events reported in that scripture. Most were low on a scale of violence.

93 Regarding the glyphs, see Joyce Marcus, "The Conquest Slabs of Building J, Monte Alban," in *The Cloud People: Divergent Evolution of the Zapotec and Mixtec Civilizations,* ed. Kent V. Flannery and Joyce Marcus, (New York: Academic Press, 1983), 107. On the source of these Monte Albán II rulers, see Ignacio Bernal, *The Olmec World* (Berkeley: University of California Press, 1969), 166.

94 Mesoamerican armor is nowhere comprehensively discussed in the professional literature. Hassig, *War and Society,* has a partial treatment. Another introduction, with extensive notes to the literature, is in William J. Hamblin, "Armor in the Book of Mormon," in *Warfare in the Book of Mormon,* ed. Ricks and Hamblin, 410–6.

95 See particularly William J. Hamblin, "Swords in the Book of Mormon," and A. Brent Merrill, "Notes on the Cimeter (Scimitar) in the Book of Mormon," in *Warfare in the Book of Mormon*, ed. Ricks and Hamblin, 329–51 and 360–4, as well as my review, "Viva Zapato! Hurray for the Shoe!" in *Review of Books on the Book of Mormon* 6/1 (1994): 328–31.

96 As of eight years ago. Other sites have since been identified. See my "Fortifications in the Book of Mormon Account Compared with Mesoamerican Fortifications," in *Warfare in the Book of Mormon*, 425–33.

97 H.B. Nicholson, "Religion in Pre-Hispanic Central Mexico," in *Handbook of Middle American Indians,* 10:444.

98 See Frances F. Berdan, *The Aztecs of Central Mexico: An Imperial Society* (New York: Holt, Rinehart and Winston, 1982), 85 n. 1.

99 Vogt, *Zinacantecos of Mexico,* viii.

100 It is shocking to discover that there is not a single competent work by a scholar that tries to pull together the vast body of material on Mesoamerican religion. Perhaps the best, and most frequently cited, work on religion is Nicholson's "Religion in Pre-Hispanic Central Mexico," 395–446, but it is essentially on the Aztec pantheon.

101 See J. E. S. Thompson, *Maya History and Religion* (Norman: Oklahoma University Press, 1970), 233; also in an interview printed in *El Heraldo* (Mexico City), 27 January 1972.

102 Nicholson, "Religion in Pre-Hispanic Central Mexico," 409.

103 See my "The Complex Structure of Religious Groups among the Nephites, 200–1 B.C.", in a forthcoming Festschrift for professor Richard Anderson.

104 See *Landa's Relación,* 259.

105 See, for example, Nancy M. Farriss, "Sacrifice and Communion in Colonial Maya Religion," in *Abstracts of Papers,* 15. Farriss remarks, "Despite many similarities noted by Spanish missionaries to Mesoamerica between native and Christian religions, one they failed to note, or chose not to emphasize, was that similar rites of sacrifice and communion constituted the central rituals of both. Slaughter of a blameless being (animal, human, divine, and combinations thereof) and the sharing of flesh embodied the principal link between the natural and supernatural orders in both cases."

106 See especially my article, "Significance of an Apparent Relationship," 219–41. Additional references can be found in my two-volume work with Raish, *Pre-Columbian Contact with the Americas.*

107 Alfred V. Kidder, Jesse D. Jennings, and Edwin M. Shook, *Excavations at Kaminaljuyu, Guatemala* (University Park, Pa.: Pennsylvania State University Press, 1977), 93. My article "Significance of an Apparent Relationship" lists many connected similarities.

108 Philip Drucker, Robert F. Heizer, and Robert J. Squier, *Excavations at La Venta, Tabasco, 1955,* (Washington, D.C.: United States Government Printing Office, 1959), 132.

109 For a general introduction to the comparison, see my "Significance of an Apparent Relationship."

110 Nicholson, "Religion in Pre-Hispanic Central Mexico," 432.

111 See *Fernando Cortés: His Five Letters,* 1:216.

112 See William L. Fash, Jr., "Deducing Social Organization from Classic Maya Settlement Patterns: A Case Study from the Copan Valley," in *Civilization in the Ancient Americas: Essays in Honor of Gordon R. Willey*, ed. Richard M.Leventhal and Alan L. Kolata (Albuquerque: University of New Mexico Press, 1983), 266.

113 The modern place-name *Lamanai* has no apparent connection to the Book of Mormon term *Lamanite.* Rather, it derives from a Mayan language and only coincidentally sounds similar. The name comes from a Mayan word that seems to mean "crocodile."

114 Peter T. Furst, "Morning Glory and Mother Goddess at Tepantitla, Teotihuacan: Iconography and Analogy in Pre-Columbian Art," in *Mesoamerican Archaeology: New Approaches*, ed. Norman Hammond (Austin: University of Texas Press, 1974), 187–215, documents the use of hallucinogenic red seeds of the *Sophora secundiflora* shrub that occurred in northern Mexico and Texas in archaeological deposits dated before 8000 B.C. They were in use in the area as late as the last century and may also have been employed farther south among some Mesoamericans. He also discusses the literature on other substances in Mexico and Central America that produced similar effects.

115 See Arthur J. O. Anderson and Charles E. Dibble, trans., *The War of Conquest. How It Was Waged Here in Mexico*, (Salt Lake City: University of Utah Press, 1978), 42.

116 The most popular treatment of this salvational interpretation is by Laurette Séjourné, *Burning Water: Thought and Religion in Ancient Mexico* (Berkeley: Shambhala, 1976), who sees Quetzalcoatl as a god in a resurrection cult that is visible most clearly at Teotihuacan. Michel Graulich insists that elements in Mexican myth that have been considered products of Spanish Christian influence represent native, pre-Columbian beliefs (see his "Afterlife in Ancient Mexican Thought," in *Circumpacifica, Band I: Mittel- und Südamerika, Festschrift für Thomas S. Barthel*, ed. Bruno Illius and Matthias Laubscher [Frankfurt: Peter Lang, 1990], 165–88). He maintains that the sources, when correctly read, tell of a divine creator couple who lived in a paradise from which they were expelled because of a transgression. They were rescued from their dismal state on earth by the self-sacrifice of the god Quetzalcoatl, or of him and his twin, and this allowed them to escape the underworld and provided a means by which humans who emulate their qualities may reach the lost paradise. A survey of related beliefs throughout Mesoamerica is found in the massive monograph by V. Garth Norman, *Izapa Sculpture Part 2: Text,* (Provo, Utah: New World Archaeological Foundation, Brigham Young University, 1976). Consult the terms *underworld* and *resurrection* in his index, and particularly note on pages 234–6 his interpretation of resurrection beliefs shown on Izapa Stela 5.

117 One is reminded of the "gigantic, crouching toadlike monster, with snapping mouths at the elbow and knee joints and gaping, teeth-studded mouth" of Aztec belief which floated on the underearth primal sea along with the *cipactli,* the great spiny crocodilian monster which bore the earth on its back. The former creature, Tlaltecuhtli, "was possibly believed to swallow the sun in the evening, disgorging it each dawn, also devouring the blood and hearts of sacrificed victims and the souls of the dead in general" (Nicholson, "Religion in Pre-Hispanic Central Mexico," 406).

118 See Louis Midgley, "The Ways of Remembrance," in *Rediscovering the Book of Mormon,* ed. Sorenson and Thorne, 168–76.

119 See Sorenson, "When Lehi's Party Arrived," 20.

120 For details on writing systems and records among the Nephites and related peoples and their Mesoamerican parallels, see my "The Book of

Mormon as a Mesoamerican Record," in *Book of Mormon Authorship Revisited,* ed. Reynolds, 391–522.

121 See Sorenson, "When Lehi's Party Arrived," 21–2.

122 See ibid.

123 See Michael D. Coe, "Early Steps in the Evolution of Maya Writing," in *Origins of Religious Art & Iconography in Preclassic Mesoamerica,* ed. H. B. Nicholson, (Los Angeles: UCLA Latin American Center Publications, 1976), 110. Coe identifies thirteen scripts, but his list is not exhaustive.

124 George C. Vaillant, *Aztecs of Mexico: Origin, Rise and Fall of the Aztec Nation* (Garden City, N.Y.: Doubleday, 1962), 172, citing Chimalpahin.

125 Berdan, *Aztecs of Central Mexico,* 158.

126 *Landa's Relación,* 28 n. 154.

127 Part 2 of the Codex Mendoza, for example, is a copy of a pre-Spanish document known as the "Tribute Roll of Moctezuma." It was written on maguey (cactus) paper and lists in glyphic form the nature and amounts of tribute payments in goods made by over four hundred towns to the last independent ruler of Mexico (see the commentaries by Kurt Ross in his *Codex Mendoza: Aztec Manuscript* (Fribourg, Switzerland: Productions Liber, 1978), 35–65.

128 Ralph L. Roys, *The Book of Chilam Balam of Chumayel,* (Norman: University of Oklahoma Press, 1973), 5.

129 This idea was first published in David H. Kelley, "A Cylinder Seal from Tlatilco," *American Antiquity* 31/5 (1966): 744–6, who considered the script a "distinct" writing system, "typologically more advanced than other Mesoamerican systems." John A. Graham thought the marks "closely resemble various oriental scripts ranging from Burma and China to the rim of the Mediterranean." Further, he felt, if the seal is authentic "we would almost surely be dealing with an instance of transpacific contact during the Preclassic" (see his comments on the paper by H. J. Prem, "Calendrics and Writing," in *Contributions of the University of California Archaeological Research Facility* 11 (1971): 133.

130 See Carl Hugh Jones, "The 'Anthon Transcript' and Two Mesoamerican Cylinder Seals, *Newsletter and Proceedings of the S.E.H.A.* 122 (September 1970): 1–8.

131 Michael D. Coe, *The Maya Scribe and his World* (New York: Grolier, 1973), 8.

132 For example, Landa noted, "We found a large number of books of these characters and, as they contained nothing in which there were not to be seen superstition and lies of the devil, we burned them all which they regretted to an amazing degree and which caused them much affliction" (*Landa's Relación,* 77–8 n. 340).

133 See Dennis E. Puleston, "An Epistemological Pathology and the Collapse, or Why the Maya Kept the Short Count," in *Maya Archaeology and Ethnohistory,* ed. Norman Hammond and Gordon R. Willey (Austin: University of Texas Press, 1979), 63–71.

134 Thus far, Randall P. Spackman's is the definitive discussion of Book of Mormon chronology; see his "Introduction to Book of Mormon Chronology: The Principal Prophecies, Calendars, and Dates" (FARMS, 1993).

135 See John B. Carlson, "A Geomantic Model for the Interpretation of Mesoamerican Sites: An Essay in Cross-Cultural Comparison," in *Mesoamerican Sites and World Views,* ed. Elizabeth P. Benson (Washington, D.C.: Dumbarton Oaks, 1981), 178.

136 See my "Book of Mormon as a Mesoamerican Record."

137 See Michael D. Coe, "Native Astronomy in Mesoamerica," in *Archaeoastronomy in Pre-Columbian America,* ed. Anthony F. Aveni (Austin: University of Texas Press, 1975), 30–1.

138 See V. Garth Norman, "Astronomical Orientations of Izapa Sculptures" (master's thesis, Brigham Young University, 1980).

139 After Vincent H. Malmström, "A Reconstruction of the Chronology of Mesoamerican Calendrical Systems," *Journal for the History of Astronomy* 9/2 (1978): 111, fig. 2.

140 In a communication to the author in 1975, Robert E. Smith suggested two possible Hebrew etymologies for the name *Cumorah* that are provocative: **Qum'ora,* "Arise O Light," or **Kum'ora,* "Mound of Light." Either would be unusually apt for a prominent mountain above which the sun rose on 22 December, winter solstice, when viewed from Tres Zapotes, Cerro de la Piedra, and Cerro de las Mesas (their modern site names).

141 Munro Edmonson, *The Book of Counsel: The Popol Vuh of the Quiche Maya of Guatemala* (New Orleans: Middle American Research Institute, Tulane University, 1971), xii.

142 See ibid.

143 León-Portilla, *Aztec Thought and Culture,* 27.

144 For more information on Maya poetry, see J. E. S. Thompson, *Maya Hieroglyphic Writing: An Introduction,* 2nd ed. (Norman: University of Oklahoma Press, 1960), 61–3.

145 See "Parallelism, Merismus, and Difrasismo," in *Reexploring the Book of Mormon,* ed. John W. Welch (Salt Lake City: Deseret Book and FARMS, 1992), 80–2. On chiasmus, see John W. Welch, "Chiasmus in the Book of Mormon," *BYU Studies* 10 (autumn 1969): 69–84; Allen J. Christenson, "The Use of Chiasmus in Ancient Mesoamerica" (FARMS, 1988); Christenson, "The Use of Chiasmus by the Ancient Quiché-Maya," *Latin American Indian Literatures Journal* 4/2 (1988): 125–50; and Christenson, "Chiasmus in Mesoamerican Texts," in *Reexploring the Book of Mormon,* ed. Welch, 233–5.

146 See John W. Welch, ed., *Chiasmus in Antiquity: Structures, Analyses, Exegesis* (Hildesheim, Germany: Gerstenberg, 1981).

147 See, for example, the following works by John W. Welch: "A Masterpiece: Alma 36," in *Rediscovering the Book of Mormon,* ed. Sorenson and Thorne, 114–31, and "Chiasmus Bibliography" (FARMS, 1987).

148 Coe, *Maya Scribe,* 22; see also his "Ancient Maya Writing and Calligraphy," *Visible Language* 5/4 (1971): 306.

149 Fray Diego Durán, *Book of the Gods and Rites and the Ancient Calender,* trans. Fernando Horcasitas and Doris Heyden (Norman: University of Oklahoma Press, 1971,), 295.

150 See Robert Stevenson, *Music in Mexico: A Historical Survey* (New York: Crowell, 1952), 76–7.

151 See *Landa's Relación,* 131–2 n. 616.

152 See Giorgio de Santillana and Hertha von Dechend, *Hamlet's Mill: An Essay on Myth and the Frame of Time* (Boston: Gambit, 1969). On Jerusalem, see *Encyclopaedia Judaica,* s.v. "Jerusalem," 9:1557–8. For the same concept among the Maya, see J. E. S. Thompson, *Maya Hieroglyphic Writing,* 71.

153 See Henning, "Apuntes sobre."

154 See Mary Elizabeth King, "Tree Worship in Mesoamerica and Some Asiatic Comparisons" (master's thesis, Columbia University, 1958); Irene M. Briggs, "The Tree of Life Symbol; Its Significance in Ancient American Religion" (master's thesis, Brigham Young University, 1950).

155 Munro S. Edmonson, "Some Postclassic Questions about the Classic Maya," *Estudios de Cultura Maya* 12 (1979): 162.

156 See E. O. James, *The Tree of Life: An Archaeological Study* (Leiden: Brill, 1966).

157 Among many other sources, see details in C. Wilfred Griggs, "The Tree of Life in Ancient Cultures," *Ensign* (June 1988): 26–31.

158 Many analytical papers are included in Stephen D. Ricks and John W. Welch, eds., *The Allegory of the Olive Tree: The Olive, the Bible, and Jacob 5* (Salt Lake City: Deseret Book and FARMS, 1994).

159 See M. Wells Jakeman, "An Unusual Tree of Life Sculpture from Ancient Central America," *Bulletin of the University Archaeological Society* 4 (March 1953): 26–49, and subsequent treatments by him. See also Norman, *Izapa Sculpture,* 165–236, and Lowe, Lee, and Martinez E., *Izapa: An Introduction,* 298–305.

160 See Briggs's convincing analysis of five main parallels in her master's thesis, "Tree of Life Symbol."

161 Norman, *Izapa Sculpture,* 17.

162 Ibid., citing J. E. S. Thompson, *Maya Hieroglyphic Writing,* 82.

163 See William R. Holland, "Contemporary Tzotzil Cosmological Concepts as a Basis for Interpreting Prehistoric Maya Civilization," *American Antiquity* 29/3 (1964): 303.

164 See Miguel Covarrubias, *Mexico South: The Isthmus of Tehuantepec* (New York: Knopf, 1946), 358,

165 See Henry O. Thompson, "Tell el-Husn—Biblical Beth-shan," *Biblical Archaeologist* 30/4 (1967): 110–35.

166 See Carmen Cook de Leonard, "Sculptures and Rock Carvings at Chalcatzingo, Morelos," in *Contributions of the University of California Archaeological Research Facility* 3 (1967): 71.

167 See Alfredo Lopez Austin,

Teotihuacan (México: El Equilibrista, 1989), 114.

168 See, for example, discussions in Norman, *Izapa Sculpture,* and J. E. S. Thompson, *Maya Hieroglyphic Writing,* 73.

169 See John B. Carlson, "The Double-Headed Dragon and the Sky: A Pervasive Cosmological Symbol," in *Ethnoastronomy and Archaeoastronomy in the American Tropics,* ed. Anthony F. Aveni and Gary Urton (New York: New York Academy of Sciences, 1982), 135–63; Peter David Joralemon, "The Olmec Dragon: A Study in Pre-Columbian Iconography," in *Origins of Religious Art,* ed. Nicholson, 27–71.

170 See *Anchor Bible Dictionary,* s.v. "Leviathan"; William Foxwell Albright, *From the Stone Age to Christianity,* 2nd ed. (Garden City, N.Y.: Doubleday Anchor Book, 1957), 271.

171 See Norman, *Izapa Sculpture,* 56, 137, 169.

172 See ibid., 89–92.

173 See Michael D. Coe, "The Hero Twins: Myth and Image," in *The Maya Vase Book,* vol. 1, ed. Justin Kerr (New York: Justin Kerr, 1989), 161–84, especially 163.

174 Alvarado's 1524 account of passing through coastal Guatemala describes crocodiles over thirty feet long, very ferocious, and greatly feared by the people (see Lawrence H. Feldman, *Papers of Escuintla and Guazacapan: A Contribution to the History and Ethnography of South-Eastern Guatemala* (Greeley, Colo.: Museum of Anthropology, University of Northern Colorado, 1974), 18.

175 See John W. Welch, "How Long Did It Take Joseph Smith to Translate the Book of Mormon?" *Ensign* (January 1988): 46–7.

176 This map's inferential derivation is explained and documented in Sorenson, *Geogra-phy of Book of Mormon Events,* culminating on page 367 with an earlier version of this map.

177 On the checkered history of LDS efforts at correlation, most of which have been inadequately informed, to put the matter in the kindliest terms, see Sorenson, "History of Ideas," 7–35.

178 See my article, "When Lehi's Party Arrived."

179 See, for example, Robert M. Carmack, *Quichean Civilization: The Ethnohistoric, Ethnographic, and Archaeological Sources* (Berkeley: University of California Press, 1973), 16–8; and Lawrence H. Feldman, "Tollan in Central Mexico: The Geography of Economic Specialization," *Katunob* 8/3 (February 1973): 1–6.

180 See my "Book of Mormon as a Mesoamerican Codex."

181 See reviews of this terminological morass in Robert Chadwick, "Postclassic Pottery of the Central Valleys," *Handbook of Middle American Indians,* 10:228–33; and Nigel Davies, *The Toltecs until the Fall of Tula* (Norman: University of Oklahoma Press, 1977). On the Chichimecs, see Pedro Carrasco, "The Peoples of Central Mexico and Their Historical Traditions," in *Handbook of Middle American Indians*, 11:459–73. Compare the irreconcilable problems with use of the term *Hebrews,* discussed in William G. Dever (and commentators), "How to Tell a Canaanite from an Israelite," in *The Rise of Ancient Israel,* ed. Hershel Shanks et al. (Washington: Biblical Archaeology Society, 1992), 26–84.

182 Tatiana Proskouriakoff, "Olmec and Maya Art: Problems of their Stylistic Relation," in *Dumbarton Oaks Conference,* ed. Benson, 122. Others have used similar language. Some see the Olmec-looking figure on the left as a woman. We could suppose that Mulek and others in his party arrived in the land without Jewish female companions and took "native" wives.

183 See Sorenson, *Geography of Book of Mormon Events,* 305–6, compare 298–9.

184 See discussions in the following works by Sorenson, *Ancient American Setting*, 42–4; *Geography of Book of Mormon Events,* 265–6, 301–2.

185 See Jerry K. Loveland, "Hagoth and the Polynesian Tradition," *BYU Studies* 17/1 (1976): 59–73.

186 Ash depths of at least ten feet are known in El Salvador; Pre-Classic cultural remains occur beneath such deposits. See, for example, Stanley H. Boggs, *Pottery Jars from the Loma del Tacuazin, El Salvador,* (New Orleans: Middle American Research Institute, Tulane University, 1967), 177–85.

187 See Sorenson, *Ancient American Setting,* 318–23; M. Wells Jakeman, "Volcanoes in the Book of Mormon," *University Archaeological Society Newsletter* 8 (25 November 1952): 8.02; John A. Tvedtnes, "Historical Parallels to the Destruction at the Time of the Crucifixion," *Journal of Book of Mormon Studies* 3/1 (1994): 170–86.

188 See Bruce H. Dahlin, Robin Quizar, and Andrea Dahlin, "Linguistic Divergence and the Collapse of Preclassic Civilization in Southern Mesoamerica," *America Antiquity* 52/2 (1987): 367–81, who pick up on a part of this material.

189 See Sorenson, *Ancient American Setting,* 223–5.

190 See Nicholson, "Religion in Pre-Hispanic Central Mexico," 428–30.

191 Ibid., 429.

192 Miguel León-Portilla, "Quetzalcoatl: espiritualismo del México antiguo," *Cuadernos Americanos* 105/4 (1959): 127.

193 Interesting material on Quetzalcoatl, including both scholarly and Latter-day Saint perspectives, can be found in Bruce W. Warren and Thomas Stuart Ferguson, *The Messiah in Ancient America* (Provo, Utah: Book of Mormon Research Foundation, 1987), 1–50; and Hunter and Ferguson, *Ancient America and the Book of Mormon,* chapters 15 and 16. However, Hunter and Ferguson align the chronology of Ixtlilxochitl's statements arbitrarily, so the dates they attribute cannot be relied on. An even fuller treatment of the subject, including many quotations from Mesoamerican sources such as Torquemada and Ixtlilxochitl, is in Donald W. Hemingway, *Christianity in America before Columbus?* (Salt Lake City: Hawkes Publishing, 1988).

194 See Sorenson, *Ancient American Setting*, 330–332.

195 See René Millon, "Teotihuacan: City, State, and Civilization," in *Supplement to the Handbook of Middle American Indians,* (Austin: University of Texas Press, 1981), 1:235.

196 See Enrique Florescano, "La serpiente emplumada, Tláloc y Quetzalcóatl," *Cuadernos Americanos* 133/2 (1964): 137–54.

197 See the following works by Laurette Séjourné, "El Quetzalcóatl en Teotihuacán," *Cuadernos Americanos* 138/1 (1965): 131–56; and *Burning Water,* 25, 83–5.

198 See *Landa's Relación,* 102–6, 218; and Hemingway, *Christianity in America.*

199 See Sorenson, "Fortifications in the Book of Mormon Account," 425–44. The most decisive piece of literature in the turnaround was David L. Webster's *Defensive Earthworks at Becan, Campeche, Mexico: Implications for Maya Warfare* (New Orleans: Middle American Research Institute, Tulane University, 1976), which established that Becan in the central Yucatan peninsula was heavily fortified in the Late Pre-Classic, around A.D. 300.

200 Pierre Agrinier, *Mounds 9 and 10 at Mirador, Chiapas, Mexico,* (Provo, Utah: New World Archaeological Foundation, Brigham Young University, 1975), 9, 99, 100; see pages 51–93, 95.

201 See Sorenson, *Ancient American Setting,* 340–3, for fuller discussion and references.

202 See Ignacio Bernal, "Teotihuacán: nuevas fechas de radiocarbono y su posible significado," *Anales de Antropología* 2 (1965): 27–35.

203 See, for example, Angel García Cook, "The Historical Importance of Tlaxcala in the Cultural Development of the Central Highlands," in *Supplement to the Handbook of Middle American Indians*, 1:263–73.

204 See Sorenson, "When Lehi's Party Arrived," 19–21, which gives various Book of Mormon references for Jaredite cultural traits among the later Nephites.

205 See ibid., 33–4.

206 See Alberto Beltrán, "Reportaje gráfico del hallazgo de Las Limas," *Boletin INAH* 21 (September 1965): unnumbered page facing page 16.

207 See Linda Manzanilla, "Corporate Groups and Domestic Activities at Teotihuacan," *Latin American Antiquity* 7/3 (1996): 228–46.

208 "Zarahemla," *Times and Seasons* 3 (1 October 1842): 927.

209 Taken from a handout entitled "Data Sheet for Sadovszky's 'Cal-Ugrian Theory'"used by Dr. Otto Sadovszky in a lecture to a class at UCLA in 1983. A copy is in my files thanks to Dr. Todd Compton. See Sorenson and Raish, *Pre Columbian Contact*, for additional sources on Sadovszky's work.

210 Two unpublished papers Mary LeCron Foster has read at scientific conferences are in my files;

they are accessible in the form of lengthy abstracts in Sorenson and Raish, *Pre-Columbian Contact with the Americas*, 1:325–6 (entries F–146B and F–146C). Other language connections meriting serious consideration are by Brian Stubbs, David H. Kelley, Mary Ritchie Key, Pierre Agrinier, and Morris Swadesh, among others, all of which can be accessed in abstracts published in the same work.

211 See note 27.

212 Lyle Campbell and Terrence Kaufman, "A Linguistic Look at the Olmecs," *American Antiquity* 41/1 (1976): 80–9.

213 See Linda Schele and Peter Mathews, *Notebook for the XVIIth Maya Hieroglyphic Workshop at Texas* (produced by photocopy, Austin: University of Texas, 1993), 33; and summarized in various places, such as Warren and Ferguson, *Messiah in Ancient America*, 62–4.

214 See my article, "Some Meso-american Traditions of Immi-gration by Sea," *El Mexico Antiguo* 8 (1955): 425–37.

215 Ibid.

216 See the following articles by Sorenson: "Significance of an Apparent Relationship," and "Book of Mormon as a Mesoamerican Codex."

217 Cyrus H. Gordon, *Before Columbus: Links Between the Old World and Ancient America* (New York: Crown, 1971).

218 See Sorenson and Raish, *Pre-Columbian Contact with the Americas.*

219 Ibid., xii.

220 See Sorenson, "Significance of an Apparent Relationship," 233 n. 10. It depends upon Eduard Seler, *Codex Borgia* (Berlin: Unger, 1906): 2:31; and Alan Gardiner, "The Baptism of Pharaoh," *Journal of Egyptian Archaeology* 36 (1950): 3–12.

221 As William F. Albright explained in a letter to the author in 1954.

222 See Sorenson, "Significance of an Apparent Relationship," 231; Stephan F. de Borhegyi, "A Study of Three-pronged Incense Burners from Guatemala and Adjacent Areas," *Notes on Middle American Archaeology and Ethnology* 4/101 (1951): 110–2; and Stephan F. de Borhegyi, "Further Notes on Three-pronged Incense Burners and Rim-head Vessels in Guatemala," *Notes on Middle American Archaeology and Ethnology* 4/105 (1951): 162–76; Chester C. McCown, *Tell en-Nasbeh* (Berkeley: Palestine Institute of Pacific School of Religion, 1947): 1:236.

223 Among a large literature which is accessible by consulting Sorenson and Raish, *Pre-Columbian Contact with the Americas,* see especially Paul Shao, *The Origin of Ancient American Cultures* (Ames, Iowa: Iowa State University Press, 1983); and Miguel Covarrubias, *Indian Art of Mexico and Central America* (New York: Knopf, 1957), 179, 187.

224 See Drucker, Heizer, and Squier, *Excavations at La Venta,* 152–61.

225 See H. Mike Xu, *Origin of the Olmec Civilization* (Edmond, Oklahoma: University of Central Oklahoma Press, 1996). Betty J. Meggers, a Smithsonian Institution archaeologist, had earlier argued a closely similar position in her "The Transpacific Origin of Mesoamerican Civilization: A Preliminary Review of the Evidence and Its Theoretical Implications," *American Anthropologist* 77/1 (1975): 1–27.

ILLUSTRATION CREDITS

Dust Cover: © 1992 Haller Buchanan Studio

Frontispiece: The Metropolitan Museum of Art, The Michael C. Rockefeller Memorial Collection, Bequest of Nelson A. Rockefeller, 1979 (1979.206.1063)

1. Photograph by H. N. Sweet. Maudslay 1889–1902, Vol. III, Plate 10

5. Phtograph by James C. Christenson

8 left. Vizcaíno 1987, unnumbered plate

8–9. ALTI Publishers

10 upper. Photograph by John W. Welch

10 center. Photograph by Daniel Bates, courtesy David A. Palmer and S.E.H.A.

10 lower. Photograph by David A. Palmer

11. Photograph by Douglas Kasteler, courtesy FARMS

13 upper left. Photograph by Daniel Bates, courtesy David A. Palmer and S.E.H.A.

13 lower left. Photograph by Daniel Bates, courtesy David A. Palmer and S.E.H.A.

13 right. Photograph by James C. Christensen

16. Photograph by Milton R. Hunter, courtesy Paul R. Cheesman

17. Photograph by John Archer, of copy of A. Tejeda version of Bonampak mural in INAH Regional Museum, Tuxtla Gutierrez, Chiapas

18 upper right. Wuthenau 1965, 165a

18 center. Winning 1968, frontispiece

18 lower left. Wuthenau 1965, 61

19. INAH

20 upper left. Photograph by © Justin Kerr K3521

20 upper center. Wuthenau 1965, 115

20 upper right. Wuthenau 1965, 42

20 middle left. Wuthenau 1965, 52

20 middle center. Wuthenau 1965, 144

20 middle right. Wuthenau 1965, 167

20 lower left. Wuthenau 1965, 134

20 lower center. Photograph by Allen J. Christenson

20 lower right. Wuthenau 1965, 135

21 upper right. Wuthenau 1965, 136a

21 center right. Wuthenau 1965, 61

21 lower right. Wuthenau 1965, 135

21 left. Bonifaz Nuño 1993, plate 21

22 top left. Seguros America 1989, 18

22 top center. Seguros America 1989, 66

22 second row left. Seguros America 1989, 121

22 second row center. Weitlaner and Olivera 1969, Pl. 69

22 third row left and center. Courtesy of Southwest Museum, Los Angeles Calif.

22 bottom row left. Seguros America 1989, 125

22 bottom row center. Seguros America 1989, 98

22 right. Seguros America 1989, 106

23. Seguros America 1989, 23

24. © Assemblée nationale, Paris

27 lower. After Ogden 1991, 142

27 upper. Praeclara de Nova maris, 1524

28–29. After Marquina 1951, Lam. 54

31. Photograph by © Justin Kerr K3534

32 upper. Artist Adriana Velásquez M., in Velásquez et al. 1988, 33; and INAH

32 lower. Los Angeles County Museum of Art, The Proctor Stafford Collection, Museum Purchase with funds provided by Mr. and Mrs. Allan C. Balch

33 upper. Campos 1988b, 19

33 lower. The Bodleian Library, Oxford, MS. Arch Selden. A. 1, fol. 60r

34 upper. Photograph by Frank Cancian

34 lower. Photograph by W. Floyd Holdman, courtesy FARMS

35 upper. Photograph by Allen J. Christenson

35 middle left. Sahagún 1905, Vol. 5, Lib. VII, Lam. LXXXIII, #96

35 middle right. Sahagún 1905, Vol. 5, Lib. VII, Lam. LXXXIII, #97

35 lower left. Sahagún 1905, Vol. 5, Lib. VII, Lam. LXXXIII, #98

35 lower right. Sahagún 1905, Vol. 5, Lib. VII, Lam. XLIV, #14

36. Photograph by Michel Zabé

37–43. Photographs by Michel Zabé

44. Photograph by John Bigelow Taylor

45–47. Photographs by Michel Zabé

48 upper. Mingei International Museum of Folk Art (Photograph by Lynton Gardiner)

48 lower left. Photograph by Daniel Bates, courtesy David A. Palmer and S.E.H.A.

48 lower right. D. Donne Bryant Stock Photo

49 upper. Photograph by Michel Zabé

49 lower left. D. Donne Bryant Stock Photo

49 lower right. Photograph by Michel Zabé

50 upper. Photograph by Daniel Bates, courtesy David A. Palmer and S.E.H.A.

50 middle. Photograph by Paul R. Cheesman

50 lower. Artist Áyax Moreno, courtesy BYU-NWAF

51 upper. Photograph by © Justin Kerr K127
51 lower. Photograph by Daniel Bates, courtesy David A. Palmer and S.E.H.A.
52 upper left. Campos 1988 b, 37
52 upper center and second row center. Photographs by David Bates, courtesy David A. Palmer and S.E.H.A.
52 upper right. Artist Adriana Velásquez M. Velásquez et al. 1988, 37, and INAH
52 drawings. Artists Michael Lyon and Andrea Darais
53 upper. INAH
53 lower. Sahagún 1905, Vol. 5, Lib. XI, Lam. CXXVI, #796
54 upper. Sahagun 1905, Vol. 5, Lib. IX, Lam. LIV, #13
55 upper. D. Donne Bryant Stock Photo
55 lower. D. Donne Bryant Stock Photo
56 upper. Photograph by Allen J. Christenson
56 lower left. Sahagun 1905, Vol. 5, Lib. VIII, Lam. LI, #90
56 lower right. Humboldt 1810, Pl. 33
57. Artist Louis S. Glanzman; National Geographic Society
58 upper left. Photograph by P. Mendez. Campos 1988b, 18
58 upper right and middle. Photographs by James D. Nations
58 lower center. After Morley 1948, Pl. 88b
58 lower right. Artist Keith Henderson, Prescott 1922, 1:335
59 upper. After Winning 1962, 13
59 lower. Photograph by Paul R. Cheesman
60 upper. Photograph by James C. Christensen
60 lower. Campos 1988b, 15
61 upper. Photograph by Martin H. Raish
61 lower. Photograph by Peter D. Harrison
62 upper. Artist Robert Wauchope, Wauchope 1938, Fig. 44a
62 lower. Photograph by Daniel Bates, courtesy David A. Palmer and S.E.H.A.
63 upper. After Linne 1934, 40
63 middle. After Sejourne 1966
63 lower. Artist Stuart Gentling
64. Museo Amparo, Puebla, México
66. INAH
67 upper left. INAH
67 upper right. Photograph by Frank Cancian
67 lower. INAH
68. INAH
69. Boehm de Lameiras 1994, 92
70 upper. Sahagun 1905, Vol. 5, Lib. IV, Lam. XXIV, #27
70 lower. Sahagun 1905, Vol. 5, Lib. XL, Lam. VI, #31
71 upper. Photograph by Frank Cancian
71 lower. St. Louis Art Museum
72 upper. Photograph by Allen J. Christenson
72 lower. INAH
73 upper. Sahagun 1905, Vol. 5, Lib. IV, Lam. XXXI, #90
74. The Bodleian Library, Oxford, MS. Arch Selden. A. 1, fol. 60r
75. Photograph by John Bigelow Taylor
76 left. The Bodleian Library, Oxford, MS. Arch Selden. A. 1, fol. 60r
76 right. Sahagun 1905, Vol. 5, Lib. III, Lam. XX, #18
77 upper. The Bodleian Library, Oxford, MS. Arch Selden. A. 1, fol. 61r
77 lower. León-Portilla 1963, 148
78. Copy of A. Tejeda version of Bonampak mural in INAH Regional Museum, Tuxtla Gutierrez, Chiapas. Photograph by Daniel Bates, courtesy David A. Palmer and S.E.H.A.
79 left. INAH
79 right. Artist Stuart Gentling
80. Photograph by © Justin Kerr K2881
81 upper left. Sahagun 1905, Vol. 5, Lib. II, Lam. XII
81 upper right. Sahagun 1905, Vol. 5, Lib. VIII, Lam. XLIV, #15
81 middle. After Hunt 1972, 221
81 lower. INAH
82 upper. Photograph by © Justin Kerr K3711
82 lower left. Photograph by F. Anton, Burland 1976, frontispiece
82 lower right. Photograph by Michel Zabé
83 upper. INAH
83 lower. Artist Keith Henderson, Prescott 1922, 210
84 upper. Photograph by Daniel Bates, courtesy David A. Palmer and S.E.H.A.
84 lower. INAH
85 upper. After drawing by Miguel Covarrubias, Romero 1958, 69
85 middle. INAH.
85 lower. Photograph by Ben Grishaaver, Rijksmuseum voor Volkenkunde, Leiden, Netherlands
86 upper. Denver Art Museum collection
86 lower. León-Portilla 1963, 26
87. Sahagun 1905, Vol. 5, Lib. II, Lam. XV, #49
88-89, edges. After various codices excerpted in Anawalt 1981
88-89 upper. Photograph by John Archer., of copy of A. Tejeda version of Bonampak mural in INAH Regional Museum, Tuxtla Gutierrez, Chiapas
88-89 lower. Codex Zouche-Nuttall, Copyright © British Museum
90. INAH
91. Photograph by © Justin Kerr K764
92 upper and middle. Photographs by Daniel Bates, courtesy David A. Palmer and S.E.H.A.
92 lower. Photograph by © Justin Kerr K2833
93 upper. D. Donne Bryant Stock Photography
93 lower. Photograph by William Floyd Holdman, courtesy FARMS
94. Photograph by H. DuBois
95 upper left. © Justin Kerr K3517
95 upper right. © Justin Kerr K3612
95 lower. Pictures of Record
96 upper. Photograph by A. Burger, Peabody Museum, Harvard University
96 middle. Photograph by Eva Eggebrecht
96 lower. INAH
97. Museo Amparo, Puebla, México
98 upper. Photograph by Allen J. Christenson
98 lower. © Justin Kerr K2837B
99 upper. After Kerr 1989, 96
99 middle. © Justin Kerr K3880
99 lower. INAH
100 upper right. Courtesy of the National Museum of the American Indian, Smithonian Institution
100 left. INAH
100 lower center. Photograph by John Annerino
100 middle right. Photograph by Michel Zabé
100 lower right. Mingei International Museum of Folk Art (Land Collection ML767)
101 left. Los Angeles County Museum of Art, The Proctor Stafford Collection, Museum Purchase with funds provided by Mr. and Mrs. Allan C. Balch
101 upper right. Sahagun 1905, Vol. 5, Lib. VIII, Lam. XLVIII, #64
101 lower right. Sahagun 1905, Vol. 5, Lib. VIII, Lam. XLVIII, #63
102 upper. Courtesy John E. Clark
102 lower. Photograph by Allen J. Christenson
103 upper. Artist T. W. Rutledge, © National Geographic Society
103 lower. Draftsman Eduardo Martinez E., courtesy BYU NWAF
104 upper. Photograph by John Archer, courtesy FARMS
104 lower. Lowe and Agrinier 1960, frontispiece
105. Artist T. W. Rutledge, © National Geographic Society
106–7 upper. Photograph by Daniel Bates, courtesy David A. Palmer and S.E.H.A.
106 lower. After Morley 1948, 333
107 right. Coe and Diehl 1980, Vol. 1, unnumbered plate following 22
109. Photograph by Justin Kerr, limestone plaque, Usumacinta River Valley, about A.D. 782, Kimbell Art Museum, Fort Worth, Texas
110 upper. After Bernal 1968, 63
110 lower. The Bodleian Library, Oxford, MS. Arch Selden. A. 1, fol. 69r
111. © Justin Kerr K2844
112. Artist Keith Henderson, Prescott 1922, 2:78-9
113. Photograph by Mark L. Rosenberg
114 upper. Mohar Betancourt 1990, front cover
114 lower. Artist Keith Henderson, Prescott 1922, 1:205
115 upper. The Bodleian Library, Oxford, MS. Arch Selden. A. 1, fol. 46r
115 lower. Muñoz Camargo 1978, Lam. 7
116 upper. Sammlung Ludwig-Aachen 1970, 57
116 lower left. Photograph by Frank Cancian
116 lower right. Monti 1969, 28
117 upper. Sahagun 1905, Vol. 5, Lib. IV, Lam. XXIX, #68
117 lower right. Sahagun 1905, Vol. 5, Lib. VIII, Lam. XLVIII, #66
117 lower left. Sahagun 1905, Vol. 5, Lib. VIII, Lam. XLVIII, #67
118 upper. Stierlin 1981, 36, #35
118 lower left. Andrews 1970, fig. 57a
118 lower right. Photograph by James C. Christensen
119. Photograph by H. DuBois, Berjonneau and Sonnery 1985, #368
120–21. © Justin Kerr K1392
121 upper right. Drucker, Heizer and Squier 1959, 217
121 upper left. Drucker, Heizer and Squier 1959, Pl. 55
122 upper. Artist Keith Henderson, Prescott 1922, 1:200
122 lower. Norman 1973, Pl. 34, courtesy BYU NWAF
123 upper. Photograph by Joseph Labrum
123 lower. Muñoz Camargo 1978, Lam. 1
125. Musées royaux d'Art et d'Histoire, Brussels
126. After Hassig 1992
127. The Bodleian Library, Oxford, MS. Arch Selden. A. 1, fol. 67r
128 upper. Flannery and Marcus 1983, 107
128 lower. Bancroft Library, University of California, Berkeley
129 upper. The Bodleian Library, Oxford, MS. Arch Selden. A. 1, fol. 2r
129 lower. Photograph by Daniel Bates, courtesy David A. Palmer and S.E.H.A, copy of A. Tejeda version of Bonampak mural in INAH Regional Museum, Tuxtla Gutierrez, Chiapas
130. Artists Andrea Darais and Michael Lyons
131 upper left. Gendrop 1970, 22, fig. 30b
131 upper, center and right. Museo Nazionale Preistorico ed

Etnografico Luigi Pigorini, Rome
131 lower. Artist Andrea Darais
132. Matheny 1975, 170
133 upper. Artist Andrea Darais
133 lower. Photograph by Daniel Bates, courtesy David A. Palmer and S.E.H.A.
134–5. Photograph by Frank Cancian
137. Leon-Portilla 1971a, 448
138 upper. Photograph by Michel Zabé
138 lower. Photograph by Allen J. Christenson
139. Photograph by Roger Asselberghs
140 upper. Photograph by Michel Zabé
140 lower. Artist Juan A. Valdés, after A. Canel, Eggebrecht 1992, 35, #29
141 right. Photograph by Roger Asselberghs
141 left. Photograph by Michel Zabé
142 upper. Codex Zouche-Nuttall, Copyright © British Museum
142 lower left. Codex Zouche-Nuttall, Copyright © British Museum
142 lower center. Sahagun 1905, Vol. 5
143. Artist Felipe Dávalos, © National Geographic Society
144 upper. Artist Carlos Navarrete, Navarrete 1976, fig. 7
144 lower. Artist Michael Lyon, after Ruz 1973, 13
145 upper. Artist Stuart Gentling
145 lower. Photograph by William Floyd Holdman, courtesy FARMS
146. Photograph by Allen J. Christenson
147 upper left. Photograph by and © Macduff Everton
147 upper right. Photograph by Frank Cancian
147 middle left. Sabloff 1990, 63, courtesy J. Sabloff
146–7 lower. Draftsman Bryan M. DeWitt
148 upper. Sahagun 1905, Vol. 5, Lib. II, Lam. XVI, #57
148 lower. After Thompson 1965, 645
149. © Assemblée nationale, Paris
150 upper. Tozzer 1941, 42
150 lower. Museo Amparo, Puebla, México
151 upper. Museo Amparo, Puebla, México
151 lower. Mexico or Guatemala, Maya, c. 600–800. Incised shell, H 16.5cm. © The Cleveland Museum of Art, 1996, The Norweb Collection, 1965.550
152 left. © Justin Kerr K2037
152 lower. Photograph by Frank Cancian
154. Winning 1968, 127, #151
155. © Justin Kerr K1822
156. INAH
157. Teotihuacan 1989, 119
157 lower right. Norman 1973, Pl. 50
157 upper right. Photograph by Daniel Bates, courtesy David A. Palmer and S.E.H.A.
159. INAH
160 upper left. INAH
160 lower. Photograph by William Floyd Holdman, courtesy FARMS
161. © Justin Kerr K5824
162 lower left. After Coe 1973, 92
162 upper. Parsons 1974, 116
162 middle. After Ricks 1969
162 lower right. After Lothrop 1926, II:378; Ekholm 1944, 378, r; Navarrete 1978, Fig. 5; Enciso 1953, 40; Méluzin 1987, 75, Fig. 9, d, & 72, b
163 upper. Codex Madrid, Museo de la Cultura, sheets 35, 36, Madrid, Spain
163 lower. Artist Louis S. Glanzman, © National Geographic Society
164 upper. After Hartung 1975, 196
164 lower. Sabloff 1990, 35, courtesy J. Sabloff
165. Brueggemann et al., 1992, 63
166. Florentine Codex, after reproductions in Aveni 1980, 32, Fig. 10
167. After Malmström 1978, 111
168 upper. Campos 1988a, 43
168 lower. Photograph by Michel Zabé
169. Museo Amparo, Puebla, México
170 lower left. INAH
170 upper right. Photograph by Martin H. Raish
170 middle right. Photograph by Kim Sandgren, courtesy FARMS
170 lower right. Photograph by Michel Zabé
171 Photographs by Michel Zabé
172 upper right. Musées Royaux d'Art et d'Histoire, Brussels
172 lower left. Sahagun 1905, Vol. 5
172 lower center. Sahagun 1905, Vol. 5
173 upper. Museum für Völkerkunde Wien, Foto Archiv
173 lower. Sahagun 1905, Vol. 5
174 upper. Monti 1969, 82
174 lower. Leon-Portilla 1963, 150
175. Photograph by Eva Eggebrecht
176. Sachsische Landesbibliothek, and Staats-und-universitäts Bibliothek, Dresden
177. After Christenson 1988
178 lower. Photograph by John Archer, of copy of A. Tejeda version of Bonampak mural, INAH Regional Museum, Tuxtla Gutierrez, Chiapas
179 upper. Photograph by Michel Zabé
179 lower. © Justin Kerr K791
180. © Justin Kerr K3228
181 upper. Sahagun 1905, Vol. 5, Lib. VIII, Lam. XLVIII, #69
181 lower. Photograph by Daniel Bates, courtesy David A. Palmer and S.E.H.A.
182 upper. Photograph by Eva Eggebrecht
182 lower. Norman 1973, Pl. 10
183 upper left. Copyright © British Museum
183 middle left. Maudslay 1989–1902, IV: Pl. 76
183 lower left. Peabody Museum, Harvard University
183 right. Photograph by Merle Green Robertson
184 upper left. Museo de América, Madrid
184 middle. Douglas Donne Bryant Stock Photography
184 lower center. Gay 1971, 55, Fig. 24
185 upper. Photograph by Michel Zabé
185 lower left. Teotihuacan 1989, 114
185 lower right. Teotihuacan 1989, 68
186 upper. Douglas Donne Bryant Stock Photography
186 lower left. Museo Amparo, Puebla, México
186 lower right. Clark 1994, 255
187 left. Photograph by Michel Zabé
187 right. Norman 1973, Pl. 2
188. By the author
189. By the author
191. Leon-Portilla 1971b, 458
192. Dumbarton Oaks Research Library and Collections, Washington, D.C.
193. By the author
194. Photograph by Daniel Bates, courtesy David A. Palmer and S.E.H.A.
194–5 and 195 upper. Photographs by Daniel Bates, courtesy David A. Palmer and S.E.H.A.
195 lower. Photograph by Daniel Bates, courtesy David A. `Palmer and S.E.H.A.
196. Photograph by Allen J. Christenson
197 upper. Photographs by Bruce W. Warren
197 lower. ALTI Corporation
198 upper. Photograph by Allen J. Christenson
198 middle. Photograph by John W. Welch
198 lower. Photograph by James C. Christensen
199 upper. Photograph by Eva Eggebrecht
199 lower. Artist Michael Lyon
200. Photograph by Michel Zabé
201 upper left. Photograph by Daniel Bates, courtesy David A. Palmer and S.E.H.A.
201 upper right. Photograph by Allen J. Christenson
201 lower. ALTI Corporation
202 upper. Vizcaino 1987, unnumbered plate
202 middle. Photograph by David A. Palmer
202 lower. Vizcaino 1987, unnumbered plate
203 upper. Photograph by Allen J. Christenson
203 lower. Photograph by Daniel Bates, courtesy David A. Palmer and S.E.H.A.
204 upper. Photograph by Ricardo Mata, Gluckman 1991, 222
204 lower. Copyright Merle Green Robertson, 1976
205 upper. Photograph by Allen J. Christenson
205 middle. Photograph by Daniel Bates, courtesy David A. Palmer and S.E.H.A.
205 lower. INAH
206 upper. Museo Civico di Numismatica, Etnografia, e Arti Oriental, Turin
206 lower. Artist Andrea Darais, after Marquina 1951, Lam. 20
207 upper. INAH
207 middle. Photograph by Daniel Bates, courtesy David A. Palmer and S.E.H.A.
207 lower left. BYU NWAF
207 lowest. Photograph by Michel Zabé
208 upper. After Morley 1948, 224
208 middle. Artist Pierre Agrinier, Agrinier 1975, frontispiece
208 lower. Photograph by Daniel Bates, courtesy David A. Palmer and S.E.H.A.
209. © Justin Kerr K2887
210 lower. Photograph by Allen J. Christenson
210 upper. Artist Keith Henderson, Prescott 1922, 2:286
211 upper. Photograph by David A. Palmer
211 lower. Photograph by Warren Aston
212 upper pair. Sahagun 1905, Vol. 5
212 middle. Artist Stuart Gentling
212 lower. Artist, Rob Wood, Wood Ronsaville Harlin, Inc.
213 upper. Artist Louis S. Glanzman, copyright National Geographic Society
213 lower. Photograph by Paul R. Cheesman, mural by Diego Rivera, Palacio Nacional de México
214 upper. Photograph by Daniel Bates, courtesy David A. Palmer and S.E.H.A.
214 lower. Artist Áyax Moreno, courtesy BYU NWAF
215. Photograph by James C. Christensen
216. Photograph by Joseph Labrum
217 left. Artist Alberto Beltrán, Beltrán 1965, 17, and INAH
217 right. Photograph by Bruce M. White, The Art Museum, Princeton University. Gift of Mrs. Gerald B. Lambert by exchange
218. Photographs by Steven W. Booras
219 upper. Courtesy Jeremy A. Sabloff and the Sayil Archaeological Project
219 lower. Culbert 1993, 50, cour-

tesy University of Pennsylvania, University Museum
220 upper. Photograph by Joseph Labrum
220 lower. Photograph by Daniel Bates, courtesy David A. Palmer and S.E.H.A.
221. Artist Áyax Moreno, courtesy BYU NWAF
222 upper left. Catherwood 1844, Pl. 5
222 upper right. Photograph by John Annerino
222 lower. After Sadovszky n.d.
223 right. Códice Matritense, fol. 191r and v; Leon-Portilla 1971b, 455
223 upper left. Campbell 1988, 254, Fig. 14
223 middle. © The Metropolitan Museum of Art, purchase, 1900 (00.5.991)
223 lower. After Schele and Matthews n.d., 33
224. After D'Alviella 1894, 226
225 upper pair. Gordon 1974, 30
225 lower. Wuthenau 1975, Pl. 14 following 48
226 upper left. After Gardiner 1950, 5
226 upper right. After Seler 1898, II:31
226 lower left. After May 1935, 13
226 lower right. After Borhegyi 1951, 112
227 upper and middle left. After Covarrubias 1954, 55
227 lower. Stierlin 1981, 19, #12

References

Anawalt, Patricia Rieff. 1981. *Indian Clothing Before Cortés: Mesoamerican Costumes from the Codices.* Norman: University of Oklahoma Press.

Andrews, E. Wyllys, IV. 1970. Balankanche, Throne of the Tiger Priest. *Middle American Research Institute Publication 32.*

Aveni, Anthony F. 1980. *Skywatchers of Ancient Mexico.* Austin: University of Texas Press.

Beltrán, Alberto. 1965. Reportaje gráfico del hallazgo de Las Limas. *Boletín INAH* 21 (September 1965): 9–17.

Berjonneau, Gérald, and Jean-Louis Sonnery. 1985. *Rediscovered Masterpieces of Mesoamerica: Mexico-Guatemala-Honduras.* Boulogne, France: Editions Arts 135.

Bernal, Ignacio. 1968. *The Olmec World.* Berkeley and Los Angeles: University of California Press: 1969.

Boehm de Lameiras, Brigitte, coord. 1994. *El Michoacán antiguo: Estado y sociedad Tarascos en la época prehispánica.* Zamora, Michoacán, México: El Colegio de Michoacán, and Gobierno del Estado de Michoacán.

Bonifaz Nuño, Rubén. 1993. *El Museo Amparo. Colección prehispánica.* México: Museo Amparo.

Borhegyi, Stephan F. de. 1951. A study of three-pronged incense burners from Guatemala and adjacent areas. *Carnegie Institution of Washington, Notes on Middle American Archaeology and Ethnology,* no. 101.

Brueggemann, Juergen, Sara Ladrón de Guevara, and Juan Sánchez Bonilla. 1992. *Tajín.* México, D. F.: CITIBANK/MÉXICO.

Burland, C. A. 1976. *Peoples of the Sun: The Civilizations of Pre-Columbian America.* New York: Praeger.

Campbell, Lyle. 1988. The Linguistics of Southeast Chiapas, Mexico. *Brigham Young University, New World Archaeological Foundation, Papers* No. 50.

Campos, Julieta. 1988a. *Bajo el signo de Ix Bolon.* México: Gobierno del Estado de Tabasco, and Fondo de Cultura Económica, S.A. de C.V.

———. 1988b. *El lujo del sol.* México: Gobierno del Estado de Tabasco Instituto de Cultura de Tabasco, and Fondo de Cultura Económica.

Catherwood, Frederick. 1844. *Views of Ancient Monuments in Central America, Chiapas and Yucatan.* London: Vizetelly Bros. and Co.

Christenson, Allen J. 1988. The use of chiasmus in ancient Mesoamerica. Provo, Utah: FARMS.

Clark, John E., ed. 1994. *Los Olmecas en Mesoamérica.* México: CITIBANK/MEXICO.

Coe, Michael D. 1973. *The Maya Scribe and His World.* New York: The Grolier Club.

Coe, Michael D., and Richard A. Diehl. 1980. *In the Land of the Olmec.* 2 vols. Austin: University of Texas Press.

Covarrubias, Miguel. 1954. *The Eagle, the Jaguar, and the Serpent: Indian Art of the Americas. North America: Alaska, Canada, the United States.* New York: Alfred A. Knopf.

Culbert, T. Patrick. 1993. *Maya Civilization* (Smithsonian Exploring the Ancient World series). Washington: St. Remy Press, Montreal, and Smithsonian Books.

D'alviella, Count Goblet, Eugene Felicien Albert. 1894. *The Migration of Symbols.* London: Westminster.

Drucker, Philip, Robert F. Heizer, and Robert J. Squier. 1959. Excavations at La Venta, Tabasco, 1955. *Bureau of American Ethnology Bulletin* 170.

Eggebrecht, Eva, and Arne Eggebrecht. 1992. *Die Welt der Maya: archäologische Schätze aus drei Jahrtausenden.* Mainz am Rhein, Germany: Roemer- und Pelizaeus-Museum: Hildesheim; and Verlag Philipp von Zabern.

Ekholm, Gordon F. 1944. Excavations at Tampico and Panuco in the Huasteca, Mexico. *Anthropological Papers, American Museum of Natural History* 38/5 (New York).

Enciso, Jorge. 1953. *Design Motifs of Ancient Mexico.* New York: Dover.

Flannery, Kent V., and Joyce Marcus. 1983. *The Cloud People: Divergent Evolution of the Zapotec and Mixtec Civilizations.* New York: Academic Press.

Gardiner, Alan. 1950. The Baptism of Pharoah. *Journal of Egyptian Archaeology* 36:3–12.

Gay, Carlo T. E. 1977. *Chalcacingo.* Monographien und Dokumentationen: Die amerikanischen Felsbilder. Graz, Austria: Akademische Druck- und Verlagsanstalt.

Gluckman, Daniel. 1991. *Antigua* (Colección Ciudades Iberoamericanas). Agencia Española de Cooperación Internacional, Ediciones de Cultura Hispánica. N.p., n.d.

Gordon, Cyrus. 1974. *Riddles in History.* New York: Crown.

Hartung, Horst. 1975. A scheme of probable astronomical projections in Mesoamerican architecture. In *Archaeoastronomy in Pre-Columbian America,* edited by A. F. Aveni, 191–204. Austin: University of Texas Press.

Hassig, Ross. 1992. *War and Society in Ancient Mesoamerica.* Berkeley: University of California Press.

Humboldt, A. de. 1810. *Vues des cordillères, et monuments des peuples indigènes de l'Amérique.* Plate 33. Paris: F. Schoell.

Hunt, Eva. 1972. Irrigation and the Socio-political Organization of the Cuicatec Cacicazgos. Chapter 5 of Chronology and Irrigation. Vol 4 of *The Prehistory of the Tehuacan Valley,* edited by Frederick Johnson, 162–259. Austin: University of Texas Press.

Juarros, Domingo. 1823. *A Statistical and Commercial History of the Kingdom of Guatemala.* London: Hearne.

Kerr, Justin, ed. 1989. *The Maya Vase Book.* Vol. 1. New York: The Editor.

León-Portilla, Miguel. 1963. *Aztec Thought and Culture: A Study of the Ancient Nahuatl Mind.* Norman: University of Oklahoma Press.

———. 1971a. Philosophy in ancient Mexico. In *Handbook of Middle American Indians,* Vol. 10, Part 1, *Archaeology of Northern Mesoamerica,* edited by Gordon F. Ekholm and Ignacio Bernal, 447–51. Austin: University of Texas Press.

———. 1971b. Pre-hispanic literature. In *Handbook of Middle American Indians,* Vol. 10, Part 1, Archaeology of Northern Mesoamerica, edited by Gordon F. Ekholm and Ignacio Bernal, 447–51. Austin: University of Texas Press.

Linne, Sigvald. 1934. Archaeological Researches at Teotihuacan, Mexico. *Ethnographical Museum of Sweden, n.s.,* Publ. No. 1. Stockholm.

Lothrop, Samuel K. 1926. Pottery of Costa Rica and Nicaragua. Conribution No. 8, Museum of the American Indian. New York: Heye Foundation.

Malmström, Vincent H. 1978. A reconstruction of the chronology of Mesoamerican calendrical systems. *Journal for the History of Astronomy* 9:105–16.

Marquina, Ignacio. 1951. *Arquitectura prehispánica.* Memorias del Instituto Nacional de Antropología e Historia 1.

Maudslay, Alfred P. 1989–1902. Archaeology (Plates). Volumes III and IV of *Biologia Centrali-Americana*; or *Contributions to the Knowledge of the Fauna and Flora of Mexico and Central America,* edited by F. Ducane Godman and Osbert Salvin. London: The Editors.

May, Herbert G. 1935. *Material Remains of the Megiddo Cult.* Oriental Institute Publication 26. Chicago: University of Chicago.

Méluzin, Sylvia. 1987. The Tuxtla Statuette: An internal analysis of its writing system. In *The Periphery of the Southeastern Classic Maya Realm,* edited by Gary W. Pahl. Los Angeles: UCLA Latin American Center Publications, Los Angeles.

Mohar Betancourt, Luz Maria. 1990. *La Escritura en el México Antiguo (1) [sic].* México City:

Plaza y Valdés, Editores.
Monti, Franco. 1969. *Precolumbian Terracottas*. Paul Hamlyn: London.
Morley, Sylvanus G. 1948. *The Ancient Maya*. Stanford Calif.: University Press.
Muñoz Camargo, Diego. 1978. *Historia de Tlaxcala* [Crónica del siglo XVI]. México: Editorial Innovación, S. A.
Navarrete, Carlos. 1978. Exploration at San Agustín, Chiapas, Mexico. *BYU New World Archaeological Foundation,* Paper 3, 1959.
Norman, V. Garth. 1973. Izapa sculpture. *BYU New World Archaeological Foundation,* Paper 30, Part 1. Album, 1976.
Ogden, D. Kelly. 1991. *Where Jesus Walked: The Land and Culture of New Testament Times*. Salt Lake City: Deseret Book.
Parsons, Lee A. 1974. *Pre-Columbian America: The Art and Archeology of South, Central and Middle America* (Handbook for the Exhibition Hall). Milwaukee Public Museum Publications in Anthropology and History No. 2.
Praeclara de Nova maris oceani Hyspania narratio. 1524. Nuremberg.
Prescott, William H. 1922. *The Conquest of Mexico.* New York: Henry Holt.
Ricks, Welby W. 1969. A possible linear script from Preclassic Mexico. Newsletter and Proc. of the Society for Early Historic Archaeology, No. 112:1–4.
Ruz Lhuillier, Alberto. 1973. *El Templo de las Inscripciones, Palenque.* Instituto Nacional de Antropología e Historia, Colección Científica: Arqueología 7.
Sabloff, Jeremy A. 1990. *The New Archaeology and the Ancient Maya*. New York: Scientific American Library.
Sahagún, Bernardino de. 1905. *Historia general de las cosas de Nueva España*, edited by Francisco del Paso y Troncoso. Vols. 5–8. Fondos de [funding by] la Secretaría de Instrucción Pública y Bellas Artes de México. Fototipia de [typesetting by] Hauser y Menet: Madrid, 1905–1907. (Volume 5 consists of the Florentine Codex illustrations bound and distributed by the Museo Nacional de Arqueología, Historia, y Etnografía de México, 1926, as vol. 5 of the unfinished work.)
Schele, Linda, and Peter Mathews. N.d. *Notebook for the XVIIth Maya Hieroglyphic Workshop at Texas, March 13–14, 1993*. Photocopied volume, copyright Linda Schele and Peter Matthews.
Seguros America. 1989. *Los hijos del sol: Oaxaca*. México: Seguros America.
Sejourne, Laurette. 1966. *Arquitectura y Pintura en Teotihuacan.* México: Siglo XXI Editores.
Seler, Eduard. 1898. *Gesammelte Abhandlungen zur Amerikanischen Sprach- und Alterthumskunde*. Vol. 2, p. 31. Berlin: A. Asher: Berlin.
Stierlin, Henri. 1981. *The Art of the Maya: From the Olmecs to the Toltec-Maya.* London and Basingstoke: Macmillan London Ltd.
Teotihuacan. 1989. México: El Equilibrista; Madrid: Turner Libros.
Thompson, J. Eric S. 1965. Maya Hieroglyphic Writing. In *Handbook of Middle American Indians*, Vol. 3. *Archaeology of Southern Mesoamerica,* Part 2, edited by Gordon R. Willey, 632–58. Austin: University of Texas Press.
Velázquez Morlet, Adriana, et al. 1988. *Zonas Arqueológicas: Yucatan*. México: Instituto Nacional de Antropología e Historia.
Vizcaíno, Antonio. 1987. *Veracruz, un panorama*. N.p. [México?]: San Angel Ediciones.
Wauchope, Robert. 1938. Modern Maya Houses: A Study of Their Archaeological Significance. *Carnegie Institution of Washington* Publ. No. 502.
Weitlaner, Roberto J., and Mercedes Olivera de Vázquez. 1969. *Los grupos indígenas del norte de Oaxaca*. México: Instituto Nacional de Antropología e Historia.
Winning, Hasso von. 1962. Figurillas de barro sobre ruedas procedentes de México y del Viejo Mundo. *Amerindia* 1:11–39 (Montevideo).
———. 1968. *Pre-Columbian Art of Mexico and Central America*. New York: Harry N. Abrams.
Wuthenau, Alejandro von. 1965. *Altamerikanische Tonplastik: Das Menschenbild der Neuen Welt* (Series: Kunst der Welt). Baden-Baden, Germany: Holle Verlag.
———. 1975. *Unexpected Faces in Ancient America, 1500 B.C.–A.D. 1500. The Historical Testimony of Pre-Columbian Artist*. New York: Crown.

SCRIPTURE INDEX

Genesis
11:4, p. 129

Numbers
10:1–10, p. 178
21:6, p. 187

Deuteronomy
14:1, p. 156

1 Kings
7:21, p. 201

2 Kings
24, p. 108
25, p. 108

2 Chronicles
36:2–3, p. 124

Job
29:8, p. 176

Psalms
47:15, p. 176

Isaiah
27:1, p. 187

Jeremiah
16:6, p. 156

Acts
2:46, p. 144

1 Nephi
1:4, p. 103
2:7, p. 146
2:8–19, p. 73
2:20, p. 6
5:9–10, p. 140
5:14, p. 156
7:16, p. 53
7:22, p. 142
8:10, p. 183
10:4, p. 166
11:9, p. 183
11:31, p. 140
12:1–5, p. 73
12:15, p. 73
12:16, pp. 146, 187
12:19–23, p. 73
12:23, pp. 17, 142, 210
13:14, p. 211
16:4, p. 73
16:35, p. 156
17:7, p. 146
17:41, p. 187
18:9, p. 179
18:17–19, p. 73
18:18, p. 156
19:8, p. 166

2 Nephi
2:11, p. 187
2:18, p. 187
4:12, p. 156
5:16, p. 146
5:21, p. 17
8:9, p. 187
9, p. 156
9:10, p. 156, 187
9:13, p. 156
9:19, pp. 156, 187
9:26, p. 187
24:9, p. 187
25:1–5, p. 222
25:2, p. 176
25:19, p. 166
25:20, pp. 187, 205

Jacob
1:13, p. 68
2:22–35, p. 68
3:13, p. 191
5, p. 69
7:4, p. 176
7:26, p. 73

Enos
1:1, p. 77
1:2, p. 153
1:20, p. 140
1:21, p. 37
1:22, p. 140
1:22–23, p. 150
1:23, p. 73

Jarom
1:1, p. 156
1:3–4, p. 153
1:8, p. 53
1:10–11, p. 140
1:11, p. 150

Omni
1:14–19, p. 158
1:15–16, p. 120
1:17, pp. 25, 140
1:17–18, p. 25
1:18, pp. 68, 156
1:20–22, pp. 162, 200
1:21, p. 165

Words of Mormon
1:5, p. 191
1:13, p. 125

Mosiah
1:2, p. 77
1:2–8, p. 73
1:5–7, p. 156
1:8, p. 146
1:10, p. 115
1:13–16, p. 156
2:1, pp. 144, 146
2:3, pp. 101, 142, 146
2:5–7, p. 146
2:6, p. 144
2:9–19, p. 112
2:13, p. 80
2:40, p. 73
4:14, p. 140
4:15, p. 73
4:17, p. 37
4:21, p. 140
4:24, p. 61
5:7–8, p. 140
5:10–12, p. 177
7:5, p. 198
7:7, p. 112
7:9, p. 112
7:10–11, p. 117
7:15, p. 80
7:21, p. 123
7:22, p. 37
8:7–10, pp. 12, 200
8:8, pp. 12, 200
9:9, p. 37
9:19, p. 156
10:4, p. 37
10:5, p. 83
10:7–8, p. 198
10:8, p. 198
10:21, p. 46
11:1–15, p. 113
11:2–6, p. 80
11:4, p. 68
11:12, p. 198
11:14, p. 80
11:15, p. 45
16:3, pp. 73, 187
17, p. 117
17:13, p. 116
17:16, p. 87
18, p. 117
18:5, pp. 187, 198
18:5–14, p. 146
18:30, p. 146
18:35, p. 103
19:6–29, p. 108
19:12–15, p. 129
19:20, p. 140
19:24, pp. 140, 189
20, p. 108
20:1–5, p. 179
20:3, p. 73
20:11, p. 187
20:14, p. 123
20:17–22, p. 80
21, p. 108
21:3, p. 57
21:25, p. 200
21:25–27, p. 12
22:6, p. 132
22:7, pp. 42, 53, 115
22:10, p. 115
23:20, p. 103
23:25–26, p. 129
23:30, p. 12
23:30–37, p. 198
23:35–36, p. 12
23:35–39, p. 80
24:1–8, p. 80
24:4, p. 158
24:6, p. 162
24:6–7, pp. 55, 158
24:8–18, p. 80
25:12, pp. 73, 190
26:1–2, p. 140
26:6–12, p. 150
27:22–23, p. 151
28:12, p. 200
28:18, p. 156

Alma
1, p. 158
1:7–9, p. 80
1:10–15, p. 117
1:15, pp. 117, 140
1:19–22, p. 137
1:26, p. 80
1:29, p. 90
2:1, pp. 12, 117
2:1–10, p. 112
2:2, p. 15
2:6, p. 68
2:13, p. 15
2:16, p. 125
2:29–33, p. 135
2:37–38, p. 156
3:1, p. 156
3:3, p. 156
3:5, p. 130
4:6, p. 90
4:7, p. 90
5, p. 150
5:34, pp. 42, 156
5:55, p. 61
5:62, p. 156
7:15, p. 146
8:7, p. 115
8:11–13, p. 15
8:17, p. 15
8:21–22, p. 37
9:10, p. 156
9:22, p. 87
10:1–3, p. 68
10:2–3, p. 156
10:2–4, p. 137
10:4, pp. 61, 68
10:11, p. 61, 68
10:13–16, p. 117
11:4, p. 158
11:6–7, p. 115
11:8, p. 115
14:1–15:1, p. 137
14:8, p. 117
14:16, p. 158
14:17, p. 117
14:18, p. 140
15:16, pp. 61, 68
15:17, p. 146
15:17–19, p. 68
15:18, p. 61
16:2–3, p. 129
16:5–8, p. 150
16:10–11, p. 156
16:13, p. 146
17:4, p. 146
17:6, p. 68
17:7, p. 130
17:9, p. 151
17:23, p. 80
17:24, p. 123
17:25, p. 80
17:25–26, p. 34
17:28, p. 80
18:2–4, p. 113
18:6, p. 112
18:9, p. 59
18:10, p. 59
18:12, p. 59
18:13, p. 112
18:21, p. 112
19, p. 83
19:1, pp. 51, 156, 199
19:5, p. 51, 199
19:15, p. 115
19:16–17, p. 153
19:18, p. 113
19:20, p. 112
19:22, p. 115
20:4,pp. 112, 123
20:6, p. 59
20:7, p. 123
20:14, p. 123
20:18, p. 156
20:26, p. 123
21:1–2, p. 198
21:2, p. 203
21:4, pp. 80, 146, 158
21:23, p. 73
22, pp. 83, 153
22:1, p. 113
22:2, p. 113
22:2–3, p. 113
22:27, p. 123
22:27–34, p. 198
22:29, pp. 12, 188
22:32, pp. 188, 198, 200
23:1–12, p. 198
23:2, p. 146
23:9–13, p. 137
23:14, p. 137
24, pp. 112, 113
24:1, p. 198
24:28, p. 158
25, p. 112
25:5, p. 117
26:4–12, p. 113
26:29, p. 146
27:1, p. 113
27:8–9, p. 80
27:20, p. 61
28:1–2, p. 122
28:2–3, p. 87
30:1, p. 156
30:2, p. 156
30:3, pp. 101, 142
30:18, p. 80
30:27–28, p. 80
30:28, p. 151
30:58, p. 68
31, p. 140
31:1–4, p. 15
31:13, p. 146
31:27–28, p. 80
31:28, pp. 90, 96
31:37, p. 77
31:59, p. 15
32:2, p. 80
32:2–3, p. 80
32:28, p. 206
32:28–42, p. 183
33:19, pp. 187, 205
34:10, p. 142
34:11, pp. 142, 156, 207
35:5, p. 68
35:6, p. 137
37:2, p. 150
37:3, p. 156
37:35, p. 77
37:37, p. 176
37:47, p. 73
38:10–12, p. 77
38:15, p. 73
39–42, p. 73
39:10, p. 77
42:27, p. 146
43:4, pp. 112, 190
43:13–14, p. 226
43:19–20, p. 130
43:22, pp. 12, 187
43:24, p. 12
43:27, p. 12
43:30, p. 125
43:31–35, p. 12
43:40–42, p. 12
43:44, p. 187
43:47, p. 113
43:50, p. 125
44:3–4, p. 125
44:3–5, p. 140
44:8, p. 123
44:15, p. 110
44:18, p. 130
44:21–22, p. 156

45:9–14, p. 73
45:10–12, p. 166
46:12, p. 127
46:16–21, p. 125
46:19–21, p. 127
46:36, p. 129
46:40, p. 87
47, p. 83
47:2–7, p. 113
47:5, p. 53
47:33, p. 124
47:35, p. 123
48–51, p. 198
48:5, p. 127
48:8, p. 132
48:10, p. 73
48:11–17, p. 80
48:16, p. 125
49:1–25, p. 129
49:2, p. 132
49:4, pp. 130, 132
49:6, p. 130
49:12, pp. 127, 130
49:18, p. 132
49:19, p. 130
49:22, p. 132
49:25, p. 127
50:2, p. 132
50:3–5, p. 132
50:7–11, p. 198
50:12, pp. 68, 112
50:25–36, p. 117
50:29, p. 200
50:32, pp. 198, 200
50:34, p. 200
51, p. 80
51:1–8, p. 112
51:8, p. 80
51:13–20, p. 112
51:14–20, p. 112
51:16–20, p. 15
51:17–19, p. 108
51:19, p. 108
51:20, pp. 108, 129
51:22, p. 112
51:22–30, p. 129
51:26–32, p. 166
51:28, p. 199
51:30, p. 127
51:32, p. 199
51:33, p. 130
51:33–34, p. 166
52:1–2, p. 166
52:13, p. 198
52:20, pp. 123, 127
52:22–26, p. 199
52:31, p. 127
53:3, p. 156
54:12, p. 83
55:31, p. 42
55:32, p. 42
55:34, p. 127
56:1–2, p. 15
56:30–36, p. 199
56:31, p. 199
56:31–32, p. 51
57:8–10, p. 127
57:25, p. 87
57:28, p. 156
58:8–9, p. 15
59:2, p. 15
60, p. 112
60:1–3, p. 15
60:7, p. 29
60:11, p. 108
60:22, p. 115
60:27–31, p. 112
61:3–5, p. 15
61:12, p. 80
62:9, p. 117
62:39, p. 85
62:42–43, p. 80
62:45, p. 153
62:48–49, p. 153
63:4, p. 57
63:4–10, p. 200
63:5–8, pp. 57, 201
63:9, p. 57

Helaman
1:2, p. 68
1:2–5, p. 68
1:4, p. 68
1:14–22, p. 129
1:20–22, p. 123
3:3–5, p. 57
3:5–6, p. 35
3:5–10, p. 201
3:8, p. 57
3:8–9, p. 201
3:10, p. 57
3:11, p. 107
3:12, p. 57
3:13, p. 162
3:14, pp. 107, 146, 191
3:15, pp. 158, 163
6:4, p. 73
6:6, p. 200
6:7–9, pp. 55, 158, 163
6:7–13, p. 30
6:10, p. 200
6:11, p. 30
6:12, pp. 34, 46, 200
6:13, pp. 34, 83, 93
6:26–30, p. 158
7:4, p. 118
7:10, pp. 61, 146
7:22, p. 108
8:14, pp. 187, 205
8:14–15, p. 205
9, p. 89
9:10, p. 156
9:22, p. 156
10, p. 89
11:4–17, p. 187
11:25, p. 12
11:27–33, p. 12
12:2, p. 30
12:4, p. 73
12:15, p. 107
13:5, p. 166
13:6–38, p. 73
13:18–20, p. 142
13:22, p. 77
13:27, p. 77
13:27–28, p. 90
13:34, p. 53
13:37, p. 140
14:2–6, p. 166
14:3, p. 166
14:5, p. 107
15:11, p. 156
15:15, p. 156
16:21, p. 80

3 Nephi
1:2, p. 150
1:4, p. 166
1:8, p. 166
1:9, p. 166
1:21, p. 107
2:5–7, p. 166
2:8, p. 166
2:15–16, p. 17
3, p. 188
3:9, pp. 118, 158, 212
3:10, p. 115
3:19, pp. 125, 150
3:22, p. 59
3:23, p. 200
4:4, p. 59
4:28, p. 117
5:4, p. 117
5:20, p. 68
6:8, p. 107
6:10–12, p. 80
6:11, p. 112
6:12, p. 80
6:15, p. 80
6:27, p. 68
7:2, p. 68
7:4, p. 68
7:9–14, p. 203
8, p. 202
8:1–2, p. 150
8:1–3, p. 166
8:7, p. 61
8:8, p. 61
8:14, p. 103
8:20, p. 202
9, p. 202
9:7, pp. 198, 203
9:9, p. 203
9:19, p. 142
18:2, p. 42
18:8, p. 53
20:16, p. 184
21:12, p. 184
21:14, p. 59
21:17, p. 59
21:18, p. 59

4 Nephi
1:1–2, p. 140
1:3, p. 203
1:12–13, p. 150
1:23–26, p. 206
1:24, p. 96
1:26, p. 80
1:33, p. 117
1:34, p. 150
1:38, pp. 73, 205
1:41, pp. 140, 146, 206
1:46, pp. 118, 158, 206, 212

Mormon
1:2, pp. 73, 77
1:2–3, pp. 150, 153
1:3, pp. 77, 163
1:5, p. 68
1:15–17, p. 153
1:19, pp. 119, 140, 157
2:1, p. 68
2:8, p. 118
2:10, p. 157
2:28, pp. 118, 123
4:14, p. 125
4:14–15, pp. 142, 210
4:15, pp. 142, 210
4:21, p. 142
5:24, p. 184
6:2–3, p. 123
6:4, p. 200
6:6, p. 163
6:11–15, p. 209
6:14, p. 127
8:6, p. 166
8:9, pp. 162, 212

Ether
1:3, p. 129
1:33, p. 129
3:1, p. 146
4:1, p. 146
8, p. 83
8:9–19, p. 158
8:11–12, p. 122
9:3–6, p. 153
9:8–10, p. 210
9:17–19, p. 46
9:20–22, p. 153
9:30–34, p. 213
10:5–6, p. 30
10:12, p. 30
10:19, p. 213
10:20, p. 57
10:22–27, p. 30
10:27, p. 30
10:33, p. 212
12:23, p. 176
12:25, p. 176
13:18, p. 212
14:30, p. 125
15:22, p. 42
15:27–32, p. 125

Moroni
6:9, p. 73
8, p. 73
9:7–10, p. 125
9:16, p. 87
9:19, p. 87
9:24, p. 162

SUBJECT INDEX

administration 108, 112, 114, 116
Africa 17, 224
afterlife 154, 156, 157, 230
agriculture 32, 33, 35, 82, 84
ambassadors 120, 123
ancestors 64, 66, 69, 136, 138, 154–57, 155, 156, 157, 183
animals 32, 33, 34, 46–49, 54, 56, 84
Anthon transcript 162, 231
archaeoastonomy 106, 167
archaeology 50, 91, 191, 202, 204, 205, 206, 210, 218–21, 224
architecture 104, 105, 106
army. *See* military
art 168–73
astronomy 106, 107, 148, 150, 164, 166
astrology 124, 125, 149, 163, 164
Atitlan, Lake 11, 93, 170, 198, 205
Aztec(s) 4, 14, 28, 33, 36, 40, 46, 49, 53, 54, 58, 63, 70, 73, 74, 76, 77, 79, 81, 83, 84, 86, 87, 99, 102, 108, 110, 112, 114, 116, 117, 118, 126, 128, 130, 134, 135, 137, 138, 142, 144, 145, 148, 149, 154, 160, 164, 170, 171, 172, 173, 174, 175, 179, 181, 192, 206, 207, 213, 217, 224

B

bandits. *See* rebels; robbers
battle. *See* war
beauty 168, 170, 171
Bible, life of peoples in 3, 4
black people. *See* ethnicity
beans 32, 36, 37
boats 56, 57
Bonampak 15, 16, 78, 88, 89, 129, 178, 218
bondage. *See* slavery
Book of Mormon and Mesoamerica 1, 3, 192, 193, 194, 214, 224
Book of Mormon geography 2, 3, 188, 189, 194, 195, 198, 200, 232
books 105, 159, 160, 161, 163, 164, 174
Bountiful 200, 201, 202, 206
bread 33, 36, 37, 54
Brigham Young University 140, 218
buildings 60–63, 104, 105, 106
bureaucracy 108
burials 144, 154, 199

C

cache 142, 143, 227
calendar 32, 70, 73, 99, 125, 149, 150, 164, 165, 166
cannibalism 212
catastrophe at crucifixion of Jesus 166, 204
Central Depression 12, 13, 196, 197
ceremony 105, 135, 140, 145, 148
Cerro El Vigia 211
charisma 108, 112, 113
Chiapas 10, 13, 22, 35, 42, 50, 58, 71, 78, 89, 92, 102, 103, 113, 116, 118, 128, 134, 135, 138, 144, 147, 182, 189, 192, 193, 196, 197, 210
chiasmus 176, 177
Chichen Itza 1, 16, 219
childbirth 70
children 70–73, 85, 99, 100
China 110, 158, 166, 224, 227
chocolate 42, 43, 54
Christianity 84, 98, 141, 150, 153
church. *See* cult
city 84, 102, 103, 107, 115
civilized/civilization 6, 12, 26, 28, 65
class. *See* social class
climate 10, 11, 12, 130, 194, 196, 203
clothing/cloth 79, 88–93
Coatzacoalcos River 202
codex. *See* books; records
coercion 108, 110, 112
community 64, 65, 136, 137, 153
concubine 83
conquest, Spanish 28, 36, 56, 69, 84, 99, 115, 122, 132, 144, 150, 158, 213
cooking 33, 34, 36, 82
Copan 102, 222
corn 24, 25, 32, 35, 36, 37, 54
Cortez 28, 115, 116, 120, 123, 144, 206
costumes. *See* clothing; ornamentation
courts 108, 116, 117
crafts 50–53, 168
crime 116
crocodile 186, 232
Cuicatec 22, 81, 128
cult 65, 136, 137, 138, 151, 158, 207, 217
cultivation. *See* agriculture
culture(s) 14, 15, 26, 26, 92
Cumorah 110, 167, 202, 210, 214, 231

D

dance 148, 178, 179, 181
death 154–57, 175, 182, 187, 189
demography 32, 103
descent. *See* ancestors
devil 187
diet 33, 37, 39–42, 84, 85, 87, 228
diplomacy 120, 121, 122
disease 46, 84–87, 136, 218
diversions 33, 98–101
divination 149, 150
dragon 185, 230
drinking alcohol 42, 44, 45, 98
drugs 136, 151, 185, 212, 230

E

eccentric flints 30, 31
ecology/environment 8, 10, 11, 66
Egypt 138, 144, 154, 160, 170, 226
elite 64, 65, 68, 75, 78, 79, 80, 81, 99, 134, 135, 138, 156, 159, 168, 191, 212
El Mirador 103, 105, 140, 147
engineering 105, 107, 148
entertainment. *See* diversions; holidays
ethnicity 16, 17, 18, 120, 207, 218, 228
Europe, Western 158, 168
exhortation 71, 73, 77

F

fabrics. *See* clothing
family 64, 66, 70, 71, 80, 82
famine 85, 87
fasting 151
fate 67, 70, 73, 168
fish/fishing 33, 35, 36, 54
flags 108, 126, 127, 129
flocks. *See* animals
food 33, 34, 36, 54, 82
fortifications 128, 130, 132, 133
fruit(s) 36, 37, 54
fun 42, 45, 76, 100
funeral 154
furniture 60

G

gambling 99
games 99, 100
garden 34, 60, 61
genealogy. *See* ancestors
geography 2, 3, 188, 189, 194, 195, 198, 200
gods 99, 124, 128, 129, 136–40, 143, 184, 227
government 68, 108, 110, 113, 115, 120
Grijalva River 12, 13, 196, 197, 201

H

Hagoth 188, 203
harlots 80, 83
health 70, 82, 84, 85, 86
heavens 138, 144, 149, 182
hill, artificial 144, 145, 146
history 160, 162, 190, 191
holidays 98
houses 32, 60–63, 113
humor 73, 99, 100
hunting 46, 131

I

idols 138, 140, 153
illness. *See* disease
incense 142, 227
individuals 65, 66, 68, 76, 136, 152, 153
insignia. *See* ornamentation
Israelite. *See* Judah, land of
Izapa 51, 60, 122, 140, 146, 157, 167, 182, 187, 193, 196
Izapan style 44, 51, 196

J

jaguar 184, 185
Jaina style 18, 80, 83, 85, 90, 92, 98, 174, 180
Jaredites 6, 17, 30, 35, 42, 118, 167, 202, 214, 215, 216, 223
Jerusalem (Old World) 27, 103, 108, 124, 144, 179, 182, 194
Jerusalem (Lamanite) 198, 205
Jesus Christ 142, 150, 187, 204, 206, 207
jewelry 94, 95, 96
Jewish. *See* Judah, land of
Judah, land of 25, 107, 108, 117, 120, 121, 141, 142, 146, 165, 174, 184, 186, 190, 192, 201, 207, 224, 225, 228
judges 108, 112, 113, 116, 117

K

Kaminaljuyu 175, 194, 195, 199, 200
king 65, 110, 112, 123. *See also* rule/ruler
King-men 112, 129
kinship 64, 65, 66, 68, 79

L

Lacandon Maya 58, 222
Lake Atitlan 11, 198, 205
Lamanites 6, 12, 15, 17, 30, 46, 50, 55, 80, 83, 101, 102, 103, 108, 112, 113, 115, 118, 123, 129, 140, 156, 157, 158, 162, 166, 192, 194, 196, 197, 198, 200, 207, 210, 230
Land Northward 188, 189, 202, 203, 212
languages 12, 24, 25, 126, 222, 223
La Venta 10, 120, 121, 143, 201, 215, 227
lawyer 108, 113, 116
learning 70, 71, 74, 76, 77
leviathan 186, 187
lineage 66, 68, 190, 191, 192, 214
lion 184, 185
literacy 108, 160, 162
literature 160, 174
loom 92

M

maize. *See* corn
market 33, 82, 83, 99, 101, 105
marriage 66, 68, 76, 77, 83, 110, 120, 123
Maya 4, 14, 18, 20, 24, 56, 57, 58, 64, 66, 72, 75, 78, 79, 82, 83, 89, 99, 111, 116, 119, 120, 121, 133, 140, 148, 149, 150, 159, 160, 161, 162, 164, 176, 177, 179, 180, 182, 187, 192, 196, 209, 212, 220, 227
meals 60
meat 37
medical. *See* disease
Mediterranean 20, 40, 224, 225
merchants 14, 33, 54, 55, 57, 118, 120
Mesoamerica defined 6
metal 52, 53, 94, 96, 130
midwife 71
military 74, 76, 78–81, 118, 124–129
Mixtec 22, 23, 88, 95
Mongoloid. *See* Northeast Asian origin for Amerindians
Monte Alban 102, 128, 160, 212, 220
Montezuma 36, 46, 84, 110, 120, 206, 213, 224
monster. *See* dragon
Mormon, historian/leader 3, 77, 99, 188, 189
Moses, law of 117, 142, 150
mother 70–73, 82, 83
mountains 104, 105, 146, 201, 223
mountainous "narrow strip" 13, 196, 201
mourning 156
Mulek 25, 108, 201, 214, 232
"Mulekites," see people of Zarahemla
music 148, 178–181
myth 163, 176, 182, 186

N

narrow pass 202
navel of the earth 182

Nawal 141, 186, 215, 217
Near East 2, 4, 28, 59, 102, 104, 108, 118, 184, 214, 223, 227
needle 92
Nehor 158
Nephi, land of 175, 188, 189, 194, 195, 196, 198, 210
Nephites 2, 3, 6, 12, 15, 17, 25, 30, 37, 42, 44, 46, 49, 50, 53, 55, 61, 68, 73, 77, 80, 83, 93, 101, 102, 103, 107, 108, 110, 112, 113, 115, 117, 118, 123, 129, 132, 137, 140, 141, 142, 150, 151, 156, 158, 162, 165, 166, 167, 176, 188, 192, 194, 195, 196, 197, 198, 200, 202, 206, 207, 210, 212, 216
Nibley, Hugh 2, 17
nobility. *See* elite; king; rule; social class
Northeast Asian origin of Amerindians 16, 17, 18, 21, 216, 222

O

obsidian 31, 51, 52, 218
oath 110, 123
Oaxaca 8, 14, 20, 22, 23, 81, 95, 128, 156, 181, 192, 203, 212
offerings. *See* sacrifice
officials. *See* administration
old age 86
Olmec 20, 103, 118, 123, 143, 168, 185, 192, 201, 214, 215, 216, 217, 223, 227
oratory 71, 76, 174, 175, 176
ornamentation 94, 96, 169, 200, 214

P

palace 110, 113
Palenque 19, 104, 144, 183
parents 73
Patolli game 99
people of Zarahemla 17, 25, 140, 158, 196, 216
personality 82, 83, 98, 99
pessimism 67, 168
pets 46, 100
play 70
poetry 174–77
police. *See* administration
Popol Vuh 177, 191 *(search for others)*
population size. *See* demography
pottery 50, 51, 219, 221
prayer 175 *(search for others: "pray ")*
priests 65, 76, 80, 113, 124, 134, 136, 140, 142, 148, 150, 151, 174
prisoners 108, 116, 117
punishment 76, 116, 117
prophecy/prophets 73, 125, 140, 148, 150, 166
pyramid. *See* hill, artificial

Q

Quetzalcoatl 140, 206, 207, 230, 232

R

race. *See* ethnicity
rain 186, 187
rank. *See* social class
rebels 108, 110, 112, 113, 118, 124, 129, 162, 202, 212
records 108, 130, 148, 150, 159, 166
recreation. *See* diversions
religion 98, 108, 113, 117, 124, 125, 134, 135, 136, 151, 163, 230
resurrection. *See* afterlife
ritual 46, 85, 98, 100, 114, 117, 120, 124, 134, 140, 145, 151, 152, 175
roads 56, 105, 107
robbers. *See* rebels
rule/ruler 65, 80, 81, 108–12, 114, 115, 116, 120, 123, 170, 190, 199, 200, 214

S

sacrifice 99, 142, 143, 145, 209, 230
sacrifice, human 125, 142, 151, 199, 208, 212
Santa Rosa (site) 12, 196, 197, 200
schools 76, 77, 148, 174
script. *See* writing systems
secret associations/groups 65, 115, 118, 119, 158, 184, 214
Semitic 20, 25, 201
sepulchre. *See* tombs
serpents. *See* snakes
settlements 102, 103
shamans 85, 136, 148, 149, 150, 151, 185
ships. *See* boats
shrines 144, 145
Sidon River 12, 188, 196, 200
skin color 17, 228
slavery 78, 79, 80, 81, 124, 229
Smith, Joseph 2, 30, 188, 222
snakes 185, 186, 187, 207, 215
social class 64, 78, 79, 80, 81, 206, 207
solemn/sober 73, 98, 99, 100
Southeast Asia 21, 146, 176
Spaniards 213, 224
speech skills. *See* oratory
spies 118, 120
squash 36, 39
state 108, 110, 112
Stela 3 (La Venta) 121, 201
Stephens, John Lloyd 30, 222
sweet foods 42, 45, 54
swords. *See* weapons
symbolism 94, 95, 96, 99, 114, 156
synagogues 146, 147

T

taxes. *See* tribute payments
teaching 73, 74, 75, 76, 77, 150, 174
technology 30, 46
temple 61, 104, 105, 107, 108, 129, 138, 144, 145, 146, 194, 203, 206, 207
Tenochtitlan (Aztec capital) 14, 27, 28, 29, 63, 145, 179
Teotihuacan 20, 63, 66, 68, 102, 139, 145, 146, 147, 157, 170, 185, 206, 207, 208, 212
textiles. *See* clothing/cloth
throne 111, 214
timber 203
Tikal 102, 147, 212
Tlatilco 21, 162
Tlaxcala 14, 62, 115, 120, 123, 127–28, 133
tobacco 136
Toltecs 192
tombs 154, 156, 199
tools 51, 52, 53, 218, 229
tortillas 33, 34, 36, 37, 40
tower 61, 107, 129, 132, 195, 214
toys 70, 99, 100
trade 12, 33, 51, 54, 57, 158, 218
tradition 168, 178, 223, 224
treaties 120, 123
tree 69, 182, 183
trials. *See* courts
tribute payments 110, 113, 114, 115, 120, 124, 126, 128, 129

U

underworld 182, 186, 187, 230

V

values 74, 76, 77, 92, 108, 148, 150, 168
vehicles 58, 59
Veracruz 8, 20, 21, 110, 151, 152, 165, 192, 202, 211, 223, 227
village 102, 103, 115
volcano 204, 205, 218
voyages across the oceans 194, 214, 216, 223, 224, 225, 226

W

war 11, 82, 87, 99, 120, 122–28, 194, 197, 198, 200, 201, 202, 210–14, 216, 230
weapons 53, 130, 131
weaving 82, 92, 93
wheel 59, 229
white people. *See* ethnicity
wine 42, 45, 53, 93, 115
wilderness 10, 12, 196, 197, 201
witchcraft 119, 140, 148
women 33, 34, 82, 83, 92, 93
worship 54, 61, 98, 134, 135, 136, 152
writing systems 160, 162, 220, 231

Y

youth 74–77
Yucatan 32, 56, 58, 62, 105, 133, 146, 150, 160, 164, 170, 183, 224

Z

Zapotecs 14, 141, 160, 169, 192
Zarahemla, city of 12, 115, 196, 200
Zarahemla, land of 12, 15, 188, 189, 196, 202, 210
Zeniffites 112, 114, 129, 198
Zinacantan 113, 116, 134, 135, 147, 152, 153
Zoramites 15, 90, 112, 137